The Dreyfus Affair and the
Crisis of French Manhood

PUBLISHING FOR THE WORLD
125 Years

THE JOHNS HOPKINS UNIVERSITY PRESS

The Johns Hopkins University Studies in Historical and Political
Science 121st Series (2003)

The Dreyfus Affair and the Crisis of French Manhood

Christopher E. Forth

The Johns Hopkins University Press
Baltimore and London

Johns Hopkins Paperbacks edition, 2006
9 8 7 6 5 4 3 2 1

The Johns Hopkins University Press
2715 North Charles Street
Baltimore, Maryland 21218-4363
www.press.jhu.edu

The Library of Congress has cataloged the hardcover edition of this book as follows:

Forth, Christopher E., 1967–
    The Dreyfus affair and the crisis of French manhood / Christopher E.
Forth.
        p.   cm.—(The Johns Hopkins University Studies in historical and
political science, 121st ser., no. 2)
Includes bibliographical references and index.
ISBN 0-8018-7433-5 (hardcover : alk. paper)
    1. Dreyfus, Alfred, 1859–1935.   2. France—Politics and govern-
ment—1870–1940.   3. Masculinity—France.   I. Title.
DC354.F63 2004
944.081′2′081—dc21   2003006216

ISBN 0-8018-8385-7 (pbk. : alk. paper)

A catalog record for this book is available from the British Library.

For Declan

Contents

Illustrations

Acknowledgments

This project was conceived through ongoing discussions with friends and colleagues whose own work inspired me to press forward. Venita Datta and John Cerullo have each offered pioneering reinterpretations of the Dreyfus Affair by drawing attention to the generally ignored issues of gender and sexuality, and this book owes much to our productive exchange of ideas. Although in places my views deviate from theirs, I remain indebted to their example and grateful for their support. Robert Nye has been for me a great scholarly inspiration and source of encouragement during the writing of this book. A number of colleagues and friends commented on parts of the book at various stages, and I am very grateful for the suggestions made by Erika Esau, Jay Geller, Ruth Harris, Jonathan Judaken, Sara Lloyd, Jill Matthews, Daniel Pick, Brian Rigby, and Anne Tirone. Special thanks go to those generous colleagues who read the entire manuscript: John Cerullo, Venita Datta, Martin Johnson, Bertrand Taithe, and Robert Wood. Thanks also to the critical and informed comments made by the anonymous reader procured by the Johns Hopkins University Press. Finally, Thomas Kselman made some very useful suggestions regarding the history of Christ imagery, and Paul B. Miller generously shared with me the manuscript of his recent book, *From Revolutionaries to Citizens: Antimilitarism in France, 1870–1914*. In an academic world where solitary work is the norm, it is refreshing to find busy people so willing to give of their time.

My editor at the Johns Hopkins University Press, Henry Tom, supported this project when it was just a disparate collection of articles and seminar papers, while Michael Lonegro provided editorial assistance that rendered the process smooth and pleasant. Peter Dreyer's excellent copyediting helped to iron the wrinkles out of the final manuscript. I have been very fortunate to work with David Bancroft's Centre parisien d'études et de documentation pour l'enseignement et le rayonnement du français (CPEDERF), an excellent service for overseas scholars requiring long- and short-term research assistance in France. Many thanks go to my CPEDERF researchers: Caroline Leckenby, Julia McLaren, and

Francine Morgan. Thanks also to staff at the Bibliothèque nationale, the Centre des archives d'outre-mer, the British Library, the Wellcome Library for the History and Understanding of Medicine, the National Library of Australia, and the Australian National University libraries for their assistance. Funds received from the University of Memphis, the Australian Research Council, the Australian National University, and the Wellcome Trust for the History and Understanding of Medicine helped bring this book and its images to the light of day, and a sabbatical fellowship at the ANU's Humanities Research Centre provided me with the opportunity to complete this book in a peaceful environment.

Home life may not always be as peaceful, but I wouldn't trade it for anything. As always thanks to Jenn for her love and support, and to our children, Declan and Logan, for keeping life interesting.

The Dreyfus Affair and the
Crisis of French Manhood

The Body Politics of the Dreyfus Affair

> In history, as in natural science, it remains true that as soon as one terri-
> tory has been explored, another comes into view on the horizon, perhaps
> even more extensive than the last. The view that everything has already
> been said on the Affair is grotesquely mistaken.
> — ERIC CAHM, *The Dreyfus Affair in French Politics and Society*

At the height of the Dreyfus Affair, readers of the conservative Catholic newspaper *La Croix* were well accustomed to articles making liberal, even gratuitous,
use of the word "traitor." After all, to these readers, what anti-Semites had for
years often said about treasonous Jews seemed confirmed when, in 1894, a Jewish artillery officer named Alfred Dreyfus was found guilty of selling military secrets to the Germans and exiled for life to a penal colony off the coast of South
America. Adding insult to injury, the disgraced officer's family insisted that the
traitor was innocent and enlisted a growing number of liberal and left-leaning
politicians and intellectuals in a campaign to reopen the case. However controversial this movement seemed when it emerged in 1896, two years later, it had
clearly gone too far when one of its key spokesman, the "pornographic" novelist Émile Zola, further scandalized the nation by publicly accusing the French
army of covering up the truth about the Dreyfus case. Well known for their anti-
Semitic bent, writers for *La Croix* inveighed heavily against this growing revisionist campaign, which seemed to have been orchestrated by the nefarious "Syndicate" of international Jewry. Dreyfus was clearly a traitor, they opined, because
he hailed from a people who were racially and culturally alien to the codes of
honor that structured French society. His was thus no solitary crime, but indis-
putable evidence of "the Jewish enemy betraying France."[1] On the cold morning of 23 February 1898, therefore, the reader who turned to page 4 of *La Croix*
would have encountered what was, at first glance, yet another article on the

Dreyfus case. A closer look at the item boldly entitled "TRAITRE" revealed something rather different: "There is nothing as treacherous [*traître*] or distressing as the consequences of influenza, and all the neglected winter maladies. Ah! if everyone had the pleasure of being acquainted with Poncelet's lozenges!"

After initial surprise, and perhaps even a chuckle, few readers had reason to be shocked by this bit of deception. Advertisements for patent medicines were regular features of nineteenth-century newspapers and often masqueraded as medical articles about various ailments that, after some discussion of symptoms and causes, ended by recommending one product in particular. Few such advertisements, however, appealed so directly to contemporary political developments. Shrewdly tapping into his readers' anxieties about treason, the *pharmacien-chimiste* Poncelet invoked what was widely described as a disorder of the body politic to pitch his own cure for the personal body. While the case of the condemned captain was cited only in the title, the advertisement promoted ideals and promised remedies that functioned nicely alongside the medicalized rhetoric that framed the Dreyfus Affair. Unlike political measures that failed to calm the upheavals of the nation, Poncelet's lozenges worked their magic by sterilizing air inhaled through the mouth, by acting as an expectorant for the expulsion of phlegm, and by distributing their healing properties throughout the body. Whereas the flu wrought a kind of "treason" that upset the physiological equilibrium considered synonymous with health (much as treasonous Jews had allegedly polluted the country), Poncelet promised to cleanse the body of pathogenic impurities and to replenish its vitality. Finally, here was a truth that anti-Dreyfusard readers of *La Croix* contemptuous of the pro-Dreyfus slogan "Truth is on the march!" could believe in. Poncelet's lozenges were, after all, "the savior of a million people every year. Bow down before the truth."[2]

Cultural historians are by now well acquainted with the role played by biological metaphors in political discourses, where discussions of the "body politic" are often cast in the explicit language of medicine, gender, and sexuality. Observations about the illness of the national body had been widespread since France's defeat at the hands of Prussia in 1870 and were a recurring theme in political and social discourses as the newly formed Third Republic limped from crisis to crisis. Since the social, political, and gender discussions of the fin de siècle were permeated by what Robert Nye describes as a "medical discourse of national decline," the Dreyfus Affair was readily cited as a grave instance of collective catastrophe.[3] Moreover, one did not need to be conservative to make use of such imagery. Never one to shrink from disease imagery in his novels, for example, even the Dreyfusard hero Zola described the Affair as a national tumor. "A miscarriage of justice has been committed," he proclaimed, adding that "as long as it has not been corrected, France will be weak and sickly and will suffer as from a secret cancer gnawing at its flesh." Though the maintenance of a healthy national body seemed to require a strict regimen of moral hygiene, Zola felt that the current situation called for more radical measures. France would ironically become sound again only by cutting away parts of itself: "If some of its limbs must be amputated in order to make France healthy again, let them be amputated!"[4] The writer André Suarès, an assimilated Jew who was himself a physician, carried the surgical theme even further in his pro-Dreyfus essays. "A sore develops on a body that is not healthy," and inept doctors had been charged with the surgery: "They operate secretly, at night, in the depths of a basement. With dirty hands they carry instruments rusted by long usage; some have even drenched theirs in mud." After botching the surgery, these physicians fled, leaving the patient in even worse health than before. "The next day, the unhealthy limb is not amputated, nor is the disease cured. On the contrary, the whole body is infected. The sore has become an immense ulcer."[5]

Ulcers and cancer are, of course, conditions more dire than influenza, but Poncelet's throat lozenges can perhaps teach us something about the Dreyfus Affair—namely, that when the body politic is perceived to be in disarray, the physical body is often proposed as a site of reform and a platform for action. What Jackson Lears writes of the American scene is equally true of the French: "As the public world outside the self becomes diffuse, distant, governed by institutions we cannot control or even influence, the body remains important as an arena we can actually control—or we think we can. It becomes a domain of self-expression, a field for developing one's own set of cultural meanings, and a source, quite naturally, of anxiety."[6] Poncelet's lozenges subtly enacted this strategy by diverting the reader's attention from the public sphere to the private body. By invoking the catchword "traitor," the advertisement reminded readers of a troubling national crisis that seemed to deepen every day, but it also reassured them by identifying a more personal and infinitely more manageable form of "treason," one that might be remedied by the product in question. Ultimately, however, the lessons of the personal body were implicitly referred back to the public sphere. If the sick private body could be cured by expelling its own "traitor," so too might the body politic recover through a large-scale purgation of all that threatened national health. *La Croix*'s readers would have surely grasped these implications, for the articles they read often called for just such a purgation when it came to the Jews of France and those who defended them.

Within this minor and apparently insignificant advertisement are condensed many of the tensions and themes explored in this book, a study of the Dreyfus Affair as a crisis of the body politic that had important yet often overlooked implications for the personal bodies of the men who became engaged in it. Its point of departure is the notion that political discourses often articulate a politics of embodied existence—a "body politics," if you will—that facilitates reflections upon the interrelations of the individual and the collective. By taking seriously the organicist metaphors that proliferated in social and political discourses at the fin de siècle, it demonstrates how deeply implicated the Dreyfus Affair was in the cultural anxieties of the day and draws attention to the ways in which this political controversy facilitated discussions about a "crisis" of manhood and a reform of the male body. Attention to these issues in no way entails the elaboration of concerns that were peripheral to the political controversy, but cuts to the heart of what the Affair was all about and how its issues were framed. In short, while this book agrees that the Dreyfus Affair was ultimately a political phenomenon, it is animated by a much wider conception of "politics" and of the avenues through which politics is expressed.

The Dreyfus Affair is not often approached with an eye to issues of gender, sexuality, and the body, but has generally remained within the domain of fairly conventional approaches to politics and society.[7] Even studies that situate the Affair within the cultural context of fin-de-siècle France often evince a blindness to the role played by gendered and somatic rhetoric in the polemics generated by this crisis, and betray little engagement with studies (such as those by Edward Berenson, Ruth Harris, Robert Nye, Daniel Pick, and Ann-Louise Shapiro) that demonstrate the centrality of the languages of medicine and gender to the political discourses of the Third Republic.[8] Moreover, studies that explore the Jewish dimension of the Dreyfus Affair often take little notice of developments in the cultural history of anti-Semitism, especially the pioneering work of Sander Gilman, that have helped to illuminate the complex nature of racial stereotyping and the channels through which racial ideas circulated.[9] The aversion, however, seems to be mutual. Historians studying matters of culture, gender, and sexuality in fin-de-siècle France have tended to sidestep the Dreyfus Affair, thus allowing it to remain largely the preserve of conventional historical methodologies. To date, the productive application of cultural and gender analyses to a political event—what historians like Roger Chartier, Robert Darnton, Lynn Hunt, Dorinda Outram, and Antoine de Baecque have done for the French Revolution—remains relatively undeveloped in the case of the Dreyfus Affair.[10]

To provide some rectification of this situation is one of the aims of the present study. By examining how the polemical writings of the Dreyfus Affair were articulated in and through mainstream cultural concerns about the diminishing quality of French manhood, this book seeks to bridge these historiographies by exploring domains of mutual concern and encouraging a more complex view of this event. It argues that by citing the many anxieties about modernity and physical health that circulated at the fin de siècle, the polemics of the Dreyfus Affair provided the French with an opportunity to elevate hitherto localized anxieties about masculine identity to national proportions, thus expressing and perhaps even accelerating changes in manly ideals that had been developing in earlier years. The richly gendered language of these writings not only gave voice to these concerns, but helped to create identities around which men on both sides of the Dreyfus issue could rally. Insofar as gender and the body remain its central concern, this book therefore considers the Dreyfus Affair as both a locus of investigation and a springboard for discussion of the shifting ideals of manliness in the years leading up to World War I. As the most important political scandal of the period, the Dreyfus Affair is a logical place to explore these issues: alongside the problem of whether or not Dreyfus was guilty of treason lurked a deeper uncertainty about the manly credentials of those whose opinions on this issue purported to represent the good of the nation. The Affair was not simply a forum where conflicting ideas about politics and society could be proposed and debated; it was an arena in which the men who embraced these ideas also felt compelled to affirm their own virility, while denigrating that of their opponents. This is not to reduce the complexities of the Dreyfus Affair to matters of gender and the body but to observe that such discourses provided a common idiom for conceptualizing and discussing issues at the heart of the Affair. It is to assert that the "politics" of the Dreyfus Affair invoked issues that were personal as well as public.

Modernity, Medicine, and Manhood

Masculinity is a multifaceted topic that eludes easy categorization. Inasmuch as every discipline seems to approach masculinity differently, few discussions of it manage to capture its many dimensions. My own understanding of the "crisis" of masculinity so often observed at the fin de siècle is intimately bound up with issues pertaining to modernity and medicine, and these three themes (modernity, medicine, and manhood) represent the conceptual axis of the book. They are nevertheless terms that need to be defined. It is no exaggeration to say that the polemics of the Dreyfus Affair were saturated with concerns about "modernity," though historians have typically understood this word in rather restricted terms. It is sometimes said that by championing the advance of democracy, humanity, justice, and truth, the pro-Dreyfus camp assumed a progressive stance that engaged heroically with the forces of superstition and tradition. In his appraisal of the Affair, Robert Hoffman admits that "'modernity' entails a mentality, one which assumes innovation to be the norm, even if sometimes still reacting uneasily against it"; yet Hoffman nevertheless attributes this mentality exclusively to the Dreyfusards while arguing that their conservative opponents manifested a "rage against things modern."[11] This perspective is a fairly common one, and it lingers on in contemporary historiography. For example, a 1998 conference at Georgetown University commemorating the centennial of Zola's famous intervention in the Affair suggested the same viewpoint through its provocatively polarized title: "The Dreyfus Affair: Human Rights vs. Prejudice, Intolerance, and Demonization." In other words, Dreyfusards have typically been seen as latter-day heirs to the Enlightenment, and have thus been located on the side of modernity (the defense of human rights) triumphing over the forces of tradition (prejudice, intolerance, and demonization). This opposition no doubt has its ideological benefits, particularly when one depicts anti-Dreyfusards as paving the way for later anti-Semitic atrocities, a view that confirms the liberal tendency to see fascism as an aberration in an otherwise rational project of Enlightenment. Given such an ominous trajectory, it is easy to see how contemporary historians might fondly and uncritically consider the Dreyfusards to be "heroes."[12]

As with many comfortable binarisms, the situation becomes more complex upon closer scrutiny. Aside from the fact that some rightly challenge the view that "the Holocaust was a failure, not the product, of modernity,"[13] this vision of heroically modern Dreyfusards becomes further clouded if we consider the multiple responses they registered to the modern world they inhabited. While rarely using the word itself, people on both sides of the Dreyfus issue wrestled implicitly with a conception of modernity that also connoted profound shifts in subjective experience as a result of the accelerated pace and sensory overload of urban life, such as that wrought by streetcars and automobiles, newspapers and advertising, crowded streets, and material abundance generally. Fin-de-siècle appraisals of the modern world often bemoaned more concrete developments, including the increasing visibility of homosexuals, the influx of working-class men into hitherto exclusively bourgeois professions, the rise of socialist movements, and the emergence of feminist politics. All of these modern changes entailed profound challenges to conventional assumptions about self, gender, and society that, insofar as they seemed to erode traditional bases of male authority, were frequently interpreted as assaults on virility itself. Contrary to the rather optimistic definition favored by historians like Hoffman, modernity was experienced as a much more complex development and elicited a spectrum of responses, many of which were couched in tellingly gendered terms. "For every account of the modern era which emphasizes the domination of masculine qualities of rationalization, productivity, and repression," Rita Felski writes of this period, "one can find another text which points—whether approvingly or censoriously— to the feminization of Western society, as evidenced in the passive, hedonistic, and decentered nature of modern subjectivity."[14] Expressed through so many dislocations and assaults on traditional hierarchies and values, modernity's "feminization" of the world provided the broad framework for observations that contemporary manhood was in a state of "crisis."[15]

Insofar as fin-de-siècle culture wrestled with the complexities of the modern world, it is misleading to situate the debates surrounding the Dreyfus Affair with reference to such a restricted view of the period. Far from being unqualified or even uneasy proponents of the modern world, Dreyfusards too expressed grave concerns about modernity and its long-term effects. Rather than giddy responses to the occasional bump on the road of progress, their concerns conveyed misgivings about the damage that modernity was doing to the virility of the nation. Not only did they acknowledge that the ever-accelerating pace of change could have disastrous consequences for city dwellers, but they used this knowledge to identify their opponents as one such damaged population. As both purveyors and consumers of lies and "fictions," the enemies of Dreyfus seemed dangerously open to the manufactured seductions of religion, the novel, the mass press, and the crowd, and thus implicitly counted among the victims of a modernity that corrupted the characters of women and weaker men. At the same time, however, anti-Dreyfusards were depicted as being so inured in traditional mind-sets as to be incapable of transcending their outmoded customs, thus evincing irrational and even atavistic tendencies that made them seem hopelessly out of step with the times. In other words, anti-Dreyfusards were at once too modern and not modern enough. Yet as men representing the march of intellect in a world that increasingly privileged mental over physical labor, Dreyfusards could hardly disavow their own connection with the modern, not merely (as we shall see below) due to their association with education and the bourgeois professions, but because the people whose rights they defended were themselves seen as epitomizing the ephemerality of modernity: images of the cerebral, nervous, and wandering qualities of Jews only cemented the association of these people with the liquefying flux of modern life. How the Dreyfusards rhetorically negotiated their problematic position is the focus of Part II of this study.

If modernity suggested to many the feared erosion of mind, body, and morality wrought by the conditions of urban existence, concerns about such processes rendered medical knowledge and therapeutic practices essential for the diagnosis and treatment of modern men. Commentaries on the debased state of French manhood were liberally spiced with medical metaphors that connected gender anxieties with the crises faced by the nation at the fin de siècle. That these metaphors often referred to disorders of the collective body has been well established; that they also redounded upon the personal bodies and gender identities of the main actors of the Dreyfus Affair (so that their writings are equally infused with anxieties about health and manhood) has gone largely unexamined. Among the mostly bourgeois men of the Dreyfus Affair, the problems of modernity and medicine intertwined at the level of lifestyles, and invoked long-standing concerns about the impact of urban life on masculinity itself.

Insofar as it entailed the expansion of largely sedentary and cerebral professions, modernity was increasingly identified as exercising a negative, even feminizing effect upon the very men who constituted the nation's elite: those who benefited most from the educational system to secure bourgeois occupations. Working at a desk rather than in the fields instilled in men sedentary habits that left them less inclined to exercise their bodies, especially since coaches, streetcars, and railroads minimized the need for physical exertion outside the workplace. Such technological changes to everyday life were complemented by higher incomes, allowing professionals to enjoy more material benefits than ever before, thus enhancing the desirability of these occupations, while increasing the risk of obesity, gout, and other disorders that came with sedentariness and abundance. Add to the mix the seemingly endless stream of cheap and perhaps enervating amusements made possible by city life—gambling, prostitution, cabarets, panoramas and dioramas, the circus, and, in time, the cinema—and one had a potent recipe for physical, mental, and moral decline that might result in alcoholism, syphilis, hysteria, neurasthenia, tuberculosis, obesity, and a range of other ailments that seemed inextricably tied to modernity itself.

Scholars often point to contemporary anxieties about hereditary degeneration as playing a crucial role in fin-de-siècle discussions about mental and physical decline, but these medical concerns were also tied to the problem of modernity. Daniel Pick has demonstrated how the language of degeneracy shifted at the end of the century, so that the deterioration that had in previous decades been located within individual bodies and bloodlines was increasingly viewed as the consequence of the morbid effects of the modern milieu.[16] By upsetting the association of degeneracy with certain easily identifiable groups or bloodlines, the growing identification of modernity as a major cause of physical and moral decay had profound consequences for men who could no longer comfortably assume a direct correlation of sex with gender. In many cases, masculinity was explicitly cast as being more of a personal project than an anatomical guarantee, the cumulative effect of the everyday measures one took to maintain health, willpower, and character. This was especially true in the post-Affair period, when one Catholic writer insisted that the renewal of French vitality required a "conquest of virility." Abetted by feminist and socialist politics at the nineteenth century's end, the much-heralded "crisis" of masculinity during this period also stemmed from this growing realization that gender identity was susceptible to inconsistencies and lapses that called into question the very category of the "normal." In her work on the crisis of manhood during this period, Annelise Maugue reasonably argues that "it is through the discourse on woman that masculinity is constrained to constitute itself sometimes explicitly as such, to define itself, to speak itself."[17] Yet whereas the general discourse of masculinity achieves a degree of conceptual coherence in its relationship with "the feminine," a closer analysis of manhood in daily life reveals a fractured identity in which competing definitions of masculinity often pit men against one another. The Dreyfus Affair provides a fertile terrain for the examination of tensions internal to manhood itself. In a contest whose participants agreed on very little, anxieties about the state of French manhood represented a significant, if rarely acknowledged, common ground.

Men of Thought, Men of Action

Masculinity, then, refers less to a stable identity than to a cultural contestation among competing ways of "being" a man. What makes the Dreyfus Affair a useful site for the examination of competing styles of masculinity are the tensions that existed among the various kinds of men who engaged in it. The "in-

tellectual," for instance, is an inescapable figure in any discussion of the Dreyfus
Affair, emerging in the writings of the period both as an object of fawning admiration and as a target of vitriolic abuse. Many accept that our modern notion
of the politically engaged intellectual was forged in the crises wrought by the
Dreyfus Affair and crystallized in Zola's essay "J'accuse," but few inquire into the
relationship between the intellectual and the gender anxieties of the fin de siècle. In one influential attempt to define the intellectual, Pascal Ory and Jean-
François Sirinelli seek a middle way between the two definitions that circulated
during the 1890s, a social definition that distinguished men in terms of the re-
quirements of a profession and lifestyle (i.e., of intellectual rather than manual
labor), and an ideological one that suggested the fervor of a "vocation" or spiritual mission (political criticism in the name of abstract values). Like other attempts
to describe the intellectual, the mediating definition proposed by Ory and Sirinelli
drifts closer to the vocational side of things. For them the *intellectuel* is not simply "the man 'who thinks' . . . but the man who communicates a thought . . . a
man of culture, a creator or mediator, placed in the situation of a man of politics, a producer or consumer of ideology."[18] This emphasis on the intellectual
life as a kind of mission faithfully conveys the manner in which intellectuals perceived themselves and wished to be perceived throughout the twentieth century.
It is also central to the recent work of Venita Datta, who in *Birth of a National
Icon* has persuasively analyzed the ways in which intellectuals on both sides of the
Dreyfus question sought to project suitably masculine public images, while condemning the effeminacy of their opponents.[19]

   References to intellectuals appear quite frequently in the pages that follow;
but this book is not about the intellectual per se, or at least not as this figure has
been commonly understood. Rather, it submits that an adequate understanding
of how intellectuals were perceived requires a closer look at the relationship between the socioprofessional conditions of the intellectual lifestyle and contemporary medical anxieties about masculinity. Of course, in the context of a country like France where, due to the cultural tendency to value mental over manual
labor, many people have long considered themselves to be *intellectuel* in one way
or another, most would agree with Jeremy Jennings that overstating the role of
profession creates a category that is "so extensive as to be virtually meaning-
less."[20] If one's aim is to define the intellectuals as a distinct social category, then
Jennings's view is correct. But if one inquires into the relationship between intellectuals and contemporary ideals of masculinity, particularly as they were perceived through the lenses of modernity and medicine, an understanding of so-

cioprofessional matters becomes especially important. As illustrated above, medicine offered a framework through which the defects of men could be cited as evidence of national decline, and it often encouraged critics to focus their attention on the unhealthy lifestyles led by modern people. Of course, many intellectuals, and aesthetes in particular, prided themselves on their distance from the rituals of bourgeois life, and by engaging in such conventionally cultural pursuits as science, journalism, or literature, they sought to distinguish themselves from men in other occupations. Yet if we consider them as embodied subjects as well as social agents, we shall see that in medical terms, intellectuals shared with "white-collar" professionals (like lawyers, doctors, engineers, and civil servants) occupations that emphasized mental exertion and sedentary lifestyles rather than physical action and muscular force. Insofar as he engaged in labor that was mental rather than manual, the intellectual enjoyed a lifestyle that had much in common with that of the bourgeois professional. In broad terms, both were "men of thought" or (to use the term employed by the American physician George Beard) "brain workers."

It is here that the presumed masculinity of the intellectual becomes problematic, for in the Western world, the man whose profession demands mental rather than physical effort has enjoyed an ambiguous reputation at best. Michael Nerlich argues that one of the reasons that the heroic soldier remains a physical and even spiritual ideal of manhood is that this figure undergirds an "ideology of adventure" that is primarily traceable to models set down in medieval romance stories. Epic adventures certainly figure prominently in Greek mythology, but, as Nerlich argues, in most cases these adventures befall heroes who find themselves compelled to pursue a series of dangerous missions. While their manly credentials were certainly confirmed by completing such arduous tests, Greek heroes generally do not set out on adventures for their own sake; rather, they are unwittingly drawn into a series of circumstances that require some sort of epic action on their part. Medieval romances, on the other hand, often feature knights who deliberately embark on and court danger in their quests and find their virility validated through heroic deeds. Much of Western history is marked by a thirst for adventure and novelty, Nerlich claims, thus providing a medieval genealogy for what is often seen as the "restlessness" of modernity.[21]

Manifested differently depending on historical period and cultural context, the ideology of adventure represents one of the most powerful and enduring myths of Western manhood. John Hoberman concisely describes the manly qualities valorized by this myth: "This doctrine, and the military culture from which it derives, have shaped the predominant image of masculinity in the West. It is important to keep in mind that this ethos of self-assertion prescribes not merely action but a style of action: risk-taking as an end in itself, a contempt for those outside this male caste, and a martial athleticism."[22] This myth of male action developed throughout the relative pacification of Western societies in the sixteenth century, thus forming a powerful counterpoint to increasing medical warnings that the sedentary, scholarly, and indulgent lifestyles of the nobility and bourgeoisie promoted immorality as well as physical and mental problems. For much of the modern era, then, the manhood of elites has been shadowed by the persistent ideal of action. By sustaining a historical opposition between heroic men of action (such as knights, explorers, and athletes) and less glorious men of thought (including priests, scholars, artists, Jews, and bourgeois professionals), the ideology of adventure contributed in no small part to the systematized and explicitly corporeal stereotype of masculinity that reached its apotheosis at the end of the nineteenth century. The fact that in the modern period few middle-class men have fully embodied this adventurous lifestyle has not diminished its attractiveness as a masculine myth. Rather, as martial physicality and bodily beauty became integral elements of the manly ideal, bourgeois men often resorted to metaphor as a means of describing their own deeds in reassuringly active and heroic terms. By the time of the Dreyfus Affair, when, across the Western world, more tangible proofs of manliness through sport, colonialism, or warfare were demanded, such compensatory tactics emerged as poor substitutes indeed.[23]

The Dreyfus Affair and the Crisis of French Manhood is concerned not with what made intellectuals seem unique to themselves and to others, but with what, in terms of lifestyle and the body, situated them on a continuum with the bourgeoisie. After all, as Edmond Goblot argued in his 1925 study of bourgeois culture, *La Barrière et le niveau*, there is no such thing as a class of intellectuals standing apart from the bourgeoisie. "There are only the intellectual professions. . . . Intellectuals are bourgeois." Insofar as they were themselves part of this professional elite, they too bore the marks associated with this lifestyle. "Nothing marks a man like his profession. . . . Daily work determines one's regime; more so than the organs, it constrains ideas, sentiments and tastes adapt to it. Habits of the body, habits of the mind, habits of language, all converge to give each of us a professional physiognomy."[24] The acquired habits that make up this "professional physiognomy" bear a striking resemblance to what Pierre Bourdieu calls the habitus, the "dispositions of an agent . . . [and] schemes of perception, appreciation and action" that are acquired over time and which function as second nature.[25] The dispositions of the habitus provide not only a structure for gender identity but an important stake in the tensions among different lifestyles in the social world.

This book therefore seeks to put intellectuals back in their bodies.[26] Its point of departure is the fact that, in addition to growing concerns about the progressive degeneration of the race and the threatening rise of feminist politics, distrust of the effects of excessive mental labor, associated with the liberal professions, was one of the most crucial catalysts of the period's gender anxieties. In other words, the habitus associated with the liberal professions, and epitomized in the lifestyles of *les intellectuels*, was identified as a major source of contemporary man's putative loss of power. The stereotypes conjured up by this association were numerous. The intellectual, it was assumed, lived a life that was sedentary, cerebral, and unhealthy; his physical weakness not only left him prey to nervousness and other disorders but rendered him unattractive to women and even cowardly. Like the stereotypical bureaucrat and Jew, the man whose work was *intellectuel* (as opposed to *manuel*) was not really a "man" in the full sense of the word, at least not when compared to traditional images of the man of action. Developing gradually since the 1880s, this tension flows throughout the polemics of the Dreyfus Affair, where condemnations of the messianic pretensions of the Dreyfusards frequently slipped into gender attacks that foregrounded the physical weakness produced by their chosen profession and unfavorably contrasted intellectuals with soldiers. That the Dreyfusards proved hypersensitive to these charges, which they defensively tried to refute with assertions about their manly deeds and virile bodies, suggests that their mission to defend the abstract values of truth and justice remained haunted by their problematic public image as weaklings. The gender of reason may have been implicitly masculine, as many feminist theorists suggest, but in this context, reason alone could not remove the stigma of effeminacy.

Drawing attention to such matters does not mean collapsing the intellectual into the bourgeois, especially since the weaknesses of the former were generally viewed as exaggerated versions of what afflicted the latter. Rather, it is a question of assessing the extent to which the intellectual could be appropriated as a means of symbolically belittling the kind of men who seemed to thrive under the Third Republic: members of the bourgeoisie who passed through the system of educational meritocracy to land positions of influence under the republican state, the so-called new social strata, or *nouvelles couches*, described during the 1880s.

That traditional elites resented these social, political, and economic interlopers is well established as a force contributing to the divisions of the Dreyfus Affair; that these elites also denigrated the manhood of the newcomers is acknowledged far less often. As we shall see, the conflict between traditionalism and republicanism was not confined to the clash of social visions; it also implied a tension between the kind of exemplary male figures who would thrive in each of those visions. The soldier could be celebrated, not merely because he symbolized a more traditional form of authority, but because he was thought to embody a classical style of heroic and robust manhood that seemed to be slipping away under the overly cerebral and enervating conditions of modernity. Conversely, if the civil servant, or *fonctionnaire*, could be condemned as the creature of a hothouse educational system, in which mental achievement outstripped physical fitness, it is easy to see why politically engaged professors would be singled out for even more brutal assaults. If attacks on the manhood of Dreyfusard intellectuals often overshot their marks, it was partly because they were meant to.

Although this book is organized in a loosely chronological fashion, beginning with the 1895 degradation of Dreyfus and ending with an overview of developments leading up to World War I, the analyses and arguments contained in it reflect thematic rather than narrative concerns. Because gender identity is deeply enmeshed within a network of cultural relationships and tensions, each chapter proceeds through layers of associations that reveal the complexity of the Dreyfus Affair as a gender issue. The lengthy chapter that constitutes Part I considers the broad gender issues that faced the French during the 1895 degradation of Dreyfus. This chapter provides a close examination of how newspaper coverage of the degradation ceremony commented excessively on the "dishonorable" and "cowardly" behavior of Dreyfus, addresses the wider implications of such critiques for the masculine credentials of Jewish men, and considers the strategies through which the Jewish press responded to allegations of Jews' cowardice and effeminacy. Part II comprises three chapters that explore the avenues through which the Dreyfusards tried to negotiate their identities as men by distancing themselves from "cowardly" Jews (Chapter 2), "hysterical" crowds (Chapter 3), and threatening women (Chapter 4), a project undertaken by some of the many writings and cartoons produced throughout the Affair. The two chapters that make up Part III shift the focus to the body itself, and reveal the tensions that haunted Dreyfusards and ultimately undermined their ability to sustain their heroic reputations during the prewar years. Chapter 5 uses the portly body of Émile Zola to discuss the relationship between diet, exercise, and shifting ideals of male body shape, while Chapter 6 engages with the emerging "culture of force" that marked French society during the prewar years, revealing the extent to which the tensions of the Dreyfus Affair continued to resonate in repeated critiques of intelligent but physically weak men.

The lines that form the epigraph to this Introduction were written by the late Eric Cahm, who in his broad survey of the Dreyfus Affair identified critical gaps and misconceptions that a century of scholarship had failed to resolve. When this fine historian died in 2001, he was busy working to improve our understanding of this pivotal event. For Cahm, the Dreyfus Affair was an open issue, one that demanded further inquiry and fresh interpretations. Just as a century ago, men and women insisted that the Dreyfus case be reopened in the light of unexamined evidence, this book seeks to review an event that might appear to be similarly closed. Of course, revisiting historical cases rarely results in the reassuring closure of a new verdict that simply replaces the prior one. It is therefore hoped that this book will complement traditional accounts by situating the Dreyfus Affair within a broader cultural setting, and that it will perhaps even encourage further scholarship on a case that is far from closed.

Part I / Masculinity and the Jewish Question

When Captain Alfred Dreyfus was accused of selling artillery secrets to the German ambassador in 1894, some explained the crime by simple reference to his Jewishness. Of course, Dreyfus was guilty, they said. Weren't all the Jews of France essentially foreigners, bound by different loyalties, and thus potential traitors? The sudden leap in anti-Semitic sentiment during the late 1880s, fueled largely through the Jew-hating writings of Édouard Drumont and propagated on a daily basis through his newspaper, *La Libre Parole*, made arguments such as these seem quite reasonable to his growing number of readers.

Although anti-Semites often made the loudest and most outrageous allegations about Dreyfus and about Jews in general, theirs were not the only opinions being voiced during this period of national outrage. Others sought to understand Dreyfus's motive without simply reducing all discussion to matters of race. In addition to citing his Jewishness, the press provided ample information about the family background of Dreyfus and his senior position in the army. Readers learned that this artillery officer hailed from a wealthy family in Mulhouse, that he had studied in the best schools, and that his impressive rise to the army's General Staff testified to his excellent credentials. What could have compelled a man who seemed to have everything to commit this most heinous of acts? Did he feel remorse for his deed? Would his behavior speak the truth that he refused to confess? The public degradation of the condemned man, whether witnessed personally or, more likely, through the press, provided an opportunity for people to judge for themselves. Although a fairly basic ceremony, the degradation of Dreyfus served a variety of purposes and elicited complex reactions on the part of spectators. A ritual of atonement whereby a wronged collective would avenge itself by crushing the guilty, the degradation also functioned as a theater where loyalty triumphed over betrayal and honor conquered cowardice.

No one doubts that anti-Semitism was at the heart of the Dreyfus Affair, but the problem of racism is not something that is easily contained in references to this or that group. By situating the problem of "the Jew" within a wider cultural context, we shall be in a better position to consider this brand of racism in more complex terms. Many agree that the Dreyfus Affair constituted the first serious eruption of modern anti-Semitism, a form of persecution that differed from more traditional forms of Jew-hating based on religious or economic grounds in that it incorporated biological arguments. However, few acknowledge that this modern anti-Semitism was also coextensive with the traditional assumption that Jewish men, whether due to age-old customs or congenital factors, were bookish, sedentary beings, whose weakness, cowardice, and effeminacy rendered them unfit for military service. This contention, in which the discourses of race and gender were intersected, was so pervasive that it is frequently found expressed even by those who denounced anti-Semitism, thus showing how racial stereotypes could cross conventional political lines. Chapter 1 considers these allegations about the defective virility of Jewish men by way of newspaper representations of Dreyfus, both during his 1895 degradation and at his 1899 retrial, and inquires into the implications that such images had for the gender identity of assimilated Jews. It argues that reports of the "cowardly" behavior of Dreyfus, even when they failed to situate this conduct in racial terms, implicitly provided fuel for overtly anti-Semitic allegations that Jews generally were cowards, thus forcing Jewish men to defensively assert their capacity for honor. As such, allegations about Dreyfus's cowardice illuminate the masculine anxieties harbored by gentile men during this time and underscore the period's tension between thinking men and men of action. Although most French Jews denounced the miscarriage of justice that exiled Dreyfus and supported the campaign of the "intellectuals" for a revision of his case, they insisted upon their proximity to military men in terms of lifestyle. The chapter concludes by looking at how, despite their disagreements, both assimilated and Zionist Jews celebrated the ancient figure of the Hebrew soldier as a worthy exemplar and necessary remedy for the tarnishing of Jewish male honor by the Dreyfus Affair, thus self-consciously embracing a gentile code of martial manhood.

CHAPTER ONE

Masculine Performances

Alfred Dreyfus and the Paradox of the Jewish Soldier

On the icy morning of 6 January 1895, in a solemn public ceremony in the court-yard of the École Militaire in Paris, Alfred Dreyfus was formally stripped of his military identity before being shipped off to Devil's Island. Journalists, digni-taries, and other invited guests witnessed this event from special seats, while an estimated crowd of six or seven thousand thronged outside the gate. The se-quence of events is fairly straightforward and has been reported in a number of histories. At the stroke of nine, Dreyfus was escorted by four soldiers with drawn sabers to the center of the courtyard, where General Paul Darras declared "Alfred Dreyfus, you are not worthy of bearing arms. In the name of the French people, we degrade you." Forced to parade before the silent troops and, when he passed the gate, the screaming crowd, Dreyfus proclaimed his innocence several times before being photographed by the anthropometric service and returned to prison. Transferred to La Rochelle eleven days later, Dreyfus was imprisoned at the Saint-Martin de Ré fortress before being embarked a month later on a convict ship for Devil's Island, just off the coast of French Guiana in South America.[1]

Historians have often underscored the prevalence of anti-Semitic sentiment in the atmosphere surrounding the degradation and have rightly noted how its eruption in France during this time represented a hostility to Jews that had been absent, or at least dormant, throughout much of the nineteenth century. Jean-Denis Bredin's very comprehensive historical treatment of the Dreyfus Affair emphasizes the racial tension of this atmosphere by citing, in addition to the abuse being screamed by the crowd, the impressions of confirmed anti-Semitic journalists like Léon Daudet and Maurice Barrès.[2] Eric Cahm sketches a more complex picture of the Paris press during the 1890s, demonstrating how the four largest dailies, *Le Petit Journal, Le Petit Parisien, Le Journal,* and *Le Matin* sought to maintain their broad readerships by appearing politically neutral, while the political press manifested a broad range of perspectives, from the religious neu-trality of republican papers like *Le Figaro* and *Le Temps* to the anti-Semitic vit-riol of *La Libre Parole* and *L'Intransigeant.*[3] Yet if these newspapers disagreed on whether the Jewishness of Dreyfus was a crucial factor in his alleged treason, they were virtually unanimous in their condemnation of the captain's conduct during the degradation, which for the most part struck them as callous and cowardly. If much of the mainstream press opted for neutrality by avoiding the politically loaded issue of Jewishness, when it came to questions of honor and manhood, it was far less restrained and registered opinions similar to those expressed by other newspapers.

Yet if the paucity of explicit references to the Jewishness of Dreyfus suggests toleration on the part of journalists, what are we to make of the ubiquitous condemnations of his "dishonorable" behavior? Is there a relationship between these two discourses, one based on race, the other on gender? Scholars associated with what is sometimes called New Jewish Cultural Studies assert that these different stereotypes are in fact interrelated, that the language employed in the creation of one "other" often borrows from the rhetoric used to construct another. As we shall see below, traditional images of the Jewish man associated him with physical weakness, cowardice, nervousness, and a lack of honor, all qualities commonly associated with women and blacks, among others. In other words, the Jew's difference from the "white man" was historically crafted in terms of his distance from both whiteness (race) and manhood (gender). Rather than being easily distinguishable phenomena, discourses of race and gender are frequently fashioned out of the same cultural material, thus revealing the extent to which the social construction of otherness is itself "interarticulated" across a spectrum of differences. The category of Jewishness in late-nineteenth-century French culture attests to the fluid nature of stereotyping. Insofar as they drew upon a pool of qualities associated with Jews and capable of being mobilized for anti-Semitic ends, repeated references to the deficient manhood of Dreyfus did not need to invoke Jewishness explicitly in order to be utilized for racialized arguments. Rather, the interarticulation of gender and race made it possible to employ a gender critique that could also function as a euphemized racial commentary, so that besmirching the manliness of Dreyfus could be read as an implicit indictment of his Jewishness. This slippage between gender and racial stereotypes was common in fin-de-siècle culture and partly explains why Jewish men of the time, long familiar with the racial implications of any discussion of honor, were quite sensitive to how Dreyfus was being described and responded by defensively insisting upon the unacknowledged honor and martial prowess of Jewish men.

Like every newspaper account of the degradation, this chapter takes the body of Alfred Dreyfus as its focus. Whereas journalistic accounts sought to depict the body of Dreyfus as it "really" was, I am more concerned with the ways in which it appeared to the men who wrote these reports, how it violated the expectations about honor and innocence that structured their perceptions, and the extent to which these representations resonated in later encounters with Dreyfus, particularly when he returned to France in 1899. The complicated responses to the degradation ceremony illuminate the interplay of conventions about, on the one hand, the behavior of honorable as opposed to cowardly men, and, on the other, the comportment of innocent as opposed to guilty parties. These conventions were to some extent grounded in precedents set in earlier court cases, but they were also reinforced by the press and by novels, both of which helped to prefigure the way Dreyfus appeared to the public. Although these expectations did not necessarily rely upon explicitly drawn racial stereotypes for their efficacy, they facilitated the reinforcement of critiques of Jewish manhood. Claims that Dreyfus seemed bereft of honor could be used to illustrate traditional assumptions that Jewish men generally were bookish, weak, cowardly, and effeminate, all without explicitly playing the race card. Indeed, such allegations not only resurfaced during Dreyfus's 1899 retrial but were implicit in the strategies of Jewish men who sought to sustain their sense of manhood in the face of the "cowardice" of one of their own. The body of Dreyfus thus became enmeshed in the intersection of racial and gender anxieties of the period; it was a crucial component in the struggles being waged by his enemies and allies.

Paris 1895: The Monster of Evil

The degradation of Dreyfus was a ceremony of dishonor. Although those charged with political crimes could no longer receive the death sentence, the degradation was often described as if it impacted directly upon Dreyfus's body. Joseph Reinach explained how Dreyfus had become a "walking cadaver" when he made his turn around the courtyard after being "tortured."[4] In fact, most newspapers referred to the ceremony itself as an "execution," a word that, according to a reporter for *La Lanterne*, was quite well chosen. After all, being degraded in such a manner was a punishment "a thousand times more terrible than death. . . . [This is] a moral death that we are going to witness."[5] This "moral death" consisted of the removal from the traitor all signs of military honor, capped off by the breaking of his sword. Reporters claimed that this spectacle was particularly disturbing to the military men in attendance, many of whom would have preferred an actual execution to this public humiliation. *Le Petit Journal* underscored this impression for its readers: "[T]his man is a coward. . . . Dreyfus is no longer a soldier. He is no longer even a man. He is a mere number in a convict gang."[6] Yet the questions of honor raised by the Dreyfus case were not put to rest by the guilty verdict, and the shaming of the captain was never a cut-and-dried instance of civic retribution. Of course, Dreyfus's reputation as a man of honor had been fatally compromised once he was declared guilty of treason, a deed that no honorable soldier would have committed. Yet for some observers, the finality of this fall from grace was deferred by the fact that Dreyfus had always steadfastly maintained his innocence, an insistence that provoked speculations about the justness of the military verdict and encouraged even greater attention to his behavior during his degradation. Those who allowed some room for doubt assumed that if he had indeed been unjustly convicted, his outrage at being publicly disgraced would have been manifest and persuasive: no truly honorable or innocent man would have been able to endure such torture silently. Among those convinced of his guilt, the problem of honor was complicated by questions of motivation and remorse, for there is evidence that a traitor who admitted his error and repented his crime would have elicited public sympathy even though the verdict remained unchanged. Whether onlookers scanned Dreyfus's body for evidence of innocence or signs of contrition, most were looking for proof that honor still resided in this man.

Since the public had been barred from the court-martial, Dreyfus was in a sense being tried twice: first before a military tribunal that assessed his case in closed session, then in a court of public opinion that judged his honor. Even before his degradation, some readers had been coached on how to read the spectacle and encouraged to assess the characters in terms of their worth as soldiers. So as not to be disheartened by the horrible spectacle, the readers of *Paris-Journal* were counseled to draw inspiration from the sight of General Auguste Mercier: "[I]t is good for everyone to recall that the safekeeping of the army and the care of our defense are in loyal hands, those of General Mercier, minister of war." Mercier, who had bowed to anti-Semitic pressure to insist upon the conviction of Dreyfus, cut an imposing figure that seemed the very essence of the true army, if not of France itself: "One look at this physiognomy, so martial and so French, will calm our minds, [and] lift our hearts, which have been so saddened by the treason of an officer of our valiant army."[7] From the start, the public was primed to recognize the bodily signs that would mark the contrast between an honorable officer and a cowardly traitor. When it came to attacks upon

honor, noted *Le Petit Parisien*, there was an inverse relationship between the behavior of traitors and that of "brave men." When a political crisis sends them to
the wall, brave men will face twelve bullets "without trembling," but when someone tries to "mark them with infamy," these same men will "bellow with grief."
Traitors, however, usually kneel and weep in a cowardly way before the firing
squad but manage to remain standing when one merely attacks their honor
rather than "their precious skin."[8] The impassivity of Dreyfus was thus considered unbecoming for an innocent or honorable man and proved problematic
even for those who were somewhat sympathetic to the man. The diplomat Maurice Paléologue was one such sympathizer, and even he believed that the captain's behavior alone was enough to convict him of treason: "To have lent himself so docilely, so passively, to such a torture, the man must have been devoid
of moral sensibility. . . . his voice might have been the voice of an automaton."[9]

That the degradation ceremony had become a veritable theater of guilt and
dishonor is not surprising. Parisian life at end of the nineteenth century was by
most accounts steeped in spectacle and marked by a widespread emphasis on visuality. The rise of department stores that encouraged the leisure practice of "just
looking" was complemented by the proliferation of cheap amusements that fascinated the public, including panoramas, dioramas, circuses, and even weekly
trips to the morgue. Some spectators would have gazed with admiration and awe
upon the bodies of the strongmen who performed for crowds on the grand
boulevards or the acrobats and trapeze artists who delighted audiences at the
Cirque Molier. Others would have relished evenings of laughter and fun at café-
concerts and cabarets, where contorted and epileptoid performances helped sate
the bourgeoisie's growing appetite for strong sensations. To be sure, the boundaries between "reality" and its sensationalized representations were blurred in
this era, inasmuch as newspaper stories were often framed by serialized novels,
or *romans-feuilletons*, that commented via fiction upon a range of contemporary
issues.[10] It is no surprise, then, that Dreyfus's performance was similarly judged
in terms of spectacle.

Coming as it did on the heels of a court-martial, however, the degradation
of Dreyfus must also be considered in the context of what the French had come
to expect of the spectacles orchestrated by their legal system. Ever since the
eighteenth century, French elites have often denigrated theatricality as a form of
ritualized artificiality that threatened the authenticity of nature and the self, thus
manifesting the "antitheatrical prejudice" that has recurred in Western society
since Plato.[11] Despite this distrust of spectacles, however, during the nineteenth

century the public had nevertheless come to expect an element of theatricality in its legal system. As Katherine Fischer Taylor has shown in her study of the Palais de Justice, these theatrical elements were integral to the ways in which French jurisprudence functioned, an observation that requires a qualification of Michel Foucault's claim that in the nineteenth century, trial and punishment had divested themselves of visual display. Elegantly dressed spectators often filled the courtroom for particularly sensational cases, sometimes equipped with picnic baskets and champagne so as not to surrender their seats during lengthy recesses. This public access to court proceedings, available since the Constitutional Charter of 1814, was also criticized on medical grounds by those wary of the "contagious" effect that discussions of criminal activity could have upon impressionable individuals.[12] During the first step of the proceedings, the clerk would read aloud the prosecutor's reconstruction of the crime, "a novelistic reconstruction of crime, motive and culpability," which could take up to an hour in certain cases. Moreover, insofar as they represented "an individual in contest with a vast social body," defense attorneys were expected to be emotive and theatrical in order to sway the jury: "the language employed in trials was an oral one informed by gesture and expression, which appealed to the imagination." One effect of this system was that the body of the accused became especially open to scrutiny. The French inquisitorial (as opposed to the Anglo-American accusatorial) legal procedure required the defendant to face the judge directly, and given the architectural structure of the courtroom, this meant that the jury and the public saw the defendant primarily in profile. The judge, however, was seen in full face. As Fischer Taylor argues, this practice "created the conditions for the old tradition of physiognomic interpretation, with its interest in profile."[13]

The training that experts and the public received in the art of reading bodies was not restricted to court cases, but easily extended to other areas of life. Indeed, in the nineteenth century, the term *physionomie* was applied loosely to a variety of things, both physical and nonphysical, and the very character of a person was often said to have its distinctive "moral physiognomy." The language of gesture, posture, and overall comportment was crucial when it came to evaluating witness testimony, and both press and public became adept at interpreting bodily signs that might provide insight into the credibility of the individual testifying. Indeed, from the 1880s onward, artists for the popular press typically produced pages of composite vignettes depicting the various characters of the trial and thus further encouraging amateur physiognomy among the public.[14] Yet reading the body also meant scrutinizing its actions, and the theatricality of the French system demanded that its players follow certain cultural scripts. For instance, in a convention fueled by precedent and reinforced through literature, it was widely assumed that a guilty verdict would reduce the accused to tears or some other outward sign of repentance, and the public expressed its displeasure when such displays were not elicited. At the culmination of the spectacle of the trial, the accused was expected to confirm the justness of the verdict and thus to speak the "truth" about his or her crime.

The press and the public were particularly interested in assessing how a convicted traitor like Dreyfus would comport himself. Having been barred access to the court-martial proceedings, which had been conducted in a closed session, journalists and spectators could only catch glimpses of Dreyfus in transit. His degradation would allow some of them to gaze directly at the "infamous man, to see if he was not a monster physically as well as morally."[15] As always the press eagerly played its part as go-between for its readers: "And we, the press, are there, ready to catch every fleeting movement, to translate the least hesitation, to magnify even the slightest sign of error or doubt."[16] This penetrating journalistic gaze was frequently described in terms of *dévisagement*, variously meaning "scrutinizing," "staring down," "disfiguring," or "scratching" a face. *Dévisagement* meant paying close attention to the most minute bodily signs: a nervous spasm at the temple, a trickle of sweat, a trembling lip, a halting step, anything that might give one insight into the inner state of the accused. Yet it also implied an aggressive gaze that analytically broke the face down into sections, whose meaning the journalists deciphered for the public. Finally, through its connotations of disfigurement, *dévisagement* ironically suggested the impossibility of ever presenting an accurate description of Dreyfus. During Dreyfus's 1899 retrial, for instance, one journalist explained the mission of the press corps: "Paris has assigned to Rennes its most perspicacious reporters and its most subtle psychologists. Their mission was to inform posterity about [Dreyfus's] moral and physical physiognomy: they have probed his heart and scrutinized [*dévisagé*] his features."[17]

We see that at least three factors played a part in structuring public responses to Dreyfus's behavior: the theatrical conventions of the courtroom, a public that had come to expect these conventions, and a press ready to interpret the performance of the accused. Putting aside the issue of anti-Semitism for the time being, it is evident that the outrage expressed by many journalists in the wake of the degradation was elicited more by unmet expectations than anything else, particularly regarding the accused's emotional control. Assuming the man to have been guilty as charged, observers expected from Dreyfus either tangible signs of repentance or outrage at having been dishonored, a performance that would have conformed to the standard "script" of the legal theater. In fact some reporters went to the degradation expecting to be torn between righteous feelings of vindication and a degree of pity at the anticipated histrionics of the condemned. "Yesterday morning I went to the École Militaire with the dread of attending a frightening spectacle," confessed one journalist: "'The condemned is going to be sorrowful, he is going to weep, he is going to wail,' I told myself, 'his strangled voice will touch my heart. I know myself: I am going to pity him.'" This reporter was unprepared for the stoical and even defiant posture assumed by Dreyfus and reacted with a very different set of emotions: "I returned from the ceremony disgusted, shocked, indignant, furious with the wretched man. . . . I looked at him through binoculars. Not a muscle shudders! Not one tear of despair! Scarcely a blink of an eyelid betrays his emotion."[18]

Undeterred by the self-control exercised by the captain, journalists scanned his body for any clues to his emotional state. A reporter for *La Petite République* picked up on some very subtle signs: "In his step we see a slight limp. He is walking all the same, a bit to one side; his left arm is apart from his torso, as if stiffened through some hypnotic influence." Was that a glimmer of remorse betrayed by Dreyfus soon after he had addressed the crowd? "His gaze has resumed its hard fixity . . . but his cheeks are moist. Was he weeping?"[19] Few others reported tears in the eyes of the accused, and most were shocked that the captain had refused to weep. We can sense why such tears of repentance would have been expected. Just as literary conventions had helped to shape the theatricality of the courtroom drama, so too popular literature had acquainted the reading public with the villain who partly paid for his crimes by being publicly reduced to tears.[20] It was a gesture that had come to be expected of guilty parties, and the sight of the weeping traitor would have provided a form of closure that confirmed the guilt of Dreyfus. Journalists had therefore come to the degradation with feelings of anticipation and dread, expecting to be uncomfortably moved by a penitent, ideally weeping, traitor. Anticipating a mixture of pity and contempt, most were outraged by Dreyfus's actual performance.

There is now a substantial body of scholarship exploring the gendered dynamics of the legal system in France, making it clear that the comportment of men and women was often taken into account as proof of the degree to which they conformed to the gender norms of the day. In certain cases, the credible performance of one's gender role could mean the difference between a jury's verdict of guilt or innocence. Edward Berenson has demonstrated this quite vividly in his exploration of the 1914 trial of Henriette Caillaux for the murder of the newspaper editor Gaston Calmette. Newspapers sympathetic to the prosecution often pointed out the composed and calculated demeanor of Madame Caillaux when she shot Calmette in his office, thereby indicating the self-possessed and therefore "masculine" nature of the murderer. Conscious of how damaging any hint of gender-bending could be for their case, the defense insisted that Caillaux's motive for killing—Calmette's scandalous publication of love letters between the accused and her future husband, the politician Joseph Caillaux—had driven this woman out of her wits, rendering her deed a veritable crime of passion (meaning that the revenge she exacted would have appealed to popular conceptions of justice). Caillaux herself employed the stock defense of the crime of passion to her benefit and presented a credible rendition of the passionate woman driven by her violated sense of honor to an irrational deed. Her eventual acquittal in part testifies to the persuasiveness of her performance before the jury.[21]

Regardless of the fact that women might still find themselves convicted of their crimes—indeed, the legal system was frequently at odds with public perceptions—women who played the appropriate role often merited the favor and pity of spectators, regardless of their culpability. Yet what role would a man have had to play in order to elicit such favor? There is every reason to agree with Jean Ajalbert's 1895 speculation that Dreyfus would have been damned no matter how he carried himself: "They insult Dreyfus for having marched with a firm step throughout this abominable promenade; they would have insulted him even if his step had hesitated."[22] But if we remain attentive to the reactions registered by many journalists, more complicated expectations seem to have been in place. Weeping might not automatically have made Dreyfus seem honorable, and it could have easily been cited as evidence of effeminacy; but one cannot discount the nearly unanimous outrage reporters registered when he failed to perform as expected. In other words, newspaper accounts of the degradation were complex cultural responses structured by a range of factors and expectations. Their perceptions would have been shaped as much by general assumptions about appropriate gender behavior as by the particular emotional conventions encountered in trials.

The recent work of Ruth Harris and Ann-Louise Shapiro on French court cases suggests that had the crime of Dreyfus been motivated by passion, some emotional display would have been essential for the public's response. As Shapiro notes, "The true *criminel passionnel* was expected to instantly and eternally regret the act—attempted suicide could attest to such regret—and to make no effort to conceal the crime, asserting thereby the essential legitimacy of the behavior."[23] The behavior of Dreyfus did not conform to this script. When he was first accused of treason, for instance, the captain was offered a pistol so that he could choose an honorable end. Yet while such performances were expected of men as well as women, they did not necessarily confirm the masculinity of the guilty man; rather, tearful outbursts could just as easily confirm a guilty man's "feminine" lack of emotional control. Whether or not a man should outwardly express emotion was a rather slippery issue at the fin de siècle. It often depended upon circumstances. A long tradition of manly comportment, one inherited from antiquity and refined during the French Revolution, demanded that men present a public front of control and impermeability, especially in the face of adversity, thus approximating the stoicism encouraged in many classical texts.[24] While this insistence on emotional control had been partly submerged due to the influence of romanticism, by the end of the nineteenth century, it had become virtually de rigueur across the Western world. In France as elsewhere, the educational system was an important site for instilling this cultural imperative into young men. All of Dreyfus's schooling had emphasized the importance of concealing emotion, and his schoolmasters had insisted that coldness was by far the preferable stance. The somber barracks and institutional feel of the prestigious Collège Chaptal inculcated seriousness at the expense of youthful spontaneity and only reinforced the need for young men to conceal their emotions.[25]

To some degree, then, male weeping could be cited as evidence of an inability to control one's emotions. Yet this general rule neither reveals the many subtleties and nuances in the actual behavior of men nor accounts for the many ways in which students might flout the very rules they were being taught. Peter Stearns has demonstrated how the Victorian emotional style emphasized the channeling of emotions like anger into productive ends, and Shapiro has vividly shown how in France, even violence could be respected if inflicted in the heat of passion. In actual practice, male emotional management neither entailed rigid stoicism nor ruled out periodic displays of passion.[26] There is also the personality of Dreyfus himself to consider. As was the case with many males, his education had always stressed mastery of the emotions. Yet as a cadet at the École polytechnique, Dreyfus was repeatedly criticized for his shyness, monotone voice, and rigid demeanor, thus revealing an inability to open himself to others that he once confessed as his greatest personal fault.[27] It is true that the French had come to expect a significant degree of emotional control in their men, but it seems that Dreyfus exceeded this expectation to a fault. So deeply ingrained was his personal reserve that Dreyfus failed to convince Lieutenant-Colonel Armand Mercier du Paty de Clam of his innocence when first confronted with the infamous *bordereau*, the document that purportedly incriminated him. To his superior, the captain's energetic protests of innocence seemed forced, altogether too "theatrical."[28] Most who witnessed the degradation spectacle also deplored the stiffness (*la raideur*) of Dreyfus. Even his loud protests, which most agreed were to be expected of a truly innocent man, seemed to ring false. Being a man thus entailed a careful management of one's emotions, which ordinarily meant the exercise of self-control, offset by an ability to recognize circumstances where passionate outbursts were appropriate and even necessary. A true man of honor, most agreed, would have spontaneously rebelled against the humiliation of a public degradation rather than endure it silently. The stiffness of Dreyfus for much of the degradation rendered his actual outbursts less than credible. However sincerely they were uttered, Dreyfus's anguished protests failed to convince those who witnessed his public disgrace. As Paléologue noted, "[W]e sensed no heat of the soul [*aucune chaleur d'âme*] there."[29]

There is an obvious retort to the above ruminations: treason is not normally considered a crime of passion. The latter usually features a spontaneous act of revenge, whereas treason requires premeditation and execution over an extended period of time. While this is no doubt true, it was admitted at the time that unwholesome passions, say, for money or influence, could compel even the most loyal soldier to betray his country. Claims such as these helped many observers to conceptualize treason as a deed grounded partly in passion, thus perhaps prompting so many to demand an emotional display that matched the motivation for the crime. Unlike the *criminel passionnel*, the traitor could not hope for a popular acquittal, but a display of remorse might at least have elicited sympathy. Military expectations were not far removed from mainstream ones with respect to the proper comportment of traitors. Several officers interviewed after the degradation explained to *Le Siècle* that the scandalous behavior of Dreyfus only confirmed his guilt in their eyes. "Whereas *les dégradés* are typically in a state of complete prostration, Dreyfus did not betray the slightest emotion, not the slightest weakness; nothing but hatred, arrogance, rage. He had the look of a criminal furious at having been caught, not that of an innocent man who protests."[30] Far from being the primary ingredient in public perceptions of Dreyfus, anti-Semitism exacerbated this more basic sense of unmet expectations. "Dreyfus, the Jew, manifested a revolting cynicism," fumed *La Croix*. Faced with his former comrades from the General Staff, soldiers of every rank, the angry crowd, and the press, "who noted the slightest gestures," this "Judas remained calm, but a calm that let itself be pierced by rage."[31]

The final, and for many spectators, the most revolting phase of Dreyfus's performance occurred when he confronted the press and the crowd while being led away. This was the moment for which the press corps had eagerly waited. "In two minutes he would pass before me," Édouard Conte recalled thinking excitedly when he saw Dreyfus approaching. "I shall see his face. I shall scrutinize it [*Je le dévisagerai*]. I shall try to decipher his features."[32] The primacy of the visual register in juridical spectacles meant that the traitor was ideally an object to be consumed with the eye, and the scandal of Dreyfus's composure was heightened by his bold willingness to stare down his audience. A more obviously penitent traitor might have suggested a soldier led astray under conditions of warfare or civil strife, perhaps even a once honorable man whose sense of duty had been compromised, as André de Boisandré put it, by "the hurricane of more or less vile passions."[33] Like many of his colleagues, this reporter incorporated into his expectations the figure of the guilty, yet repentant, *criminel passionnel*, someone who had come sincerely to regret the fruit of his personal weakness. Such a man would surely be too ashamed to meet the eyes of onlookers, his shame being based on the gravity of his crime, and perhaps on the spectacle he had made of himself by weeping publicly. The composed traitor, however, suggested a being of utter calculation, one who defiantly returned the gaze that was meant to reduce him to an object. "He is passing several paces in front of us, his head high," observed an unnamed reporter who was stunned to find his gaze returned by the accused: "His confident gaze stares us down [*dévisage*] with menacing flashes." This final performance of Dreyfus seemed to disclose everything:

> And now the impression is complete, clear, incontestable: the man who has looked at us in this way, the man who, between the guards, walks with his body upright, his legs confident, his arms stiff, his fists clenched as if ready for attack, this man is not *un passionnel* who, having erred, can repent; this man is a monster of evil, *un cérébral* who struck and does not want to admit defeat. The traitor does not want to acknowledge that he is justly punished. He does not want to repent.[34]

The tension of the degradation seemed to revolve around these two poles of motivation: a traitor who was *un passionnel* would be condemned but nevertheless pitied; one who betrayed his country with cold calculation was altogether beyond redemption. This could provide further grounds for assuming, as some did, that this man had never truly been French in the first place: a reporter for *Gil*

Blas even explained that the Alsatian Dreyfus was in fact German rather than "a Frenchman like us."[35] Yet despite the crowd's screams of "Judas!" and the racist slurs of the conservative press, many newspapers were able to deplore the behavior of Dreyfus without ever mentioning his Jewishness. This does not mean that the anti-Semitic imagery that circulated widely at this time played no role in these accounts, but that references to gender performance could serve as more tactful replacements for racial slurs. At the same time, it is also evident that anti-Semitism was partly dependent on judicial conventions and the performance of the accused, where the press almost unanimously agreed. Even the anti-Semitic *La Libre Parole* admitted that a different "attitude would have inspired pity. His only inspired disgust."[36]

After this, the final and most scandalous phase of the degradation, Dreyfus was led away to be measured by Dr Alphonse Bertillon's anthropometric service before being returned to prison and shipped off to Devil's Island.[37] For those who regretted that a death sentence had not been handed down, there was still some consolation to be found in imagining how the traitor would live out the rest of his days. "After all, who knows what dreadful tortures the future holds for him!" wondered one reporter with relish. "Imagine the terrifying nightmares that will haunt him when his conscience, which is [now] perhaps only benumbed, awakens. . . . What pain, what physical torture could be comparable to what he will endure then! Imagine his days spent in despair, his excruciating nights disturbed by horrible recollections." The departure of Dreyfus from the stage served as a purification for a scandalized audience, retribution for a violated body politic: "The disappearance of the traitor was greeted by an immense relief. The air seemed purer, we breathed easier."[38]

Jewish Manhood and the Western Ideal

In the four years he spent in exile, Dreyfus was indeed plagued by black thoughts and physical pains, but not because he was being eaten away by guilt. Rather, Dreyfus not only insisted repeatedly in his letters to his wife that he was innocent but that his honor had been impeached, thus striking a blow at his identity as a man. It is not altogether surprising that a convicted traitor would be considered unworthy to wear a military uniform, and that his deed would be viewed as proof of just how little he embodied the honor of the army. Yet due to the captain's Jewishness, the case of Dreyfus exceeded this basic tension between the traitor and the true soldier. Thus far, the issue of race has been bracketed from this account of the degradation, for while anti-Semitism indeed played a role in helping to explain the virtually incomprehensible act of treason, it did not figure explicitly in the press's response to the degradation. Rather, after all the "facts" were in and the guilt of Dreyfus seemed without question, the public expected the accused to conform to the standard script of guilty parties; yet insofar as the legal theater was a stage that sought to pass for reality, this performance had to be credible enough so as not to appear "performed." Onlookers expecting to be caught up in the spectacle resented the sort of "bad" performance that might draw attention to the system's inherent theatricality. Indeed, during Dreyfus's degradation in Paris, and again during his retrial in Rennes, the most common complaint about him was that he seemed to be merely performing, which ironically meant that he had failed to perform properly. When Dreyfus loudly proclaimed his innocence, noted one reporter, it "did not vibrate with the slightest emotion. This is a *cri de théâtre*, uttered by a bad actor who has played his role badly."[39]

Despite the relative absence of explicit anti-Semitic imagery, the specter of race was never banished from these newspaper accounts. Press reports of the degradation sketched a series of oppositions between innocence and guilt, loyalty and treason, honor and cowardice, and true and sham remorse, oppositions that were sufficiently protean to admit a further tension between "real" men and Jewish men. That Dreyfus's performance came under such scrutiny testifies in part to the gender anxieties of the fin de siècle, where, as Robert Nye argues, "assessments about a man's masculinity took on an unusual importance in social life. At least for middle and upper-class men, being anatomically 'of the male sex' was necessary, but was not in itself sufficient to satisfy the ideals of masculinity articulated routinely in public discourse."[40] Although overt racial rhetoric was absent from most newspaper accounts, the captain's inept performance, which suggested a profound disjunction between the officer's uniform and the man inside, functioned easily alongside anti-Semitic discourses about the duplicitous nature of Jews and their general unfitness to serve in the military. This particular concern emerged more clearly after 1896, once the pro-Dreyfus campaign began in earnest, thus making the defense of the degraded captain appear to be an attack on the army and a critique of military manhood itself. It is thus possible to understand "performance" on a number of levels, from the acting out of cultural scripts in the courtroom to more generalized scripts governing the performance of gender identity. Among mainstream newspapers with a commercial interest in appearing politically neutral on the Jewish question, obsessing over Dreyfus's "dishonorable" performance may have been a convenient way of employing a gender critique as a substitute for riskier racial observations. At the very least, the fact that the presumed weakness, timidity, nervousness, and cowardice of Jewish men were popular features of anti-Semitic discourses made these accounts readily available for more explicitly racist purposes.

In the Western world, Jewish men have often received bad reviews for their gender performances, largely due to the perceived distance between Jewish manhood and the martial ideal. In a culture shaped by an ideology of adventure, the soldier occupies a central role in the pantheon of acceptable male types and offers a style of manhood that is as physical as it is moral. Well into the modern era, European countries had identified military men as prime examples of male physical fitness, and soldiers were often viewed as models of bodily reform against which other men could be measured.[41] Yet the soldier was also one who submitted to sacrifice, subordinating his fear for the sake of a higher goal. The "disinterested" pursuit of a cause and a willingness to sacrifice oneself bravely would come to epitomize a tragic conception of life. To shrink in the face of danger was a sign of cowardice, and "any soldier who reckons with death is not a true soldier."[42] However, Jewish men have traditionally been considered incapable of living up to this warrior ideal. In the distinction he drew between the Semite and the Aryan, the anti-Semitic journalist Édouard Drumont invoked many of these Western martial ideals to show how the latter had a monopoly on the ideals of heroism, justice, liberty, and beauty. The Aryan forges into unknown territories on "voyages of adventure," Drumont claimed, and, in his embodiment of the chivalric tradition, is a being who "risks his life, who fights for a cause, who sacrifices himself," much like Parsifal on his quest for the Holy Grail.[43] Yet the Jew was also disqualified from normative masculinity on other grounds. Considered rootless, mercantile, and cerebral, he has been viewed as disconnected from the soil and its cultural symbolism, thus rendering him a stranger to the lifestyle of the physically hardy and quietly heroic rural laborer, whose robustness was often contrasted to the sedentary decadence of the urban bourgeois. Despite efforts to refute these images of Jewish passivity, notably in Israel, the figure of the cerebral, urbane, weak, and nervous Jew continues to circulate in Western culture as the countertype of both the "tough Jew" and the Gentile man of action.

Many scholars trace the image of the effeminate Jewish male to the Middle Ages; yet Daniel Boyarin contends that the historical tension between the bookish rabbi and the violent soldier represents a much older contest among competing versions of manhood. In *Unheroic Conduct: The Rise of Heterosexuality and the Invention of the Jewish Man,* Boyarin argues that traditional Judaism offers a normative ideal of nonphallocentric masculinity that could serve as an alternative to the violent model based on the knight that has developed in the Western world. Boyarin's claims are largely drawn from the allegorical tales found in the Babylonian Talmud, the vast textual project that epitomized the new emphasis on the local synagogue and rabbinical culture following the destruction of Jerusalem by the Romans in 70 C.E. Boyarin argues that in the Talmud, "the image of the ideal male as nonaggressive, not strong, not physically active is a positive product of the self-fashioning of rabbinic masculinity." The Talmud denigrated the pugnacious style of manhood demonstrated by Roman soldiers and, later, by knights, as uncivilized, as it did Jews who sought to copy such behavior. Yet unlike the Christian tradition, where the bookish monk was refused an identity as a legitimate sexual object, the gentle rabbinical scholar was cast by the Talmud as the quintessential object of female desire: the qualities that would in gentile culture only qualify a man to withdraw from women represented in Jewish culture the perfect preparation for the ideal husband. This is not to say that Talmudic scholars failed to enact distinctive gender hierarchies when representing their own activity or that traditional forms of Judaism celebrate equality between the sexes; nor, indeed, is it to argue that the Hebrews themselves did not have a distinctive martial tradition or that Jewish men are incapable of violence in everyday life. Rather, it is to say that in the Diaspora, the gender order was itself structured in opposition to the conventions of mainstream gentile culture, thus representing what Boyarin sees as "a principled and deliberate reversal and rejection of those norms." Traditional ideals of Jewish manhood were thus self-consciously articulated against the Roman and Christian courtly male norm, which was in turn cast as the "other." What has been for centuries described as the "effeminacy" of male Jews was, rather, an alternative mode of masculinity, which Boyarin regards as preferable.[44]

Boyarin sketches tensions between competing styles of manhood that are useful for thinking historically about the implicit gender dimension to Jewish assimilation. He also helps us to understand the experience of male Jews in France, where Judaism had since 1792 been formally sanctioned as a form of private religiosity that was ideally insulated from the putatively universal concerns of the public sphere. This entailed a significant expansion of the liberties enjoyed by Jews and served as a beacon to Jews in other countries throughout the nineteenth century. Moreover, ever since their formal emancipation at the time of the French Revolution, Jews have served and even risen to ranks of considerable authority in the French army.[45] Yet Jewishness was often viewed with suspicion even among ostensibly sympathetic gentile commentators, which is why these facts should not lead us to conclude that Jewish males were necessarily considered from the start eminently *fit* to serve in the military. Many scholars have noted how the project of Jewish assimilation, which was subscribed to by modernizing Jews as well as by many prominent Dreyfusards, generated a series of paradoxes that have yet to be resolved.[46] Ever since the eighteenth century, sympathetic observers have recommended an acceptance of the Jews in France. Yet despite their best intentions, even these well-meaning commentators posited the corrupt actuality of this group with an expectation that the Jewish condition might improve at some future time, implying a distinction, as the abbé Henri Grégoire observed in 1788, between an outward cultural layer of "burlesque traditions," "physical degradation," and "odious practices" that concealed an inner core qualifying the Jews as members of the "universal family" of humanity.[47] Assimilationism thus self-consciously recognized the superiority of the gentile cultural model as well as the current abject state of the Jews, and anticipated a time when they would be purged of the social, psychic, and somatic qualities that maintained their difference in gentile culture—that is, their "Jewishness." As Grégoire had suggested, despite their sickly bodies and "effeminate temperaments," the Jews should only be judged in relation to their willingness to redeem themselves in the future.[48]

As a by-product of shedding the conspicuous signs of Jewishness from their bodies, the "regeneration" of the Jews explicitly meant overcoming effeminacy, suggesting that full acceptance in the nation entailed conformity to widely circulating ideas about the newfound virility being crafted during the French Revolution. Against the "effeminacy" of the Old Regime with its impotent king, despised, lascivious queen, immoral clergy, and foppish aristocracy, the new republican order emphasized manly virtues that were considered synonymous with patriotism itself.[49] For Western Jews, assimilation to this revitalized body politic required not merely an acceptance of gentile French culture but the adoption of its gender codes as well. "To be a man rather than an outsider or a member of a stigmatized minority," writes Zygmunt Bauman, "meant to be able to control one's passions, to keep one's nerves in check, to be strong (yet not overbearing) in body and mind."[50] In other words, it meant being able to master a gender performance that non-Jews would ultimately accept as convincing—or, as Sander Gilman puts it, to demonstrate styles of comportment that would allow one to "pass" as a man.[51]

These developments shed light on the so-called "Infamous Decrees" that Napoleon instituted in 1808, one of which insisted that conscripted Jews be forced to perform their military duty rather than pay for a replacement as other men were permitted to do. One scholar has noted that in requiring conscripted Jews to serve, the emperor "attributed great virtues to the prolonged presence of the Jews in the army."[52] Though it is unclear what these "great virtues" were or who was meant to benefit from them (the Jews or the army), it is evident that Napoleon was in fact furthering the "regeneration" of the Jews through mandatory schooling in male codes of civility. Anti-Semites had claimed as much around 1900, arguing that while Napoleon particularly disliked the Jews' aversion to military service, he had unwisely opted to "correct" rather than expel them, and thus sought "to assimilate the Jews to the French, to discipline them, to moralize them."[53] Much in keeping with the Enlightenment project of cultural assimilation—and, indeed, with the Jewish Enlightenment project, the Haskalah—hitherto "effeminate" Jewish *males* might through compulsory military service be transformed into "virile" French *men*.[54]

In the eyes of some nineteenth-century observers, the legal emancipation of the Jews had not yet brought about the anticipated physical reform, leading to sweeping medical claims such as, for example, that "*le type israélite* has lost its vigor and its beauty."[55] Though Jews were sometimes credited with uncanny powers of assimilation, the persistence among them of certain traditional qualities could be taken as proof of their inability to pass in gentile culture, evidence of an almost innate propensity toward "bad acting." In one of several attempts to reverse the rising tide of popular anti-Semitism around 1890, Anatole Leroy-Beaulieu (a future Dreyfusard) qualified, in accordance with many pro-assimilationist writers, the contemporary shortcomings of Jews by reference to environment rather than blood. Yet here, as elsewhere, the formative role of the milieu was limited by the supposedly innate qualities of these people. There was "something Protean" in the Jew, Leroy-Beaulieu asserted in his book *Israël chez les nations*, for he "adapts and assimilates himself to everything" and "consequently he succeeds in everything." Assimilation could never be complete or even entirely persuasive, for the Jew could accomplish all these metamorphoses "while scarcely ever losing the impress of his race, just as he preserves on his body the mark of his religion. He has the remarkable faculty of taking on a new skin, without at bottom ceasing to be a Jew."[56] Hence the dialectic between visibility and invisibility that appears so often in discussions of Jewishness, where the Jew can either be criticized for refusing to merge into mainstream culture or condemned for having assimilated so completely as to become invisible. The latter criticism was most often leveled by anti-Semites, for whom it was precisely the invisibility of the Jew that was most disturbing, and for whom performance and dissimulation found their logical conclusion in treason.

Yet what was this Jewish core that resisted and ultimately gave the lie to attempts at assimilation? By virtue of his failure to fully divest himself of the congenital traits of his "race," through his inability to convincingly "pass" as a man in gentile culture, the case of the Jewish male sheds light on what the French imagined as normative manhood at the turn of the century. Leroy-Beaulieu cited a number of qualities that situated the Jew outside of conventional gender roles. Physically, he asserted, the Jew was weak, with a diminished musculature and a narrow chest, which, while springing from a sedentary urban lifestyle and even unhealthy conditions, "often gives him a somewhat unmanly appearance." Centuries of persecution no doubt contributed to this enfeebled condition, which was why Jewish men "cannot help becoming small, puny, weak, and frail; it would be ridiculous to expect in them the splendid torso of the Greek or the fine bearing of the Englishman." Finally, there were aesthetic issues to contend with, and while the Jewish man's physical weakness could be partly explained by reference to his milieu, his "ugliness" seemed more congenital, less mutable. "The race is not handsome. . . . Their ugliness is one of the secret grievances that set so many women against them." [57] No amount of assimilation, it seems, would have compensated for this congenital trait.

A further critique assumed paradoxically that Jews were more potent than gentiles yet less capable of satisfying women. In a country haunted by the specter of depopulation, the sexual potency of French men was often taken as a privileged site of masculinity and the material foundation of honor; yet while the fecundity of the Jews was often remarked with surprise, it did not confirm their manhood in the same way. Rather, here was a sexuality that popular stereotypes had already deemed perverse: Jews were freely associated with prostitution, pornography, and debauchery, all of which threatened to corrupt the French bloodline and to hasten its premature degeneracy. Circumcision was also easily caricatured as being akin to castration, thus undermining a Jew's ability to adequately please women. One image depicting postcoital pillow talk shows a clearly satisfied woman exclaim with surprise to her rather smug-looking paramour, "That was splendid—I thought you were a Jew!" (Fig. 1). It is unclear whether the man is in fact Jewish, although he does share some of the facial features artists conventionally used to denote Jewishness. Nevertheless, the woman's astonished

Ça, c'est épatant, je te croyais juif!...

Fig. 1. Grun, "Ça, c'est épatant, je te croyais juif!" Reproduced in Perrine Simon-Nahum, "Les Juifs," in *L'Affaire Dreyfus et le tournant du siècle (1894–1910)*, ed. Laurent Gervereau and Christophe Prochasson (Paris: Bibliothèque de documentation internationale contemporaine, 1994), 153. By permission of the Bibliothèque de documentation internationale contemporaine.

satisfaction amply illustrates the perceived contradiction between Jewishness and manly sexual performance. Yet just as "Jewishness" appeared as a fluid set of qualities, the circumcised Jew also appeared as a circumciser who threatened gentiles with emasculation. Not only had Drumont himself declared that the Jews sought to circumcise all Frenchmen, but *Le Précurseur*, the weekly organ for the Parti National Antijuif, offered considerable advertising space to purveyors of anti-impotence cures.[58] Such evidence points to the performative dimension of stereotyping, where the categorization of certain groups as "other" is also an attempt to prevent one from *becoming* that other.

Other qualities linked to Jews seemed less congenital and more of an effect of their environment and lifestyle. These "puny athletes" had somewhat compensated for their muscular weakness with great scholarly and commercial achievements, it was conceded, but their overdeveloped intellectual life contributed to the extreme nervousness so often considered virtually synonymous with Jewish psychology. In the Jewish man, muscular weakness accorded his nervous system a certain prominence: "[H]e is all nerve. . . . The Jew is the most nervous of men, perhaps because he is the most 'cerebral,' because he has lived most by his brain," Leroy-Beaulieu declared. Often cast as the quintessential neurasthenic, the Jew was one of the most telling symptoms of modern urban life and seemed to fore-shadow the fate of all modern men: "The Jew is the most nervous and hence the most modern of men. . . . it will not take the Christians long to catch up to the Jews in this respect."[59] The prospect that gentiles would one day "catch up to the Jews" in terms of nervousness did not clear Jewish men of the charge of effeminacy, but rather proved a dismal commentary on the possibility of all men one day figuratively becoming "Jews." Leroy-Beaulieu thus indicated what Susan Kassouf describes as the "discursive proximity" between Jews and gentiles when it came to the maladies of sedentary and cerebral lifestyles, a proximity that was often disavowed by the non-Jewish intelligentsia seeking "to preserve a dangerous, yet effective fiction of its healthy and manly exclusivity."[60] This sense that "Jewishness" itself was a protean quality that other men might share betrays an implicit uneasiness about the current state of French manhood. After all, when thinking of exemplars of physiological manhood, Leroy-Beaulieu readily cited men from ancient Greece and modern Britain rather than from his own country. In other words, his anxiety about modernity amounted to fear of all *French-men* eventually becoming "Jewish."

The basic tenor of such "pro-Jewish" writings did not change very much by the time of the Dreyfus Affair. Even Émile Zola, who was so often identified as a staunch opponent of anti-Semitism, sketched a complex and contradictory image of Jewishness. In his 1896 defense of the Jews, Zola cataloged a list of grievances harbored by many anti-Semites: that Jews' allegiance was grounded more in their religion than in the nation, that they married among themselves and maintained close family ties, and that they were above all "a wise and practical race; in their blood they carry a need for lucre, a love of money, a prodigious business sense." Admitting that "all of this is true," Zola also insisted that these faults be explained as the effect of anti-Jewish persecutions over the ages. Like Marx before him, Zola viewed Jewishness as partly synonymous with huckstering, so much so that one needed only possess this quality to qualify as a "Jew." In response to a Catholic banker's claim that Jews were better than gentiles at business, Zola quipped, "I know certain Christians who are very distinguished Jews." Ideally, Zola affirmed, the Jews would eventually disappear as a distinct social type, an assimilation blocked by anti-Semites themselves. "If there are still Jews today, it is your fault. They would have disappeared, would have blended into the rest of the population if they had not been compelled to defend themselves, group together and stubbornly cling to their race." Only by giving up all that made them different from gentiles would Jews finally achieve parity in the nation: "The day the Jews are merely people like ourselves, they will be our brothers. . . . Let us embrace the Jews so as to absorb and blend them into our ranks. . . . This and this alone will achieve unity."[61]

When Dreyfusards verbally defended Jews against anti-Semitic attacks, they did so against the backdrop of an implicit historical trajectory of assimilation: Jews could be defended as human beings so long as they promised some day to divest themselves of their "Jewishness." This somewhat paradoxical position of being at once for "the Jew" but opposed to "Jewishness" was quite prevalent at the turn of the century, and illustrates how, as Linda Nochlin has perceptively noted, one could be anti-Jewish when it came to *representations* of "Jewish" character traits without necessarily manifesting outright hostility to actual Jewish people or subscribing to anti-Semitic ideology. This was particularly the case in graphic images of Jews, even when they were created by artists who were themselves Jewish. The "signifiers that indicated 'Jewishness' in the late nineteenth century were too firmly locked into a system of negative connotations," writes Nochlin; there was no visual language available that might have allowed one to construct an image that was at once recognizably Jewish and positive.[62] As Zygmunt Bauman has indicated, situations such as these suggest that the conventional distinction between anti- and philo-Semitism is quite inadequate, and must be situated in a more foundational "allosemitism" that from the start posits the Jew as "other" and as requiring special treatment, whether through persecution or toleration.[63]

Paradoxes of Military Manhood

In light of such imagery, much of which also resonated elsewhere in French culture, the Jewish soldier necessarily appeared as a somewhat paradoxical figure. How could a man so renowned for cowardice, muscular weakness, and physical repulsiveness ever pull off such a role? Given the kinds of issues raised during the Dreyfus trials, however, most damning would be the charge that Jews were, thanks to centuries of virtually enforced duplicity and abuse, necessarily incapable of honor.

Yet if the manliness of the Jewish male was in a state of crisis at the fin de siècle, was the reputation of the French soldier above reproach? Military rhetoric certainly made it seem so. The ideal soldier was first and foremost a superior physical specimen, one who must be physically fit and ready for action. "Repose and idleness diminish physical forces and courage," Marshal de Marmont noted in 1845. "Health, energy, and moral value ordinarily follow from a life hardened by fatigues and devoted to movement."[64] The ideal soldier was also marked by heroic self-control and sacrifice that assured that he would risk his life for his country, thus evincing a style of self-discipline that was repeatedly contrasted to the moral laxity of civilian life. Fostering such traits in boys and young men had been considered essential in the wake of the Franco-Prussian War, during which the martial qualities of the military had been called into question. Not only had the disciplined and loyal soldier been made into a positive role model in the standardized schoolbooks of the early Third Republic, but the passing of the military service law of 1872 made five years of military service compulsory for all young men.[65] By the 1890s, self-control had become a veritable fetish of military manhood. "Discipline will be the soldier's religion," declared the 1893 edition of the standard manual for noncommissioned officers. "The regiment is the school of subordination, of the virile spirit, of male pride."[66] When during the Affair, the immorality of high-ranking officers was becoming evident, supporters intoned these ideals like a mantra. "The honor of the soldier," one anti-Dreyfusard insisted, "is composed of courage and abnegation."[67]

The defensiveness of some anti-Dreyfusards sprang to a large degree from years of antimilitarist writings that had attacked the sort of man being produced by compulsory conscription, either from the perspective of bourgeois elites who disliked rubbing shoulders with lesser social types or workers who refused to fight for a nation that did not represent them.[68] Yet critiques of military manhood were not the sole product of disgruntled elites or resentful proletarians. As Eugen Weber has shown, up until 1889, rural people harbored traditional prejudices against soldiers and deeply resented the conscription that took their sons away from the fields and often returned them with haughty, lazy, and immoral attitudes.[69] Physicians, too (perhaps unwittingly), lent antimilitarist sentiment some scientific backing. While Jews were often seen as the quintessence of the nervous type, the physicians Adrien Proust (father of Marcel) and Gilbert Ballet invoked a study that showed how army officers ranked higher than artists (and just under students) when it came to neurasthenia.[70] According to a recent survey of late-nineteenth-century medical discourses, physicians even agreed that the military profession figured prominently as a predisposing cause of male hysteria.[71]

If an association with feminizing nervous disorders was not enough, there remained the lingering suspicion that life in the barracks meant frequent encounters with vice. Licentious sexuality was potentially even more damaging to the soldier's manly reputation than the drunkenness and gambling that also seemed to characterize military life.[72] The conflict between virtuous self-control and proving one's virility through repeated sexual encounters was certainly not exclusive to the military; it was lived by many men in the nineteenth century.[73] Yet the military's reputation for sensual escapades was fixed in the public imagination and represented an embarrassing contrast to the virtual religion that the army had made of discipline. As we have seen, in the hands of the army's opponents, this incongruence could become grounds for damning critiques.[74] These critiques were intensified in the aftermath of World War I, when, faced with the sadism and immorality of warfare, many commentators wondered whether the soldier's sacrifice was indeed founded on heroic self-discipline or on the selfish gratification of base instincts.[75] As accounts of soldiers' indiscretions were received against the backdrop of acute anxiety about both morality and manhood, revelations about the military's sordid side dealt a significant blow to its honorable reputation.

As perhaps the most damning evidence that all was not well with military manhood, the question of homosexuality was broached frequently in both learned and popular circles. "Military training is rarely manifested in acts of rape or assaults on decency, but it frequently gives rise to pilfering intended for the demands of prostitutes. The most corrupt soldiers become pederasts."[76] Experts also noted with concern how readily many soldiers succumbed to "vice" when on duty in overseas colonies like Algeria and Indochina, where scorching temperatures, the absence of women, and the proliferation of "dirty" Arab or black prostitutes transformed heterosexual soldiers into "sodomites by necessity" with adolescent male partners. Yet while some assumed that such activities would cease once these men were safely back on French soil, less optimistic minds believed that the colonial experience had more lasting effects on the morality of returning soldiers.[77] In his presentation of data gathered by a range of European sexologists, Dr Léon-Henri Thoinot revealed that, far from being immune to sexual "inversion," men in uniform were highly prized and often willing partners in same-sex liaisons. "A penchant that seems very common in *le monde uraniste*, at least in Germany, is the seeking out of soldiers: the reason for this is without a doubt—as certain uranists confess—that the soldier, at least in Germany, is often easily seduced and ready, in exchange for some money, to satisfy the desires of *l'inverti.*"[78] Thoinot's twice-uttered qualification that such is the case "at least in Germany" conveniently invoked sodomy's reputation as *le vice allemand* and temporarily displaced anxiety about gays in the military onto the nation's most feared enemy. It also deployed a longtime strategy of homophobic discourses by situating homosexuality as a dangerous "foreign" and above all secret community, a "Freemasonry of vice" that threatened to disrupt the sanctity of the heterosexual norm.[79]

This displacement was nevertheless a rather weak endorsement of the French soldier's heterosexual credentials, particularly in light of a former police chief's 1887 account of homosexual establishments in Paris that catered mainly to the needs of soldiers. This author, too, sought to soften the damage that such revelations might inflict by insisting that his information was meant neither to tarnish "the honor of the army" nor to suggest that the armies of other nations were exempt from these practices.[80] Other reports offered no comforting disclaimers. In a chapter on pederasty, "one of the most repugnant forms that vice assumes in Paris," another popular exposé freely associated soldiers with "workers, sordid *déclassés*, ragged children" and others in the "abject part of society" who engaged in this practice.[81] There is little doubt that Dreyfus had become a convenient scapegoat for an army whose prestige had been severely compromised at Sedan; yet revelations such as these also suggest that the ideal of military manhood was being challenged on levels that were far more intimate than battlefield performance.

Awareness of the soldier's association with vice partly explains the compensatory pleasure with which the French fantasized about *le vice allemand,* as well as the amusement with which the nation received news of the homosexual scandals that rocked the German army between 1907 and 1909.[82] It also explains how associations with homosexuality might have served the interests of the officers who framed Dreyfus for treason. Historians of the Affair have often noted, usually with more amusement than analysis, how a homosexual affair between the German and Italian military attachés, Maximilien von Schwartzkoppen and Alessandro Panizzardi, came to light after their love letters were intercepted along with the incriminating *bordereau* by French military intelligence. Strangely, these letters ended up being included in the secret dossier that was withheld from the defense team in 1894, and they thus constituted the "puerile pieces without any interest" that were later discussed in closed session during the 1899 retrial.[83] While few historians have done anything substantive with this information, Nicholas Dobelbower proposes that one of the reasons these letters and the so-called "canaille de D." document were withheld from the defense team was to implicate Dreyfus with this homosexual liaison, thus reinforcing the association of Jewish men with effeminate and un-French conduct. In the eyes of many worried observers, there remained a convenient slippage between homosexuals, who in their "cosmopolitan society" practiced a vice that belongs "to no proper country, but imposes itself on all,"[84] and Jews, a "cosmopolitan" and "effeminate" people renowned for being without country and suspected of corrupting every nation they entered.

The association of Dreyfus with homosexuality was more of a strategic move than a serious charge. While hardly unblemished, the captain's private life was by all accounts impeccably heterosexual and even inspired sexual jealousy in his comrades. By having affairs with several society women, this wealthy officer, who had become even more wealthy through marriage, seemed capable of "paying" for the women of his choice.[85] For those with an axe to grind, the rhetorically interchangeable categories of Jewishness and homosexuality could conveniently signify foreignness and even treason: "French homosexuality," Dobelbower claims, "in other words, is not French, but rather always symbolically foreign." The love letters that were used to pack the secret dossier that ultimately condemned Dreyfus served no other purpose than to implicate this Jew with foreign homosexuals, a group that formed yet another "Syndicate" bent on the destruction of French values. In this way, the allegation of treason would be rendered doubly odious. Dobelbower's brief but insightful analysis leads to a startling conclusion: "The bed that Dreyfus was made to lie in was initially prepared for an invert but it was able to accommodate a Jew just as easily."[86] This was no simple exclusion of Jewish men from the ideal of military manhood, but arguably the effect of anxiety about French manhood itself. Indeed, one limitation of Dobelbower's otherwise illuminating interpretation is its failure to account for the army's own troubled reputation for homosexuality, that is, the scandalous proliferation of this "unmanly" and "un-French" practice among the defenders of the nation themselves, who were supposed to be the most manly and the most "French." Not only were Jewish men often thought incapable of living up to the military ideal but, insofar as the military was itself haunted by the specter of sodomy, a fair number of gentiles were as well, thus giving rise to a situation that challenged the boundary between "real" men and these threatening "others." In other words, such anxieties sprang not from a firm sense of the homosexual's essential *difference* from "normal" men, but from the fear that such differences could never be fully established.[87] To some extent the uncritical and sometimes hyperbolic celebration of the manly soldier may be seen as an overcompensation for this fundamental anxiety.

Rennes 1899: The Soul of Steel

If Dreyfus was neither homosexual nor physically unfit, what was it that made him seem less than a manly soldier? Anti-Semitic claims that Dreyfus lingered too long over his morning toilette, that he showed great care about his clothing, or that his facial hair was rather sparse, were no doubt aimed at making him seem effeminate in the public eye.[88] Much of the problem, however, sprang from growing divisions within the army itself, where under the Third Republic new, technically trained officers had risen to positions of authority. Gone were the days when military elites were composed of those who had spilled blood for the nation; rather, this status was increasingly accorded to graduates of academies like Saint-Cyr, the École polytechnique, and the École supérieure de guerre.[89] In other words, Dreyfus struck some observers as more of a scholar than a true soldier, an impression that seemed to confirm stereotypes about how among Jews calculation and interest surpassed honor, courage, and strength. As we shall see in Chapter 2, however, these misgivings about the new military elite were part of a broader cultural anxiety about the quality of the men being produced by the nation's secular schools, whose intelligence seemed to outstrip their physical vitality. In other words, the gender anxieties that Dreyfus provoked were exemplified by, rather than simply reduced to, his Jewishness. Like many other *écoliers*, he bore the telltale signs of study on his body: "[H]is back depicts the curve of the *polytechnicien* who has leaned for a long time over notebooks and books."[90] At times, the intelligence of Dreyfus was singled out for particular scorn: one reporter asked his readers to gaze upon "this former student of the École polytechnique and the École de guerre, this savant, this intellectual" and to revel in the thought of him living the rest of his life in guilt, as "a prey to remorse!"[91]

The soldierly status of Dreyfus became important in the campaign to retry his case, so when the captain finally returned to face retrial in 1899, such factors became especially crucial. Officers like this were clearly poor substitutes for the real thing, some concluded, which made Dreyfus's own performance seem even more like bad acting. In the eyes of anti-Semites, Jews were consummate actors and possessed an uncanny ability to blend into whatever role they found themselves playing. In addition to the charge that the overall attitude of Dreyfus seemed to confirm his guilt was the related claim that he was a fraud who cynically played the part of an honorable army officer. As someone so "hermetically sealed to our conception of honor," as Drumont had put it,[92] in French culture a Jew could at best pretend to be a man. His apparent inability to "pass" as a soldier was exacerbated by the fact that his body seemed "strained in his too new uniform," thus making it appear more like a costume.[93] "This disharmony, this dissociation between the uniform and that which is inside explains everything."[94]

Aware of the need to cast the accused in a favorable light, which necessarily meant being able to sustain his image as an honorable and worthy man, supporters of Dreyfus were nevertheless ambivalent about how to address the military bearing of the captain. Strategically there was some logic to painting Dreyfus in a military hue, for doing so would have surely helped appeal to the cultural expectations of a reading public well-versed in novelistic representations of heroism. It would have also helped to rehabilitate Dreyfus's persona as a man whose soldierly appearance was an adequate expression of his being. Ever critical of theatricality, Maurice Barrès charged that this attempt to cast Dreyfus as "an enraged militarist, *un chauvin*" was consciously orchestrated by Dreyfusard leaders;[95] yet, given the wide currency of the ideal of the manly soldier (which was contrasted to the current state of the army), one may argue that such "strategies" of seeing were also largely unconscious, being intimately embedded in a network of expectations and tacit interests that were not easily reducible to conscious design. Dreyfus appeared to a writer for *Le Matin* as, "if possible, more military, even more '*dans le rang*' than ever," evincing a degree of self-control that made him seem almost classical, "a figure of marble proud in his impassivity, more closed off than a wall." Most important, and contrary to impressions elicited in 1895, this man was no emotionless automaton, for his "protestations could be vibrant, with an emotion without equal, with anger accumulated during these past five years. I am certain that they did not move out of '*l'alignment.*'"[96] Moreover, in a provocative and perhaps hyperbolic remark that predictably drew the fire of anti-Dreyfusards, Joseph Cornély buoyantly declared that throughout the Rennes trial, the ex-captain had conducted himself as a colonel![97]

Other revisionists were wary of such tactics and found the gap between the conduct of the accused and public perceptions of heroism simply too great to be breached by a mere rhetorical flourish. An alternative strategy was to attack the stereotype itself by insisting that true heroism need not conform to models laid out in popular fiction. Not only did this approach help to vindicate the moral courage of the Dreyfusards but it seemed to resolve the problem of Dreyfus's apparent theatricality by highlighting the virtues of *refusing* to perform. Here the stoic posture of Dreyfus was reinterpreted as a sign of virtue. Despite the fact that "the soul of this martyr is enclosed in an envelope of iron" and marked by a "superhuman will," Henri Varennes conceded that the public had, through the novels of Georges Ohnet and Jules Mary, come to expect certain conventions of physique and comportment when conceiving of their ideal hero. "We would like him to look like a hero, but this hero of the most frightful adventure only has the look of an impeccable functionary. Having come here as if to a theater, some are, without realizing it, disappointed that he should be himself and not playact [*qu'il ne joue pas la comédie*]." By confronting popular expectations of innocence rather than heroism, Joseph Reinach pressed this strategy even further. Not only did Reinach see in Dreyfus's impassive face "the envelope of iron for this soul of steel . . . more enclosed than a wall,"[98] but, by cleverly enlisting the revival of French classicism in the Dreyfusard cause, he co-opted a cultural trend that was often (but not exclusively) associated with the political right. If clarity and simplicity stood at the center of the French cultural tradition, then in his refusal to play the part of the storybook martyr, Dreyfus was nothing less than a study of Frenchness. In an affair so often marked by melodrama and spectacle, Reinach remarked sardonically, Dreyfus had "the bad taste to be *un classique*, to not abase himself by being a merely decorative innocent, the innocent of a drama from the boulevard who beats his chest, invokes heaven and the stars, breaks down in sobs, pours out tears and tears apart his clothes." In refusing to play such a role Dreyfus affirmed the purity of the facts, for "true innocence . . . finds repugnant the use of a theater artifices and role-playing."[99]

Some of his defenders thus claimed that Dreyfus was a true hero precisely because he *failed* to act like one. Later, in his multivolume history of the Affair, Reinach revised his earlier claim in a way that emphasized the distance between true and sham honor by reconciling Dreyfus with military manhood: "The trial called for an actor, and he was a soldier."[100] For other allies, however, the less "military" Dreyfus appeared, the more he gained in credibility and even in humanity. "Here is Dreyfus," noted one, "he advances with the same confident step. But to us he seems less cold, less automatic, less military."[101] Even his health problems, which entered into the reportage of both sides of the press war, did not necessarily diminish Dreyfus's aura of vigor. For example, the captain's digestive problems, which would have been recognizable as stock symptoms of nervous disorder, were treated in a manner that minimized too close an association with true debilitation. Unavoidable admissions of weakness were thus usually tempered with affirmations of vitality. "Captain Dreyfus suffers from stomach problems. He has adopted a milk diet," observed *Le Matin*, but "his energy is intact and his intelligence remains luminous."[102] Such affirmations of the energy and willpower of Dreyfus resonated in many revisionist writings, and one even noted that his "physical courage is equaled only by his moral courage."[103]

Rehabilitating Jewish Manhood

The contested status of Dreyfus as a soldier had profound implications for the gender identities of other Jewish men, especially since well-publicized incidents of cowardice necessarily implicated them as well. If a highly placed Jewish army officer could be seen as a coward, then what did this say about ordinary Jews? Decades of nearly uninterrupted peace had surely encouraged acculturated Jews to see themselves as having more or less succeeded in their assimilation, and, in terms of manhood, the case of Captain Armand Mayer vividly illustrates this sentiment of having "arrived." Stung by allegations in Drumont's *La Libre Parole* that Jewish officers used bribery and other machinations to achieve promotions, Mayer died in 1892 fighting a duel with the anti-Semitic marquis de Morès, thus making a very public show of honor that earned him the accolades of the Jewish community and no doubt silenced more than one critic of Jewish manhood.[104] Mayer was a *polytechnicien* like Dreyfus, and his demonstration of honor was so convincing that even Leroy-Beaulieu was forced to concede, in response to a letter from a rabbi protesting his depiction of Jewish manhood, that such exceptional cases made it impossible to claim unequivocally "that a sense of honor is foreign to the Jews."[105] What Mayer's heroic sacrifice did for Jewish manhood was deeply undermined by the Dreyfus case, which is why the alleged cowardice of this traitor exacerbated an already besieged sense of Jewish manhood. By examining the Jewish press during this period, particularly the *Archives israélites* and the *Univers israélite*, we shall see how Jewish males tried to persuade themselves that, despite the example of Dreyfus and the stereotypes of the past, they really were men. It is true that the pro-Dreyfus campaign was largely waged by politicians, professors, and men of letters, but we shall find that the style of manhood Jewish men claimed for themselves was for the most part military in nature.

The obsessive reassertions of courage and honor in Jewish writings at the end of the century were as much reactions to a certain style of Zionist rhetoric as a rebuttal of anti-Semitic truisms. If, on the whole, Zionism never became a mass movement in France during this period, its frequently pointed critiques of the debased state of the people struck a nerve at a time when French Jewish masculinity was most vulnerable. Both Theodor Herzl and Max Nordau, Zionism's two leading lights, cited the Dreyfus Affair as a defining moment in their campaign for Jewish regeneration. In 1899, Nordau directly invoked the Dreyfus Affair in his address to the Second Zionist Congress in Basel, not only as a vivid example of the need for Zionism, but as a demonstration of the depths to which Jewish manhood had fallen in the modern world. "The Dreyfus Affair was the revelation of a state of mind hitherto unsuspected. It rises up as a warning and a lesson to that category of Jews who continue to believe in their definitive and unqualified admission into the most advanced states of the West." What Nordau found particularly galling was the relative failure of French Jews to respond to the anti-Semitic attacks visited upon them, a hesitation that signaled a categorical lack of honor. "Attacked as a group, Judaism should have defended itself collectively," Nordau proclaimed; "it should have risen up, as a single man, to defend its well-being. . . . The whole of Judaism let it be said that all Jews were naturally traitors—it found nothing to say on its own behalf." In the great political contest wrought by the Affair, the vast majority of the Jews remained "flabby spectators" of those heroes who risked all for the sake of justice. Notable exceptions to this collective feebleness were Bernard-Lazare ("a good man, that one, a strong man"), Jacques Bahar ("our gallant comrade in the struggle"), and

Joseph Reinach ("who has manfully taken his place in the highest rank"). Such heroic exceptions threw the more general cowardice of French Jewry into relief: "And it is thus that this Dreyfus Affair has served to determine, to our horror, the exact extent of our weakness, our irresolution, our apathy, and especially our mutual aversion."[106]

Nordau's allegations about Jewish passivity during the Affair were of course somewhat hyperbolic and designed to support his more general claim that Western Jewry had become enfeebled over the course of several centuries. There is in fact ample evidence of Jewish resistance to anti-Semitism throughout the fin de siècle, ranging from journalistic attempts to counter the effects of Drumont's anti-Semitic proclamations to the use of physical violence in response to verbal and physical abuse. Yet, as Michael Marrus has concluded, despite these periodic and highly localized outbursts of resistance to anti-Semitism, during the Affair, the vast majority of French Jews preferred a more passive posture, and many eschewed involvement altogether.[107] Hyperbolic or not, Nordau's remarks struck a nerve and elicited some angry responses from Jewish leaders unwilling to accept allegations of cowardice and effeminacy without qualification.

In the eyes of many Dreyfusards who, as we shall see in Chapter 2, fancied themselves as heroic fighters for justice and honor, the detachment of the Jews made little sense. The writer Jean Ajalbert, who had failed to overcome his anti-Jewish feelings, was particularly irked by the apparent failure of "certain dirty Jews" to get involved in the Affair, an abstention that he read as a typical sign of Jewish cowardice. Despite having the right and even the duty to defend themselves against anti-Semitic outrages, Ajalbert complained, French Jews had done nothing on their own behalf. "We have seen little of them; they have marched off—as they tend to do—under a variety of pretexts, to such an extent that for their cowardice they deserve the panegyrics of *La Libre Parole*." A controversy that was at heart "their affair," Ajalbert concluded, had devolved to non-Jews, who were evidently better qualified to stand up for honor.[108] Jewish journalists energetically protested such charges with the claim that "Israelites are not afraid to expose themselves to the blows of their enemies to hasten the deliverance of their unfortunate brother."[109]

For many acculturated Jews, faith in the republican system of justice may have outweighed the desire to assert their dignity as a separate group, but it did not prevent their feeling a lingering sense of guilt at not having collectively risen up "as a single man." Such self-consciousness about their own lack of action compounded an already beleaguered sense of masculinity and elicited the types of defensive reactions evident in the pages of Jewish magazines. Anxieties about the body and concerns about exhaustion were widespread at the end of the nineteenth century, and the Zionists were hardly the first to express concern about such matters. Yet for the Jews, a people widely considered more prone than others to a range of feminizing nervous disorders, the prospect of physical and mental exhaustion acquired even greater social significance. Whereas among gentiles such disorders ideally signaled only *temporary* (and thus treatable) pathologies, among Jews they might seem merely to confirm assumptions about the "normal" condition of that group. Contrary to the case of certain gentiles, situating Jewish manhood within a therapeutic framework did not necessarily hold out the possibility of the realization of a healthy masculine ideal through rejuvenating practices: still viewed as congenitally predisposed to a range of nervous and physical disorders (yet mysteriously immune to others), Jewish men could just as easily find their therapeutic aims thwarted by the inherited traits of their own bodies.

It is thus not surprising that Jewish magazines revisited the problem of manhood at precisely those moments when the honor of Jewish men was most under fire. For instance, during the late 1880s, a number of defensive essays appeared in the wake of Drumont's *La France juive*. "In its most male and heroic form," declared one observer, "courage is . . . a Jewish virtue, just as patriotism is another." Yet for this writer, the burden of proof lay with the Jews themselves, who were implored to reform their lifestyles: "[I]t is our duty to rehabilitate ourselves in the eyes of public opinion."[110] As we have seen, the death of Armand Mayer was an important moment in this rehabilitation, but, as Leroy-Beaulieu indicated, the sacrifice of a single man could just as easily be viewed as exceptional and therefore not representative of the group as a whole. Sometimes men required assistance in their rehabilitation, and, like many periodicals of the time, the *Archives israélites* carried advertisements promising health and happiness at a price. An especially striking advertisement from 1897 offered the readers of the *Univers israélite* an exciting new medallion promising to restore their "vital energy and health." Regularly wearing "Professor Heskier's Electric Star of David" (Fig. 2) would bring about "the normal functioning of the blood and the nervous system." Moreover, thanks to this mysterious talisman, "the senses are stimulated, physical and moral force are restored, and the result is a state of health and happiness." All of these effects were nicely captured in the advertisement's arresting illustration of a robust young man rejuvenated by the good vibrations of the electrified pendant hanging around his neck.

Fig. 2. Advertisement for Professor Heskier's Electric Star of David, in *L'Univers israélite*, 24 September 1897, 29.

A plethora of nostrums, tonics, and talismans were marketed to the French population generally during this period, and most appealed to the broadest clientele possible. Heskier's advertisement spoke directly to Jews, suggesting that his product would reverse the dominant stereotypes about that group's effeminacy and cowardice. Nevertheless, it only appeared once in *L'Univers israélite*, and most Jews would have been more likely to seek a rest cure through the numerous Jewish spas and sanitariums advertised in various periodicals.[111] In more concrete terms, the growing willingness of Jews to defend their honor through dueling at the turn of the century—especially during the Dreyfus Affair—reveals how such assertions of physical health and courage could be put readily into practice. Unlike in Germany, where dueling with a Jew was considered beneath a true man of honor, French codes of masculinity provided opportunities for Jewish men to prove themselves. As Robert Nye points out, "There is a certain irony in the fact that in their Jew-baiting anti-Semites were, in effect, schooling their victims in civil equality and then legitimizing them in the subsequent duel. To duel with a man meant to acknowledge his worthiness as a man of honor, so that what anti-Semitic rhetoric denied in principle, anti-Semites acknowledged in practice."[112] When Jews took up these challenges and fought valiantly, Pierre Birnbaum notes, "the anti-Semites who laid bets on the Jews' cowardice, their feminine character and their homosexuality, did so to their own cost, in so far as they involuntarily contributed to proving their statements false."[113]

Despite the association of virility with assimilation, religion dovetailed with prophylactic and therapeutic practices in the refashioning of Jewish manhood. As T. J. Jackson Lears has argued, by the end of the nineteenth century, even religious leaders had appropriated aspects of the primarily secular therapeutic ethos for their own purposes.[114] Though Lears makes this claim in reference to the United States, similar developments are discernible in the French context. One article in the reformist *Archives israélites*, for instance, expressed the belief that one must connect bodily vigor with spiritual healing in order to help regenerate the Jews. In this case, the spiritual cure would follow the summer holidays, during which Jews rejuvenated themselves at the beach and in health spas. "After the physical cure that invigorates and stimulates, which reestablishes equilibrium in the human organism subjected to a rude ordeal over several long months by labor, worries, or pleasures, comes the moral, spiritual cure that Judaism offers to its children at the dawn of autumn and that is bound to purify their thoughts, to clear up their spirit, to impart new energy to their good instincts, to calm the fire of their passions, and to elevate and purify their soul[s]."[115]

Assimilation therefore clearly had its limits, and many Jewish leaders advocated a middle way between ethnic particularity and complete assimilation. In fact, some commentators emphasized the courage implicit in steadfastly asserting one's Jewish identity in the face of racist prejudice. For instance, in the *Archives israélites*, Hippolyte Prague condemned Jews who changed their names so as to appear less obviously Jewish in social circles, a "disgraceful capitulation," which he predicted would ultimately prove useless. By admonishing such overly zealous assimilators, Prague voiced a common assumption of the day: that the peculiarities of the Jewish body would always give the lie to such superficial gestures as altering one's name from "Lévy" to "Levillain" (thus taking a swipe at Isaïe Levillain, the rival editor of the *Univers israélite*). Insofar as Jewishness functioned as an ethnic as well as a religious marker, it contained an indelible quality that would always distinguish the Jews as a people apart. As such, trying to conceal one's heredity through a change of name was like using a disguise to cover up a large nose: such gestures would only draw more attention to the identity being hidden. "This Jewish quality you want to conceal," Prague continued, "well, you carry it most often on your physiognomy in singularly characteristic traits. All the fake noses in which you try so ridiculously to dress yourselves up will do nothing to help you. It's cowardice spent in pure loss."[116]

Despite these qualifications, attempts to harmonize Jewish manhood with the Western heroic ideal were far more common. In a series of essays for the *Archives israélites* on "The Military Virtues of Jews," Maurice Bloch underscored the long history of heroism and martial prowess exhibited by Jews throughout the ages and acknowledged by numerous gentile commentators, such as Silvestre de Sacy and Germaine de Staël. Special attention was given to the most famous martial episodes of Jewish history, from Masada and the Maccabean revolt to Bar Kochba. "Never surrender! Indeed, that's one of the distinctive traits of the Jewish character. The Jew has tenacity, he has endurance. But isn't it this above all that [which] constitutes the born soldier?"[117] Rather than the lost virility and enervation lamented by Nordau and the Zionists, such character traits constituted for Bloch evidence of the Jew's boundless energy and action, the timeless essence of the Jewish male congenitally incapable of something as cowardly as treason. "Now how do we explain so much courage, so much energy, so much heroism? I see only one response: fidelity to the flag!—The Jew does not know treason."[118] Several months later, Nordau himself delivered a public lecture on the Jewish soldier in very similar terms: Jewish military prowess had been unimpeachable in antiquity and could become so once again in modern times. Contrary to stereotypes about the excessive nervousness and delicate sensibility of Jews, paraphrased a journalist in attendance, "the Jew controls his nerves and woes through his will; he has a cold and deliberate courage that masters the quakings and distractions of the flesh [*la carcasse*]."[119]

As evidence of these broad assertions of virility, journalists took every opportunity to provide concrete examples of Jewish manhood in action. A brief article in the *Archives israélites* recounted the story of a Jewish engineer who had saved a trainload of passengers from a forest fire: "At a time when Israel is so odiously vilified by the press of lies, isn't it worth remarking that the brave engineer who accomplished this tour de force and who proved himself with such happy audacity was a Jew by the name of Lopès?"[120] In 1899, another Jewish hero, an artillery captain like Dreyfus, was celebrated in the pages of the *Archives israélites*, as was a Dutch Jewish brigadier the following year.[121] In the same vein, the *Univers israélite* ran a series of brief articles profiling selected Jews of the day. The Grand Rabbi of France, Zadoc Kahn, was characterized by a number of laudatory qualities, including "infinite religious tenderness" and "ardent patriotism." As a orator, the author explained, Kahn also had the ability to inspire his audience with his boundless vitality and optimism: "His male vigor and his very optimism are the safeguard of Judaism."[122] Such gestures persisted through World War I, evincing an ongoing obsession with refuting the association of Jews with weakness and cowardice.

Nordau's appeal for the development of a "new muscle Jew" was thus hardly an unprecedented notion at the turn of the century; it had been a de facto aspect of acculturated Jewish male identity throughout the nineteenth century. The tension between assimilationists and Zionists was not primarily one of being for or against the muscular Jew, but revolved around whether this figure was a contemporary reality or an ideal to be achieved in the future. The widespread reaction against Nordau thus had less to do with the specifics of his plan than with his insulting claim that modern Jewry was currently in a state of effeminacy. Hence the critique formulated by the journalist Louis Lévy, who, while agreeing that Jews were especially nervous, sensitive, and impressionable, maintained that "it was not necessary to exaggerate this sensitivity and to make of the Jew one of these pansies [*femmelettes*] who are made to swoon by a loud noise or a slightly disagreeable odor."[123] In other words, assimilated Jews objected less to Nordau's emphasis on virility than to his assertion that modern Jews lacked such a trait.

Nordau's statements on the Jewish condition were closely scrutinized in France, and when the Zionist responded to an 1897 survey on the question of

Jewish decadence in Germany, the *Archives israélites* decided to conduct its own survey. Focusing on the issue of moral decadence, Hippolyte Prague commented that the "refinements of civilization" had brought about a veritable "deformation of the Jewish character." Yet since all Westerners suffered from such advances, how could one seriously maintain the uniqueness of Jewish decadence in an environment marked by the "general collapse of characters"? What was needed in the face of this "contagion" was "a virile and rapid action" capable of arresting this steady moral decline.[124] Even traditionalists admitted that a major reform was in order, but highlighted the specific problems faced by Jews themselves. "Be strong!" was the injunction of an author writing for the *Univers israélite*, in an article that could have been written by Nordau himself:

> Over the course of many centuries of cerebral labor imposed by circumstances (exclusion from crafts, persecutions . . .), [Jews] have lost the habit of physical exercise. . . . Indeed, we have observed among them a progressive diminution of bodily health, a disturbing augmentation of nervous illnesses. In the future, it will be necessary [for them] to fortify their muscles and nerves. Only at this price will they resist an internal debilitation that will corrupt the vigor of the race and deliver them without defense into the designs of their adversaries.[125]

This chapter has shown that the crisis of Jewish masculinity was exacerbated rather than inaugurated by the Dreyfus case, and, insofar as the Jewishness of the captain was often emphasized, his alleged treason and dishonorable performance at the degradation necessarily reflected badly upon the honor of other Jewish men. In the discourses provoked by this gender crisis, the recuperation of Jewish manhood required the active renunciation of a scholarly lifestyle and the cultivation of health and physical prowess in accordance with the martial manhood demanded by the military. Ironically, to some extent it also meant that Jews had to distance themselves from the "intellectuals" who rallied behind Dreyfus, a group of men who, as we shall see in Chapter 2, were also considered effeminate due to their nonmartial and relatively sedentary professions. By self-consciously promoting the soldier as the ideal of Jewish manhood, acculturated Jews subscribed to the broader masculinist discourse that was shared by both anti-Semites and those who championed the Jewish cause. Against this backdrop of gender anxiety, the figure of Alfred Dreyfus stood out quite starkly. Since the officer had been taken as an exemplar of Jewish cowardice, the recuperation of Dreyfus in many respects meant an affirmation of the manliness of

Jews generally. Though at Rennes the broken body of Dreyfus affirmed the sufferings endured by the man, his steadfast denials of guilt seemed to signal the persistence of a type of bold virility that vindicated all Jews. "Yes! Dreyfus has the audacity to deny the fantastic charges that have weighed upon him! . . . These Jews have every audacity. When they are attacked, they defend themselves, and they succeed in proving that they have not committed the crimes for which they have been condemned."[126]

Part II / Dreyfusard Fantasies

In mid 1899, the campaign of nearly two years for a revision of the Dreyfus case had finally borne fruit, and the condemned captain was being returned to France to face a retrial in the city of Rennes. After confessing to having forged documents that had sealed the fate of Dreyfus years before, Colonel Hubert Henry was imprisoned and soon after committed suicide. Dreyfusard spirits were understandably riding high, after years of preaching in the wilderness.

Although the careful construction of Dreyfus's legal case was of obvious concern to the inner circle of revisionist leaders, they and many other Dreyfusards seemed particularly concerned with how Dreyfus himself would appear at the hour of his anticipated vindication. What impact would years of exile under punishing conditions have had upon the man? As we have seen, when Dreyfus behaved just as stoically as he had four years earlier, sympathetic journalists rushed to put a positive spin on this development by viewing it as evidence either of the captain's ironclad military discipline or of his laudable refusal to perform for the crowd. As the management of public perceptions was of the utmost concern to everyone entangled in the Dreyfus controversy, encouraging the "correct" interpretation of bodily signs was crucial for both sides.

Yet such solicitousness about the captain's appearance exceeded the bounds of political strategy. By obsessing over the manly conduct of their living symbol, the Dreyfusards acted as if they themselves had a stake in his performance, as if one false move on his part might redound upon their own reputations as honorable men. As the chapters that comprise Part II reveal, this need to project a favorable public image was central to the revisionist campaign long before the Rennes trial. As popular expectations about heroism called for more martial forms of manhood than *intellectuels* or Jews seemed capable of providing, the Dreyfusard campaign to alter popular perceptions that Dreyfus was guilty doubled as a gender project that posited the superior manhood of those who defended the captain against the effeminacy of those who condemned him. Just as many Jewish men insisted upon their patriotism and martial prowess and downplayed their reputation for bookishness and physical weakness, however, so, too, many non-Jewish Dreyfusards distanced themselves from the "unmanly" aspects of their own intellectual professions and from the Jews with whom they were associated.

Dreyfusards' projections of their own manhood were accomplished by reference to the broad cultural concerns that preoccupied many bourgeois commentators. As these chapters reveal, Dreyfusism appropriated these anxieties for its own ends by demonstrating that, whereas their enemies displayed the worst aspects of modernity, Dreyfusards themselves remained steadfast and resolute in their commitment to truth and manly values. By speaking of "Dreyfusism" in these chapters, I do not imply that favoring a revision of the Dreyfus case necessarily entailed unity of purpose or social identity—a close look at the divisions and infighting within this group both before and after the Affair should dispel the notion of a homogeneous pro-Dreyfus camp. Rather, use of the term refers to the pool of conventional and often repeated images that constituted the shared repertoire of the revisionist campaign. "'Stock languages,'" Richard Griffiths observes, "had emerged on both sides of the battle-lines that had been forming in France well before the Affair and which were to continue for a good time thereafter. By their exclusiveness, these modes of discourse confirmed people in their prejudices and in their abhorrence of 'the other side.'"[1]

The Jewish man's reputation for being cerebral and sedentary, and therefore weak and even cowardly, was not simply an effect of a hybrid discourse of race and gender; it was often generalized into a veritable condition of modernity itself. In this sense, "Jewishness" was understood as a set of negative qualities that extended beyond Jewish bodies, thus making it possible for anyone to be metaphorically transformed into a "Jew." As Chapter 2 demonstrates, the men who identified themselves as "intellectuals" implicitly subscribed to a medical category in which excessive mental activity was often associated with neurasthenia, impotence, and a host of other ailments. In other words, as self-professed men of thought, the Dreyfusards situated themselves within a cultural category that included bourgeois professionals as well as Jews, an imbrication with potentially disastrous consequences for their public image as heroic men. Representing grotesque versions of the bourgeois professional, intellectuals became easy targets for anti-Dreyfusard critics, who repeatedly employed stereotypes of the foppish aesthete or feeble scholar as counterpoints to the manliness of soldiers. Sensing their distance from the more culturally valued man of action, Dreyfusards sought to improve their public image by emphasizing their manly credentials, a project accomplished in part through the rhetoric of sacrifice and the strategic use of Christ imagery. Just as Jewish men insisted upon their patriotism and martial qualities, Dreyfusards affirmed themselves as men of action by co-opting the language of sacrifice, duty, and abnegation traditionally espoused by the military. Yet if Dreyfusards hoped to redeem themselves by seeming to court persecution bravely, they were also interested in altering the image of the man they defended. The second half of Chapter 2 addresses the rhetorical effects obtained by casting Dreyfus as a suffering Christ figure, especially in regard to Théodore Reinach's short story, "Gonse-Pilate," where the pathologies so often attributed to Jews were symbolically redeemed through the captain's "death" at the hands of the anti-Semitic mob.

In this manner, the negative qualities associated with "Jewishness" were displaced from Dreyfus and the Dreyfusards onto the anti-Semites themselves, ironically revealing them to be the true "Jews."

Despite this rhetorical ingenuity, however, Dreyfusards remained troubled by the intensity with which the anti-Semitic crowd voiced its opposition to the prospect of a revision of the Dreyfus case, and, in their ongoing project to craft a positive social image, they invoked the negativity of the crowd as a means of underscoring their own masculine qualities. As Chapter 3 argues, Dreyfusard discourses on the crowd tapped into a deep pool of contemporary anxieties about modernity, and in particular expressed concerns about an overstimulating urban landscape and the inability of most men to resist its seductions. Describing a veritable sensory overload powered in part by popular fiction, newspapers, prostitution, and the "moral contagion" of all forms of external suggestions, this critique of modernity allowed the revisionists to underscore the autonomy, sacrifice, and willpower that seemed implicit in their resistance to public opinion. The many exasperated critiques of the crowd reveal a common logic: men who were caught up in popular irrationality betrayed their own inner weaknesses, showing themselves to be dangerously susceptible to suggestion and thus as emotionally "porous" as women. Conversely, those who retained their autonomy posited the firmness of their personal boundaries and the superior physicality that was the foundation of all good character. Insofar as they sided with, and benefited from, the indignation of the crowd, military men were prime targets of this critique and thus served as foils for the superiority of the Dreyfusard man. As the last section of Chapter 3 reveals, the most glaring example of the depths to which military men could sink was the real traitor, Major Charles-Ferdinand Walsin-Esterhazy, whose personality and moral character were mercilessly scrutinized to reveal his mental and emotional proximity to the irrational crowd he had deceived.

Damning figurations of military men and irrational mobs were important weapons in the Dreyfusard arsenal, and their tactical use allowed revisionists to project an image of manhood that alleged superiority to that of more traditional men of action. Combining intelligence, autonomy, and courage in a healthy body, the Dreyfusard seemed like the perfect man for modern times. What to do, then, with the significant number of women who also marched under revisionist colors? How to reconcile their activities with claims that bringing truth to the light of day was essentially a man's job? Chapter 4 addresses these questions by examining how women factored into Dreyfusard politics, both as actors and as icons. It contends that the troubling presence of active women in their ranks compelled many Dreyfusards to compensate for this intrusion on the level of the imagination, particularly through graphic depictions of women in more conventional roles. On one hand, as the case of the journalist Séverine makes clear, female Dreyfusards played an important role in the gender politics of the Dreyfus Affair, where they affirmed the virility of their comrades while deploring the cowardice of their enemies. On the other hand, although politically engaged women could function as bona fide experts on manhood, this feminine presence in revisionist circles was also used as further ammunition against the weaknesses of the intellectuals. In other words, while many Dreyfusards welcomed allies like Séverine, this acceptance was not without reservations that supportive women might be better off restricting themselves to their "proper" spheres of competence, namely, empathy and tears, rather than articles and deeds. This anxiety about women out of place had a broader resonance with other gender concerns of the period. In addition to the feared "unsexing" of women who engaged in mental pursuits or political action, it reflected long-standing republican concerns about how the conservative, religious, and emotional tendencies of women threatened to corrupt boys and men. Unable to actually forbid active female involvement in revisionist politics, Dreyfusard artists employed symbolic means of reinserting women into more conventional roles. As a means of illustrating their own heroism and of "managing" the feminine within their own ranks, these artists made ample use of the female allegory, Truth. Often depicted as trapped in a well and incapable of emerging without male assistance, Truth reaffirmed the weakness of women, the cowardice of her captors, and the heroism of her Dreyfusard emancipators.

CHAPTER TWO

Sanctifying Dreyfus

Intellectuals, Jews, and the Body of Christ

In their campaign to win over the hardened hearts of the French public, the Dreyfusards often engaged creatively with the nasty rhetoric generated by their opponents. By vilifying Alfred Dreyfus as a "Judas," anti-Semites had created a label that would stick to the captain for the next decade. Pro-Dreyfus writers often reversed this imagery, however, by presenting the captain as a kind of Christ figure. In many respects, this strategy made good rhetorical sense: what better way to counter the epithet "Judas" than with "Christ"? The personal experiences of Dreyfus made such a reversal seem especially appropriate. Having heard the first guilty verdict while facing a massive painting of the crucified Christ, the innocent captain surely noticed the gulf between his actual predicament and the "Judas" he was accused of being. "Now my Calvary is finished" is what bystanders heard Dreyfus utter after his degradation, and readers would later find the disgraced man's published diary and letters filled with references to the "crucifixion" he had endured.[1] Such imagery made the "execution" of Dreyfus seem more like a sacrifice (Fig. 3). As the Dreyfusards were the ones who preached the innocence of Dreyfus in the face of hostile opposition, however, they were not satisfied with having just one Christ figure. In addition to defending the captain against "the country that crucifies him,"[2] Dreyfusards also insisted upon the Christ-like sacrifices being made by men like Colonel Georges Picquart, Émile Zola, Joseph Reinach, and others who were persecuted for their convictions. Suffering unjustly for a cause made one seem heroic, and the Dreyfusards tried to cultivate this impression in the general public.

The soundness of this Dreyfusard tactic becomes far less obvious if we consider the complexity of the passion story they invoked. According to biblical accounts, especially in the overtly anti-Jewish gospel of Matthew, the betrayal and condemnation of Christ are perpetrated mainly by Jews, either single-handedly by Judas or collectively by the crowds in Pilate's courtyard. Not only does the plot structure of the passion story *require* the presence of the Jews as antagonists, but, insofar as the crowd in Matthew (27:25) accepts responsibility for the blood

Fig. 3. H.-G. Ibels, "Pitié: Le Coup de l'éponge," in H.-G. Ibels, *Les Légendes du siècle* (Paris: Le Siècle, 1901). By permission of the Houghton Library, Harvard University.

of Jesus, it prefigures the guilt that Jews have been made to bear throughout the Christian era. That Jesus was himself Jewish does not disrupt this basic opposition, for the Christian tradition has implied that whatever meaningful connection Jesus had with the Jews was nullified once they called for his death. With Christ virtually divested of the taint of Jewishness, it is no surprise that medieval performances of the passion play so often turned into the very real suffering of local Jews, upon whom Christians would heap the accumulated resentment of the previous year.[3] Anti-Jewish in its basic structure, or at least treated as such by generations of Christians, the story of Christ's betrayal and death has always been available for the purposes of Jew haters. Albeit deplorable and dangerous, its appearance in anti-Dreyfusard imagery is hardly remarkable.

What is remarkable is that this religious narrative was appropriated by the Dreyfusards themselves, many of whom were resolutely anticlerical and manifestly opposed to anti-Semitism. As Richard Griffiths insightfully argues, this genre of Dreyfusard polemic implied that, contrary to anti-Semitic claims, the "real" Jews were those responsible for the captain's plight.[4] This important observation not only highlights the basic categories of the Christian narrative but recognizes the structural necessity within it. Whenever someone is cast as "Christ" in the passion story, the role of "the Jews" must also be filled. Casting non-Jews like Picquart or Zola as Christ figures nicely served the purposes of Dreyfusard symbolic politics, while leaving the basic parameters of the Christian plot intact. In such figurations, "Christ" and "the Jews"—however the latter were defined—could still be viewed as clearly distinct categories. Casting the Jew Dreyfus in the role of Christ, however, was a far more problematic maneuver, inasmuch as it suggested an identity between protagonist and antagonist that violated the structuring principles of the Christian narrative.

Fortunately for the Dreyfusards, Jewishness was at the fin de siècle a protean category that lent itself to a variety of ideological uses, from the condemnation of Jews per se to the critique of qualities, such as sedentariness, physical weakness, bookishness, and cowardice, that, while traditionally attributed to Jews, could also be shared by non-Jews. That intellectuals and bourgeois professionals shared these qualities was highly significant, for it suggested to critics one way in which modern men might be considered "Jewified." As Chapter 1 has revealed, this conceptual play made it possible to defend the Jewish people while condemning the "Jewish" qualities they displayed. Chapter 2 develops this idea further by inquiring into the function of Jewishness in the Dreyfusard use of Christ imagery. It argues that, by likening their heroes to Christ figures, Dreyfusards appropriated the transformative potential of the passion story as a means of altering public perceptions of revisionist men, who, as a result of being described as sedentary "intellectuals," were considered to be at a remove from the robust men of action epitomized by the soldier and the officer. Depicted as Christ figures, Dreyfusard males could lay claim to the courage, sacrifice, and self-negation that were so frequently associated with the military, thereby proving that they, too, were men of action by distancing themselves from the "unmanly" qualities of the Jews they defended. Insofar as the qualities associated with Jewishness were potentially found everywhere, however, this transformation of the Dreyfusards also operated through the displacement of these undesirable qualities onto other groups. This was particularly clear when Dreyfus himself was depicted as Christ, as in Théodore Reinach's short story "Gonse-Pilate," where the "Jewish" qualities of Dreyfus are displaced onto the anti-Semitic crowd.

Homo Sedentarius

Historians accustomed to viewing the Dreyfus Affair as primarily a problem of anti-Semitism have tended to ignore the complexity with which Dreyfus himself was perceived. Recall that the distance between Dreyfus and military manhood was not founded solely on the captain's Jewishness, but also on his status as a *savant*, a *cérébral*, and an *intellectuel*, inasmuch as he represented the new breed of highly educated officer. This was, moreover, no mere social observation, for, like the ethnic markers of Jewishness, the effects of such bookishness were thought to be clearly legible on the body. As one reporter noted, "his back depicts the curve of the *polytechnicien* who has leaned for a long time over notebooks and books,"[5] while another bemoaned the fact that Dreyfus seemed more like a functionary than a military hero. Recall, too, how, in the face of anti-Semitic charges of effeminacy, many Jewish men sought to redeem their masculinity by emphasizing the martial glory (and thus military fitness) of the Hebrew past while downplaying their reputation for study and sedentariness. Military manhood found its foil not only in the image of the cowardly and effeminate Jew, then, but in the related figure of the sedentary and unhealthy scholar or functionary. In other words, the superior virility of the loyal soldier was constructed as much in terms of profession and lifestyle as of race; as early as 1895, it served to cast doubt on the masculinity of Dreyfus and, in time, on the very "intellectuals" who would become his defenders. Insofar as scholarliness was integral to stereotypes of Jewish men, there existed a fluid relationship between Jewishness and intellectuality that has gone largely unexamined, but that is nevertheless crucial for understanding the uneasy alliance between French Jews and their non-Jewish colleagues during the Affair.

We shall see how Dreyfusard rhetoric invoked the tortured and crucified body of Christ as a means of managing the discursive proximity of intellectuals and

Jews; yet this cannot be accomplished without first considering the problematic status of "the intellectual" in the context of fin-de-siècle anxieties about individual and national health. It is striking, for instance, that the collection of subscription lists known as the "Manifesto of the Intellectuals" got its name from the fact that most who signed also included their professions, a strategy whereby Dreyfusards tried to establish their authority to pass judgment on the political world by reference to the fact that they were principally engaged in intellectual rather than manual labor. The conservative literary critic Ferdinand Brunetière underscored the role of academics in the group he dubbed *les intellectuels*,[6] but in actual fact those who demanded that the Dreyfus case be retried represented what one might call the "white-collar" professions of the bourgeoisie; they included poets, publicists, architects, schoolteachers, lawyers, doctors, and pharmacists. Despite their own tendency to focus on the well-known scientists and writers in their ranks, Dreyfusards too acknowledged doctors, lawyers, and magistrates in the revisionist camp.[7] Georges Clemenceau's attempt to popularize the term *intellectuel* as a badge of honor thus represented real progress in the nascent social identity of Dreyfusards, who quickly followed suit to assert the primacy of rational judgment over the purportedly distorted thinking bred by religious fanaticism and blind allegiance to nationalism. None of this is meant to suggest the homogeneity of the pro-Dreyfus group. As Christophe Charle has argued, this public gesture of solidarity allowed otherwise mutually exclusive social types and political perspectives to conceal for a time the features that would have divided them under normal circumstances.[8] This is a very instructive observation, for it shows how these people tried to project a public image of unity and authority that would be viewed as distinctly "Dreyfusard," although that term glossed over potentially divisive differences. Moreover, it implies that while the figure of the engaged intellectual was in some respects founded by this "Manifesto," the survival of that figure depended on its being articulated repeatedly in the numerous pamphlets and tracts being produced by Dreyfusards.

The very concept of the *intellectuel* was fraught with negative connotations. Used as a substantive during the 1890s, *intellectuel* was a pejorative term that conjured up images of social disorder, decadence, and nervous illness: precisely what anti-revisionists like Maurice Barrès had in mind when they used it to describe their opponents.[9] Moreover, by seeking to ground the legitimacy of their authority in a particular form of labor, Dreyfusards invoked a long-standing contrast between men of thought and men of action. Although modern men have often registered a common disdain for the principled idleness of the traditional aristocracy, they have remained considerably divided over the relative merits of mental as opposed to physical labor. Of course, not needing to work with one's hands was a defining feature of bourgeois male identity;[10] yet the ideology of adventure that structured the expectations and emotional investments of many Western men lingered on in the social imagination, and represented a persistent source of anxiety among men involved in contemplative, nonmanual activities. Faced in the early nineteenth century with forging a definition of manhood that did not rely primarily on demonstrations of physical strength and risk-taking (qualities crucial for working-class men as well as for soldiers), many bourgeois males defensively incorporated the rhetoric of combat and conquest into discussions of economic activity, while implicitly valorizing rationality as an inherently masculine trait.[11]

What was the relationship between intellectuals and other kinds of men? Most historians have preferred to view the former as inhabiting a world quite removed from the mainstream, as if they were, to quote a contemporary, "an aristocracy that is distrusted, and that unfortunately doesn't know how to inspire confidence."[12] This view of the scholar or artist as a different sort of being extends back to antiquity and is in many circles an enduring mark of the cultural distinctiveness of such pursuits. Yet the gap between philosophers and ordinary men was also thought to be displayed on the body, whose insistent demands for sensual pleasures were thought to be subordinated to the search for truth. As a result, we have inherited a view of the intellectual as a singularly stunted physical being. "Aristotle wondered why men of genius tended toward melancholy," Steven Shapin reminds us, "and Seneca asked why God afflicted the wisest men with ill health. These questions continued to circulate in the seventeenth century and beyond. The [seventeenth-century] natural philosopher Walter Charleton announced that the 'finest wits' are rarely committed to 'the custody of gross and robust bodies; but for the most part [are lodged] in delicate and tender Constitutions.' Dead White Males, that is, were generally Sick White Males."[13]

To some extent this view of the distinctiveness of certain intellectuals is true enough, for during the Dreyfus Affair much was made of those savants who departed their laboratories to combat injustice. Moreover, as Charle and others have observed, it was during this period that the modern engaged intellectual as a relatively autonomous social group first emerged.[14] Contemporary critiques of intellectualism were also couched in such terms, where old elites scorned those newcomers with pretensions of being an "intellectual aristocracy." Yet dwelling on the social distinctiveness of intellectuals also means casting a blind eye on the long-standing *continuities* between academics, writers, and journalists and the wider world of the bourgeois professions, all of which required the acquisition of intellectual capital and engagement in mental rather than physical labor. Above all, men who formed part of the emerging state and business bureaucracies, many of whom were themselves Jewish, lost in prestige what they gained in power and income, largely due to the fact that they were seen as subordinate to more powerful men.[15] Despite the fact that the Dreyfus Affair facilitated the emergence of the modern engaged intellectual as a semi-autonomous social being, this common reliance on mental labor and the physical problems it sometimes entailed continued to connect *les intellectuels* with the bourgeois professions generally.

The history of medicine reveals ongoing concern about modern sedentary lifestyles and illustrates the ways in which intellectuals could be considered less robust than other men. Since at least the eighteenth century, the lifestyles of worldly people have been the subject of medical scrutiny, mainly because the combination of physical sedentariness and unhealthy habits resulted in a range of health problems that were largely unknown to peasants, workers, and "savages." The Swiss physician Samuel Tissot informed his readers that the passions, worries, and rich diets of well-to-do city dwellers could lead to nervousness, gout, and migraines, as well as a host of respiratory, digestive and visual problems.[16] Stemming from a slightly different set of causes, the ailments suffered by men of letters were not far removed from those of *gens du monde:* nervousness, poor digestion, and physical weakness awaited any man who disregarded the needs of his body for purely mental pursuits. As Anne C. Vila has observed, these medical warnings "played an important role in forging and disseminating the image of the intellectual that would predominate from the late eighteenth century to our day: that of a delicate, oversensitive, borderline invalid, ill-suited to the rigors and shocks of worldly life."[17]

Concerns about the health of both writers and worldly people proliferated during the nineteenth century and were often expressed in the many manuals of hygiene that warned of the dangers with which sedentariness and mental labor threatened men of the upper classes, whether savants, writers, artists, administrators, bureaucrats, lawyers, or doctors themselves.[18] Even though the agitated minds and sorry physiques of urban professionals were deplored, however, for much of the nineteenth century, nervousness was still held to attest to the more delicate (and therefore superior) sensibilities of the bourgeoisie. This is perhaps one reason why male nervousness did not become widely perceived as a mark of effeminacy until later in the century, particularly after nervous exhaustion, or "neurasthenia," became identified as a disorder that primarily afflicted men. With neurasthenia evidently on the rise among the bourgeois elite during the Third Republic, it was impossible simply to relegate neurasthenics to the margins of social life. Instead, one sees a growing uneasiness about bureaucrats and functionaries who had lost touch with the warrior ethos of their distant ancestors.[19] As we have seen, this unease was manifested most vocally in the military, where the technocrat Dreyfus was singled out as a prominent example of how functionaries had eclipsed older, more "honorable" elites in this bastion of French manhood. The specifics of the French experience resonated with developments across the Western world, where, in addition to preoccupations with homosexuals, criminals, and the insane, physicians began to focus more closely on those who had been long considered normal. As George Mosse observes, during this time, attention was increasingly drawn to "otherwise respectable middle-class men who could not live up to the manly ideal because in some manner they were considered sick or unmanly. They seemed to narrow the gap between true masculinity and its foil in a dangerous way."[20] Despite the cultural demand that men defend their honor through dueling, the men who rose to positions of power and prestige in the new republican system seemed quite removed from the warrior ideal, primarily because their livelihood was based on mental rather than physical labor. Perhaps for them the need to affirm their honor through dueling was even more pressing.

Whether they were professors, poets, or bureaucrats, men committed to mental labor were often seen as a population at risk. When physicians intervened to ameliorate the problem, the educational system that fostered such cerebralism was a logical target. By the 1880s, partly in response to the growing awareness of neurasthenia, the schools that produced the nation's elite came under scrutiny for promoting a dangerously excessive cerebralism that might, it was thought, result in intellectual exhaustion (*surmenage intellectuel*). This concern was understandable considering the emphasis that most *lycées* placed on philosophy and, contrary to practice in England and the United States, the relative lack of interest in instilling sporting values into young men. Attempts to incorporate physical education into the *lycées'* curricula, particularly after 1870, met with failure generally, inasmuch as most schools lacked either the facilities or the will to do so.[21] Moreover, the *bataillons scolaires* created in 1882 to make gymnastic and military exercises compulsory met with only limited success, and they were scrapped altogether after the frightening chauvinism generated during the Boulanger crisis. Only later in the decade did some students begin to create soccer clubs in their *lycées*, a move applauded by Pierre de Coubertin, who, in addition to founding the modern Olympic games, was also a strong advocate of the moral and physical benefits of English team sports.[22] For many critics, however, this was not enough, and the perceived relationship between schooling and the cultivation of weak men remained a concern among social observers and medical experts. Among many specialists, neurasthenia was a logical progression of the mental fatigue incurred during one's school days. In addition, mental strain and sedentariness seemed to promote general physical debility, and in several studies, the thoracic capacities of schoolboys were found to be alarmingly limited, thereby potentially exempting them from military service. All of these factors served to "annihilate individual initiative, *force of will*, moral energy, [and] firmness of character [emphasis in original]."[23] It was no wonder that boys were growing up to be neurasthenic, one physician noted: "Look at the soft, enervating, effeminate education to which we submit the child whose faculties are just beginning to develop."[24] The result of this *surmenage intellectuel* was a steady deterioration of the French elite, leading one physician to note with irony that, when it came to neurasthenic men, "the classes that are called *dirigeantes* furnish the strongest contingent."[25]

The crisis of manhood so often decried at this time was thus part and parcel of a wider social transition, which was also taking place in other countries. "Masculinity was at the turn of the century obviously going through a period of deconstruction and reconstruction," Angus McLaren explains. "The context was one in which the older disciplinary mechanisms employed by elite males to control women, workers, and young people—especially those of the church, family, shop, and farm—were breaking down and being replaced by teachers, policemen, and doctors."[26] In many respects, the Dreyfus Affair played out this tension between old and new elites, and the *intellectuel* represented the crystallization of a more general social development: the growing desirability of the liberal professions under the Third Republic and a corresponding increase in university enrollments. What made the *travailleur intellectuel* a problem in this regard was that, aside from being physically underdeveloped and prone to nervousness, he seemed to position himself against old elites and competing styles of manhood, particularly those epitomized by the manual laborer and the soldier, thereby implicitly discouraging men from entering these professions and creating a glut in a range of white-collar occupations. Critics of academic overproduction argued that promising comfortable careers to young working-class men who pursued tertiary degrees (despite the limited spots available) did little more than create a population of unemployed and frustrated professionals—doctors without patients, lawyers without cases, teachers without students—a veritable "intellectual proletariat," whose professional frustrations might be channeled into socially disruptive ends.[27] Moreover, despite the fact that republican school-books celebrated the soldier's willingness to defend his country, after 1889, compulsory military service was reduced from five to three years, and in time university students could receive an exemption for two of these years. The social problem posed by the intellectual proletarian readily dovetailed with medical discourses about the menace of excessive cerebrality, thus demonstrating how a crisis of the male body could also have unsettling implications for the body politic. "This is a leprosy for France," observed the publicist Henry Bérenger. "It enfeebles the body, dissolves consciousnesses, impoverishes the race."[28]

This gathering criticism of mental work helped further divide men along professional lines, and, in a move reminiscent of eighteenth-century critiques, often meant the valorization of the healthy manual laborer over the white-collar worker. Anson Rabinbach has argued that by the late nineteenth century, fatigue had lost much of its validating potential in the lives of workers;[29] yet during this time, some bourgeois men responded to this crisis of masculinity by implicitly celebrating the kind of fatigue, as a consequence of intellectual work, that brought on nervous and digestive disorders, as opposed to strictly muscular woes. In a regular medical column in the highbrow *Annales politiques et littéraires*, Dr Henri de Parville assured his readers that mental labor was just as burdensome, if not more so, than manual exertion. "It's always the same prejudice," he lamented. "For the worker, intellectual labor does not count." Little did the manual laborer know what hardships were endured by the white-collar professional, for whereas the former worked outdoors and remained free in his toil, the intellectual worker was "a prisoner to his chair." The effects of such work had a cumulative effect, and the difference between the two men at age forty would be quite striking: "The worker is solid, healthy; *l'homme de plume* is deformed; he digests badly, and is already gouty or rheumatic." In terms of fatigue and the expenditure of energy, there could be no comparison between these two forms of work, for "mental labor uses up its man more quickly than does muscular labor." Parville insisted, with a touch of defensiveness, that a worker who swapped places with a professional for just one year would not be able to hack it. The worker would quickly discover that the "building site and the workshop are preferable to the office."[30]

he might never have become an intellectual at all. This sense of being removed from the manly ideal of the warrior continued to haunt this young man, in whom feelings of physical inadequacy sometimes became confused with his identity as a Jew. In the early days of the revisionist campaign, Benda was made to feel quite self-conscious at his first meeting with his fellow Dreyfusard Georges Clemenceau, a well-known journalist and renowned duelist. Having grown to adulthood with a keen awareness of the gap between thinking men and men of action, Benda also felt that Jewish republicanism, which was "abstract, metaphysical, inhuman," could not measure up to the palpable heroism of more robust Frenchmen. Clemenceau seemed to agree, for at their first meeting, Benda had "the feeling [that Clemenceau] experienced pity in the presence of this race of men, as well as embarrassment and a certain esteem."[34]

Despite his celebration of the life of the mind, in his memoirs Benda evinced a general regret that becoming an intellectual entailed so many refusals of (or the inability to achieve) an energetic warrior ethos. Most important, in this regard, Benda cited a continuity between the scholar and the white-collar professional, both of whom seemed to lack this martial spirit. Yet Benda's misgivings were not unique, and many of the tensions that he recalled decades later were also voiced by some Dreyfusards in the heat of the Affair. Some clearly resented being made to feel less manly in the presence of more robust contemporaries, a distinction underscored starkly during their military service. The writer René Ghil commented bitterly on this antagonism and spoke in collective terms that his comrades would understand: "We know the contempt, the irreconcilable hatred even, that most men of the sword profess for men of thought." Under circumstances where a premium was placed on physical tests of manhood, creative men felt compelled to play the man as convincingly as possible: "It is thus that litterateurs above all take every precaution to conceal this defect during the time they spend in the regiment."[35] It is likely that many others shared this sense of embarrassment that being an intellectual sometimes implied. While scholars like Paul Gerbod rightly note that an ethic of heroism expanded under the Third Republic,[36] men of the time understood that not all heroisms were created equal. Despite their endorsement of moral rather than physical courage, intellectuals were far less secure in the validation that moral courage was meant to provide.

In many ways, then, the emergence of men who identified themselves as "intellectuals" cut against the grain of prevailing cultural wisdom about the dangers of excessive mental labor, a mind-set encapsulated in the hygiene reformer Philippe Tissié's concise prescription for national health: "More athletes, fewer aesthetes."[37] Of course, the anti-Dreyfusard camp included a great many professors and men of letters; yet many of these purposely rejected the term *intellectuel*. The novelist Maurice Barrès, for instance, who was hardly a stranger to the life of the mind, memorably lauded the virtues of being intelligent rather than *un intellectuel*. The tensions that divided competing styles of masculinity along professional lines reverberated in the heat of the Affair, where the specter of the intellectual proletariat was repeatedly conjured up by those critical of the defenders of Dreyfus. The crowd psychologist Gustave Le Bon launched his attack on Dreyfusard *demi-savants* by noting that the anarchist Émile Henry was "an unsuccessful candidate from the École Polytechnique; a man unable to find any employment for his useless and superficial science, and consequently the enemy of a society which was not wise enough to appreciate his merits."[38] Another observer, writing in the immediate wake of the "Manifesto of the Intellectuals," underscored the tension between honorable soldiers and those young men who "come to the Faculty, to all the Faculties, to flee the barracks," thus alleging the unpatriotic and even cowardly character of such men. Nothing less than a wholesale shift in public opinion would alleviate the problem of the intellectual proletariat, continued this writer, and central to this campaign would be a rehabilitation of the virtues of physical work, "to preach that manual labor is no less noble than that of the pen or the tongue."[39]

Finally, the physical problems associated with mental work, particularly muscular weakness and nervousness, were brought to bear against the Dreyfusards. The negative implications of shattered nerves for masculinity were eagerly invoked by Barrès in his characterization of his opponents. When at the height of the Affair, the nationalist hero Paul Déroulède rudely interrupted a pro-Dreyfus rally, Barrès reported how "some 'intellectuals,' weak masters of their nerves, displayed on their faces the convulsions of satyrs and, under the scorching light, in this terrible atmosphere of the masses, delivered themselves to the rut of hatred."[40] Later, Barrès would contend that these "rebellious pedants are the most sterile of men [*les plus inféconds des hommes*]."[41] Anti-Dreyfusards were quick to emphasize how nervous, "pale intellectuals" failed to measure up to the more physically robust style of manhood embodied in the unjustly condemned military. Cartoons of neurasthenic intellectuals, figured as egg-headed, exceptionally thin, physically weak, and repulsive to women, abounded in the anti-Dreyfusard magazine *Psst . . . !* (Figs. 4-6). These caricatures were taken to contain a germ of medical truth, for it was commonly accepted that excessive mental labor augmented the volume of the brain while diminishing musculature throughout the body. With a bit of imagination, one could easily produce arrestingly grotesque extensions of this idea.[42] Other caricatures alleged that in "intellectual salons," women were generally neglected, inasmuch as the men preferred their own company, thus subtly associating the allegedly weak, impotent, and unappealing bodies of intellectuals with outright homosexuality. The women in one cartoon think angrily in unison: "A kingdom for a lieutenant of dragoons!" (Fig. 7). Ridiculing the defective manhood of the intellectuals was a favorite tactic of anti-Dreyfusards: while one facetiously declared his opposition to the pro-Dreyfus camp as the president of a "group of neurasthenics," another saw his intervention as a way to help "reawaken traditional French virility."[43] Most important, condemnations of the intellectual as a specific social type often slipped into a wider critique of the bourgeois "brain worker" or intellectual proletarian, thus constituting an extension of the conflict between intellectuals and men of action on a national scale.

Once Were Weaklings

Nervous, physically slight, and perhaps even cowardly, the stereotypical intellectual not only embodied all that was wrong with the bourgeoisie, but displayed qualities that were frequently condemned in Jewish men. Despite its often overtly bodily connotations, however, as a cultural construction, Jewishness had no *necessary* seat in the Jew's body, just as metaphors of "femininity" and "blackness" also operated with some independence of their original referents in women and Africans. In conjunction with these related metaphors of otherness, Jewishness was a contested concept that circulated with some fluidity in the Western cultural imagination, to be invoked whenever circumstances demanded its presence. Hence, not only were the Jews themselves seen as dangerously protean and fluid, but the very category of "the Jew" could be expanded to encompass a much wider range of individuals.

That relatively few Jews signed the "Manifesto of the Intellectuals" illustrates the hesitation on the part of many to become embroiled in a controversy that might signify Jewish solidarity. Many became more actively engaged months later, mainly after Dreyfusism began to seem more like the defense of republican ideals.[44] As we have seen, this hesitation was sometimes misunderstood as another instance of traditional Jewish cowardice. Yet the relatively poor showing of Jews among these *intellectuels* did not prevent their enemies from making damning associations nonetheless. Recalling the indeterminate quality of the

Noble dégoût

L'INTELLECTUEL : — « Je ne veux pas me baigner dans la même mer qu'un général!... »

Fig. 4. Caporal Poiré [Forain], "Noble dégoût," *Psst . . . !* 20 August 1898, 4.

construct called "Jewishness" is important for understanding how stereotypes about Jews converged so readily with assumptions about intellectuals during the Dreyfus Affair. Not only were Jews traditionally credited with extraordinary intellectual powers, but in France they were also closely linked with anticlerical educational reform, Kantian moral philosophy, and the "immoral" trends of literary modernism.[45] Together intellectuals and Jews seemed to stand for the triumph of effete cerebrality over virile corporeality, cosmopolitanism over nationalism, and the destabilizing effects of modernity over the putative certainty of tradition. The contemporary psychiatric claim that Jews were congenitally predisposed to neurasthenia only accentuated the connection between them and Dreyfusard brain workers.[46] Indeed, among certain sectors of the population becoming an intellectual was tantamount to becoming "Jewish" in the broadest sense of the term, a belief explicitly professed by one anti-Semite who called for "the extermination of the Jews and the Jewified [*les enjuivés*]."[47] A famous anti-

Extra Muros

— Adieu, Monsieur!... dit–elle.

Fig. 5. Caporal Poiré [Forain], "Extra Muros," *Psst . . . !* 18 June 1898, 4.

Semitic cartoon entitled "Intellectual Baptism" summarized this perspective vividly: by signing the "Manifesto of the Intellectuals," men of already dubious character effectively transformed themselves into Jews (Fig. 8).[48]

Figuratively speaking, then, intellectuals and Jews seemed to inhabit virtually interchangeable categories, whose similarity was rendered even more apparent by the assumption that both types of men were excluded from the warrior ideal of action. We have seen how many Jewish men chafed at being too closely associated with bookishness and sought to reaffirm their martial qualities by emphasizing their honor and virility. One response to this discomfort was to subtly distance themselves from the very men who rallied in defense of Dreyfus. Some revisionists were appalled by this hesitation, and proclaimed how ironic it was that the Dreyfusards were being opposed by both Jews and anti-Semites. Insofar as the negative implications of scholarly activity could also invoke the meek and nonviolent Jew, however, this dynamic could just as easily move in the opposite direction: Dreyfusards correspondingly sought to distance themselves from the Jews, or at least from the unmanly connotations of Jewishness. Obses-

Pendant la Grève

— Fiche–moi la paix..... Je suis Française!

Fig. 6. Caporal Poiré [Forain], "Pendant la Grève," *Psst . . . !* 22 October 1898, 4.

sively disavowing any connection with Jews, a gesture that was manifestly meant to illustrate the "disinterested," and thus laudable, nature of the revisionist campaign, also had the subtle effect of creating this distance. Yet in masculine performances, simple denials of unmanly qualities have never sufficed, and just as Jewish magazines reiterated the concrete deeds of valor of Jewish men both historically and currently, Dreyfusards likewise had to put their manly credentials to the test. They, too, felt compelled to produce positive examples of heroism and robustness for public consumption.

Cultivating an ethos of action and sacrifice assisted Dreyfusards in their own masculine performances. Yet transforming enfeebled intellectuals into more robust men, if only rhetorically, required expanding the meaning of "action" itself. When, in early 1898, Georges Clemenceau lauded the intervention of the intellectuals, he still had to contend with the prevailing stereotype of thinkers, who, given "the character of their work, their mental habits, [and] lifestyle," were at some remove from "men of action." Clemenceau thus embraced a broader view

Salons intellectuels

CHŒUR DES DAMES : — « Un royaume pour un lieutenant de dragons! »

Fig. 7. Caran d'Ache, "Salons intellectuels," *Psst . . . !* 10 December 1898, 2.

of action, and noted approvingly that by rallying around Zola, such men had "emancipated themselves" by being moved by the "virtue of action."[49] The journalist Paul Brulat observed with satisfaction how, unlike the fearful *honnêtes gens* who refused to act, he and his comrades audaciously confronted peril.[50] These acts of moral courage were often explicitly contrasted to the physical courage demonstrated by other men of action, and many Dreyfusards insisted that such

Page d'histoire

« Baptême intellectuel »

Réédition de : « Sauvons la patrie en danger ! »
Seulement... c'est tout le contraire.

Fig. 8. Caran d'Ache, "Page d'histoire: 'Baptême intellectuel,'" *Psst . . . !*
12 February 1898, 3.

forms of bravery were far superior. Some, like the writer René Ghil, became overly optimistic. Envisioning a shift in the social value accorded intellectual activity during the Affair, Ghil anticipated an increase in the manly credentials residing therein. The time would come, he predicted, "when it will be more glorious to disseminate thought than to spill blood."[51]

This fantasy of a world where mental heroism was valued above physical courage was pleasing to many Dreyfusards, but in an age marked by an increasing focus on the healthy body as the guarantor of national vitality, it did not prevent them from insisting repeatedly that men of thought could also enjoy a virile physicality. In fact, many Dreyfusards not only described the manliness of their project in overtly physical terms, they frequently engaged in duels as a means of affirming their honor, while refuting allegations of their physical weakness. Indeed, no fewer than thirty-one serious duels pertaining to the Dreyfus Affair were reported between 1894 and 1906, many of which were fought by Jews, suggesting that assaults upon one's honor were typically answered according to established codes of masculinity.[52] The martial prowess of Clemenceau himself was noted long before the Affair, and in the duels he fought in the midst of the crisis, he did not fail to perform. From his bookshop near the Sorbonne, the socialist Charles Péguy was always ready to snap into action whenever a Dreyfusard professor was abused; Péguy often rallied his troops with the military order "Fall in!"[53] Bourgeois men generally preferred the conventions of the *point d'honneur* to the crudities of direct physical aggression, which is not to say that fist-fighting could not also be grounds for enthusiasm: the Dreyfusard Henri de Bruchard was celebrated as "a courageous intellectual who is not afraid to throw a punch [*qui n'a pas craint de faire le coup de poing*]."[54]

Since the Dreyfusards labored for well over a year in the face of public and governmental opposition, these positive examples of courage were often eclipsed by frequent descriptions of how heroically these men suffered for their beliefs. In this sense, Dreyfusards arrogated to themselves the very discipline and sacrifice so often professed by the army, and thus instituted a veritable cult of heroic suffering. The conservative republican Joseph Cornély, who had applauded the military appearance of Dreyfus, insisted that Dreyfusism too was "an opinion of abnegation and sacrifice."[55] How fortuitous it was, then, when Dreyfus's principal defense lawyer, Fernand Labori, was shot by an unknown assailant on the streets of Rennes in 1899. Despite the fact that Labori survived this assault (although the bullet could not be removed), the Dreyfusards now had a hero who had literally risked his life for the cause. Outpourings of support congratulated the heroism of this new martyr, and Marcel Proust's letter to Labori gushed with admiration for this "invincible good giant" who "no longer even has to envy military glory the magnificent privilege of soldiers: Giving one's blood."[56] The fact that few of Dreyfus's champions would actually shed blood in his name did not diminish the presumed manliness of the revisionist campaign—even bold speeches and essays were cited as proof of heroic action. "Finally!" exclaimed Clemenceau in response to a pro-Dreyfus speech delivered by the educator Ferdinand Buisson. "Here are Frenchmen who rise up and speak when to speak is to take action." Significantly, Clemenceau identified this newfound action as being in itself transformative: "Men! There are men in France! So many weaklings who trembled before the barbarous threats of the Army and the Church [*le sabre et le goupillon*] are regaining their courage."[57] Zola had sown the seeds of heroism, and now heroes were cropping up everywhere. "Courage is contagious," declared Paul Brulat. "Under the mass of lies and calumnies, heroes are multiplying."[58]

The Dreyfusard desire to combine military and intellectual virtues with manly sacrifice made Colonel Georges Picquart an easy hero to embrace. As a military man, Picquart differed from his contemporaries in that he represented a more intellectual type of officer. Like Dreyfus, he was a *polytechnicien*, and his erudition and love of music transformed him into a unique kind of Dreyfusard hero: a bona fide man of action who was also an intellectual.[59] The fact that Picquart suffered for his convictions by being sent to Tunisia and later imprisoned for over a year only enhanced his reputation for heroism. He was unburdened by the stigma of Jewishness or any personal association that might have motivated his involvement, and no Dreyfusard seemed quite as virile as he. In 1899, a massive subscription campaign was waged to honor this "heroic artisan of the revision," and Octave Mirbeau praised the "firm and tranquil courage" of this man who quietly welcomed persecution for his convictions. "You can condemn me, he seemed to say to them, and I am ready to submit to everything, because against persecution and misery my soul is strong. . . . Do what you will, then."[60] As Joseph Reinach noted, this man "refused to prostitute his conscience. . . . Here is a hero, a martyr, the hero of Law, the martyr of Truth."[61] "A figure above all others radiated a pure brilliance," Francis de Pressensé declared. "It's Colonel Picquart. We asked for a hero: here he is."[62] Regardless of these accolades, Picquart was by no means an unproblematic hero. In the hands of his enemies, the very culture and erudition that impressed his revisionist comrades were easily cited as proof of overrefinement and, when coupled with his unmarried status, even homosexuality. In this sense, Picquart—who was sometimes called "Marie-

Georges"—was no different than any other overrefined intellectual. Commenting on his deposition during the Rennes trial, a skeptical Maurice Barrès found in this man signs of a "delicacy of psychology" that "certainly evades the man of action."[63] The novelist also described the Dreyfusard fascination with Picquart as a veritable cult, which even included fetishistic tendencies, particularly in the distribution of photos of the colonel with shreds of his uniform and bits of his epaulettes attached as holy relics.[64] There is something to Barrès's observation, for more than one admirer professed that the colonel exercised "a sort of fascination over those who approached him," a fascination that was also rejuvenating: "With every conversation I felt my soul fortified by coming into contact with his."[65] Although this sentiment was expressed by a woman, Mirbeau's own prison interview with Picquart elicited a similar response, as well as the conclusion that, "along with our dear Zola, he is the martyr and the hero."[66]

Most Dreyfusards would have agreed with Mirbeau. As the favored object of abuse for anti-Dreyfusards, many of whom had long detested the man for his popular and sometimes controversial novels, Émile Zola was indeed revisionism's most conspicuously suffering hero. Unlike Picquart, however, Zola had no background as a military man, had a rather flabby body, and was renowned for gustatory excesses and nervous disorders. This reputation was bolstered by the grim medical facts reported in an 1896 book by Dr. Édouard Toulouse, a thorough study of Zola that depicted him as a "superior degenerate" who suffered from nervousness and other health problems.[67] Although, as we shall see in Chapter 5, Toulouse generally praised Zola's character and willpower, the novelist's questionable physical and mental stability made him a somewhat problematic hero for the Dreyfusards. Invoking the "disturbing" conclusions that Toulouse made about the novelist's nervousness, for example, a writer for the anti-Dreyfusard newspaper *L'Eclair* used such medical findings to explain what madness had compelled Zola to intervene on behalf of Dreyfus.[68] The journalist Ernest Judet took this biological argument even further, alleging that Zola's father had been a criminal and that the novelist had inherited similar immoral traits. Inspired by his deed nevertheless, Zola's supporters were moved to take steps toward reconfiguring his image. The writer Saint-Georges de Bouhélier dubbed Zola a "hero," whose action, "better than one accomplished with arms, illuminates the virtues of the race."[69] As Octave Mirbeau observed during an interview with Zola, the deed even exercised a profound rejuvenating effect on the man himself: "[S]ince these events, Zola is less nervous, less febrile than usual, he is more in possession of himself—body, mind, and soul. . . . He is ready to sacrifice his liberty, to give his life for the triumph of his cause, which is that of humanity."[70] Zola had clearly been toughened up by the whole experience, and Clemenceau noted admiringly how, faced with Judet's allegations about his father, "the author of the immortal pamphlet *J'accuse* received the blow without weakening."[71]

Alongside the more active deeds of dueling and street-fighting, passive suffering like shedding blood, receiving blows, and enduring persecution helped to make Dreyfusism seem like an ordeal that could transform brain workers into heroes. It also elevated these men above too close an association with cerebral yet "cowardly" Jews, men who, despite their protests to the contrary, seemed to shrink from any action on their own behalf. So important was this ethic of sacrifice among both Jewish and non-Jewish Dreyfusards that one could conclude that it was more important to receive blows than to land them on an opponent. Among many revisionists, in short, courting persecution became something of an obsession. Paying homage to Zola's heroic deed, a redactor for *Le Rappel* declared that "we are happy also to be . . . insulted, scoffed at, bespattered. . . . Let's march without cease, and always with a firmer step, *non pas certes!* without care for the wounds received, the sufferings endured."[72] In their campaign for a "just and healthy cause," the Dreyfusard heroes whose portraits appeared in Gerschel's photo gallery *Les Défenseurs de la justice* had all "withstood blows, received wounds, grieved and suffered."[73] Ordeals such as these, like all "good suffering," were best endured quietly. As another observer remarked, the suffering hero "displays neither his wounds nor his tears; he pays them no mind. [His combat] is entirely inward and silent."[74] So this ethic of sacrifice had become so widespread that Zola himself, once "J'accuse" was deemed libelous by the court, began to wonder if he had really suffered enough. Should he submit to a one-year prison sentence or flee to England? Several others had already paid dearly for their convictions: Picquart was persecuted for his inquiries and ultimately had his pension annulled, and, in addition to being harassed on the street, pro-Dreyfus politicians like the republican Joseph Reinach and the socialist Jean Jaurès both lost their seats in subsequent elections. Opting in the end for exile over imprisonment, Zola regretted that his decision to flee would reflect badly on his heroic reputation.[75]

The Crucified Jew

The example of Christ provided a useful metaphor for the suffering the Dreyfusards had sustained and thus contributed to the masculine reputation they were trying to cultivate. Like the savior before them, revisionists too marched in the name of something higher, defied the curses of a misunderstanding populace, and ended up persecuted for the ideals they espoused. Christ's sacrifice had redeemed humanity, and the Dreyfusards likewise suffered in the name of universal values like truth, justice, and humanity. Nevertheless, Dreyfusard Christ imagery mobilized a complex interplay between manhood, Jewishness, and the universal that illuminates many of the tensions within Dreyfusard discourse. Indeed, just as Jesus's redemptive sacrifice seemed to prove his own "sacred" nature, Dreyfusards likewise accepted their sanctified status eagerly, even as their enemies were, as an added bonus, metaphorically transformed into "Jews."

Over the centuries, Christ has been pressed into the service of an array of causes: he is one of the most widely exploited of historical figures. It is true that representations of Christ during the central and later Middle Ages were feminized in certain milieus and at specific periods,[76] but the nineteenth century provides many examples of a masculinization of Jesus, expressing a renewed emphasis on the virile body. This was especially true in Anglo-Saxon countries. In America, the therapeutic ethos of the late nineteenth century helped bring about a rapprochement between religion and the more secular need to maximize the vitality of the self, a development vividly illustrated in the psychologist G. Stanley Hall's representation of Jesus as a vigorous adolescent superman.[77] When appropriated as a masculine exemplar, Christ epitomized the qualities of detachment, renunciation, sacrifice, and heroism demanded of any "true" man faced with the jolting conditions of the modern world. Indeed, one might even cite the English "muscular Christianity" movement decades earlier as further evidence that associations between Jesus and manhood were quite acceptable during this period.[78]

At first glance, France provides a counterpoint to such tendencies. Not only did many French Catholics emphasize the "feminine" qualities of Jesus in their devotional practices, but republican men had for years distrusted the association between priests and women, who threatened to overturn liberal ideas from within the family itself. In fact, during the nineteenth century, many Frenchmen had relegated Christianity to the feminine sphere, while claiming, along with Alfred de Vigny, that honor itself had become the new religion among men.[79] Under the Third Republic, this feminization of religious faith was also effected on medical grounds. Jan Goldstein shows, for example, that the famous neurologist Jean-Martin Charcot earned the approval of the republican elite by showing through retrospective diagnosis that the ecstatic experiences of religious mystics were actually instances of "hysterical" psychological states. It was only a matter of time before Jesus himself would be lampooned by writers like Léo Taxil or thoroughly medicalized by scholars like Dr Binet-Sanglé, who, declaring that the entire Christian tradition was founded on a "diagnostic error," contended that Jesus himself suffered from almost every mental disorder that was feared at the fin de siècle. Binet-Sanglé even intimated that homosexuality was on the list of Christ's many afflictions.[80]

One might conclude from such evidence that, unlike Protestants in Britain and the United States, the French did not seek to render their practice of Christianity "muscular"; yet such developments account for only part of the rather complicated relationship between the French and the figure of Christ in the nineteenth century. For instance, although Ernest Renan's positivist retelling of the life of Jesus proved an affront to many Catholics, its very favorable image of Christ as a respectable man (and, significantly, one whose Jewish ancestry could not be proved) nonetheless circulated widely in the cultural imagination.[81] Moreover, the blatantly secular figure of the "Dreyfusard Christ" had important antecedents in what Michael Paul Driskel terms the "desacralization" of Jesus in the nineteenth century. Moves to humanize the savior had roots in the short-lived "sans-culotte Christ" of the French Revolution, and continued during the romantic period, when "Christ" and "the people" were rhetorically blended. In this synthesis, Jesus emerged as either a symbol of the suffering masses or a heroic rebel fighting for the popular cause. This "Republican Christ" was most often invoked as a symbol of the manly fight for liberty, as an *homme révolté* whose struggle for social justice had little in common with conventional notions of domestic femininity.[82] In short, while there was a complicated relationship between the figure of Christ and masculine identity, it is nevertheless evident that iconographic traditions and the convergence of religious and therapeutic discourses at the end of the nineteenth century helped to make it possible for Dreyfusards to appropriate Christ in secular terms.

Religious metaphors moreover provided a useful way to frame the entire Dreyfusard experience. As John Cerullo has shown, the rhetoric of the Dreyfus Affair was steeped in the language of religiosity, and among revisionists, the figure of the crucified Christ became a perfect metaphor for the trials they had endured.[83] Colonel Picquart was sometimes figured as the suffering servant of Justice made to tread in the footsteps of Christ. "Step by step, station by station, he walks his *Via Dolorosa*, he climbs his Calvary."[84] Yet the full Jesus treatment was reserved for the author of "J'accuse." In the eyes of many, Zola's intervention not only vindicated the right of intellectuals to pass judgment on the political world but seemed to be a gesture ripe with redemptive potential: "By the fullness of the Deed, by the energy of the Word, Zola was transfigured into a modern Christ."[85] This impression was only enhanced by perceptions of Zola's manly conduct in the face of mass opposition, and prompted Octave Mirbeau to write approvingly to Claude Monet: "He is like a Christ."[86] The theme of Zola-as-Christ even resonated in the international press, with one Italian artist presenting a remarkably muscular Zola standing bound and defiant before a screaming mob.[87] In other cases Christ imagery was mixed with representations of allegorical female figures like Truth, who, as we shall see in Chapter 4, proliferated during this period. It seems that Truth too could be personified and crucified like Christ, as one Dreyfusard remarked: "What! Truth glides to the summit of a calvary!"[88] As a postcard by the illustrator Denizard Orens suggests, the savior Zola could play both roles simultaneously (Fig. 9). In this print, Zola stands in the foreground of this scene, his arms upstretched in a gesture of victory. Naked except for a piece of cloth around his pelvis, Zola has miraculously lost the considerable girth he had acquired with literary success. The empty crucifix looms in the background, and we realize that the novelist has emerged from his ordeal to be thoroughly assimilated to the slender body of the victorious Christ. In one hand, he even holds the mirror traditionally associated with Truth, an ideal usually represented by female allegory.[89] Through this rather excessive imagery one point becomes clear: as the result of his heroic deeds Zola has been doubly transformed into the embodiment of the universal to become at once Jesus and Truth. In the Dreyfusard imagination, one really could be redeemed through "Christ."

Most important, this redemption even applied to Dreyfus himself. In a provocative reading of the Affair, Sander Gilman contends that the body of Dreyfus was fundamentally transformed through his public degradation and imprisonment on Devil's Island, and that his experiences provide "a model for the decline of the healthy body of the acculturated, westernized male Jew into the sick, decaying body of the essential Jew he is concealing, the *exemplum* of racial predestination."[90] Though there is much in the Affair to recommend this interpretation, such a view pertains more to anti-Dreyfusards who, while at times willing to think of the captain as a negative or anti-Christ, were generally content to consider his body as a justly tortured object. Among Dreyfusards, the situation was far more complex. When depicted as Christ, Dreyfus's broken body could be cited as testimony to his manly ordeal rather than as evidence of his

Fig. 9. Denizard Orens, Zola postcard, in John Grand-Carteret, *Zola en images: 280 illustrations, portraits, caricatures, documents divers* (Paris: Félix Juven, 1908). By permission of the Houghton Library, Harvard University.

Jewishness. We have seen how the oppositional logic of the passion narrative allowed a victorious Christ to emerge against the backdrop of Jews who functioned collectively as an antagonistic anti-Christ, thus permitting the imaginative disengagement of Jesus from the negativity of his Jewishness. Dreyfus could not be made to play the role of the universal Christ without undergoing a similar transcendence of his Jewish particularity.[91]

Since the Christ-like qualities of Dreyfusard heroes tacitly excluded all taint of abjection ("Jewishness"), it is arguable that, by being cast as Christ, Dreyfus was made symbolically to transcend his own ethnic particularity to become an embodiment of the universal, a process apparently made possible only through the application of pain. This perhaps explains the considerable interest Dreyfusards took in the condition of Dreyfus's body after his ordeal on Devil's Island. Joseph Reinach noted with admiration how during his long voyage home, Dreyfus had struggled against illness and nervousness in his quest "to conquer himself [*à se dominer*]."[92] In the courtroom, the sight of Dreyfus moved Maurice Paléologue to gasp: "Ecce homo!"[93] Even the female journalist Séverine, who had never fully divested herself of anti-Semitic sentiment, marveled at how different the captain seemed during the Rennes trial, particularly when he responded to allegations of treason: "In a minute, his legs shook, his accent became more vigorous; if one dare say it, he 'humanized' himself."[94]

A similar movement from Jewishness to humanity was sketched by Joseph Reinach's brother Théodore in his short story "Gonse-Pilate," a revisionist rendition of the passion account that appeared in *Le Siècle* just days after the publication of Zola's "J'accuse."[95] Exploring this text in some detail may put us in a better position to evaluate the discursive effects of the passion metaphors that abounded in Dreyfusard polemic. General Charles Gonse was the deputy chief of the General Staff who had blocked early attempts to prove the innocence of Dreyfus, while knowingly defending the real culprit, Major Charles-Ferdinand Walsin-Esterhazy. Gonse was also one of those generals singled out by Zola for acting as an accomplice to the cover-up, in his case "because of the esprit de corps which makes the War Office the Holy of Holies and hence unattackable."[96] Figured as Pontius Pilate in Reinach's tale, Gonse-Pilate epitomized the questionable honor of the French military committed to sealing the fate of Dreyfus. Described as a brave man, "at least in war," "Gonse-Pilate, we see, lacked civic courage. Such is the case with many military men." Such personal shortcomings were only exaggerated by the volatile social climate of the capital city, for the "people of Jerusalem were spiritual, credulous, and savage" (43–44). Due to a lingering "thirst for blood" among the people of Jerusalem, the authorities had agreed long before to the annual spectacle of a crucifixion.

Enter "a little Galilean, a military scribe by profession—history has not retained his name." Aside from being detested for his overweening ambition and unconventional religious creed, this Galilean was "very ruddy, very ugly, and very myopic," physical defects apparently traceable to his unfortunate ethnic background. After all, Reinach explained, "he was from Galilee, and we know that the inhabitants of this province were very much despised in Jerusalem. They had hooked noses, an uncouth gait, and a terrible accent [*Ils avaient le nez crochu, la démarche disgracieuse, et une prononciation fort corrompue*]" (45–46). The Galilean was arrested on trumped up charges and, because he was "from Galilee," soon elicited the wrath of the gullible populace. Despite the efforts of "an honest centurion" (Picquart) to expose the truly guilty party, "a certain Barrabas" (Esterhazy), Gonse-Pilate yielded to public opinion and the pressure to cover up for the army. He offered the crowd a choice between the Galilean and Barrabas, and predictably they demanded that Barrabas be set free. Failing to reason with the multitude, Gonse-Pilate "took water and washed his hands in the presence of the crowd, saying, 'I am not responsible for the blood of this man, it is your concern!' And all the people replied: 'Let his blood be on us and on our children!'" Here the transformation of Dreyfus into Christ is effected through suffering: "And the Galilean was delivered to the people for whom he was crucified after being scourged. They say that Gonse-Pilate did not sleep well that night" (50–51).

Reinach's remarks about Jewish bodies may appear as an ironic depiction of the period's most vivid prejudices. After all, why would a Dreyfusard who was himself Jewish sketch such a pejorative physiognomy, especially in a tract whose manifest purpose was to condemn anti-Semitism? Yet such statements could have only been truly ironic if Reinach himself disagreed with them, and it is therefore to Reinach's own perspective on Jewishness that we must turn. A philologist at the École pratique des hautes études, Reinach was no casual commentator on the Jewish condition. Through his multivolume history of the Jews and outspoken advocacy of assimilationism over Zionism, this writer was by the turn of the century considered eminently qualified to pass judgment on anti-Semitism. Some insight into Reinach's depiction of Dreyfus may be found in his 1894 article on the Jews for *La Grande Encyclopédie*. Though stating from the outset that the Jews "do not form a race properly speaking," in this piece Reinach cited certain unfavorable characteristics that were explained by reference to environment:

The most prominent physical and physiological features of the Jews are the result of customs, of conditions of secular existence, rather than true ethnic particularities: thus are explained, for example, the nervous, often painful expression of many Jews, their timid and awkward gait, their too animated or vulgar gestures, their weak muscular force, their predisposition to cutaneous and nervous sicknesses, and dementia leading to suicide. These characteristics, the product of centuries, will gradually yield according to changes of milieu and manners. Today French, Italian, and English Jews differ little from their compatriots from other religions, while Polish or Russian Jews, who are destitute, badly housed, [and] malnourished, carry all the signs of physical degeneration.[97]

Reinach maintained that some customs contributed to Jewish health: the "circumcision of Jews, their sobriety, their dietary laws, have been able to and could still preserve them from certain diseases" (273). Nevertheless, in this account, the qualities that define Jewish visibility are generally negative and indicate a link between Jewishness and pathology, especially among the eastern European Jews who had been migrating westward in growing numbers since 1881. While western European Jews were often represented as virtually indistinguishable from Catholics and Protestants, these "degenerate" eastern Jews were unwelcome reminders of all that assimilated Jews were endeavoring to overcome.[98]

Scholars like Reinach who rejected anti-Semitism also tended to challenge the assumption that the primary qualities of the Jews could be explained by reference to race. Though such individuals regularly invoked environmental factors, they generally presented the most visible markers of Jewishness, whether explained by heredity or environment, as highly pathological and at odds with the normative traditions of Western civilization. That is, to be recognizably Jewish was to be marked by pathology and thereby situated outside society's mainstream. Reinach evidently shared this view. Despite depicting many Jewish qualities as socially constructed, he still claimed that Jews' success in commerce was largely due to their "hereditary superiority" in and "hereditary aptitude" for such pursuits; and he further asserted that Jews also tended toward excess in these areas, manifesting "a lustful, excessive taste for lucre, a shrewdness that degenerates into duplicity, a tendency to think that everything is for sale and that it is legitimate to buy everything" (274–75). Ironically, though, Reinach had to admit that even the process of assimilation that he celebrated could have a serious psychological cost: "Abrupt intellectual and religious emancipation produces other effects of imbalance: by severing the bonds linking him to traditional Judaism, the Jew often finds in his emptied conscience neither a curb nor a guide to stop it; he abandons himself, like an escaped horse, to all the effervescence of his imagination and logic, to all excesses of thought and action" (274). Despite apparent superiority over their eastern European counterparts, even assimilated Jews were perceived to have a propensity for nervous illness and sensual excess.

For Reinach, the assimilation of Jews into the mainstream of human progress was a veritable cleansing process whereby the pathological qualities of the people would eventually cease to exist. Under optimal living conditions, Reinach maintained, most of the physical signs of Jewishness would be wiped away, leaving a purified body virtually indistinguishable from the European norm. But Reinach's reform project did not stop with the body, for in his desire to eliminate Jewish particularity, this anticlerical intellectual took aim at Judaism itself. The Jew's religion, he assured his readers, had long ceased to be significantly different from Christianity, and "tends to transform itself into a sort of colorless deism differing little from the Protestantism of the extreme left; perhaps the day is not far off when attempts at a fusion will arise." True emancipation would mean that "the Jewish sentiment would gradually lose its harshness and end up, without a doubt, extinguishing itself completely." At the end of the day, Jews would become "absorbed into the mass of their fellow citizens of different faiths," while Judaism would "consider its 'mission' accomplished and die without regret, shrouded in its triumph" (279). Despite his defense of the Jews during the Affair, it is nevertheless evident that, like Zola and many others, Reinach wanted them to disappear as a recognizably distinct human type.

Reinach's scholarly ruminations on the Jewish question both illuminate and obscure the meaning of "Gonse-Pilate." Despite his progressive political stance, Reinach offered in both these texts an image of the Jewish body that is not only unflattering but somewhat at odds with the traditional image of Christ. Whereas the Christian tradition remembers the body of Christ as being pure, Reinach deliberately transformed that of Dreyfus into a pathological specimen. That is, disregarding the assimilated character of the "real" Alfred Dreyfus, Reinach denied his textual Dreyfus the liberating invisibility purportedly enjoyed by acculturated Jews. Instead, the signs of the captain's deviance were inscribed on his "ruddy," "ugly," and "myopic" face. Nor are any of the other Jews in the story examples of the healthy acculturated type celebrated earlier; they too bear the stigmata of the degenerate eastern Jewry that Reinach deplored: "They had hooked noses, an uncouth gait, and a terrible accent."

Since Reinach evidently agreed with such assumptions about Jewish bodies, it is difficult to conclude that "Gonse-Pilate" was written simply in the ironic mode. For this reason, I suggest a reading that reconciles Reinach's assimilationist teleology and ambivalence about Jewishness with the passion narrative that frames "Gonse-Pilate." Pathological Jewish particularity, we have seen, is not only a precondition for the harmonious synthesis that Reinach envisioned for the future, but is the affliction of all the Jews in his story. One might say that Jewishness is here reminiscent of the "fallen" state of humanity prior to the coming of Jesus, whose suffering and death is highlighted for its redemptive power.

In this sense, the Christian narrative is an especially appropriate vehicle for Reinach's philosophy of history, itself being a narrative in which the fallen nature of the Jews promises to be redeemed in a universal body. For Reinach, Jewishness was the unwholesome chaff that would in time fall away from the Jews, revealing the kernel of universal humanity within. And, more important, in this text, Dreyfus is made into a sacrificial figure, whose suffering is closely associated with the universal.

While an ironic reading of "Gonse-Pilate" cannot be entirely dismissed—for there is much that *is* ironic in this allegory—such an interpretation does not account for the numerous tensions in this and other texts written by Reinach. It is more appropriate to consider "Gonse-Pilate" a particularly vivid example of the contradictions and ambiguities circulating within Dreyfusard discourse, for in its pages, the author's sincere desire to ridicule anti-Semitism collides with his own misgivings about Jewishness. These misgivings arguably sprang in part from Reinach's own role in the Affair. Indeed, it is worth noting that Reinach did not put his own name to the tale he had spun. As far as the reading public could tell, this story was written, not by the Jew Reinach, but by "An Intellectual," an anonymous hero who also suffered unjustly.[99] There is thus a parallel between the author and Dreyfus himself, the unnamed "scribe" of Reinach's tale.

How Anti-Semites Became "Jews"

Christ was thus an appropriate symbol for intellectuals frustrated by the persistence of the particular in their politics of the universal. As Louis-Albert Revah has argued, the Dreyfusards often shifted public attention away from the Jewish question to more universal issues: "The more it appeared to them that anti-Semitism was the motor force of the Affair, the more they insisted on the universal character and import of the event."[100] By making Dreyfus stand for the universal, revisionists symbolically absolved their hero of his Jewishness, that is, of his pathological particularity. Through this process, Dreyfus himself became sanctified, or "purified," as Zola once put it. At once pure and purifying, the body of Christ effectively staged the sufferings of a Jew on the way toward humanity, a secular "god" whose sacrifice for a time cemented the unity of Dreyfusard intellectuals. Cleansed of his Jewish nature, Dreyfus was rendered fit to be included in the pantheon of Dreyfusard heroes.

Yet the transformation of Dreyfus into Christ did not mean that the taint of Jewishness was simply expunged from Dreyfusard discourse. Instead, "the Jew" emerges as an integral aspect of Dreyfusard thinking, for the negative qualities associated with "Jewishness" were displaced onto another troublesome category of fin-de-siècle social life: the anti-Semitic crowd. The Christian tradition remembers Judas's action as a decisive moment in the passion of Jesus, providing posterity with an archetype of betrayal for centuries to come. Yet the legacy of anti-Semitism that emerges with this narrative also depends upon the Jews as a collective agent in the condemnation and death of Christ.[101] The ramifications of this for Dreyfusard polemic were significant and reinforced the associations made between their heroes and Christ. In the face of the anti-Semitic crowd, as Émile Duclaux observed, "Zola could perhaps respond, 'Father, forgive them, for they know not what they do.'"[102]

Despite their ambivalence about the Jews, for obvious reasons Dreyfusards could not depict actual Jews as participants in the betrayal and condemnation of Dreyfus-Christ; rather, in Dreyfusard polemic, intellectual saviors suffer, not at the hands of the Jews as such, but at the bidding of an anonymous yet irrational mob. As Chapter 3 will show, the crowd was generally represented as a "feminine" entity, prone to hypnosis, "contagion," and "hysterical" outbursts; along with women, "primitives," and Jews, it counted as one of the major threats of the fin de siècle. Moreover, given the numerous outbreaks of anti-Semitic rioting and the early mass opposition to the revisionist cause, the crowd was quickly cast as the antithesis of the heroically marginalized Dreyfusards.[103] "And in France," wrote one revisionist, "heroism now means defying the instinctive crowd from the heights . . . of reason, justice, and truth."[104] While anti-Dreyfusards condemned the betrayal of "Christ" (France) at the hands of "Judas" (Dreyfus, the Jews), Dreyfusards at once separated, reversed, and collectivized these terms. For them the fate of "Christ" (Dreyfus or Zola) was sealed by "the Jews" (the crowd). Not only did republican Dreyfusards manifest a profound distrust of the masses, but they condemned such disorderly behavior through the vivid historical antecedent in the Bible: "It is [the majority] that in 1870 led us to [the French defeat at] Sedan and not to Berlin," declared a professor of pharmacy, "it condemned 'Jesus' to death and pardoned 'Barrabas'!"[105]

Despite their manifest opposition to anti-Semitism, many Dreyfusards nevertheless commented on the "Jewish" or "Judaic" aspects of the anti-Dreyfusard crowd. According to *La Revue blanche*, for example, "There is in this anti-Jewish clamor a Judaic character of religious exclusivism that drags anti-Semites down to the level of Jews of the earliest centuries. There is in this racial persecution a Judaic superstition about origins that takes us back to the time when Jews believed in the Talmud."[106] Consider, too, the glowing portrait of Zola painted by Paul Marin in an open letter to Édouard Drumont, where the masculinity of the Christ figure was emphasized: "It is against this Hercules . . . that today you play the role of the Jew in regard to the Messiah!"[107] Religious metaphors allowed many revisionists to posit the "Jewishness" of anti-Semitism in fairly oblique terms. The crowd, according to one commentator, "exiles Aristides and deifies Caesar; it forces Socrates to die and prostrates itself before Napoleon; it supports [General] Boulanger's flocks and drags Jules Ferry into the mud. It delivers Barrabas and condemns Jesus!"[108] In some instances, however, the specter of Jewishness shone through quite clearly: "I dare to hope that it [public opinion] will find itself on the side of Justice. But universal suffrage offers such surprises! Between Barrabas and Jesus, the Jews, alas, have not hesitated!"[109] Whoever was cast as "Christ" in these Dreyfusard passion plays, the anti-Christian Jewish crowd was usually played, paradoxically, by an anti-Jewish "Jewish" crowd.

A similar displacement takes place in "Gonse-Pilate," where the only concrete Jew to be found is the unnamed Galilean himself. With the Jewishness of Dreyfus neutralized through his transfiguration into Christ, the role of the Jews is now entirely taken over by the antagonistic crowd. Though both are implicitly specimens of degeneracy at the outset, the crowd and the Jews follow diametrically opposed trajectories in this text. Degraded and defeated, as a Christ figure, Dreyfus must emerge victorious in the end, while the vengeful crowd invites everlasting guilt for the death of the savior: "Let his blood be upon us and upon our children." Even the body of Dreyfus, physically defective and unattractive at the beginning, implicitly becomes the body of Christ at the end. A subtle reversal is perhaps the unspoken conclusion to "Gonse-Pilate," for ultimately the Jews and the crowd swap places. Anti-Semites are made to absorb the "Jewishness" of the Jews.[110]

This chapter has contended that the Dreyfusard appropriation of the passion narrative represented an attempt to sustain the image of a coherent collective identity centered around normative conceptions of masculinity, while subtly displacing the specter of Jewishness that frustrated such a projection. Depicting themselves as heroically masculine in body and mind, revisionists recognized that the dominant image of the Jewish body was incompatible with this self-representation, and symbolically effaced the ethnic particularity of Dreyfus by placing him on the cross. At the same time, lingering anxieties about Jewishness were transferred onto the anti-Semitic crowd, whose often violent behavior was cited as proof of its degeneracy and hysteria. Hardly philo-Semitic in any simple way, then, many Dreyfusards displaced the repugnance they felt for Jewishness as they campaigned for the revision of the Dreyfus case. As a founding event in the construction of Dreyfusard identity, the "Manifesto of the Intellectuals" struck anti-Dreyfusards as the metaphorical transformation of intellectuals into Jews. Given the multivalent nature of Dreyfusard discourse, however, we might speculate that the gendered and universalistic claims of this petition also transformed Jews into men.

CHAPTER THREE

Educating the Will

Crowds, Contagion, and the Dreyfusard Body

The eruption of popular anti-Semitism in France is one of the most widely cited and disturbing aspects of the Dreyfus Affair, and no discussion of crowd imagery should distract us from the fact that there were concrete reasons to be shocked at the behavior of the crowd. Armed with mounting evidence refuting the original verdict and feeling that revelations of the truth would turn the tide of public opinion, Dreyfusards were stunned at the widespread violence of the anti-Semitic mobs that, beginning in late 1897, rallied in every major French city against the revisionist campaign. Nevertheless, the fact that the masses so vociferously opposed the revision, often destroying property and physically attacking Jews, was perhaps less surprising to these men than the more painful betrayal of university students, many of whom on several occasions poured into the streets of the Latin Quarter to protest the recent interventions of Zola.[1] Such young men, destined for professional careers, had clearly abdicated rational reflection for the irrational leveling of the mob. "Intellectual machines, more servile than manual laborers," fulminated Achille Steens, director of the illustrated review *Le Sifflet*, "they are contemptible because they have willingly renounced their free will. They could have been independent but they want to be part of the crowd."[2] That intelligent men of any age would nullify their own autonomy by succumbing to the crowd was one of the most disturbing developments during this contentious period and, as we shall see, cut to the heart of what many Dreyfusards considered the foundation of true manhood. Steens's statement encapsulated sentiments shared by many Dreyfusard intellectuals, who were beginning to forge a fragile sense of social identity just as the crowd made its noisy debut in the political drama. In many respects, the projection of what might be called a Dreyfusard body was enabled through the troubling presence of this labile force.

Dreyfusards, we have seen, scarcely had a kind word to say about the masses, especially during the early days of revisionism. This might seem paradoxical, for Dreyfusism was largely composed of liberal republicans, socialists, and anarchists, people with a definite social mission who could not distance themselves entirely from the masses. More often (but not always), however, even these champions of public opinion distinguished "the people," whose legitimate desires merited respect, from the unruly mob, whose rebelliousness and irrationality called for vigilance, surveillance, and control. As one writer observed, "all those who feel themselves to be part of the *people* . . . should be Dreyfusards [emphasis in original]."[3] At the same time, they saw themselves as playing a leading role in guiding public opinion and gladly accepted their position as members of *la classe dirigeante.* "To believe in public opinion is foolishness or cowardice," declared Paul Brulat unequivocally, but as a republican he felt compelled to give a fuller explanation of such antipopulist sentiments. "I hear you," he explained, "public opinion is Universal Suffrage, it's the fundamental principle of the Republic. That's true, but the duty of republicans is not to submit to it, flatter it, or be dragged along by it, but to enlighten and direct it."[4] Brulat's concerns about being dominated or "dragged along" by the crowd resonated elsewhere in Dreyfusard rhetoric, for it was precisely this subtle threat of being overcome that frightened most social commentators during the last decades of the nineteenth century.

Anxiety about the crowd went far beyond concrete instances of collective action, such as during the Boulanger Affair or industrial strikes, and the fear of being overcome had implications that were as subjective as they were social. As Daniel Pick explains, by the end of the century, "the crowd" had become "a sociological category in the understanding of society. This was no longer in response to a specific threat (some isolated strike or riot), but a commentary upon modernity itself and the supposed dangers of socialism and mass democracy."[5] Pick's reference to modernity is crucial, for while Dreyfusards self-consciously identified themselves with the rationalist, cosmopolitan, and progressive notion of modernity inherited from the Enlightenment, they also struggled against a competing definition that had been generated by Baudelaire years before. This was a notion of modernity characterized by the fleeting and ephemeral qualities of urban existence, nicely encapsulated in Marx's famous claim that under capitalism, "all that is solid melts into air." Far from being simply a problem of mass politics, the crowd thus suggested a liquefaction that was ultimately more personal, even fantasmatic in nature, a protean threat of engulfment that paralleled the period's anxieties about modernity and cut to the heart of conventional assumptions about masculine autonomy. Andreas Huyssen's analysis of the elitist tendencies of modernist art illuminates the many levels on which male anxieties about the crowd may be read: "The fear of the masses in this age of declining liberalism is always also a fear of woman, a fear of nature out of control, a fear of the unconscious, of sexuality, of the loss of identity and stable ego boundaries in the mass."[6] Through a slippery chain of associations, the crowd came to embody the opposite of all that distinguished the true man from his many foils.

Chapter 2 illustrated how Dreyfusards sought to resolve the tension between the soldier and the scholar by asserting the virility of moral courage and self-sacrifice, while distancing themselves from all connection with "Jewishness." Identifying with a masculinized Christ figure was an important aspect of this strategy, for it allowed these men to negotiate the precise terms of their difference from anti-Dreyfusism by reference to their own heroic sacrifices and to the abject nature of the crowd. This chapter unpacks this crowd imagery in greater depth to explore its various dimensions. As we shall see, the Dreyfusard critique of the masses entailed a wider critique of modern life, which eclectically employed medical, social, and gender discourses to project its fantasy of a self-contained and biologically superior Dreyfusard man, a man with an iron will who, though not a soldier, nevertheless embodied the physical and moral health considered synonymous with true manhood. At once a master physician and a specimen of perfect health, such a man would be a virtual savior to France during its time of need. Ultimately, the critique of the crowd extended far beyond the problem of collective politics, for by subtly interweaving anxieties about literature, prostitution, seduction, and disease, these discourses provided the means of asserting the inherent weakness, not only of military men, but of the entire anti-Dreyfusard camp. As we shall see toward the end of this chapter, the weaknesses of military men were seen as embodied in the person of the real traitor, Major Walsin-Esterhazy, whose scandalous "fictions" deceived the crowd and himself.

The End of the *Flâneur*

No understanding of how the French bourgeoisie perceived the masses at the fin de siècle is complete without some consideration of the crowd psychology that circulated widely at the time of the Dreyfus Affair. Robert Nye and Susanna Barrows have each made invaluable contributions to our understanding of this genre of social theory during the early Third Republic, and have clearly shown how the works of Gustave Le Bon, Gabriel Tarde, and many others employed medical categories and gender stereotypes as a means of expressing their misgivings about the rise of mass politics at the dawn of the twentieth century.[7] My treatment of crowd psychology seeks to extend this scholarship by focusing on both masculinity and the crowd as dynamic processes, particularly as the latter encapsulated the fear that modernity might liquefy all that was tentatively established by the former. To this end, I suggest that this dynamic dimension of the crowd may also be understood by revisiting the problem of the *flâneur*, or gentleman stroller, a widely recognized figure on the urban landscape whose decline around the middle of the nineteenth century paralleled the rise of the masses and was accompanied by the proliferation of the *badaud*, or gawker. Exploring the qualities attributed to this polar opposite of the *flâneur* around midcentury, I contend, helps to illuminate how many observers would understand the crowd decades later.

Of course, the act of urban strolling has been reported in every modern city, but as a distinct social type, the *flâneur* has generally been described as a quintessentially Parisian phenomenon.[8] As it was celebrated in the first half of the nineteenth century, the superiority of the *flâneur* was defined in terms of a more sophisticated sensibility, corresponding to an elevated social status, qualities that gave the gentleman stroller a clear advantage over the lesser social types who happened to be on the streets with him. Always a male figure, and often either wealthy or cultured, the *flâneur* resisted the temptations of women and shopping in order to dive into the waves of fluid humanity and safely emerge elsewhere with his integrity intact, both morally and subjectively.[9] While the *flâneur* might experiment with the boundaries of self and other by immersing himself in the crowd, this playful blurring was always only a game that could be ended whenever he liked. As we shall see, the truth of the *flâneur* would always reside in his capacity for bounded interiority and possession of a strong will capable of sustaining a sense of self despite the encroachments of physical impulses and external stimuli.

Yet the story of urban spectatorship is only half told through an explication of the *flâneur*, for on his walks the gentleman stroller would sometimes encounter his antithesis in other individuals wandering the streets. Sometimes writers, such as Balzac, would mark a distinction between these passive ordinary *flâneurs* and the more active "artist-*flâneur*," while others relied upon a different social taxonomy by speaking instead of *le badaud*, literally, a "gawker," who was as quintessentially Parisian as the *flâneur*.[10] According to the *Trésor de la langue française*, the adjective *badaud* is etymologically traceable to the sixteenth century, when Rabelais used it as a synonym for "fool" (*sot, niais*); yet the link between the *badaud* and the *flâneur* is made explicit in the *Trésor*'s definition of *badaud* as a substantive: "That person who pauses in his strolling [*flâneries*] to gaze at the most mediocre spectacles." *Badauderie* signaled a lack of discernment in one's appreciation of urban spectacles; it was the act of someone "a bit foolish, lacking judgment and personality, who believes everything he is told and is eager to follow the ideas of others."[11] The *flâneur* and the *badaud* thus represented, not only two distinct styles of wandering, but two diametrically opposed responses to modernity itself. Insofar as the *badaud* became transfixed by the visions of the city, his activity portended at once both the end of *flânerie* and the potential fate of those *flâneurs* who failed to remain detached in the face of modernity. In other words, the *badaud* was a failed *flâneur*.

The difference between the *flâneur* and the *badaud* was underscored in the numerous "physiologies" published in the first half of the nineteenth century, popular studies that enumerated the various social types encountered in the urban landscape. According to an anonymous, self-professed *flâneur* contributing to *Le Livre des cent-et-un* (1832), the gentleman stroller had to be distinguished from doctors and lawyers who spent their free time loitering among theaters, shops, and bridges: "those are *musards* [dawdlers], but *flâneurs*, never."[12] Above all, the true *flâneur* had to resist the tantalizing power of rumor, which compelled the ordinary man to rush to the scene of some spectacle or other, leading this writer to "insist on the profound difference that separates the *badaud* from the *flâneur*."[13] The discerning eye of the *flâneur* was thus also based to some extent on a resistance to the kinds of stimuli leading to *badauderie*. In his contribution to one of the best known physiologies, *Les Français peints par eux-mêmes* (1842), Auguste de Lacroix found himself unable to describe the *flâneur* without also invoking the *badaud*. Despite the claim that "Paris belongs to the *flâneur* by the right of conquest and of birth," Lacroix also makes it clear that the *badaud* is equally unimaginable outside of Paris.

> The *flâneur* is to the *badaud* what the gourmet is to the glutton. . . . The *badaud* walks for the sake of walking, is amused with everything, is captivated by everything indistinctly, laughs without reason and gazes without seeing. . . . The *badaud* does not think; he only perceives objects superficially. There is no communication between his brain and his senses. Things only exist for him simply and superficially, without any particular character and without nuances.[14]

The difference between the *badaud* and the *flâneur* evokes the gap between irrational impulse and calculating volition: "Without a doubt the *flâneur* [like the tourist] also likes movement, variety, and the crowd; but he is not tormented by

an irresistible need for locomotion; he willingly circumscribes his domain."
Though the *flâneur* may have indeed been a mere idler in an age of bourgeois industry, production was less important for Lacroix than the tasteful accumulation
of memories: "The *flâneur*, it is true, produces little, but he amasses a great deal."

The *flâneur* incarnated the individualistic ideal of being *in* the crowd without necessarily being *of* the crowd, helping illustrate the intellectual's predicament vis-à-vis the masses and modernity. The parallel between the man of letters and the *flâneur* is articulated by Priscilla Parkhurst Ferguson, who reminds
us that urban tales could only be told "by those immune to the stress and the
seductions of the city, who can turn those seductions to good account, that is,
into a text that will exercise its own seductions."[15] Resistance to seduction thus
went to the heart of the identities of both the *flâneur* and the intellectual. Most
important, the *flâneur* stood for the triumph of intellectuality and textuality over
appetite and specularity: "Who are you, finally, you who reads these lines? And
who am I who writes them? A *flâneur*." We find at the end of this essay that the
flâneur has been nothing less than Lacroix's own self-presentation. Both the cultured reader and the man of letters embody *flânerie* in its fullness and reveal the
secret of how this wanderer retained his self-identity: the transformation of spectacle into text. This implicit aspect of *flânerie* was further explicated a few years
later by Alfred Delvau, who in *Les Dessous de Paris* (1860) explained that the "most
poignant realities are not spectacles for [the man of letters]: they are studies."[16]
The fullest definition of *flânerie* thus entailed not only a mastery of oneself, but
an intellectual conquest of Paris and its "social labyrinth." It was a way of making the flux of the city manageable through the precise calculations of a scientist.[17]

Not all commentators celebrated the quasi-scientific detachment of the
flâneur. Charles Baudelaire, for instance, invited his readers to remember the
pleasure that the *flâneur* took in his contact with the crowds. Sensitive to the nuances of modernity, Baudelaire complicated the vision of heroic singularity and
separateness by associating the *flâneur*'s experience of the crowd with intoxication: "The pleasure of being in crowds is a mysterious experience of pleasure in
the multiplication of numbers. Everything is numbers. Numbers are in everything. Numbers are in each individual. Drunkenness is numbers."[18] Baudelaire's
flâneur seeks in the crowd the intoxicating experience of multiplicity rather than
the singularity of conventional subjectivity; his is "un *moi* insatiable du *non-moi*."[19]

The crowd is his domain, just as the air is that of the bird and water that of the fish.
His passion and his profession is *to marry the crowd*. For the true *flâneur*, for the im-

passioned observer, it is an immense pleasure to take up one's abode in numbers, in the flowing, in movement, in the fleeting and the infinite. To be outside of one-self and nevertheless to feel oneself everywhere at home; to see the world, to be at the center of the world and to remain hidden in the world, such are some of the lesser pleasures of those independent, passionate, and impartial spirits, which lan-guage can but badly express [emphasis in the original].[20]

To the *flâneur*, the crowd is a feminine being, a prospective bride capable of elic-iting what we might call an "oceanic feeling" in the male, a pleasurable collaps-ing of the self into the fluidity of the nonself. Moreover, this exhilarating sensa-tion of losing oneself in the multitude resonates with the hashishin's "idea of evaporation," which Baudelaire relates in *Les Paradis artificiels*. Yet in this text we encounter a *flânerie* of a purely psychological nature, in which the actively per-ceiving artist is contrasted with the passively receptive addict who ends up being consumed by the very substance he has willingly ingested.[21] Though Baudelaire comes closest among his contemporaries to relinquishing the control of the sov-ereign self over its domain, the intoxication of his *flâneur* is a temporary experi-ence, after which the self must be reconstituted in all its singularity. Baudelaire's *flâneur* is not unlike the artist who, "by the strength of his will can deliver him-self, after having long been under the dominion of opium or hashish." In *Les Par-adis artificiels*, the artist-*flâneur* emerges victorious, while the addict remains in a relationship of dependence on the substance analogous to that of the *badaud* vis-à-vis the "intoxicating" urban spectacle.[22]

The distinction between *flânerie* and *badauderie* allowed mid-century com-mentators to posit a difference of kind separating reason from appetite, depth from superficiality, and textuality from unmediated spectacle. Yet the develop-ment of department stores and the Haussmannization of Paris during the Sec-ond Empire resulted in a new urban environment created in the image of the grande bourgeoisie, constituting an early society of the spectacle in which the once noble practice of *flânerie* would be declared a failure.[23] This new condi-tion required a more nuanced social taxonomy able to account for the process of psychic disintegration itself. In *Ce qu'on voit dans les rues de Paris* (1858), Victor Fournel heralded the decline of *flânerie* and the reign of *badauderie*. While the *flâneur* observes and reflects the spectacles of the street, he noted, "he is always in full possession of his individuality. That of the *badaud*, however, disappears, absorbed by the external world, which entrances him, which whips him into in-toxication and ecstasy. Under the influence of the spectacle, the *badaud* becomes an impersonal being; he is no longer a man: he is part of the public, he is one of the crowd."[24] For Fournel, the *flâneur* and the *badaud* were less statically oppositional types than mental states situated on a continuum: the gawker is the *flâneur* whose core of individuality has been evacuated by the spectacle. Not longer a creative wanderer freely consuming the city, he has become a mere recorder of stimuli, "a mobile and impassioned daguerreotype, which retains the slightest traces."[25] Stable ego boundaries were compromised once the spectacle penetrated to the subjective interior; autonomous creativity was liquidated and replaced by mere imitation.

Seduction, Consumption, and Collapse

Why this detour through the world of urban strolling? Because the manner in which Achille Steens and others described anti-Semitic students during the Affair (young men who, having "renounced their free will," now simply "want to be part of the crowd"), invoked the problematic status of the *badaud*, described decades earlier as one who is "no longer a man [but] one of the crowd." Some observers, like the physician Charles Féré, were content to explain crowd behavior with reference to borderline personalities who exhibited a morbid predisposition to suggestion. "To join in a crowd," Féré maintained, "is already the manifestation of an innate tendency."[26] For many others, however, becoming part of the crowd implied the forfeiture of willpower and individuality for the sake of something other, namely, the dissolution of boundaries so that one became, like the *badaud*, "absorbed by the external world, which entrances him, which whips him into intoxication and ecstasy."[27] This rather hyperbolic imagery was rhetorically useful for the Dreyfusards, not only because it posed a structural contrast to their heroic Christ figures, but because it offered a way of thinking about the relationship between failed manhood and devouring femininity that facilitated the celebration of the superior bodies of the Dreyfusard rank and file. By casting the crowd as "a labile, chaotic, and undifferentiated force that threatens the boundaries of autonomous individuality,"[28] as Rita Felski puts it, such discourses facilitated the emergence of what we might call a "Dreyfusard body" as the only one capable of resisting seduction and suggestion.

Metaphors of seduction, suggestion, imitation, consumption, and contagion permeated fin-de-siècle culture and conferred upon discussions of modernity a degree of anxiety that transformed the urban world into a particularly frightening place. Whether inquiring into criminality or crowd behavior, hysteria or masturbation, physicians, social commentators and legal experts tried to account for the avenues through which morbid ideas were transmitted and the varying degrees to which individuals could resist those ideas. These metaphors proved remarkably interrelated and even interchangeable, allowing for frequent slippages between, for example, the temptations of shopping and the problem of prostitution, both of which employed seductive techniques that appealed to the sensual desires of prospective clients. Individuals who succumbed to such external entreaties were often described as lacking character and willpower, while the process of seduction was likened to the spread of disease through contagion.

Inherited or acquired physiological defects were often cited as principal causes of a person's vulnerability to dangerous ideas. In his study of contagious murder, for instance, Paul Aubry used the language of microbiology to describe moral contagion as the "penetration of a morbid element into a prepared soil."[29] That is, with healthy individuals considered to be more or less immune to contamination, the majority of those identified as having succumbed to contagious influences also suffered from hereditary degeneration, nervous disorders, or some other acquired affliction, all of which fostered a special receptivity in the person. Lodged thus in a similarly unhealthy "soil," the morbid "seed" would act much like a microbe: "[T]here the idea will germinate, grow, ripen and, at a certain moment, secrete the toxins that will transform a normal brain into a criminal brain."[30] However, this was no simple "penetration" at work here, for while moral contagion was in many respects "produced from the outside in," as two other specialists noted,[31] it also acted primarily upon those whose defenses had been compromised and whose capacity for self-control was diminished. In this sense, moral contagion represented a double capitulation to the outer world of "contagious" ideas and to the inner world of affects and drives: the external "other" seemed to form an alliance with the sensual "other" within. Not only does this suggest an eruption or uprising as well as a penetration, but it indicates that on an unconscious level, the individual welcomed the collapse of the will that contagion entailed.

For many people, moreover, this collapse was not only welcomed but deliberately induced. At the fin de siècle, Parisians of many classes relished the temporary suspension of everyday volition that was promised by frequenting cabarets and café-concerts or attending the shows of magnetizers and hypnotists, thus reveling in what Rae Beth Gordon describes as "the corporeal unconscious." In a culture where discussions of hysteria and hypnosis took place in newspapers and magazines, many would have recognized the association between the almost epileptic gestural exaggerations of performers and the hysterics so theatrically displayed at the Salpêtrière hospital. They would have also felt themselves moved, as if automata or puppets, to the sound of lively music or the sight of grimacing and contorted performers, thus experiencing the guilty pleasure of allowing their bodies to overwhelm their minds. Gordon explains the ambivalence that such sensations could instill: "The total domination of body over mind, of sensation over reason and reflection, had—and has—a tremendous appeal in popular entertainment. . . . The spectator's physical experience is exciting and stimulating yet anxiety-provoking; the experience of the body involuntarily imitating the convulsive movements and facial contortions that characterized epilepsy and hysteria could not help but remind spectators of the all-too-common attacks of these illnesses that found their way into the popular press."[32]

Popular entertainment thus blurred the boundary between normal and pathological states and pointed disturbingly to more dangerous activities. The suspicion that anyone could succumb to seduction, or, as one doctor vividly put it, that "the most virtuous being conceals a dormant criminal,"[33] invoked some of the most recent findings in psychology pertaining to hypnotic suggestion. Indeed, alongside the idea of imitation, suggestion was the most widely cited mode of transmission for morbid ideas, and medical discussions about suggestion served as a point of intersection for debates about contagion and the paralysis of the will. Although Jean-Martin Charcot's ideas about suggestion attracted great notoriety at the fin de siècle, particularly due to the physician's dramatic public hypnotism of hysterical female patients at the Salpêtrière, his theories were quite conservative when compared to those of his rival from the city of Nancy, Hippolyte Bernheim. Arguing against Charcot, who claimed that only hysterical patients could be hypnotized, Bernheim presented evidence that healthy individuals were also subject to visual and verbal suggestion, and that such suggestion often took place in the waking state without the use of hypnosis. "Sensorial hallucinations" were thus not only experienced by hysterics, but were an everyday reality for all people as they lived their lives. Striking a blow against the idea of subjective autonomy, Bernheim's findings thus blurred the distinction between the subjective interior and the outside world in a way that helped shape the manner in which moral contagion would be conceived. "We are all suggestible," he contended. "No one can escape the suggestive influence of others."[34]

The contemporary legal and psychological ramifications of the debate between Bernheim and Charcot have been addressed in a number of historical works and need not be explored further here.[35] Suffice it to say that these two poles of interpretation were often blended in the popular imagination. This was certainly the case with the work of Gustave Le Bon, whose immensely popular *Psychologie des foules* (1895) employed insights borrowed from both Charcot and Bernheim. Admitting on the one hand the degenerate and deranged qualities of those who lead crowds—and stressing that such leaders are simply elevated from within the social ranks of the crowd itself—Le Bon also conceived of the crowd as a dangerous process of psychological leveling that could afflict any individual regardless of class. "In a crowd every sentiment and act is contagious," Le Bon observed, "and contagious to such a degree that an individual readily sacrifices his personal interest to the collective interest."[36] Much in keeping with Bernheim's ideas about the inherent suggestibility of both men and women, Le Bon attested to the power of suggestion in crowd formation. "From the moment that they form part of a crowd," Le Bon wrote, "the learned man and the ignoramus are equally incapable of observation. . . . by the mere fact that an individual forms part of a crowd, his intellectual standard is immediately and considerably lowered." Though he often elided the crowd with the lower classes, Le Bon's remarks indicate that crowd formation represented a return to the primitive state of the race, where the most regressive forms of savagery could manifest themselves under the psychological conditions provided by modern urban society. A hitherto intelligent man was not only dragged down by the crowd socially but was, in a sense, propelled backwards in time, for "as far as ideas are concerned, [crowds] are always several generations behind learned men and philosophers."[37]

Although he became an ardent anti-Dreyfusard during the Affair, Le Bon's ideas about crowd psychology remained very much *au courant* in educated circles. For the Dreyfusards, the crowd came to represent sensuality itself and seemed especially susceptible to contagion or seduction. According to Émile Duclaux, who as director of the Institut Pasteur knew a thing or two about contagion, "When someone caresses any one of these evil passions, the public is like a gong and responds to each stroke with a long vibration."[38] With such a vast array of passions to be satiated and items to be consumed, the likelihood of contamination was greatly increased through the less restricted flow of mass consumption. Guided less by reason than by instinct, the crowd could be seduced through the manipulation of the press. Though apparently assuming the role of seducers, however, anti-Dreyfusard journalists who indulged mass passions could not unproblematically lay claim to the masculine position in this scenario, a point frequently articulated by Dreyfusards. Rachel Bowlby has aptly described the instability of the seducer/seduced relationship in modern anxieties about consumption: "[T]he boundaries of subject and object, active and passive, owner and owned, unique and general, break down in this endless reflexive interplay of consumer and consumed."[39] As Le Bon had observed, the leader too was hypnotized by a seductive idea that takes "possession of him," evidence that such leaders were themselves degenerate and most often recruited from "the ranks of those morbidly nervous, excitable, half-deranged persons who are bordering on madness."[40] That a repressed identity united leaders and followers hardly surprised the Dreyfusards, who seemed to concur with the law professor Maurice Vauthier's observation that the crowd "can on occasion include 'well-born' people and 'cultivated' minds."[41]

Like many at the fin de siècle, Le Bon insisted upon the inherently feminine nature of the crowd, even when it was composed entirely of men. In fact, this association of the crowd with female psychology played a role in many of the period's political discourses. Like woman, therefore, the crowd was not merely open to seduction but was itself seductive in the riches it promised those who dared satisfy its dangerous passions. By appealing to base appetites, the crowd became more like a prostitute who seeks to entice men. From the standpoint of artistically "pure" literature or "disinterested" scholarship, those who so shamelessly catered to the passions of the general public had compromised a noble spiritual vocation for the tantalizing lure of money and had in the process transformed themselves into "prostitutes."[42] Such was the perspective offered by Paul Brulat, who noted with disgust how certain men of letters had allowed their profession to decline into a mere business: "What they value is success, bookstore sales."[43] Yet one might wonder who was actually "seduced" in this prostitute/client relationship: the client who succumbed to illicit pleasure or the prostitute who debased herself for money? The journalist Édouard Drumont seemed fit to play both roles simultaneously. A promiscuous disseminator of that infectious "disease" anti-Semitism, he also "got rich off the commerce of the most odious personalities."[44] So too did those newspapers that parasitically "prey[ed] on the ignorance of the crowds and the atavistic passions of the race."[45]

Many men at the end of the nineteenth century were seduced by the very idea of seduction. Possessing the ability to resist seduction implied a form of self-mastery that could be useful in one's social relations, thus compelling some men to become veritable seducers in their own right. If popular pleasures entailed a willing loss of control, success in the world seemed to depend upon an ability to master others, or so many had come to believe. The famed psychologist Alfred

Binet confirmed this view when, after describing a range of personality types in terms of their inherent suggestibility, he pointed out that *"les suggestionneurs . . . have a greater chance of succeeding in life than do les suggestibles."*[46] This belief that it was better to be a virtual hypnotist than *un suggestible* was echoed in advertisements in popular health magazines and self-help manuals that taught men how to increase their personal magnetism and to secure wealth and happiness by learning how to manipulate others. Having intelligence and strong opinions are very useful for success, counseled one such author, but they are not enough: "[Y]ou must exert a sort of fascination over your peers; you must dominate them, impose your views upon them. . . . To have all of that, one must possess personal magnetism."[47] Although the erotic conquests of the libertine were frequently condemned in the nineteenth century, the allure of sexual seduction seems to have remained paramount for many men, even if such seductions only took place in the world of fantasy. In his study of prostitution, Alain Corbin cites the rise of seduction fantasies in brothels at the end of the nineteenth century, where clients increasingly paid for scenarios in which prostitutes played the role of helpless virgins to their seductive overtures.[48] Whether these fantasies reflected a compensation for feelings of weakness in their actual relations with women or of powerlessness in the world generally, it is clear that the cultural demand for mastery penetrated to the heart of male subjectivity.

Sometimes even the Dreyfusards succumbed to a seduction fantasy, particularly when it came to the fickle and feminine crowd. In this regard, Laurent Tailhade's hope that one day "the pleb would kiss the footsteps of the poets"[49] was simply a more aesthetic vision of René Ghil's later vision of a world where "it will be more glorious to circulate thought than to spill blood."[50] As one pamphleteer admitted: "[W]e imagined the great savant, the great artist, the great writer benefiting from the crowd already grouped around him in order to emit words of social truth and revolt."[51] Of course, most Dreyfusards would not have seen this as "seduction" per se, but as the rational enlightenment of the people. Nevertheless, the reality they confronted frustrated such hopes. What they usually saw in the crowd was a dangerously consuming being, one that threatened to subsume them as well. In the cultural imaginary, dread of the consuming masses paralleled anxieties about devouring femininity that, whether embodied in the syphilitic prostitute or the independent New Woman, plagued male identity at the turn of the century. For example, despite the fairly composed behavior of the female customers in *Au Bonheur des dames*, Zola's novel about a department store, women are depicted as always being capable of exploding into unrestrained lust for commodities, thus threatening to overstep the bounds of propriety established by male commerce.[52] Since urban spectacles and mass culture were closely associated, it was frequently implied that the masses could consume an individual, much as, in Zola's novel, a throng of female customers threatens to crush hapless males underfoot. "Crowds are somewhat like the sphinx of ancient fable," Le Bon had warned. "It is necessary to arrive at a solution to the problems offered by their psychology or to resign ourselves to being devoured by them."[53]

The dream of directing the masses was thus linked to the fear of being devoured by them. Rhetorically useful for illustrating how Dreyfusards sacrificed themselves for their cause, this form of engulfment was also undoubtedly a frightening prospect. For Paul Stapfer, the aggressively consuming crowd was truly a monstrous spectacle: "Oh, the majority, that hydra with millions of heads, hissing and howling jaws, crazed tongues, dull, meager, and empty minds, that's my nightmare." As with many fin-de-siècle images of otherness, Stapfer's crowd led a strange double existence as both object and subject of consumption. A "purely passive animal, which stagnates, [whose] function is *to consume*," *la foule* was also described as *badaude*, and therefore totally consumed by the spectacle of the street.[54] A devourer of objects and images, then, the crowd was itself devoured by the objects of its fickle desires. More alarmingly, men risked being sucked into the maelstrom and destroyed. Daniel Halévy described the crowd as a "swelling sea that throws wrecks onto the bank. We were the wrecks, and every instant someone else would be ejected, pursued, violently rejected."[55] Evidently, Dreyfus himself had been the first wreck, for as another put it, during his degradation "the huge, ghastly monster composed of these crowds had swallowed, annihilated, and ripped him apart."[56] Le Bon had described the gravity of the situation years before, and many Dreyfusards seemed to agree: a man's failure to penetrate the enigma of the crowd might ultimately lead to his own dissolution.

Educating the Will

How could any man be expected to cope in an environment so fraught with dangers? Moreover, if the new psychology stressed that anyone could succumb to the external suggestions of modernity—in other words, that any man could be "devoured" by the crowd or "seduced" by spectacles—what was it that supposedly rendered the Dreyfusard immune to these forces? How could any man truly *be* a man? To an extent, masculinity was perceived as the result of effort rather than the simple possession of anatomical maleness. When confronted with modernity's many sensual temptations, a man could only remain a "man" through sheer force of will, which at the fin de siècle meant possessing a strong mind firmly seated in a healthy body. This capacity for willpower suggested an ability to maintain strict boundaries around the self that fulfilled the prophylactic function of insulating the male from external excitations while giving him a firm hold over inner passions. In their condemnation of the crowd, Dreyfusards suggested that they alone possessed these traits and could thus lay a more legitimate claim to manhood than their opponents.

So heavily do most versions of masculine identity rely upon the capacity for willpower that when Achille Steens accused anti-Semitic students of having "renounced their free will" by forming a mob, he was in fact disputing their status as men. By giving in to the crowd, he implied, they had succumbed to the "low" within themselves. It is therefore unsurprising to find that, during this period of gender crisis, pathologies of the will would be so widely diagnosed, both by medical men and social commentators, and that they would figure so prominently in the polemics of the Dreyfus Affair. Strictly speaking, paralysis of the will (or "abulia") was considered a disorder in its own right that left the patient bedridden with little or no desire to do anything at all. Yet more frequently this condition appeared as the most common and troubling symptom of nearly all of the period's other afflictions, from neurasthenia and hysteria to degeneracy, agoraphobia, and sexual "perversions." Despite a number of cases where the problem of female volition was raised, as in kleptomania and crimes of passion, the obsession with willpower primarily concerned men. Indeed, nineteenth-century discourses of masculinity repeatedly stressed the need for a male to *be a man*, as if manliness were the result of an act of will. As Angus McLaren observes: "To be a man required effort and labor that was not required of women. One did not goad on a woman by force of will to 'be a woman'; she was born one. Exertion and activity was required to 'be a man.' In effect the public accepted implicitly the notion that manliness was a constructed identity because a male had to 'prove' repeatedly at work and at play that he was a 'man.'"[57] McLaren does not suggest that gender identity is somehow less culturally constructed in the case of men, but that in the nineteenth century, femininity was explicitly aligned with nature, feeling, and nervousness. In other words, by being reduced to reproductive processes or weakened nerves, female character was constructed as a more or less inevitable reflection of biology. Because masculinity tended to be defined mainly through action, however, men were usually expected to reaffirm their manliness through concrete deeds that positioned them squarely on the side of culture.

The overall effort required to "be a man" was the sum of all the ways in which willpower could manifest itself, and included the ability to withstand pain and to display courage in the face of danger, either on the battlefield or when fighting a duel. As we saw in Chapter 2, the demonstration of civic courage, an audacity that risked the scorn of one's contemporaries in the name of a higher good, could also serve as evidence of manhood. But exercising willpower did not necessarily imply the victory of a "masculine" mind over a "feminine" body, for, unlike certain philosophical discourses, the materialist terms of modern medicine made it impossible to sustain such a simple dichotomy. Rather, whether used to undergird physical or moral courage, exercising the will entailed strengthening the body so as to master the body, much in line with an observation by Rousseau that circulated widely in the medical self-help literature of the day: "The weaker the body, the more it commands; the stronger it is, the more it obeys. All the sensual passions lodge in effeminated bodies."[58] In other words, one might say that willpower meant steeling "the body" as a means of overcoming the sensuality of "the flesh."

The practical logic that implicitly distinguished the body from its own sensuality was reinforced by medical wisdom wherein volition emerged as more prominent in the psyches of men rather than women, mostly due to the assumption that the weaker bodies of women (and other counter-types like Jews, homosexuals, criminals, and the insane) meant that they were closely tied to the flesh in ways that "normal" men were not. Above all, as one physician noted, an inability to exert effort left one "powerless" in the face of the "unhealthy incitations" of the outside world.[59] In the eyes of many worried observers, the entire modern world seemed committed to toppling this already unstable faculty. As one author noted in an 1898 study of masturbation, modern people faced a world that was thoroughly charged with eroticism. "The milieus in which we live are enervating; the air we breathe is charged with desires that stimulate our senses and create for us imperious needs that we neither want nor know how to struggle against. Pleasure is our only thought, enjoyment our supreme goal."[60] In his famous work on degeneration, Max Nordau pointed to urban hyperstimulus as wearing away the nerves of Westerners: "Even the little shocks of railway traveling, not perceived by consciousness, the perpetual noises, and the various sights in the streets of a large town, our suspense pending the sequel of progressive events, the constant expectation of the newspaper, of the postman, of visitors, cost our brains wear and tear."[61]

Professional men whose nerves were shattered through neurasthenia counted among the most disturbing victims of this modern hyperstimulus. Viewed from a social as well as a medical perspective, neurasthenia represented not only physical and moral weakness but a certain *vulnerability* or "porousness" that undermined normative conceptions of the bounded male self. Of course, neurasthenics manifested a variety of symptoms, including headaches, insomnia, loss of appetite, indigestion, and constipation, that did not in themselves pose immediate threats to their sense of manhood. Yet from the viewpoint of contemporary understandings of masculinity, two sets of related symptoms proved most vexing about the neurasthenic man. There was, on the one hand, his extreme susceptibility to external physical stimuli, manifested in an inability to withstand loud noises, crowds, movement, and even changes in the weather. On the other hand, neurasthenics suffered from more internal weaknesses, especially psychic disorders like memory lapses, anxiety, short attention spans, and a slavish submission to their own passions, all symptoms of a troubling inability to exercise willpower and a collapse of personal boundaries. Spatial and martial metaphors abounded in the medical discourses on nervous disorders, and often referred to "floods," "waves," and "invasions" of excitations from the outside as well as crumbling inner resistance to such dangerous stimuli.[62] In other words, as the hygiene reformer Jules Payot asserted, resisting the power of the external crowd depended upon conquering the "undisciplined and ungovernable pleb" within. Admitting that of young men resisting modern temptations was like enduring daily "crucifixions," Payot encouraged these future Christ figures to keep busy so they could erect a "dam of granite" against the flood of sexual suggestions that swirled around him.[63]

The tension between the *flâneur* and the *badaud* shows how compromised boundaries and weakened inner forces were intimately related, attesting to a spatial dimension to masculine identity that is rarely observed in the existing historiography. In keeping with the materialist terms of the nineteenth-century human sciences, this spatial dimension was to a great extent constructed through the interarticulated domains of medicine and morality. The ideal male was one who in medical terms was seen as capable of maximizing his vitality and resisting illness. According to Anne C. Vila, during the late eighteenth century, the normative male body was defined in part by its natural ability to "resist or overcome unwelcome irritants and obstacles, whereas women cede involuntarily to the multiple stimuli to which they are subject because they have no more power to resist than do children."[64] This association of proper physiological manhood with optimal health and vitality persisted throughout the nineteenth century and posed a stark contrast to artistic and literary depictions of invalid and consumptive women whose physical ailments only seemed to confirm the inherent frailty of femininity.[65] Indeed, medical texts frequently described female physiology as existing in a constant state of flux that, especially during hysterical episodes, challenged any strict separation between inside and outside. Here a woman would be subject to uncontrollable flows of tears, urine, mucus, menstrual blood, and speech, all of which corroborate Janet Beizer's observation that in nineteenth-century medical discourses, women were truly "leaky vessels."[66] Whereas men were expected to remain firm, upright, and self-contained, women were considered amorphous both in body and mind.

This medical view of an ideal male body insulated from pathogens was inextricably bound up with a parallel discourse about the maintenance of strong ego boundaries, a psychical investment in one's bodily peripheries that effected a gradual closing (and, one might say, a closing off) of the male, at once from the outer world of dangerous stimuli and from the inner world of threatening passions. Without a doubt, as Norbert Elias has shown, in the Western world, both men and women experienced a shift in their sense of personal boundaries during the early modern era where, amid changing social circumstances resulting from a more pacified society, rising thresholds of repugnance and shame were manifested among the upper classes as a growing aversion to their own bodily functions and to the bodies of others. The changes wrought by new developments in table manners and etiquette were extended by the introduction of hygienic practices in the eighteenth and nineteenth centuries that endeavored to maximize the order and cleanliness of the social body, while further compartmentalizing the bourgeois self as a discrete bodily unit.[67] As the schoolbooks of the Third Republic suggest, children were taught to view health and subjectivity as the results of constant vigilance and self-surveillance, and illness as evidence of a moral flaw. "The microbe can invade us despite everything," cautioned one text. "It is necessary to resist. . . . Be strong and disease will not vanquish us. But if we are not strong, it is our own fault. We deliver ourselves to our vices and they kill us."[68]

This process of boundary formation reached its apotheosis by the end of the nineteenth century, when across the Western world male displays of emotion, particularly grief and fear, were increasingly being viewed with derision. In the early nineteenth century, for example, Evangelical Christianity in Britain had seen no contradiction between manliness and displays of tears and often congratulated the father who was moved to emotion. Not so by the end of the century, where British men were increasingly expected to maintain strict control over such emotions.[69] In France, too, representations of the weeping man underwent significant changes. The emotional release whereby in earlier decades (and in certain situations), a man might have easily melted or dissolved into tears was by the 1880s replaced by metaphors of explosion, catharsis, and violent eruption. Anne Vincent-Buffault has vividly captured this shift in her history of tears: "Explosion, tearing, trembling, shaking, suffocation, smothering, the body was overcome with crises, with convulsions, with nervous spasms. . . . A man wept when he could not act. The metaphors which illustrated male sobs revealed an image of the sealed body which began to explode."[70] Whether a question of pent-up emotions or resistance to external influences, changes in the elite male habitus, often directly linked to perceived crises of manhood, were here manifested in the formation of a new sensibility, a new way of managing emotions and of maintaining boundaries around the self that could nevertheless be breached under circumstances of extreme pressure or constitutional weakness (recall the disappointment that many felt when Dreyfus failed to weep during his degradation). This manly exercise of self-control was short-circuited through the emotional disturbances that were frequently generated by neurasthenia. As Vincent-Buffault astutely observes: "In the excess of his nervous despair, the man who sobbed found himself relegated to femininity and childhood."[71]

Despite the general association of manhood and willpower, medical texts made the collapse of the will seem more likely than its triumph. As Théodule Ribot declared in his classic study *Les Maladies de la volonté*, the will is no natural psychological given but is rather "the result of art, of education, of experience. It is an edifice constructed slowly, piece by piece. Observation, both objective and subjective, shows that every form of voluntary activity is the fruit of a conquest."[72] What one "conquered" in the act of volition was the substratum of desire, images, and fantasies that constituted humanity's primitive heritage, a reservoir of irrationality threatening to engulf the person whenever the will wavered. Yet from Ribot's physicalist perspective, the will was not a simple idea standing over and above the body; it was itself a reflection of material processes. Indeed, having maintained that moral precepts needed to be *felt* in order to have any sway over the individual, Ribot concluded that the "predominance of the affective life does not necessarily exclude the will: an intense, stable, permitted passion is the very basis of all energetic wills."[73] In light of the various diseases of the will observed at the fin de siècle, Ribot affirmed the rather frail nature of such a faculty and reiterated the need for constant personal vigilance: "[T]he will is not an entity reigning by right of birth, though sometimes disobeyed, but a resultant always unstable, always ready to decompose itself, and, to say truly, a happy accident."[74]

Willpower was therefore something that needed to be developed through the cultivation of healthy habits, and at the fin de siècle, physicians nearly fell over one another advising young men on how to do it. By far the most significant and widely read manual for cultivating willpower was the 1893 book *L'Éducation de la volonté* by Jules Payot, one of Ribot's former students, which went through thirty-seven editions in less than twenty years and was translated into most European languages. Aware of the overtly cerebral turn taken by the nation's elite, Payot addressed his advice to young men between the ages of eighteen and twenty-five, most of whom he assumed were bourgeois and would go on to some white-collar profession or "intellectual labor." Admitting that emotion per se was not incompatible with volition, Payot identified "sensuality" as perhaps the most significant obstacle to masculine autonomy. "Passion, that's animality victorious," Payot declared, "the blind urge of heredity that darkens intelligence, oppresses it, and, moreover, enslaves it; it is the suppression of humanity within us, the debasement of what comprises at once our honor and our raison d'être: when it growls, we assume a different rung on the zoological ladder." A strong will would help curb the impulses of the flesh, thus providing a foundation from which one could also resist masturbation, prostitutes, alcohol, and other tempting diversions. Unlike many anticlerical physicians who associated religious faith with a decidedly "feminine" credulity, Payot applauded the example of the Church as an educator of masculinity: "Virility is there, and nowhere else: it is in this mastery of oneself—and the Church is right to see in chastity the supreme guarantee of the energy of the will."[75]

Like many other hygienic reformers who distrusted the contaminating influence of the city, Payot saw urban life as fraught with seductions and excitations that could cause young men to abandon themselves to their own sensuality. "Most men are governed by what's outside of them," he lamented: they were "marionettes" moved primarily by "involuntary desires and external suggestions."[76] Being master of oneself implied "the reconquest of the self from the thousand suggestions of the external world,"[77] and proper hygiene was considered essential for building up one's capacity for resistance. The young man should keep his body scrupulously clean and exercise regularly, thus engaging in what Payot called the "primary school of the will." Many of Payot's prescriptions were negative, however, and he generally cautioned young men about a range of dangerous influences that had to be carefully avoided, including the reading of novels, oversleeping, sedentariness, overeating, eating spiced foods or excessive meat, alcohol, coffee, and consorting with "libidinous comrades." All of these nefarious influences tended to produce a "scattered" or "dispersed" personality that was ill-equipped to remain committed to a particular goal in life. Physical and mental idleness was perhaps the best way to leave oneself open to being "invaded" by sexual suggestions, for such passionate solicitations "only have a chance of entering when the mind is empty."[78]

Due to its very fragility, the will alone could not be invoked in the battle against sensuality. Like many physicians influenced by the work of Bernheim, Payot subscribed to a very controlled form of prophylactic suggestion that could be employed to build up the self's ability to cope with the menace of moral contagion through the cultivation of healthy habits, a measure that was most appropriately termed "moral vaccination."[79] Sometimes administered to women in the hope that they might resist the "hypnotic" temptations of would-be seducers through the implantation of virtuous ideas, something akin to moral vaccination could be prescribed to young men for very similar reasons. While Payot did not use this term, his emphasis on the therapeutic and prophylactic use of suggestion subtly invoked such an idea. In order to dissipate the "haze" of the modern world, he wrote, one must retire from external distractions into a quiet state of "meditative reflection" and "in this state of calm, substitute for mediocre suggestions the suggestions of a great thinker, and allow this benevolent influence to penetrate to the depths of the soul."[80] Against the vagaries of uncontrolled contagion-through-seduction one could administer rational and measured doses of countersuggestion to inoculate oneself against future contamination.

Telling the Truth

Evidently, those who allowed themselves to be swept up in public opinion had not read Payot. Possessing an iron will implied the dual capacity to resist external influences and to subdue inner passions, thus proving that such feats of volition were securely grounded in a healthy body. That men were naturally endowed with bodies capable of such willpower was taken for granted, though this did not rule out the possibility that weak or careless men might be more "womanish" in this respect. Dreyfusards employed such ideas to their advantage, for although their own moral courage may have paled next to the more impressive heroism of military men, by invoking the materialist foundation of willpower, they could still stake a claim to a superior physicality. Moreover, just as being a healthy man with a firm will equipped one for survival in a sensually charged urban landscape, resisting its seductions suggested an ability to discern science from religion, reality from fiction, and truth from lies. This triple threat of religion/fiction/lies was often identified as the motor force behind the extreme credulity of the crowd and the entire anti-Dreyfusard camp, and it was readily likened to more physical contaminants like syphilis. By emphasizing the fundamental weakness of those who succumbed to such "contagious" ideas, Dreyfusards were able to claim that their opponents were physiologically inferior beings.

The morally suspect practice of reading novels was exacerbated by the crowd's apparent credulity in the face of the lies being spun by the anti-Semitic press. Jan Goldstein's historical inquiries into the politicized nature of the hysteria diagnosis under the Third Republic helps to frame the Dreyfusard association of lying and credulity with femininity, religiosity, literature, and nervous disorders. In the retrospective diagnoses performed by Charcot and his colleagues at the Salpêtrière, historical cases of mysticism and demonic possession were reinterpreted as psychotic episodes that were at heart more about hysterical delusions than anything divine, thus undercutting in medical terms the supernatural basis of Catholic religiosity. Thanks to the veritable alliance forged between psychiatrists and the republican state during the 1880s, religious faith had become implicated in the very literary folly so often condemned by its adherents. Republicans had for years contrasted their own putative potency and fertility with the unnatural, irrational, and unfruitful ethos of the religious mind. The same imagination that, when left unchecked, allowed one to be duped by novels was revealed to be at work behind the religious spirit itself, thus positioning science as that which dispels the fabulations of both the novelist and the priest.[81]

Being misled by fiction was but one step removed from succumbing to the lies of religion. As we saw in Chapter 1, literature was often condemned as a force that led people into error, particularly as the novels of Georges Ohnet and Jules Mary seemed to have shaped popular expectations of heroism and manly conduct. Yet literature was a more widespread problem in the nineteenth century, and, whether in the form of novels, plays, or newspapers, it was often criticized for the detrimental influence it had on impressionable minds, particularly among "endangered readers" like women, adolescents, and degenerates. Physicians and social critics agreed that the reading processes of such people placed them at risk. As Jann Matlock observes, "Their reading might be a process of sexualization, infection, or magnetism. The text might drug or poison them. They might find themselves, by contagion, diseased, sexually corrupted, criminalized, hysterical, or mad. Depending on the degree of complicity attributed to them, they could be seen as having indulged their corrupt nature with the food of literary debauchery, as having been seduced, or as having been violated."[82] This vigilance about reading practices pervaded the nineteenth and early twentieth centuries and clearly powered Dreyfusard rhetoric, where the circulation of tainted ideas became a matter of public hygiene. As the socialist deputy Francis de Pressensé pointed out, "we have seen newspapers like *L'Intransigeant*, *La Libre Parole*, *L'Éclair*, and *La Patrie* launch assaults of lies, suppress essential facts, pour out slanders and, in short, poison all the springs of the public mind."[83]

Other critics condemned the use of novelesque tactics clearly designed to captivate the imaginations of gullible readers. It was even suggested that the military plot to frame Dreyfus for treason had been torn from the pages of a *roman-feuilleton*—not from one of the many espionage novels that circulated during this time of spy mania, but from Louis Létang's *Les Deux Frères*. Serialized in *Le Petit Journal* between January and July 1894, *Les Deux Frères* recounts the story of a young woman who, after falling in love with another man, seeks to break her engagement to a captain attached to the minister of war. Significantly, forged handwriting and the charge of treason are central to her strategy. After anonymously alerting his superiors to the existence of a traitor in their midst, she arranges to have a letter forged in the man's handwriting promising to deliver secret documents to the chief of German intelligence. Since late 1894, Dreyfusards sometimes claimed that this novel provided the General Staff with a set of circumstances that would allow them to frame Dreyfus.[84]

Any form of literature that deceived became intimately related to lying, so much so that for many republican critics, the two became virtually synonymous vices. For a woman to lie was considered quite "normal," at least insofar as pathology was thought to be a constant feature of female nature; a male liar, on the other hand, signaled true deviance, the result of a malignancy that had precipitated a fall from normative masculinity. There is now ample evidence to suggest that the nineteenth century's close association of novel reading with women was based less on any precise data about reading practices than on a cultural association of literature with femininity (as opposed to the "masculinity" of science and reason).[85] In short, whereas women were certainly not the only ones considered susceptible to the contaminating power of novels, men who succumbed to the sensual temptations of imaginative literature could easily be considered half-men as well. Throughout the turn of the century, numerous self-help manuals directed at young men warned of the dangers of novels and often counseled against reading them in the prophylactic interest of proper "hygiene." The reading of novels, noted one concerned physician, "perverts the moral sense, can make one contract bad habits, and is capable of leading to a disorderly, even dissolute, life that often makes the most robust young men into 'old men' prematurely."[86] Jules Payot was quite emphatic on this point, drawing clear parallels between literature and hypnotic suggestion that threatened to corrupt the fledgling volition of young men. Reading novels not only lured young men away from their duties, Payot charged, but encouraged them to reside in a fantasy world of their own making: "How many young people thus live out a novel, constructed piece by piece, over the course of several weeks. . . . Ah! how the passions of our novelists seem pale and faded alongside our own novels of the eighteenth year!"[87] Max Nordau too considered the reading of novels to be a most dangerous pastime for degenerates and hysterics, among whom he counted many males. Marked by an excessive "emotionalism" that overpowered their feeble wills, male hysterics manifested a tendency toward imitation that made it difficult for them to discern reality from fiction:

> A result of the susceptibility of the hysterical subject to suggestion is his irresistible passion for imitation, and the earnestness with which he yields to all the suggestions of writers and artists. When he sees a picture, he wants to become like it in attitude and dress; when he reads a book, he adopts its views blindly; he takes as a pattern the heroes of the novels which he has in his hand at the moment, and infuses himself into the characters moving before him on the stage.[88]

The degeneracy of individuals was easily inflated to collective proportions as a way of characterizing the reading public generally, those "crowds" of gullible people who accepted all the lies being told by the army's General Staff and the anti-Semitic press. Conceding the vocal presence of creative writers among the Dreyfusards, Jean Ajalbert sardonically observed how the Ministry of War also seemed committed to imaginative works, referring to the patent lies told by "*les chroniqueurs* and habitual story-tellers" in their ranks.[89] The pathological liar and the gullible dupe thus seemed to suffer from very similar emotional disorders, which, whether they seemed hysterical, neurasthenic, or degenerate in nature, all represented forms of effeminacy that separated them from purportedly more "healthy" men who both recognized and told the truth. The very integrity of the body politic demanded the expulsion of these abject bodies. "There must be an end to so many lies," declared Clemenceau. "If France remains France, she will vomit out the liars."[90]

In the language of revisionism, the Dreyfusard male existed on a different plane altogether. Professionally committed to the search for truth rather than being contaminated by lies, many Dreyfusards saw themselves as eminently qualified to take a stand on the Dreyfus issue. After all, resistance to seduction was a guiding principle of the professional academic, whose scholarly specialization necessarily removed him from the sphere of general consumption. Émile Durkheim could thus demonstrate how the disinterestedness of his colleagues produced the truly self-contained man: "accustomed by the practice of scientific method to reserve their judgment . . . it is natural that they succumb less easily to the seductions [*entraînements*] of the crowd or the prestige of authority."[91] Like the quintessential *flâneur*, the intellectual engaged himself in the public sphere while remaining unmoved by the flow of mass modernity rushing by. "With their honor intact, these public men preferred the sober and silent approbation of their consciences to the acclaim of the delirious crowds."[92] "These are tranquil people," explained Duclaux, "enemies of noise who normally keep their windows closed."[93] Distance from the mundane, it seems, signified intellectual chastity and a commitment to the search for eternal verities, a lifestyle emphasized in this description of an anonymous Dreyfusard: "A stranger by profession and character to the violence of current controversies, devoid of all political ambition, living above all for the science to which he has devoted his existence, he is a simple 'intellectual.' Let's use this word, since it has received high consecrations."[94] If anti-Semitic and chauvinistic writers had "seduced" public opinion by appealing to its base instincts, Dreyfusards seemed to remove themselves from the scene of seduction altogether. Representing themselves as stoically chaste and incorruptible, Dreyfusards found cultural validation in their refusal (or perhaps inability) to seduce, a relatively easy abstention to make when the masses were so resolutely opposed to them. Such was the manner in which necessity could be repeatedly transformed into a curious type of masculine virtue among unseductive and unseducible intellectuals.

Ultimately, all of this testified to the superiority of the Dreyfusard body. Assailed on a number of fronts by moral and microbial pathogens, the future health of the Third Republic was conceived in explicitly biological terms, suggesting that those who would cure the body politic had to themselves possess sound physical bodies.[95] The national crisis did not require men who were crudely physical, they implied, but men with healthy minds in healthy bodies. One writer sang the praises of revisionism's most visible hero in the language of physical vitality: "Émile Zola, whose virile work burns magnificently toward the Truth, has just shown the idiots and degenerates that pure blood still flows in his veins and that his brain continues to vibrate youthfully."[96] Contrasted with such vitality, the enemies of Dreyfus were deeply flawed men. For example, on the night of the degradation, the publisher P.-V. Stock became acquainted with the soldier who had lied about Dreyfus confessing to treason, Captain Lebrun-Renault. After a night of dining and some frivolity at the Moulin Rouge, Stock grew to distrust this "feeble and indecisive man, a jolly and florid fellow, an alcoholic without willpower, without an ounce of civic courage."[97] In an article stressing the evolutionary aspects of the Dreyfus Affair, Julien Benda argued that "the Affair is, at heart, a biological war," for it is in "the physiological complexion of the individual that we must seek the ultimate cause of one's attitude regarding the Affair." That anti-Dreyfusards like Jules Lemaître admitted to having "obeyed an instinct" by opposing the revision constituted proof that the current crisis was also a war of the healthy body against the tyranny of the flesh: "[T]he Affair . . . has come to enervate each individual in the region of his most intimate tissues, and allows organic sensibility, once put in motion, to frequently deceive the consciousness of the subject himself." While the "theocratic ideal" of the anti-Dreyfusards had functioned in the past as "a true agent of social welfare," the rationalist perspective of the Dreyfusards was "better adapted to the new conditions of earthly life." Hence, as embarrassing throwbacks to a more primitive stage of evolutionary development, Benda suggested, "all anti-revisionists are inferior organisms."[98]

Insisting that the enemies of revisionism suffered from weak bodies as well as weak minds, Dreyfusards made strategic use of the organicist imagery that circulated so widely at the fin de siècle. From this perspective, the anti-Dreyfusard students we encountered at the beginning of this chapter could easily seem like nothing more than "little degenerates, with defective brains and pitiful physiologies."[99] Indeed, as Armand Charpentier observed, "never has the Syndicate of weak brains formed such a solid and tangible mass than in this affair."[100] Most important, the Dreyfusard body manifested physical and moral health that even surpassed that of army officers who, though apparently fit physically, "have only sinned through their incompetence, through intellectual weakness."[101] Here was an opportunity to redeem engaged intellectuals from all hint of nervousness by displacing this quality onto their enemies. Whereas during the Rennes trial, Dreyfus had manfully retained his composure, thus "employing the formidable control that he had over his nerves,"[102] officers who had reacted violently to the very prospect of a revision could thus be deemed "nervous men, perhaps a bit excited by ardent polemics in the press, and who without a doubt could be calmed by a little shower administered by a sure hand from the heights of the rue Saint-Dominique [the address of the War Ministry]."[103] The pathological credulity of the crowd was thus intimately related to the shortcomings of its leaders. According to Joseph Cornély, the emotional public had been deceived by "a certain number of *neurasthéniques à plume*," whose hold on their emotions was also quite tenuous: "As they have never had any other guides than their own passions, they do not understand men without passions."[104]

Equipped with a superior body, the Dreyfusard hero was a man of character who rose above the muck of the modern world. Having frustrated long-standing hopes for a hero, Francis de Pressensé observed, the Dreyfus Affair only presented generations of Frenchmen with "baseness, ugliness, egoism, cowardice, violence, dwarfs in a muddy morass under a pallid sky and a pale sun." In the face of such moral and physical slackening, it would be best if the entire social body were to become erect, for "it would . . . be more virile, in this milieu of crumbling minds and characters, to straighten up stoically and launch a proud challenge to all the united forces of evil."[105] Fortunately, men like Picquart, Reinach, and Zola had already risen to the challenge. According to a Belgian newspaper editor, Zola epitomized the "vigorous development of character in an age where all tends to stunt character, where men who struggle and suffer for personal conviction seem rare."[106] "Honor to Zola!" declared another admiring journalist. "Because in this epoch of cowardice and degradation, he was, of all of us, the courageous man and the strong man."[107]

Esterhazy's Novel

Allegations of the nervous weakness and intellectual limitations of military men worked very well alongside critiques of the highly suggestible masses and helped to project the notion of the superior manhood of the Dreyfusards. The machinations of Colonel Hubert Henry seemed to prove this point. The son of rural parents who had clawed his way up the ranks of the military, Henry embodied the more traditional military ideal that had been recently challenged by the new breed of academically trained officer. As Armand Charpentier recalled, Henry naturally felt uncomfortable when appointed to his new bureaucratic post in Paris, and he had sought to compensate for his academic limitations. "After the agitated life of colonial expeditions and the placid existence of provincial garrisons, he found himself, at age forty-eight, called to duties whose exercise demanded a certain degree of intellectual culture. Desiring to complete his training, which he knew was incomplete, he flew indiscriminately [*il butinait au hasard*] from book to book." After beginning with serious works, such as the writings of Marcus Aurelius, Henry allowed his penchant for police stories to take the upper hand, leading him to novels like Louis Létang's *Les Deux Frères*, which, we have seen, arguably provided a narrative that would help him frame Dreyfus.[108]

Yet Henry was not the sole target of Dreyfusard ire. If anti-Dreyfusards found their most rhetorically useful "foreigners" in the persons of the "German" Dreyfus and the "Italian" Zola, their opponents made very good use of the real traitor, Major Walsin-Esterhazy. Some scholars have proposed that, whereas Esterhazy indeed tried to sell information to the Germans, he was actually a double agent seeking to distract attention from France's new 75mm field gun by feeding the enemy obsolete artillery plans.[109] This might explain why, even after he fled to England once his involvement was discovered, Esterhazy tried to cultivate the impression that he was "a good soldier, a brave soldier. . . . I was moreover a soldier devoted to his superiors, a soldier disciplined to the point of heroism."[110] Many pointed out that this sense of discipline did not extend to Esterhazy's personal life, where the major frequently indulged his passions for gambling and womanizing. Even more doubts, however, were cast upon his much vaunted loyalty. Inquiries into his private life revealed that Esterhazy, who hailed from a noble Hungarian family, harbored some very definite opinions about France. In November 1897, the Dreyfusards published a letter that the major had written thirteen years earlier to his then mistress, Mme de Boulancy, disclosing his true feelings about the French: "If someone were to come tell me this evening that I would be killed tomorrow as a[n] Uhlan captain running through Frenchmen with my saber, I would certainly be perfectly happy. . . . I would not hurt a puppy, but I would have a hundred thousand Frenchmen killed with pleasure."[111]

We have seen how important the reading of bodily features was at the turn of the century, and this was especially so in the case of Esterhazy. Just as the physiognomy of Dreyfus suggested to some his treasonous potential, so, too, Ester-hazy's body provided clues to his inner state. The journalist Séverine, for one, was quite taken aback by the physiognomy of the man (henceforth nicknamed "the Uhlan"), which in her description came close to the stock representations of the Jews she also despised. "A strange physiognomy. . . . An animal of prey, certainly; he has a bird's head, with a great beak of a nose." The foreignness of the man, suggested in these readings of his body, assumed an even more racial tone as her analysis continued: "I have a living enigma before me. . . . Esterhazy surely seems to be of foreign origin, of a race that has naturalized a notorious and hereditary courage; not displeasing, but coming from farther away than Flor-ence: from the *puzta*, from the Orient of scimitars, of bags sewn without much style, and of bad coffee."[112] Observations like these were fairly typical at the height of the Affair, and few Dreyfusards were persuaded by either Esterhazy's protests of innocence or his references to a mysterious Veiled Lady who had sup-posedly warned him of a plot being hatched against him. "The veil of the lady is already quite crumpled," quipped Jacques Bahar, "we already perceive her moustache."[113]

Most revisionists took shots at Esterhazy during the Affair. Nevertheless, credit for the most extensive account of Esterhazy must go to Joseph Reinach, a noted republican politician and Dreyfusard who, given his Jewish background and outspoken defense of the exiled captain, was often the butt of anti-Semitic abuse. Reinach's seven-volume *Histoire de l'affaire Dreyfus*, which is counted among the more authoritative contemporary accounts of the crisis, devotes well over 100 consecutive pages to the family history, character, and health of Ester-hazy, all of which were scrutinized in terms of contemporary anxieties about physical decline and moral bankruptcy. Most important for our purposes is that fact that woven throughout these analyses is a concern about the relationship be-tween Esterhazy's self-fashioning and literature itself. For Reinach, Esterhazy's intrigues and lies were not merely deceptions, but veritable "novels," springing from the unhealthy ground of his feverish imagination and weakened body. In the person of Esterhazy, literature and lying were knotted together with a sick and even effeminate temperament that ended up deceiving a gullible populace. By placing Esterhazy under the microscope, Reinach transformed every detail of the major's life into evidence that might explain his behavior during the 1890s, a mode of inquiry that had much in common with the medical case histories of the time and helped render the anti-Dreyfusard cause "pathological" as well as wrong-headed. Above all, Reinach's case study of Esterhazy as an inveterate story-teller pointed to the diseased source of mass sensation and thus bolstered the Dreyfusards' view of themselves as healthy defenders of Truth.

Reinach shared with his republican colleagues a clear distrust of the power of religion and literature to obfuscate the truth, and in his work, he frequently employed literary metaphors to describe both lying and credulity. In Reinach's estimation, the many conservative novelists and literary critics who flocked to the anti-Dreyfus camp manifested all the excesses of aesthetes who lacked "the scientific spirit" and who were therefore unable "to reason any better than the ignorant and brutish crowd."[114] It is therefore unsurprising that subtle connections between literature and lying recur in Reinach's analysis of Esterhazy and are used to explain how the Dreyfus Affair became a mass sensation. In an age when physical health to some extent meant descending from a healthy bloodline, it was significant that Esterhazy's whole family history and even his account of his own life were founded on lies: "[T]his entire novel that he repeated one hundred times and embellished with details . . . is only a tissue of impostures" (2: 20). In Reinach's account, this tendency to lie in accordance with literary models characterized both Esterhazy and his Hungarian ancestors, as if lying could be an inherited trait. Indeed, the last legitimate representative of the French Esterhazys had emigrated to Russia in the eighteenth century, while a "bastard line" had remained to carry on the name. Yet even the name Walsin, which Esterhazy claimed was traceable either to a soldier or an actor, proved to be purely literary in origin, a derivation of "Valsin" that was frequently used by eighteenth-century poets and novelists. By changing the name to "Walsin," Reinach concluded, "the novelesque nickname thus took on a fake Magyar air" (2: 13), an imposture further accentuated when the officer's father and uncle pretentiously attached the moniker to their family name.

In this age of escalating nationalism, pretending to be French proved even more scandalous than falsifying one's ancestry, and was redolent of many charges leveled by anti-Semites against Jews. The "Uhlan letter," we have seen, seemed to speak volumes about Esterhazy's true feelings about the French, and suggested to Reinach that the man had never truly overcome his Hungarian heritage, thus remaining "French in name only." Here too Reinach drew upon biological assumptions to clarify the strange case of Esterhazy, a man who, as the living result of "successive interbreeding," had been transformed into "the primitive type of the species" (2: 39). Although Esterhazy's mother had descended from a pure French bloodline, his father was the product of no fewer than sixteen Franco-Hungarian unions, and he thus brought to his new family a tainted heredity. Had

Esterhazy been of pure French stock, Reinach implied, he might not have been so compelled to betray his country and then to conceal his crime with lies in a cowardly way. Unfortunately for him, however, these "few drops of Magyar blood dominate the mixture, and impress upon it their stain [*lui donnent leur teinte*]." All of this not only helped explain the moral failings of the traitor, but accounted as well for all that was "exotic" about the man's appearance. Esterhazy's body was not only "too thin for his massive head" but betrayed a host of other unsavory features, including "the aquiline nose, truly the beak of a bird of prey, the small and sunken eyes of a marten, black, impenetrable, with a gaze always in motion, with something underhanded about it, the gestures, sometimes brusque, sometimes insinuating, the slight accent . . . and, above all, that thing in man which is truly his own, the faithful translation of the ego: his manner of speaking and writing" (2: 40). Not only are these features—a beaklike nose, sunken and shifty eyes, awkward gestures, and a foreign accent—similar to traits typically attributed to Jews, but they worked well with Reinach's earlier description of Esterhazy as possessing "a certain aptitude for speculation . . . he was a financier just as he was a soldier, a reneger on debts [*boursier-marron*], and a ruffian" (2: 28–29). So often the target of anti-Semitic abuse, Reinach struck back by displacing his own anxieties about Jewishness onto the true traitor.[115]

What Reinach found most telling about Esterhazy's personality was his unhealthy predilection for literature, a pastime that repeatedly intruded into the major's daily life: "With a feverish imagination, he improvised . . . novels in which he was the hero: he ended up believing in these fictions" (2: 24). As we have seen above, this inability to tell truth from lies signaled the presence of an imagination that exceeded the bounds of reason and common sense, a character flaw typically attributed to women, children, and those suffering from hereditary degeneration. Not surprisingly, Reinach revealed that the traitor also suffered from physical defects, which in part explained his susceptibility to feminizing literature. Having been afflicted with tuberculosis, which might have been inherited from his Hungarian father, a "sick man" lurked behind Esterhazy's façade of heroic vitality: "[T]here are certain links between afflictions of the lung and those of the brain" that were confirmed by modern medicine. "Contemporary science has established that tubercular intoxication . . . is often the determining cause of morbid overstimulation, of an extreme enervation of the intellectual or moral faculties, with or without surface lesions" (2: 25). Esterhazy's capacity for resistance and the exercise of willpower had been fatally undermined by his health problems, thus rendering him a plaything of external stimulations and inner passions. Unbalanced by his illness and by the accumulated defects of his bloodline, Esterhazy was a man in the process of coming apart: "The sickness was eating away at him; for a long time only one of his lungs functioned; he supported himself with alcohol, he ate too much, devouring his food. An inner fire slowly burned. . . . mocking and tragic, pathetic and filthy, he peddled his novel" (3: 9).

Reinach's damning characterization of Esterhazy is thus performed subtly and proceeds through a series of significant details that connect his tainted blood and corrupted body to sensuality, the reading of novels, pathological lying, and outright cowardice. For instance, had Esterhazy been a true man of honor, he should by all accounts have backed up his soldierly image with deeds. We know a great deal about how crucial a factor dueling was in nineteenth-century codes of masculinity, and even when no one was harmed, the willingness to publicly defend one's personal honor through displays of violence was integral to preserving one's reputation as a man of honor.[116] It was thus significant that Esterhazy, who was presented by the anti-Semitic press as an expert swordsman, had "never had a single duel" (2: 91). If Esterhazy's sick body lent a certain inevitability to his treasonous machinations, it also paled next to the more robust physiques of his comrades. Whereas Colonel Henry was "tall, corpulent, giving the impression of health and force," Esterhazy seemed congenitally predisposed to betrayal, an observation that Reinach shared with many other Dreyfusards: even before he committed the deed itself, Esterhazy seemed to have had "the physique for the job" (2: 77). It came as no surprise that Esterhazy, "the tempter, the perverter," who seduced himself with his own lies, had ended up corrupting his friend Henry, a man who up until then had been "a brave soldier . . . fearless under fire." Making much of Henry's rural background, Reinach was able to present him as a healthy son of the soil who, having grown up away from the seductions of modernity, had been led astray by the sensual distractions promised by Esterhazy: "This peasant, who had only known a life of hard labor and hardly any common diversions, glimpsed a new world of pleasures that had seemed hitherto inaccessible and that he could enter whenever he liked" (2: 80–81). Henry's death by his own hand after the discovery of his forgeries was a tragic end for a once honorable soldier who had been seduced and corrupted by the traitor: "[O]f these two actors, one has carried his secret to the grave, the other lies as he breathes" (2: 82).

However reprehensible it might have been, Esterhazy's corruption of Henry was nothing compared to his masterful seduction of public opinion. Esterhazy's novel thus worked impeccably alongside the contagion of other lies and anti-

Semitic abuse that had so profoundly polluted the body politic. "The microbes flying out of Drumont's inkwell had poisoned the whole atmosphere," Reinach declared; "everyone breathed this polluted air" (3: 261). Having been repeatedly accosted by anti-Semitic street mobs during the trial of Zola for libel, Reinach shared this conventional view of the crowd. Indeed, one of his most vivid memories conflated a fear of multitudes with a vision of devouring femininity bent on robbing him of his honor: "I still see a furious young woman who pursued me, who wanted to rip from me my ribbon of the Legion of Honor, while the crowd howled 'Death to the Jews! Death to the traitors!'" (3: 349). Moreover, fears about the crowd provided him with the means of connecting Esterhazy's novel about himself to its natural audience. "It acted, with a speed that surprised the hypnotist himself, as if upon a hysteric whose personality doubles itself in an induced slumber" (3: 28). Whereas isolated individuals might be capable of preserving their own reason and personalities, "the collective soul of the crowd is not the vehicle [*la moyenne*] of these diverse mentalities: it is something else, truly a different being, something quite new" (3: 28). Such informal "fictions" worked effectively with a population steeped in novelistic conventions: "[T]he episode of the Veiled Lady enchanted the public," something that would have been easily recognizable from "a hundred novels and melodramas" (3: 11). What was at stake in all of this was the imposture of honor and manhood that had been facilitated through literature. Of course, Esterhazy maintained that he was a martyr suffering at the hands of cowards: "I have against me all human cowardice and hypocrisy, I shall struggle [against them] to my last breath."[117] As Reinach maintained, however, fictions such as these convinced the multitude that he was in fact a true man of honor, despite the fact that the "only soldierly thing about Esterhazy was his language. The crowd took him for a true soldier unjustly accused" (3: 11).

In Dreyfusard discourses, Esterhazy was both symptom and victim of fin-de-siècle decline. Open to external stimulants and prey to his own base passions, his sick and porous body was incapable of true willpower and exposed his kinship with the credulous masses he seduced. His flight to England, where he lived out the rest of his days under an assumed name, was seen as a final act of cowardice that simultaneously confirmed the guilt and the defective manhood that his opponents had observed. Unlike such traitors, the Dreyfusards promised a manly resistance to all the fin-de-siècle dangers that were symptomatic of a threatening modernity and condensed in the figure of the devouring crowd. The hero-

ism of such men was partly predicated on their distance from the masses, suggesting that the very notion of a popular hero would have been oxymoronic for
many Dreyfusards. Charles Péguy's 1910 recollection of the Dreyfusard campaign thus resonated with many of the assertions being made in the heat of the
Affair: "We were heroes. . . . It escaped no one that military virtues resided within
us. In us and not only in the army's General Staff."[118]

CHAPTER FOUR

Adventures of the Naked Truth

Women and the Dreyfusard Imagination

Women rarely count for much in conventional histories of the Dreyfus Affair. They are often presented as secondary characters in a male-dominated plot, but it is nevertheless evident that, as agents and as symbols, women played important political roles in both camps during this tumu!tuous period. After all, it was a psychic medium named Léonie who revealed to Mathieu Dreyfus that his brother's conviction had been assured on the strength of a secret dossier withheld from the defense team, while the real traitor remained at large. Mathieu's resolve was immeasurably strengthened by this information, which was later confirmed by Félix Faure, the president of the Republic.[1] Women were also quite active on both sides of the Affair once it erupted into a national crisis. The anti-Semitic writer Gyp (Sybille-Gabrielle de Riquetti de Mirabeau) was among the most notorious and vocal commentators on the Affair, and despite her status as a woman, she was frequently hailed by her male colleagues as a boon to the anti-Dreyfusard cause.[2] Supportive women sent adoring letters to Zola shortly after "J'accuse" was published, just as they sent letters and flowers to Colonel Picquart while he was in prison.[3] Moreover, many women registered their positions in the various petitions generated during the Affair, though this was often accomplished through the anonymity of generic social designations such as "Une mère de famille," "Une Française," or "La femme d'un Général" rather than their own names.

Women also played more symbolic and allegorical roles in the Affair. Some were featured as tools of espionage (like Madame Bastian, the cleaning lady who delivered the incriminating *bordereau* to the General Staff), as emotional figures like despairing wives (Lucie Dreyfus) and grieving widows (Madame Henry), or as symbols of wantonness (the various mistresses of Dreyfus and Esterhazy). Others imagined that women played a more nefarious role, and one anti-Dreyfusard even claimed that they had been employed to use their seductive powers to convert men to the Dreyfusard cause. In one case, it was alleged, an adulterous wife was threatened with having her infidelity made public if she failed to persuade her husband to sign a petition in defense of Zola.[4] Finally, other women were wrapped in mystery and thus served almost exclusively symbolic purposes, such as *La Dame blanche* (Amélie Darthaut), a well-known presence at many Paris court cases who also attended the Dreyfus trials[5] and, even more mysteriously, *La Dame voilée*, an apocryphal figure who, in a much discussed midnight meeting, supposedly warned the traitor Esterhazy of a plot being orchestrated against him. Women such as these captured the public's imagination and helped to frame the deeds of male actors during the Dreyfus Affair.

Dreyfusards were outraged to find that certain prominent women had allied themselves with the enemy cause. Insofar as women seemed to embody the threats to subjective integrity that were most feared in the culture of modernity, their engagement in anti-Dreyfusard machinations triggered the typically hyperbolic reactions that female incursions in male domains often inspire. This was the case with wealthy *salonnières* like Madame de Loynes and the duchesse d'Uzès, who with the eruption of the Affair excommunicated most Dreyfusards from their weekly meetings and helped to fund the Ligue de la Patrie française. The journalist and playwright Gyp was the most prominent and detested of anti-Dreyfusard women. In addition to her typically vitriolic newspaper articles and anti-Semitic plays, Gyp was alleged to walk the poorest streets of Paris, without a corset and in sleeveless gowns that exposed her muscular arms, in search of street thugs who might be hired to disrupt Dreyfusard meetings. Casting Gyp as a monstrous female, Dreyfusards called her "a Valkyrie drinking human blood."[6]

When dealing with the presence of women in their own camp, however, Dreyfusards were more circumspect. Here were allies who had also risked a great deal by throwing their support behind the revisionist cause, perhaps even more so since their involvement meant assuming a political stance that took them outside of the domestic sphere most believed they were destined by nature to inhabit. Alongside the problem of women who violated gender roles, however, was the effect of this transgression on the image of Dreyfusism. How to sustain the distinctive aura of manly suffering and action if women too could be shown to suffer and act in a similar way? Since the concept of masculine identity made little sense if women could possess some of its basic attributes, many Dreyfusards reacted with ambivalence to the presence of outspoken women in their ranks, and while they could not forbid female involvement outright, they tried to negotiate the terms of that involvement by way of the graphic arts. This chapter explores the various aspects of female engagement in Dreyfusard politics, not only by investigating women as actors who rallied alongside men every step of the way but by regarding them as allegories who, by being frozen graphically, could be more effectively managed and even domesticated. It considers the activities of the journalist Séverine, the most visible female Dreyfusard, as well as the anxieties that many republican men harbored about the potentially negative influence that too much female contact could have on males. The second half of the chapter examines how, as a partial response to these concerns, Dreyfusard artists sought a restoration of the gender order through the female allegory Truth, a weak female figure who could only be brought to light through the intervention of heroic Dreyfusards. By considering the adventures of the naked truth, this chapter shows how women who refused their "proper" place in life could be restored to it through fantasy.

A Woman of Action

During the Affair, women participated on both sides of the crisis; but the most visible and consistently active group made their presence felt in revisionist politics through the feminist newspaper *La Fronde*, founded by Marguerite Durand in late 1897. The most famous female journalist of the time, Séverine (Caroline Rémy), wrote a daily column for the paper and quickly became the best-known female commentator on the Dreyfus Affair.[7] Refusing to remain on the margins of political journalism, Séverine and other writers for *La Fronde* (the *frondeuses*) were present at every major public event of the Dreyfus Affair, including the trials of Esterhazy, Zola, and Dreyfus himself in 1899. The emotionalism, religious piety, and suggestibility that were typically attributed to women during the nineteenth century meant that writers like Séverine had to reassert their capacity for the journalistic detachment that was demanded of (but rarely practiced by) men during the Affair. An interview with the Dreyfusard hero Zola provided Séverine with an opportunity to distance herself from such assumptions about women. "I am not blinded by uncontrollable or limitless devotion," she asserted. "I remain very much the mistress of my judgment. I discuss, I evaluate—no fetishism hinders the exercise of my free will or the critical spirit that is always awake in me." Séverine thus initially distanced herself from Zola, even admitting displeasure at how women were typically represented in his novels, before presenting a generally favorable view of the Dreyfusard hero.[8]

The Zola interview was not the only occasion for Séverine's defense of the Dreyfusard campaign. In fact, Séverine's collected essays on the Dreyfus Affair, *Vers la lumière: Impressions vécues* (page nos. cited parenthetically below), consistently emphasized the honor of her Dreyfusard colleagues, locked as they were in a virile struggle against cowardly foes. It is therefore noteworthy that this collection opened with an early essay that set the tone for much of the volume: a short piece from 1895 in which she criticized soldiers who had struck Dreyfus while he was in their custody (pp. vii–xv). Séverine recognized that this essay, tellingly entitled "Un Lâche," contained a series of "moral charges" that would ironically constitute a primary theme of many of her subsequent Dreyfusard writings: the cowardice and weakness of the military as opposed to the manly heroism of the revisionists. Throughout these essays, Séverine reinforced images of the virility of her male colleagues, a gesture illustrated during the Rennes trial, when she made "pilgrimages" to the lodgings of prominent Dreyfusards. One such walk took her to the house of the chemistry professor Jacques Cavalier, "a being of energy and perseverence," who had become a Dreyfusard "not out of puerile imitation, but out of virile confidence in such a deed" (pp. 348–49).

Séverine was a journalist who believed, along with most of her male peers, that bodily features conveyed information about moral qualities, a contention that allowed her to demonstrate through physiognomical analyses the healthy virility of Dreyfusards and the sickly cowardice of their opponents. In addition to her critique of Esterhazy's body (discussed in Chapter 3), Séverine marveled that one of the architects of the military cover-up, Lieutenant-Colonel du Paty de Clam, "this unhealthy being (even if he is not actually ill); . . . this 'subject' worthy of scientific observation," had once been a judge (p. 83). And when Dreyfus's principal defense lawyer, Fernand Labori, was shot on the streets of Rennes, Séverine noted the manly vitality and courage that he had maintained throughout the Affair and dubbed him a "professor of energy," using an expression popularized by Maurice Barrès two years earlier (p. 379). In comparison to the manly sacrifice of Labori, who had been "crucified" for his efforts on behalf of the truth, the opponents of Dreyfus were mere cowards: "Where are your living hosts? Where are your heroes?" she asked (p. 384). Séverine delighted in using typical Dreyfusard rhetoric to show that intellectuals were in fact more manly than officers: "weak or timid souls" remained silent about the innocence of Dreyfus, she claimed, but "more robust and better-tempered spirits" would continue to protest this violation of personal rights (p. 30).

Despite the commentaries she delivered on the heroism of her male comrades, Séverine also envisioned herself as an equal among these men, and took great joy at being recognized as such. She recounted with pleasure how, outside of the of the Palais de Justice, she was once recognized by a young man who ex-

claimed: "It's Séverine . . . who has fought for justice!" This relatively minor in-
cident represented a "rare victory" for a journalist committed to the search for
recognition without reference to her sex (p. 338). On another occasion, Séverine met a woman in the streets of Rennes who was surprised to discover that
she was a Dreyfusard. "You madame?" the woman marveled, "That's not possible, with such a soft manner." Séverine patiently explained the Dreyfusard case—
"the superior ideal we serve"—to the woman and was happy to see her standing
in the street deep in thought after the conversation had ended (p. 429). Viewing
herself as a veritable fighter for the Truth, Séverine also respected women who
seemed to possess similar qualities, and singled out *La Dame blanche* as a case in
point: "She displayed fine courage during the tumults of the Zola Affair. . . .
Among all the brave women, she was the most brave, militant to the point of
winning favor even among the most committed" (p. 330).

Despite frequent attempts to position herself on equal footing with her male
comrades, Séverine on occasion also cited her own situation as a woman and a
mother in ways that merit special attention. Sympathy for the Dreyfus family
prompted her to cite her female identity in addition to her role as an intellectual. Like many Dreyfusards, she found it difficult to bracket her anti-Semitism
for the sake of a higher cause and tended toward the standard revisionist line that
Dreyfus should be retried *despite* his unsavory Jewish qualities. Séverine's anti-
Semitism stemmed mainly from her anarchist critique of capitalism. "And if I do
not like the color of their skin any more than I like . . . the Jewish spirit, that is
no reason to sanction their torture" (p. 68). Indeed, even the efforts of the Dreyfus family seemed suspect to her, and Séverine admitted to having once refused
to receive Madame Dreyfus, a "prudent cruelty" that she would probably commit again because "[t]here was, and still is, too much money in their house."
Whatever pity Séverine experienced, however, was quickly attributed to her fe-
maleness: "[A]s a woman, as a mother, I felt sorry for her even as I criticized her,
and [I] understood her effort on behalf of her absent husband" (p. 35).

Séverine's pity was thus hardly gender-neutral, but was explicitly cast as feminine and thus served as a basis for her difference from Dreyfusard men. Since
stereotypes about female nature always colored the public reception of *La Fronde*,
it is worth pausing here to consider how Séverine's statements about her femininity functioned within the discourses of this period. On the one hand, such
statements could stand as evidence that Séverine saw her female identity as a true
weakness: after all, the period of the Dreyfus Affair was also a transitional one
for Séverine herself, who despite her public stance as a female journalist only

pressed for women's suffrage years later.[9] In this manner, she might be seen as exemplifying the tensions within the "familial feminism" that marked the fin de siècle, a moderate politics that was generally content to work within the doctrine of separate spheres rather than recommend full sexual equality.[10] Yet since Séverine's assertions of objectivity in the presence of Zola suggest that she hardly subscribed to stock images of inherent female weakness, her uses of sexist stereotyping may also be viewed as ironic and strategic. That is, by deliberately playing the role of a weak being who could see the truth *despite* her femininity, she was able subtly to undermine her opponents' positions. If a "mere" woman could understand the situation clearly and rationally, what did that say about anti-Dreyfusards who stubbornly clung to outdated conceptions of the army's infallibility? "I, who am only a woman and a civilian," she once noted, "I understood it clearly!" (p. 94). Within the masculinist discourse of Dreyfusism, Séverine carved out a space for intellectual women, but in so doing, she cultivated the image of her enemies as the "true" effeminates. "In my soul and conscience, with all my weak forces, with all the energy of my sincerity, I believe that Alfred Dreyfus is innocent!" (p. 421).[11] In this sense, Séverine saw herself as at similar to, yet distinct from, her male comrades, as someone who was at once an "intellectual" and a "woman."

By insisting on her right to take a stand in this political crisis, Séverine gave voice to an opinion held by many French women regardless of their views on Dreyfus. One may thus concur with Françoise Blum that, in the various petitions produced during the Affair, the presence of women's names alongside those of men was of great symbolic import.[12] Some even embraced intellectual qualities as their own, such as the anti-Dreyfusard who boldly identified herself as a "very intellectual French woman, the daughter of a French officer."[13] Significant numbers of women on both sides insisted on becoming engaged in the struggle alongside men. On the occasion of the subscription lists honoring Colonel Picquart, the widow Michelet addressed this brief missive to the newspaper *Le Rappel:* "Since women are permitted to sign, quickly put my name on the list. Put it among all the others. It belongs there."[14]

Women Who Love Too Much

Women were indeed permitted to sign such petitions, but their participation in the politics of the Affair was usually viewed as auxiliary to the more militant role played by men. As we shall see, women were often implored to take up a less conspicuous stance in the national crisis by espousing conventional supporting roles. Even Séverine suffered from unequal treatment, and despite her substantial reportage, her contributions were sometimes viewed among Dreyfusards as being of a strictly feminine nature. The publisher P.-V. Stock remembered Séverine well from evenings at the restaurant Les Trois Marches in Rennes. "What an exquisite comrade! . . . She was truly an admirable woman, charitable to a fault and a writer of a very great talent."[15] Victor Basch, however, remembered Séverine's presence as being more soothing than anything else, "a great comfort to the little Dreyfusard army. In this milieu of anxiety, she had the heroism of smiling."[16] Nevertheless, the prospect that a woman would regard herself as *une intellectuelle* was a particularly vexing one. We have seen repeatedly in this book how ambiguously mental labor has been situated in relation to mainstream conceptions of masculinity, often prompting intellectuals and bourgeois professionals to emphasize their heroic and martial qualities, sometimes defensively. If intellectuality threatened to feminize men, however, it had the opposite effect on women, for whom mental labor implied the development of virile qualities that interfered with their "natural" roles as wives and mothers. Just as intellectuals were depicted as egg-headed weaklings by cartoonists, intellectual women, *les cervelines*, were often shown with inflated heads. Regardless of their position on the Dreyfus issue, the existence of women who identified themselves with intellect signaled a dangerous transgression in its own right, an "unsexing" of women through excessive mental work. This transgression was not only damaging for women but also threatened the men with whom they associated. Geneviève Fraisse reminds us that during the nineteenth century the word *féminisme* was also a medical term used to describe a state of arrested physical development in males, denoting a feminization of the male body. While many critics agreed that intellectual labor and feminist politics threatened to displace women from their assigned gender role, feminism could also suggest a state of bodily regression for men, a connotation with obvious implications for the projected image of Dreyfusard masculinity. While intellectuality and feminism both threatened to create virilized women, they also suggested the dangerous emasculation of men.[17]

The manhood of men was thus intimately related to the status of women, particularly to the ability to maintain distinct yet mutually defining spheres of activity, mental capacity, and emotional states. Insofar as women were considered naturally suited to be only wives and mothers, the blurring or collapse of these boundaries had consequences of national proportions. "What will befall our country when the woman finds herself led astray from her natural destination," wondered one anxious author, "when the girl could suppose that there exists for her something other than the noble and healthy mission of being a wife, of being a mother."[18] Women who had been persuaded that something else awaited them thus evaded their natural destiny and contributed to the falling French birthrate. That Germany experienced a demographic boom during the same period elevated the French situation to critical dimensions and carried the "woman question" to national prominence.[19] A variety of theories were put forth to explain this national crisis, ranging from concerns about impotence and male homosexuality to lesbianism and the New Woman. Yet concerns about males becoming feminized at the hands of women were not confined to the threatening topic of feminist politics. Indeed, even women performing maternal functions could still leave their little boys in a weakened state, bereft of willpower and initiative. Depopulation, as we shall see, remained the central problem around which many critiques of women clustered, but this was often a matter of quality as well as quantity. Once properly schooled in their civic duty to procreate, it was believed, women would no doubt give birth to more boys. But were women really equipped to transform boys into men?

It has often been remarked that domesticity achieved the status of a cult among the nineteenth-century bourgeoisie, particularly among men who looked to the home as a haven from the harsh, often immoral, realities of life in the world. With the urban landscape increasingly described as exercising an over-stimulating influence on the nerves of modern men, this need for a relatively peaceful domestic retreat became even more important as the century progressed. Deborah Silverman has argued that interior design around 1900 reflected this domestic ideal and, in its mix of rococo and modern elements, proposed that "the interior could be at once a domain of tranquility for overwrought nerves and an arena for nervous stimulation."[20] The wife, it was hoped, would play the appropriate role as a minister to her mate's needs by replenishing him through her tender and even spiritual ministrations. Such had been her mission since early in the century, and many expected this supporting role to continue.

Unfortunately, the angel of the *foyer* was not all she was cracked up to be. Throughout the nineteenth century, liberals were consumed by the idea that women represented atavistic elements in society whose emotional and conservative natures rendered them unfit for what Judith Stone has described as the "republican brotherhood."[21] The close association between women and priests persuaded republicans like Jules Michelet that the liberalization of male political sensibilities was jeopardized by this collusion: by appealing to the spiritual nature of women, Michelet feared, priests might persuade them to steer their husbands away from the republican cause. For fear of losing what ground they had gained once the Third Republic stabilized in the early 1880s, some republicans stepped up their critique of women. Viewing acceptance of the republic as a categorical imperative, Jean-Paul Laffitte cautioned the republican readers of *La Revue bleue* about the potential resistance of women to this national ideal. Laffitte noted with approval that the majority of bourgeois Frenchmen, united by the triple bonds of daily work, political interest, and military service, were convinced that "the republic is the government that best suits our country and our time." It was, moreover, the handiwork of men of all social classes who had found common ground in deeds rather than words. Homosociality itself would be ensured through republican political action: "Rich or poor, ignorant or educated, action reconciles men."[22] Less dynamic than men, however, women were linked to one another by the tenuous bonds of *la charité*. They were thus badly suited to the rigors of republicanism and even seemed predisposed against it. "For [the women] of the middle class of whom I speak, nothing in their upbringing, habits, or sentiments pushes them toward democracy, and many things drive them farther away from it." Intellectual limitations, credulousness in the face of religious ideas, and perhaps innate conservatism rendered women strangers to the great republican project. As a potentially corrupting force that worked through seduction rather than rational persuasion, women threatened to circulate the contagion of anti-republican thought, perhaps turning their husbands or, worse still, their sons against it.[23]

Though ideally the republicanism of fathers would be strong enough to offset the retrograde tendencies of women, during the nineteenth century, the father's role in family life was also undergoing a transition. Under the *ancien régime*, fathers had virtually discretionary powers over all members of the household and played an active role in the moral education of their children. With the consolidation of the Third Republic and compulsory secular education, however, the paternal influence on the education of children was being steadily eclipsed by schoolteachers. They, and not fathers, would be the ones to sow the seeds of republicanism in their sons. Through the expansion of lay educational institutions under the Third Republic, the child became a veritable conduit for the state's liberal ideology, thus exercising a subtle influence over the family itself. With mothers and schoolmasters engaged in shaping young minds, fathers found themselves reduced to their roles as providers.[24] Admittedly, it is not clear how many fathers were bothered by this development. Even if some would have preferred to play a more central role in their children's lives, they received little encouragement from their peers. Gustave Droz tried to convince men of the therapeutic benefits of playing with one's children, but his was a relatively lone voice amid a chorus of others who frowned upon such frivolity.[25] The task of raising children would be left to the mother and the government. Republican educators who aimed at maximizing social solidarity underscored how the state had usurped this paternal position. They agreed with the philosopher Émile Boutroux that "no one has the right to raise children for themselves, not even the father. We raise them for the preservation and progress of humanity, for society and country, [and] for the accomplishment of the duties that await them in life."[26]

The mother and the state were thus meant to work together for the physical and moral health of the child. But first it was necessary to bring more children into the world, and the campaign to reverse the dwindling birthrate was implicitly geared toward augmenting the number of children, especially sons, born to French families. While there is evidence that for some natalists a simple increase in the number of males would help to revitalize the nation, a fixation on sheer numbers draws attention away from the fact that, for many others, increasing the birthrate was also a matter of quality. In such circles, there was a grave concern that even the few male children who were being born might not grow up to be the right kind of men. Widespread concerns about the degeneration of the French fueled concerns about the physical health of pregnant women, and in some circles supported the claim that women should be taught to take extra care of their health, even to the point of engaging in exercise regimens.[27] Philippe Tissié was quite concerned about the biological menace to manhood posed by unhealthy women: "[S]ociety should protect the mother from the moment of conception up until delivery. *In every man, one must always consider the former foetus* [emphasis in original]."[28] Delivery was, of course, just the beginning of the mother's mission, and to ensure that newborns survived to maturity, the science of "puericulture" introduced women to the nutritional needs of growing children. Praising the superior quality of mother's milk, for instance, many experts extolled the virtues of maternal breast-feeding after delivery.[29]

Transforming boys into men was cited as a desire of women everywhere. "To create a human being, to love him, to protect him, to make of this fragile beginning a robust and valiant man, what a sweet and beautiful mission!"[30] As we have seen repeatedly in this book, however, the French acknowledged that anatomical maleness was no guarantee that boys would grow up to be men capable of defending and revitalizing the nation. Doctors, educators, and other experts were thus attentive to the ways in which manhood might be frustrated through a range of morbid influences.[31] As such, the emotional natures of women were often cited as playing a leading role in the retardation of manhood. Physiologically, this could take place unwittingly, even before the baby was born. Strong emotions during pregnancy, it had been observed for centuries, could directly result in a miscarriage, and doctors contended that in other cases, the mother's emotions could have a negative influence on the neurological stability of the fetus.[32] More common was the complaint that when left unchecked, the excessive tenderness that mothers "naturally" lavished upon their babies could foster overly sensitive boys and weak men. When this did not produce nervous disorders or vices that were often connected to emotional weakness, it could result in especially credulous or idealistic men, easy prey for religious indoctrination. The tacit partnership between mothers and schoolteachers threatened to break down on this point, and old fears about the influence of priests over gullible women were resurrected in the name of promoting a more virile (that is, republican) upbringing.[33] "They suffer, they are excessively sensitive," said one critic of pampered middle-class boys. "They have grown up under the maternal eye; they have learned to pray, to believe. . . . mothers love these poor little boys too much."[34]

To have more sons without loving them too much: for some this was the paradoxical solution to the national crisis. The rejuvenation of France surely required more men, but men who were republican and tough, able fighters in their daily lives and in national conflicts. "Our France is becoming depopulated," declared Jacques Porcher, all because of the "ridiculous and deplorable" cult of the child: "We no longer have children because we love them too much." Both parents were guilty here—"the woman, who has made a god of the child, and the man, who let her do it"—but the one most to blame was the mother, the undisputed "minister of the interior," into whose hands the labor-weary man "abdicates" himself. Conceding that the Frenchwoman was "exceptionally endowed" with a number of admirable qualities, Porcher warned men of her most serious defect: "She is too tender." What many men had viewed as a blessing, as one of the feminine charms that made the household a joy, was for this author a potential curse:

> Do not be deceived: there is the danger for you first of all, for your children above all. . . . With a word, a gesture, a smile, a glance, she captivates and seduces: how to resist? . . . [While the] nervous tenderness of your wife perhaps risks enfeebling

your energy, extinguishing your ambition, [and] enervating your audacity, at least you have the means of regaining possession of yourself. Outside of the house you escape this so soft [*douce*] but so enervating [*amollissante*] influence. And besides, your mind is formed, your character has taken its shape: you can resist.

Men who had once found in the family a haven from an often brutal world were now being warned of the dangers of domesticity. The double bind that this generated must be noted: with urban modernity already being described as exercising an enervating influence over men, similar warnings about the softening effects of the household left manhood with little refuge. During this time, more and more men were looking beyond the home for experiences and friendships that might nourish their sense of manliness, whether through sports, travel, or all-male dining clubs. Yet even if a father could restore his own virility by periodically escaping the home, his little boy remained trapped in the smothering embrace of maternal affection. "And slowly he submits to the influence of this tenderness, which never rests. . . . We say it with force: the mother makes her child twice. He owes her his body, he also owes her his soul." It was a slippery slope from the solace of motherly love to the creation of effeminate men, for the excessive exposure of the son to his mother weakened the boy and, by extension, the nation itself. "There are the men that our women of France have made! Thirty-year-old children, without will, without initiative, without energy." Quite unable "to look obstacles in the face and to tackle them head on [*les aborder en face*]," these half-men joined the swelling ranks of life's failures, the dreaded intellectual proletariat described in Chapter 2. "The consequence is clear. Lawyers without clients, doctors without patients, professors without students, writers without editors. . . ." How did all of this contribute to the nation's population problem? Because ultimately such coddled men would never find a woman more loving than *maman*. As a result they would be less likely to get married and start their own families.[35]

While some feared the creation of credulous sons who might rally around the Church, others were concerned about the forfeiture of other manly traits. Father Henri Didon, a staunch advocate of physical force both through military and athletic training, warned mothers to be vigilant of their children's "natural laziness," which must be conquered at all costs. As children tend to be fearful, they, like all of humanity, must be forced to prove their capacity for valiance, and this can only be done by cultivating the spirit of combativeness. "Do not be afraid of this spirit," Didon counseled mothers. "Never forget that the combative are the strong, and that the strong are the good, but that the lazy are the cunning and the weak, and that the weak are dangerous because they are traitors."[36] This cultivation of the combative spirit was one of the great moral values of sports; yet here too women proved to be an obstacle. We have already seen how Didon classified the adversaries of sports into *"les passifs, les affectifs, et les intellectuels."* And who were *les affectifs?* "That's you, ladies. The mother is the greatest enemy of sports. How many mothers have said to me: 'And above all, my son will not play football!'"[37] Mothers were thus held partly to blame for the soft and unhealthy lifestyles of men and were identified as a population in need of reeducation. Hoping to educate the French about "the art of making a man," Abbot H. Mocquillon addressed himself directly to mothers: "Do you want your frail, delicate, and mawkish children to recover the colors and forms that indicate health and force?" he asked. *"Get them used to sport."*[38]

As we have seen frequently in this book, manly autonomy was defined in negative, even defensive terms at the fin de siècle; it suggested the ability to resist a host of "feminine" and feminizing seductions, from the sensory overload and sensual pleasures of urban life to the softening effects of mothers and wives. Given the preponderance of this gendered imagery in the Dreyfus Affair, it is thus not surprising to see family issues mobilized against one's enemies. While some reveled in claims that Zola's intervention had been presaged in the alleged criminality of his father, others found that blaming mothers for the misdeeds of their sons could be a most appealing strategy. Applauding the martial values inherent in sport, Didon contended that women stifled in young boys the values that would prepare them to defend the nation. By identifying *les intellectuels* as another antisportive group (see Chapter 2), this anti-Dreyfusard implied that revisionists were themselves the result of overprotective mothering. The socialist Urbain Gohier famously argued the opposite point, seeing in the maternal influence the breeding ground of the militarist mentality that fueled anti-Dreyfusism. "Now men in all countries are what their mothers have made of them. Why would mothers allow savage instincts and ferocious prejudices to grow and take root in the brains of their sons, rather than tear them out?" Not only did mothers and teachers encourage boys to be soldiers, Gohier claimed, but many men entered into military service because the uniform itself suggested to them "numerous feminine conquests." This was all part of the age-old role of women as the source of "the warrior play-acting of males," a pathetic theatricality that marked older men like the anti-Dreyfusards François Coppée, Jules Lemaître, and Henri Rochefort. Such defenders of the army, Gohier alleged, had been much too ugly and awkward in their youth to attract women, and "their physical defects and cowardice excluded them from military service." In their senility, these frustrated old men slipped into forms of patriotic and even sexual sadism, the latter laced with homosexual lust: "[T]hey cannot see the skirt of an ugly slut [*une maritorne*] or the trousers of a dragoon without slobbering with ecstasy." Gohier did not doubt that such pathetic displays were the result of bad upbringing: "What could the mothers of these wretched children have been like?"[39]

For Gohier, as for many others, the moral and physical worth of men, not to mention the future of the republican ideal, could be safeguarded through the careful education of girls as proper wives and mothers.[40] Yet the paradox remained: if the femininity of women was in fact a liability for their sons, how could they be entrusted with cultivating virile qualities in these boys? In other words, as one expert wondered, "How could she, a being of weakness, train beings of will?" The answer was that women themselves had to be trained, for it is "through the education of women that the education of men must begin."[41] Educating women thus became a central problem during the closing years of the nineteenth century, and it was rarely proposed for the simple purpose of extending a male prerogative to women. The Camille Sée Law of 1880, which provided for the state-sponsored secondary education of women, was among other things a republican anticlerical strategy aimed at wresting women from the clutches of the Church.[42] As the liberal social philosopher Alfred Fouillée explained, the natural religiosity and conservatism of women made such measures essential. "A mind dominated by sentiment, where the scientific tendency is less developed by the effect of nature and education, where, on the other hand, the moral idea is exalted, above all in the form of pity and charity, such a mind is naturally inclined to search above the world for a living justice and living love; such a mind is naturally religious."[43] Yet extending education to women generated a new problem. While women's allegiance to the republic might be secured by instilling liberal ideas into them, this also meant that more women might refuse traditional gender roles by venturing into the job market, a development that could aggravate the already serious population crisis. The New Woman of the turn of the century thus represented a dangerous inversion of acceptable gender identity, and in the cultural imagination, this figure was joined by those weak men who failed to control their wives. Railing against the Sée Law, Gustave Le Bon invoked studies on hysteria and hypnosis by arguing that the formal education of women resulted in the very *surmenage intellectuel* that was said to afflict both sexes equally: "If the man, by virtue of his physical vigor, can often escape the effects of *surmenage intellectuel*, it is not the same for the woman."[44] Joseph Reinach's response to the law was more blunt: "The true *diplôme supérieur* for the education of girls is the marriage contract."[45]

Less extreme were the sentiments of republicans like Alfred Fouillée, who, although they proclaimed the benefits of social solidarity, nonetheless argued that women were intellectually inferior, asserting that they experienced mental regression soon after menstruation. Émile Durkheim also emphasized the role of physiology in the sexual division of labor, claiming that "the two great functions of psychological life had become as if dissociated from each other, one sex having taken over the affective, the other the intellectual function."[46] By claiming to minimize conflict within society, and thus implicitly hoping to neutralize the threat of socialism and "individualist" or "integral" feminism, these solidarists were willing to accept limited reform for more moderate "familial feminists," who were committed to enhancing the function of women in the family rather than putting an end to patriarchy in general. From a nationalist perspective, however, even this moderate feminism was, like homosexuality, an un-French and "cosmopolitan" development and represented yet another reason to challenge the republican state.[47] Other moderates found a way to allow female education, but with many restrictions. The noted linguist Michel Bréal, for instance, applauded female education but suggested that, since women generally lack "independence of judgment and the habit of thinking for themselves," they should be directed toward "branches of study for which [they] have a special aptitude," such as foreign-language education. Here the childlike qualities attributed to women could be put to good use: "The teaching of languages demands attention, memory, pliancy, patience, devotion, the art of becoming a child with the children: all feminine qualities." Admitting the benefits of allowing women to collaborate in teaching, Bréal nevertheless maintained that "the important point is to know how to put them in their proper place."[48]

Women and Truth

With their own manly credentials in the balance, settling on the proper place of women was an important component of the Dreyfusards' self-image. There is little doubt that the "woman question" weighed heavily on most discussions of manhood at the fin de siècle, which is why the presence of high-profile women like the *frondeuses* had implications for the public image of the Dreyfusards. Despite claims that these women were not inspired by feminist politics, anti-

Dreyfusards cast doubt on the credibility of their opponents by denigrating the public role of women in their ranks.[49] The feminist newspaper *La Fronde* had been founded exactly when Zola began a series of public statements that would help to galvanize pro-Dreyfus forces as they pressed for a revision. Its appearance at this time helped create the impression that these bold women were part and parcel of the Dreyfusard intellectuals who would appear in greater numbers early in 1898. For those with an interest in condemning these challenges to military authority, the upsurge of apparently feminist action could only appear as a symptom of a deeper moral crisis. Without citing its political orientation, Maurice Barrès welcomed *La Fronde*, "so long as it did not have the ridiculous pretension of wanting to play the role of a masculine newspaper. . . . How should it present itself in the press? As the feminine brain judging all things from the particular point of view?" The notion of women participating on an equal footing in a male journalistic world was intolerable to the novelist, who tellingly saw it as a laughable, if not unsettling, form of cross-dressing: "No! I cannot imagine a [Henri] Rochefort in a petticoat!"[50] The Dreyfus Affair presented the perfect opportunity for these women to debunk such claims. By rallying under the putative disinterestedness and universality of the Dreyfusard cause, they, too, could seek to transcend their "particular point of view."

The enemy camp, however, would not reward them for their efforts. When anti-Dreyfusards were not excoriating Zola, Picquart, or Reinach, they laid into the *frondeuses* as dangerous inversions of the gender order. In 1899, a fund-raising campaign was launched by *La Libre Parole* to provide for the widow and child of Colonel Hubert Henry, who had committed suicide after his role in the forgery of documents falsely implicating Dreyfus was revealed. Anti-Dreyfusards exploited this scene of violently disrupted family life by soliciting funds to assist the widow Henry in her libel suit against Joseph Reinach, who had "slandered" the dead colonel by drawing public attention to his crime. With the Henry fund, anti-Dreyfusards also seized an opportunity to mark the distinction between this woman in her conventional role as suffering mother against the "unnatural" beings associated with *La Fronde*. One mother, for instance, asserted that by contributing to this fund, she was showing "the difference between her sex and the divorcées of *La Fronde*."[51] Similarly, a priest tried to console the widow Henry by arguing in verse that "Any woman writer who does not believe in God / Has ceased being a woman, and is nothing more than a bluestocking."[52]

We have seen how Dreyfus's intellectual defenders were already ripe for caricature as weaklings and half-men; by being associated with divorcées and bluestockings, they risked sliding even closer toward femininity in the estimation of the public. Vilified by public opinion and the anti-Semitic press during the first half of 1898, Dreyfusards of the first hour were not in a position to reject the assistance of any well-meaning supporters. Nevertheless, some took steps toward the management of femininity by delineating what they saw as the proper role of women in Dreyfusard politics. On 24 March 1898, Jean Psichari, a professor at the Collège de France, published an "Appel aux femmes de France" in *Le Siècle*. Dreyfus's letters from exile, Psichari explained, had been delivered to his wife only as edited and censored copies of the originals, thus depriving Madame Dreyfus of the full account of her husband's travails. "One thing is certain," observed the professor, "that in these letters Dreyfus *does not have the right to speak of how he passes his days.*" According to Psichari, the active role of female Dreyfusards was most appropriately manifested in such matters of the heart. Since men had "torn themselves apart" in their campaign for justice, he claimed, they had often over-looked the need for goodness and pity in their struggle. Fortunately, though, le-gitimate female participation in Dreyfusard politics was defined by this emo-tional space left unoccupied by men: "O women, it is your turn now. . . . Open wide your souls to hereditary generosities. Do not debate, do not reason, suffer. Therein lies the truth. . . . You are there for the purposes of softening. Unite! Address yourselves to those whose duty it is to hear you. Demand that this woman be allowed to see the letters of her husband."[53]

A number of women stepped up in the name of this ideal, and over the next two days, *Le Siècle* featured testimonies from many women who demanded that Lucie Dreyfus be reunited with her husband while in exile.[54] While Psichari's appeal was not directly addressed to the *frondeuses*, the very generality of his plea suggests discomfort at the threatened usurpation of what had been long con-sidered a male prerogative. With men heroically sacrificing themselves on the field of politics and ideas, matters of sentiment should be entrusted to the puta-tive experts in this area, to those who were considered superior to men in com-passion and spirituality. If France was to be restored to republican order, women must retain the softness considered proper to their sex: men would fight, and women would soothe their wounds. This sexual division of labor implied in the doctrine of separate spheres allowed Dreyfusards to mark ever more clearly the difference between themselves and the feminine. Though such a distinction was clearly more rhetorical than real, it suggests the Dreyfusards' need to foster a particular social image by distancing themselves from women. It also demon-strates how, for all of their political differences, Dreyfusards and anti-

Dreyfusards were equally vexed about women who strayed from their conventional place in society.

An examination of the caricatures generated during the Affair indicates that Psichari's misgivings about female action were shared by others in the Dreyfusard camp. The use of female imagery as a means of waging political warfare was hardly a novel tactic by the end of the nineteenth century, nor was it employed exclusively by Dreyfusard cartoonists. We have seen, for instance, how the anti-Semitic magazine *Psst . . . !* featured violent representations of the effects of Dreyfusism on the moral integrity of France. It also took advantage of female allegories like Marianne (the symbol of the republic) by depicting her being threatened in a number of ways by Jews and socialists. As demonstrated in a series of vivid cartoons, the travails of Marianne included being thrown down a hole, being forced to consort with wealthy Jews, being flogged by Jews, and having her hands sawn off.[55] These cartoonists also employed more generalized female figures to undermine the manhood of their enemies and in so doing skillfully invoked the conventional belief that French women desired "real" men, blessed with courage and robust physiques.

While apparently fired by sexual pride, these tactics were not the sole product of male fantasy. Indeed, at times, women willingly offered their services as experts on virility. One subscriber to the Henry fund insulted the virility of Jews by describing herself as *"Une parisienne* who does not like the circumcised."[56] In her novels, the anti-Dreyfusard Gyp cast aspersions on masculinity of Colonel Picquart, whose education and alleged homosexuality rendered him less manly than more robust officers.[57] Séverine, of course, had a very different view of Picquart: "That one is a man," she assured the readers of *La Fronde.*[58] In other words, the images produced by men to some extent mirrored sentiments volunteered by women. Anti-Dreyfusards eagerly employed female figures as virility experts. An illustration from *Psst . . . !* entitled "Extra muros" depicts a woman bidding a puerile and apparently frustrated intellectual adieu, presumably after he has clumsily tried to seduce her or, if they have had relations, he has failed to perform (Fig. 5). This assertion of the Dreyfusards' unattractiveness or even impotence was repeated some months later, when a woman is shown on the verge of embracing a soldier while scornfully repelling the advances of an intellectual, saying: "Leave me in peace. . . . I am a Frenchwoman!" (Fig. 6). Graphic affirmations of manhood often required such flexibility in their representations of women, and ultimately female figures could be pressed into a variety of services. Chaste and self-negating when they needed to be, "good" women were also re-

— Ma vie aura désormais un but : épouser le colonel Picquart.

Fig. 10. Caran d'Ache, Untitled, *Psst . . . !* 3 December 1898, 4.

quired to confirm men's potency and desirability, even if doing so risked calling their own moral standing into question. Even representations of the *frondeuses*, who as intellectual women were usually cast as mannish or unattractive, could still attest to passion as a driving force of women's involvement in the Affair. In one caricature, an extraordinarily plain, thin, and balding woman, obviously a journalist, sighs forlornly on a divan: "Henceforth my life will have a goal: to marry Colonel Picquart" (Fig. 10).

The figure of Truth was by far the most popular element of Dreyfusard iconography, and its examination offers a unique perspective on the sexual politics of the Affair. Truth was always naked and armed with a mirror held outward, thus indicating her ability to reveal truth to others. Echoing a proverb stating that "La vérité est au fond d'un puits" (Truth is at the bottom of a well), French tradition typically featured Truth emerging from a well into the light of day, an element that appeared repeatedly in Dreyfusard imagery. As artists such as H.-G. Ibels, Paul Barre, and Hermann-Paul demonstrated, the naked Truth had a single overt purpose: to signify the truth about Alfred Dreyfus that had been buried by his anti-Semitic enemies in the army. Yet it is worth recalling the highly ambiguous aspects of allegory in the Western tradition, a figure that traditionally says one thing while meaning something quite different. Writing on the French Revolution, Lynn Hunt points out that the female form of many allegories did not imply that real women had any access to the idea expressed through such representations. Rather the "proliferation of the female allegory was made possible . . . by the exclusion of women from public affairs. Women could be representative of abstract qualities and collective dreams because women were not allowed to vote or govern."[59] Nearly a century after the Revolution, French women were still excluded from political life, a state of affairs that allowed female allegories like Marianne to proliferate under the Third Republic.[60] During the Dreyfus Affair, the "other-speaking" quality of allegorical Truth was manifested not only in the desire to prevent real women from taking active roles in Dreyfusard politics, but in the discrepancy between the allegory's female form and the fact that Truth was widely considered a distinctly *masculine* virtue. One thus discerns an ambiguity at the heart of this symbol, whose form was female but whose essence was generally perceived as masculine. In short, the ideal of truth was safely represented by an abstract woman because, according to the logic of allegorical representation, it was assumed that real women could not be relied on to tell the truth.[61]

At least since the eighteenth century, the Western cultural imagination has retained a special association between women and deception that makes the presumed "femininity" of lying during the Affair much more comprehensible. Commentators sometimes argued that instances of female lying were due partly to the cultural demands imposed on women, requiring them to conceal certain bodily functions for the sake of preserving modesty, and to use cosmetics, fashion, and culture to foster public impressions that might draw attention away from potentially less attractive features linked to their age, health, family wealth, or body shape. Most, however, were willing to connect the propensity to deceive with assumptions about female nature, concluding that women lied to compensate for physical weakness or did so out of their inherent suggestibility, which allowed them to believe sincerely in their own fabrications. Indeed, in her study of female criminality, Ann-Louise Shapiro demonstrates how the end of the nineteenth century, medical and legal discourses about the duplicity of "deviant" women were frequently shaped by durable assumptions about qualities possessed by "normal" women: "The criminal woman was like all women, only more so: she was suggestible, weak in the face of temptation, deceitful, prone to excess, intellectually limited, and morally stunted."[62]

Such stereotypes about female nature also pervaded the science of legal testimony that was being developed at the time of the Affair, a discourse that counted women among those unstable individuals most likely to be "false witnesses" and who were thus considered quite unreliable on the stand. The so-called La Roncière Affair provided a historical precedent for such a belief and was often cited by legal experts who doubted the testimony given by women in court. In 1834, a cavalry cadet named Émile de la Roncière had been accused of writing threatening letters to the adolescent Marie de Morell, the daughter of his commanding officer. After his expulsion from the École de Cavalerie, he was charged with assaulting the girl in her bedroom and sentenced to ten years' imprisonment. The fact that La Roncière steadfastly maintained his innocence helped to generate doubts about the young man's guilt, and in subsequent decades the La Roncière Affair was often cited by skeptical doctors who felt that the cadet had been wrongly condemned solely on the unreliable testimony of a girl. As in the Dreyfus case, everything here came down to analyzing the handwriting of an incriminating text, and despite disagreement among experts as to its true author (some said the writing was La Roncière's, while others identified it as the daughter's script), an innocent man may have been incarcerated while the guilty party avoided prosecution. The lesson that legal doctors drew from the case of La Roncière was clear: due to a range of problems grounded in female nature, testimony given by women and girls ought to be treated with deep skepticism.[63]

Significantly, the La Roncière Affair was revisited by Dreyfusards as a means of condemning the obfuscating tactics of their opponents. In a lengthy text that revealed in minute detail the circumstances of the accusation and the role of hysteria in Marie de Morell's lying, a former philosophy professor, Stéphane Arnoulin, made connections between this older case and the contemporary scene that would not have been lost on his readers. Just as scholars, artists, and men of letters had rallied decades before around the falsely accused lieutenant (and against the "hysterical" fabrications of a woman and the "ignorant and stupid" crowd who believed such tales), modern intellectuals struggled against "feminine" lies being told about Alfred Dreyfus.[64] Given the masculinist trappings of Dreyfusard self-representations, the presumed femininity of lying conveniently shifted their opponents into another category of men altogether. As we saw in Chapter 3, the Dreyfusard imagination saw lies everywhere at this time. Not only had the General Staff lied about the guilt of Esterhazy (who, in turn, had spun even more fantastic tales), but Colonel Henry had forged documents that fur-

ther incriminated Dreyfus. Dreyfusard graphic imagery often featured veritable seas of forged documents, all inscribed with the word *faux*, suggesting that
the nation was literally being swamped by lies, thus collapsing the stereotype of
feminine deception into an older association of menacing women with the en-
trapping or engulfing imagery of water, filth, and mud.

In addition to symbolizing qualities that women were thought to lack (truth-
fulness and discernment), images of Truth allowed men to comment on other
aspects of contemporary womanhood. Bram Dijkstra has amply documented the
wide circulation of images of dangerous women in fin-de-siècle cultural life, and
has persuasively shown how the arts and sciences subtly colluded to produce images of women that served to discredit or even to disarm the feminine during a
period of perceived gender crisis.[65] It is therefore worth considering the relationship between Truth and other female figures in the cultural imagination, as
well as the implications of these representations for contemporary understandings of manhood. Such an inquiry reveals a host of complicated and often contradictory images of real and ideal women. In particular, the image of Truth to
some extent cited the cultural icon known as the "Parisienne," an ambiguous
contemporary figure who at once epitomized the much vaunted beauty and style
of *la bourgeoise*, while apparently responding to none of the maternal and domestic instincts that supposedly marked all "good" women. Such male ambivalence about the Parisienne reflected the double bind in which bourgeois women
found themselves during the nineteenth century. Caught between cultural demands that she make herself pleasing to the male gaze and moralistic condemnations of female vanity, the ideal woman was one who appeared "naturally"
beautiful, while subtly concealing the effort required to pull off such a performance. This perhaps explains the great voyeuristic interest in gazing upon
women in the process of beautifying themselves, for throughout the nineteenth
century, artists depicted the *bourgeoise* gazing into a mirror while dressing, ap-
plying cosmetics, and fixing her hair, all implying a troubling self-absorption and
narcissism, which was rendered explicit in numerous scenes of women kissing
their own mirror images. Although the process of beautification was obviously
performed for the sake of men, such artificiality and self-absorption were also a
source of considerable male anxiety at the end of the century, mostly because
they reinforced the connection between women and deception, but also because
it implied a degree of erotic autonomy that called into question the place of the
man as the center of a woman's world. Indeed, stock images of the Parisienne
were not far removed from the more frightening specters of the feminist and the

New Woman, both of which represented a threatening self-sufficiency and incursion of women into male domains.[66]

The most common images of Truth tacitly invoked these figures of feminine danger, if only by way of contrast, and illustrated the Dreyfusard wish that proper women restrict themselves to activities considered more appropriate to female nature. In light of the already problematic qualities associated with intellectual men (nervousness, muscular weakness, etc.), the Dreyfusard sense of manhood arguably depended upon policing this gender boundary, if only aesthetically. In an obvious departure from the fashionable Parisienne, Truth does not gaze longingly into the mirror she holds but conspicuously directs it outward, thus refusing the assumed narcissism of the fashionable *bourgeoise* and recalling the comfortable image of the self-negating *femme de foyer.* Yet despite being nude and generally situated in a rural locale, Truth does not simply represent an Arcadian ideal of unadulterated "nature" that refutes the corrupted "cultural" image of the Parisienne. Rather, as her hair is almost always shown as carefully coiffed (rather than as flowing), she suggests less the polar opposite of the *bourgeoise* than her veritable rehabilitation, a partial restoration of a potentially dangerous woman to her proper nature.[67]

In many respects, Truth was the *bourgeoise* stripped down to her essentials, shorn of the deceptive ornamentation of her more worldly counterpart and thereby domesticated. Yet this image of the *nuda veritas* nevertheless remained deeply ambiguous, for the very gesture whereby the ornamental and deceptive Parisienne was chastened also served to eroticize the very act of appropriating the Truth. In *Monuments and Maidens,* Marina Warner analyzes several historical instances where Western artists depicted the acquisition of Truth as a violent act redolent of rape, often showing the allegory trying to wriggle out of the iron grip of Father Time.[68] Often abstaining from such violent appropriations, Dreyfusards were able to employ the image of a sexually assaulted female to their rhetorical advantage. After all, the rape of Truth was an important ingredient in Dreyfusard celebrations of Zola's intervention, for in the words of one supporter, the novelist had primarily made his "noble, generous [and] heroic" gesture because "it seemed to him that Truth had been assaulted [*violentée*]."[69] In a sketch for *L'Assiette au beurre,* the artist Jules Grandjouan depicted Truth walking proudly among the people in all her naked glory, only to be jeered at by incensed priests and magistrates who failed to admire her worthy qualities. "First of all she's indecent!" yells one, "And dangerous!" adds another. Their outrage is a manifestly moral one, their response, violent: "She is debauching the young men! Strangle her!"[70] Anti-Dreyfusards were most often said to detest the Truth, going so far as to bury her beneath the weight of sabers; yet they are also the ones most often accused of venting their hatred through violation. This was not a violation with the simple aim of appropriation (indeed, anti-Dreyfusards did not seek the Truth), but one that sought to sustain the hiddenness of Truth.

Figuring Truth: Universals and Particulars

Women could thus represent Truth without necessarily embodying it. While women served to authenticate and comment upon the inherent qualities associated with men, they nevertheless remained somewhat removed from the real. Of course, the use of allegorical women was still largely predicated on the distance of actual women from conventional political activity, but during the Dreyfus Affair, allegory performed different functions, one of which was the direct interaction of the real and the ideal. Whereas many allegorical figurations depict idealized females alongside famous men, there is rarely any interaction between these figures. Not so during the Dreyfus Affair, where historical figures like Zola were portrayed as the active defenders of an ideal that could not manifest itself without mortal assistance. It is this subtle inflation of particular men to universal proportions that is most striking about the ways in which Dreyfusards used the figure of Truth.

A running theme in Dreyfusard rhetoric concerns the distortion or suppression of Truth by malicious anti-Dreyfusards bent on defending the reputation of the army at any cost. This is evident in Hermann-Paul's depiction of the anti-Dreyfusard Ligue de la Patrie française, whose members have ominously gathered in the woods near Truth's well. "How are they going to disguise me?" wonders the allegory.[71] Paul Barre's "La Vérité quand même," however, is an example of the more widespread theme of the confinement of Truth in her well (Fig. 11). In his caricature, two anti-Dreyfusards pile sabers, drums, and military caps on top of the well, while Truth struggles in vain to emerge. Such illustrations express ambivalence about Truth's potential to persevere on her own, and generate speculation that external assistance may be needed. Even Barre's anti-Dreyfusards are uncertain of the effectiveness of their own efforts. As one says anxiously to the other, "Despite all our efforts, I'm quite afraid she's getting out, the bitch!"

A few months later, it seemed as if Truth had indeed recovered as she leapt from her well to overwhelm Major Esterhazy, a scene that comments less on the

LA VÉRITÉ QUAND MÊME!

MÉLINE. — Malgré tout, j'ai bien peur qu'elle ne sorte, la rosse!...

Fig. 11. Paul Barre, "La Vérité quand même," *Le Sifflet* 5 (17 March 1898): 3. By permission of the Houghton Library, Harvard University.

sudden action of the female figure than on the cowardly qualities of the traitor.[72] Indeed, this scene of female agency is unusual in a repertoire where one is more likely to encounter male Dreyfusards working to release a frail woman. In an Ibels cartoon from December 1898, Truth is again trapped in her well and, with the year quickly coming to an end, helplessly calls to anyone above: "Hey, up there! Will it happen this year? (Fig. 12). Since by this date Dreyfusards were

N° 48. — 30 DÉCEMBRE 1898.   PARAIT LE VENDREDI   Le numéro : 10 centimes

LE SIFFLET

ABONNEMENTS
Un An : France, 6 francs; Étranger, 8 francs.

DIRECTEUR
ACHILLE STEENS

BUREAUX
10, Galerie du Théâtre-Français.
(Palais-Royal, Paris.)

Impatience

— Hé, là-haut! ça sera-t-il pour cette année?

D'APRÈS UNE LITHOGRAPHIE INÉDITE DE H.-G. IBELS.

Fig. 12. H.-G. Ibels, "Impatience," *Le Sifflet* 48 (30 December 1898): 1. By permission of the Houghton Library, Harvard University.

not much closer to securing a revision of the Dreyfus case than they had been months before, Ibels chose to underscore the weakness of this female figure. Despite the apparent powerlessness of Truth, escape certainly seems possible in this drawing, especially since the artist has indicated the unobstructed top of the well (as evinced by the light streaming from above) and even provided a rope tied to a bucket. The print's title, "Impatience," suggests that the bucket was not recently tossed down by friends on the surface, but has remained unused for some time. Ibels's illustration suggests that the female form of Truth is an obstacle to the manifestation of what many considered to be its virile essence.

This graphic disabling of the feminine was completed by the direct intervention of Dreyfusard heroes whose mission was to bring a weakened Truth to light, a situation triumphantly revealed in Ibels's "Ressaisissement" of April 1899 (Fig. 13), where cowardly anti-Dreyfusards disperse as revisionists help Truth climb out of the well. As this illustration suggests, the universal may indeed endure, but ironically needs the assistance of the particular in order to manifest itself. Truth may have been on the march, as Zola had proclaimed, but not without first being released from her well by sympathetic male supporters. The odd presence of a troubadour, the one who actually helps Truth to step out of her well, suggests that a degree of courtship (rather than force) was required to coax this bashful entity from concealment. There is thus a qualitative difference between these scenes and the active style of female allegory imagined in other works, such as Eugène Delacroix's *Liberty Leading the People* (1830). In this famous painting, the abstract universal interacts in historical time with particular actors for the purpose of inspiration and leadership. The people need Liberty to inflame and inspire them, not the other way around. With few exceptions, the adventures of the naked Truth revolve almost entirely around the inability of the allegory either to defend herself against anti-Dreyfusard forces or to manifest herself without the intervention of heroic male helpers. The naked body of Truth becomes the passive object of desire and the focal point of contests among the male actors of the Affair. She is pursued without pursuing, acted upon while generally remaining incapable of agency herself. Finally, whereas Delacroix's Liberty retains her abstraction by actively leading the people, the woman called Truth is disabled to such an extent that she ends up resembling ideals of womanhood celebrated throughout the nineteenth century. In Dreyfusard imagery, Truth does double duty by serving at once as a symbol of the universal and as a representation of more normative conceptions of femininity.

Fig. 13. H.-G. Ibels, "Ressaisissement," *Le Sifflet* 19 (7 April 1899): 1. By permission of the Houghton Library, Harvard University.

In the hands of Dreyfusard artists, this female abstraction takes on the characteristics of historical women, thus suggesting once again an implicit commentary on the proper role of women in society. Such representations seemed to provide an aesthetic version of Psichari's appeal to women, and an implicit commentary on the need to minimize the sort of female agency being demon-

Madame est avec moi.

Fig. 14. Hermann-Paul, "Juin 99. L'Arrêt de la Cour," in *Deux cents dessins* (Paris: Éditions de La Revue blanche, 1900), 63. By permission of the Houghton Library, Harvard University.

strated by the writers of *La Fronde*. An object of desire whom many men want to "possess," the body of Truth finally becomes a trophy for heroic Dreyfusards. In a very suggestive print by Hermann-Paul (Fig. 14), we see that by the time of the Rennes trial, the newly emancipated (but still naked) Truth has become domesticated, appearing as a proper lady on the arm of a pro-Dreyfus magistrate who informs the attending guard that "Madame is with me." This statement performs a double validation of the Dreyfusard, first by confirming the man's legal authority to bring an otherwise unwelcome visitor to the proceedings, and second, through its eroticization of Truth, by attesting to his ability to secure such a woman in the first place. As opposed to the insulting caricatures of intellectuals in *Psst . . . !* here perhaps was proof that Dreyfusards could indeed get dates!

Rather than merely representing the universal, however, Truth actively conferred universality upon her champions through the sheer power of association. As heroic representatives of the universal, their victory in the struggle for Truth ennobled and elevated these men above particularity, and transfigured them into veritable icons of the universal, even as Truth herself slipped to the level of mortal women. This female allegory did little to elevate real women, but it had a profound effect on the ontological status of Dreyfusard heroes, even (or perhaps especially?) when the female figure was replaced by a male. Denizard Orens's idealized illustration of Zola for a postcard series (Fig. 9) demonstrates the universalizing power that female allegory could confer upon deserving mortal men. Zola stands in the foreground of this illustration, arms stretched upward in a gesture of victory. Naked except for a piece of cloth around his pelvis, the once pudgy Zola has become the svelte body of Christ taken down from the cross, which stands empty in the background. In his hands he holds two symbols associated with Truth: a flaming torch and the telltale mirror.[73]

Many questions could be asked of Orens's depiction of Zola as Christ. Chapter 2 analyzed this ambiguous image in terms of its religious content, arguing that Zola's gesture had been likened to a sacrifice of Christ-like proportions, particularly in its defiance of popular opinion and its explicit invocation of universal values. The association with female allegory, however, raises questions about the extent to which such imagery adequately supports projections of Zola's manhood. As Tania Modleski has suggested, "we need to consider the extent to which male power is actually consolidated through cycles of crisis and resolution, whereby men ultimately deal with the threat of female power by incorporating it."[74] In this image, has Zola *become* Truth or has he simply appropriated her mirror? Armed thus with Truth's mirror, perhaps this intellectual hero has usurped the traditional female position to confirm once and for all the essentially masculine qualities of Truth. Perhaps, too, this image depicts the Dreyfusard fantasy of a campaign where women truly remained in their place, symbolically as well as socially.

Madelyn Gutwirth has aptly summarized the relationship between allegorical figurations of women and women as they appear on the historical stage: "For women, the abstract representational force of female allegory must always be mitigated in some measure by its mimetic implications of prescription or proscription, the images' teaching regarding the containment of women's acts. Allegory thus represented a species of representational incarceration for women."[75] This certainly seems to have been the case with Dreyfusard imagery, where projections of masculinity were necessarily accompanied by attempts to neutralize uncomfortable associations with femininity. The proliferation of such imagery not only demonstrates the extent to which visions of national health and vitality were predicated upon an ongoing struggle to define and defend competing definitions of masculine identity, but illuminates how gendered categories framed the putatively more central issues of anti-Semitism, patriotism, and the defense of the republican order. With the heroism of the Dreyfusards established rhetorically through their distance from Jews, crowds, and women, it might seem that revisionism's gendered imagery was successful. Yet as we shall see in the next two chapters, at the fin de siècle, metaphorical manhood was no substitute for the more muscular conception of masculinity that was coming into fashion.

Part III / Remaking the Male Body

If the 1899 trial represented the culmination of revisionism's short-term aspirations, it also revealed cracks in the uneasy alliance of political tendencies loosely united under the Dreyfusard banner and underscored the misgivings that some revisionists harbored about the suitability of Dreyfus as a symbol. To the outrage of most Dreyfusards, the Rennes trial produced yet another guilty verdict, leaving the exhausted captain and his family more demoralized than ever. Dreyfus's decision to accept a formal pardon rather than fight for a complete reversal of the 1894 verdict was nevertheless treated with contempt by militant Dreyfusards like Clemenceau, Picquart, and even his lawyer, Fernand Labori, all of whom wished to use the captain for ideological reasons. Dreyfus's reluctance to lend himself to such purposes after his release only accelerated the disintegration of the Dreyfusard campaign. Although Dreyfus pressed for, and in 1906 finally received, a full rehabilitation, spending time with his family and regaining his health were his immediate concerns after his release.[1]

If the official pardon was a bone of contention in Dreyfusism's inner circle, it also placed the enemies of Dreyfus on the defensive. Much to their chagrin, anti-Dreyfusards watched with dismay as public opinion shifted over the course of 1899 in favor of the revision. Indeed, the presidential pardon had only been made possible after the June 1899 elections produced a government dominated by cabinet ministers convinced of the captain's innocence. Some believed that part of the public's acceptance of the revisionist program had to do with images of heroism. Contending that "the maximum of intelligence . . . courage and, dare we say it, chivalry was on the same side as civil and military patriotism," the royalist Charles Maurras condemned the sham heroism of the Dreyfusards. Maurras explained the perceived heroism of the Dreyfusards as the result of several advantages: their defiant stance, the solitude of their campaign, and their early failures. Nevertheless, such men were "false heroes, heroes without heart and without reason."[2] In a striking repetition of Dreyfusard polemic, Maurras concluded that the revisionists had conquered public opinion only by enchanting the crowd with the illusion of heroism. Maurras was not alone in this view. The revolutionary syndicalist Édouard Berth maintained that the Dreyfus Affair was "a struggle between *les intellectuels et les militaires;* but, *chose prodigieuse,* the intellectuals seemed more heroic than the *militaires,* who were shown to be smooth talkers rather than men of action; and, in truth, there is nothing less military than our modern *militaires;* they are intellectualized, civilized, that is to say that they have lost the true sentiment of heroism and honor." Berth concluded that the only truly heroic act left in "our modern world in full degeneration" is that performed by "the producer on strike," the only "true modern hero." Significantly, such a heroic producer was the "*non-theoretical man,* the antithesis of the intellectual," a category of men that now seemed to encompass *les militaires* as well.[3]

Agitation on both sides of the political divide ensured that the Affair would not end with the 1899 pardon. Internecine squabbles and resentments within the revisionist party did not prevent the government from enacting religious and military reforms aimed at undoing the structures that made the Dreyfus Affair possible, thus in effect punishing anti-Dreyfusards. The rigid anticlericalism of Émile Combes, which was capped off by the separation of Church and state in 1905, was an affront to the revival of Catholicism that marked this period. For the radical right, the rehabilitation of Dreyfus in 1906 by the Cour de cassation (which the royalist Léon Daudet nastily dubbed the "Cour de circoncassation"),[4] dealt a formidable blow to the nation's integrity. If Émile Zola's body had been an divisive issue before and during the Affair, it was doubly so in its aftermath, when the government supported the interment of his remains in the Pantheon. This symbolic gesture outraged anti-Dreyfusards, who were far from conceding defeat in the Dreyfus Affair. The subsequent erection of monuments to Dreyfusard heroes across the nation only exacerbated this situation. "Nothing is finished" fumed the royalist Henri Vaugeois in 1909, and he was right.[5]

Part II considered the importance of gendered imagery to the Dreyfusard project. By insisting upon their heroically suffering yet physiologically superior bodies, the defenders of Dreyfus sought to distance themselves from Jews, crowds, and women, all of whom seemed to possess qualities that were readily displaced onto their anti-Dreyfusard enemies. In this way, the Dreyfusards tried to project a public image of manhood in the face of traditional associations of men of thought with weakness. Aside from engaging in duels and the occasional fistfight, however, most of these manly performances remained largely rhetorical or graphic, and, in an era where conceptions of manliness increasingly demanded proof of a more tangible nature, gestures such as these struck many as amounting to mere words rather than action. In other words, attempts by Dreyfusards to sustain a manly public image were fatally undermined by the emergence of a more muscular conception of masculinity during the 1890s, one that proved its virility through deeds that required force rather than simple assertions of physical vitality.

Although images of the health and comportment of the male body have been central to this account of manhood during the Dreyfus Affair, previous chapters have mainly considered these qualities as projections of Dreyfusard discourse rather than features actually embodied by revisionist men. Part III shifts the focus from the rhetoric of vitality in Dreyfusard polemics to this new emphasis on muscularity in the wider culture, and demonstrates where Dreyfusard projections of manhood ultimately foundered on the emergent discourse of force. By expanding the focus beyond the immediate concerns of the Affair, it considers how the gendered tensions wrought by the crisis reverberated in France for more than a decade, ultimately being invoked in the name of the "nationalist revival" of the prewar years. Chapter 5 begins this shift by inquiring into changing ideals about how the male body should appear. How did Dreyfusards' assertions of their own physical superiority relate to other changes that were taking place in the physical ideal of French manhood? Using as a springboard the portly body of Émile Zola, often cited as the embodiment of energy and virility, it examines the fin de siècle as a transitional period during which the once favorable figure of the prosperously corpulent man was slowly being eclipsed by that of the muscular and energetic athlete or bodybuilder. Within this context, the eating habits of bourgeois men were viewed as merely exacerbating the decadence wrought through their sedentariness, thus moving them even further from the martial athleticism that was presupposed in the ideology of adventure. Despite the centrality of dining out as a homosocial ritual in the nineteenth century, growing concerns about the physical decay of the bourgeoisie centered attention on the unhealthy lifestyle of this social elite, particularly as a gluttonous appetite began to signify an abandonment to sensual desires that was criticized as one of the unfortunate consequences of modernity. With lifestyles that otherwise tended to clash, in this case, litterateurs and bourgeois men were both castigated for existing only in their stomachs. These shifting ideals were even manifested in some of the polemics directed against Zola, thus compelling his allies to downplay the novelist's obesity and reputation for gluttony by emphasizing the sheer willpower he demonstrated by dieting. For them, Zola's mastery of his own body was an essential prerequisite to his manly stance during the Affair and was cited as further evidence of Dreyfusard virility.

Although Zola's heroic weight loss could suggest the superiority of the Dreyfusard body, by the dawn of the twentieth century, the French were looking for more impressive evidence of manhood. Interest in gymnastics and team sports had developed modestly in the 1880s and 1890s, but after 1900, they experienced explosive growth, amid lingering fears that Frenchmen were overly cerebral and physically stunted. As a new emphasis on physical fitness took hold of the male imagination, the figure of the *intellectuel*, considered virtually synonymous with the functionary, was further reduced to its professional dimension.

The cultural crisis wrought by the Affair reverberated throughout the prewar years. The political authority of the "Republic of Letters" seemed to have solidified with the creation of a pro-Dreyfus cabinet, the pardon of Dreyfus, and the parliamentary victory of the *bloc des gauches* a few years later, but the subsequent crises over clerical, military, and labor matters that ravaged the radical republicans brought *la révolution dreyfusienne* into disrepute and splintered the Dreyfusard coalition. Although historians have often acknowledged that the enemies of the radical republic waged their rhetorical campaigns partly by undermining the virility of the Dreyfusard state, thus demonstrating how the fallout of the Dreyfus Affair continued to color political debates right through World War I, these developments have usually been considered as elements of "prefascist" political discourses, without mentioning the gendered nature of such discourses. Chapter 6 outlines how continuing challenges to the manliness of victorious Dreyfusards were waged within an emerging culture of physical force, but examining the twists and turns of the radical republic from the perspective of gender politics is a task beyond its scope. After sketching the broad parameters of the culture of force, this final chapter focuses closely on the physical culture movement as one of the contexts in which the intellectual came under the heaviest fire. It concludes with a look at how political and gender critiques of intellectuals converged just before World War I in the so-called "generation of 1914," where young men defined themselves in terms of gender identity as well as generational politics.

CHAPTER FIVE

The Belly of Paris

Manhood, Obesity, and the Body of Zola

When Séverine interviewed Émile Zola in his home in early 1898, shortly after he published "J'accuse," she detected a note of asceticism in the rather Spartan interior of his study that seemed to conflict with her earlier impressions of him (which she obviously thought her readers would share). "Zola, an ascetic?" she asked. "Really? Yes. Don't be too quick to smile or gasp." The cultural ideal of the ascetic intellectual is an old one indeed. As Steven Shapin observes, it reflects the belief that "the truth-seeker is someone who attains truth by denying the demands of the stomach and, more generally, of the body."[1] Yet extending this image to the naturalist novelist would have struck many as laughable. After all, Zola's reputation as a successful novelist with a passion for fine food was quite well known, as was the rather considerable girth that he had acquired along the way. In fact, next to Sarah Bernhardt, Zola was the most frequently caricatured of French celebrities, which made him a readily recognizable figure at the end of the nineteenth century, so much so that when, some of his critics nastily dubbed him (after one of his novels) "the belly of Paris," everyone knew what they meant. Before-and-after caricatures often contrasted a younger, gaunt Zola scrounging for literary success with the older novelist who had grown fat through book sales. During the Dreyfus Affair, one cartoonist depicted Zola as a grotesque circus strongman, whose aberrant obesity is enhanced by the presence of tattoos, all of which suggested, in a carnivalesque fashion, the novelist's exotic distance from mainstream culture (Fig. 15). Contrary to these conventional images of Zola, Séverine noted a profound change in the novelist that seemed to explain the heroic gesture he had just made. "And one should believe it when I say that this new Zola . . . reveals himself, asserts himself in such a way that I never noticed before. . . . He is not pleasing to look at; he is not ugly either; in any case, he is neither pudgy nor brutish. In the end he is simply well-shaped, like one of those hunting dogs of Saint-Germain [the military academy], of a superior race."[2]

Fig. 15. C. Léandre, "Emile Zola," *Grand Guignol* 1, no. 6 (12 February 1898), cover. By permission of the Bibliothèque nationale de France.

Throughout this book we have seen how in the Dreyfusard imagination, the defense of republican ideals against the forces of religion and the military was no simple matter of political conviction; rather, taking up such a position was offered as proof of virile manhood grounded in a healthy body. Séverine's own comments may be interpreted in light of the caricatural attacks frequently launched against Zola's body, which served as a lightning rod for the period's anxieties about consumption and digestion. The belly was at once implicit and explicit in this imagery. Referring to the stomach and intestines, and functioning as a metonym for digestion itself, the belly has enjoyed an ambiguous history among the body's many parts. Ranking rather low in the hierarchy of senses proposed by the ancient Greeks, the stomach and intestines have often been denigrated as the organs closest to man's animal nature, despite Plato's admission that it was the duration of the digestive process that provided people with leisure time for philosophizing.[3] In conjunction with the genitals, the stomach has been taken as the seat of restive appetites that stand in a problematic relation to the body as a whole. When controlled through a rigorous dietetic regime, the appetites of the belly might testify to self-mastery, and, when used to adjust one's humoral balance, even to a form of self-fashioning. Allowed to roam freely, however, the belly's appetites threatened to subvert the whole completely, subordinating the masculinized rationality of the self to its own unruly passions. The fin-de-siècle cultural imagination was saturated with images of what might happen to men when such appetites were permitted free rein. From the seductive lure of department stores and belief in the sexual insatiability of prostitutes to the public's "devouring" of pulp novels, consumption had become a problematic category that found its apotheosis in the bloated belly.[4]

To cultural conservatives, Zola's belly sometimes signified the sensual complacency that had come with material success, but the novelist's intervention in the Affair shifted attention to other body parts, also embedded in the oral-digestive imaginary. Anti-Dreyfusards often denounced Zola as *la gueule*, a pejorative term for a gaping mouth that, in addition to its connotations of loud-mouthed or even bestial ranting, defined the opening of the digestive tract. Hence the French proverb "La gueule fait périr plus de gens que le glaive"[5]—words kill more people than the sword—and the use of the term *gueulard* to refer to a glutton as well as a loud-mouth. This polysemy is important for understanding how the *gueule* could be employed in relation to Zola, for the novelist and his works were scandalously associated with excretion and with excrement itself, thus allowing the alimentary trope to follow its logical course through the digestive process. Zola's well-publicized body signified to his enemies the baser aspects of organic life, from gaping mouth and substantial belly to fecal droppings, and threatened to undermine the lofty ideals to which he appealed. By drawing attention away from such issues, Séverine depicted the novelist as someone who had transcended the coarser dimensions of human corporeality. Quite in line with the tendencies of her Dreyfusard comrades, Séverine implicitly cast him as a man whose newly toned body signified his victory over the "flesh." Where others found proof of Zola's heroism in his renewed vigor and determination, Séverine happily observed that the "new Zola" was no longer fat, but "simply well-shaped."

Digestive imagery offers a rich and largely unexamined terrain for inquiries into fin-de-siècle culture. After an introductory survey of the relationships among eating, digestion, excretion, and personal identity, this chapter considers the relationship of Zola's body to the emerging cult of slenderness and muscularity, which targeted the obese belly as one of the conspicuous signs of sensual excess and a lack of self-control. While few today would deny the crushing impact that this anti-obesity campaign has had on the bodies and self-images of Western women, it is an exaggeration to claim, as one scholar has recently done, that men "are under no such size restrictions and are allowed—often encouraged—to take up as much space as they can get away with."[6] This chapter does not so much seek to redress a scholarly imbalance as to explore the relationship between male obesity and conflicting ideals of masculinity at the time of the Dreyfus Affair, and provides a glimpse into the tensions that haunted Dreyfusards' affirmations of their physical superiority. The decline of the fat man or, more specifically, the emerging idea that manhood and obesity were mutually exclusive qualities, must be understood within the tangle of a series of cultural anxieties, from standard medical warnings about the emasculating potential of the sedentary lifestyle to a renewed emphasis on bodily strength and vigor at the dawn of the twentieth century. Despite the dubious nature of the digestive organs, a large belly had for years served as a symbol of male power, health, and prosperity. By the end of the century, boasting a large belly could no longer be seen as an unproblematic sign of any of these qualities. Zola himself seemed to have sensed this imminent shift, for by the time of the Affair, he had been adhering to a strict dietary and exercise regimen for nearly a decade. That this fact was amplified by many of his admirers as further proof of Dreyfusard willpower testifies to the importance of the manly body to revisionist rhetoric.

"The Colon is King"

The campaign at the end of the nineteenth century that emphasized slimmer and more muscular bodies was built upon age-old preoccupations with the eating habits and lifestyles of social elites, and while physicians and health reformers were at the forefront of this movement, the growing contempt for flabbiness and bulk as evidence of moral softness was equally evident in nonmedical circles. However important acquiring the proper body shape would become during this period, this was no simple matter of external appearances but implied as well a collection of assumptions and prescriptions about the inner workings of individuals that the mirror did not reflect. Before considering the relationship between thinner bodies and the rhetoric of the Dreyfus Affair, we must consider how the anti-obesity campaign fitted into a wider culture of the abdomen, where culinary sensibilities were often at odds with the dictates of digestive hygiene. In particular, I shall address the relationship between diet and digestion and an emerging focus on physical force as the guarantor of manliness.

Variations in the cultural understanding of "force" during the nineteenth century, and the growing belief that one must acquire this quality in order to be considered truly healthy, attest at once to subtle developments in French ideals of vitality as well as a reconsideration of a common term employed during the Dreyfus Affair. When employed in relation to living beings, "force" referred broadly to "energy" and the "power to act," but here it was open to many shades of meaning. Suggesting on one level the basic quantum of energy that would enable a living being to act on its environment (a synonym for physical vigor and robustness), "force" could also denote a wider range of physical, moral, and intellectual qualities, such as "force of character" or "force of the soul," that were not necessarily grounded in muscle power. In other contexts, however, "force" suggested constraint and was even considered synonymous with coercion and violence.[7] *La force* was thus an ambiguous concept at best: while denoting power, strength, and vigor, virtues espoused by many men during the Belle Époque, it could also imply authority, command, and violence, thus calling to mind the brutal imposition of armed might that many associated with the army. It was also a slippery concept, for the physiological benefits of force always contained the potential for abuse: from the modest and benign ability to act on one's environment, it could be twisted into acts of violence and repression. Whereas Chapter 6 considers how the slippage between these two related conceptions of force allowed for sustained critiques of cerebral men during the prewar years, here we shall consider how a growing emphasis on energy helped to structure changing perceptions of the ideal male body.

In strictly physiological terms, "force" referred to the circulation and expenditure of energy within the bodily economy, where a surplus or deficit in one area could mean the difference between health and illness. While it was possible to speak of force in gender-neutral terms and thus extend it to discussions of female physiology, the perceived relationship between vitality and manhood was, as we saw in Chapter 2, virtually isomorphic. Insofar as it implied action and willpower, force was a quintessentially masculine quality, an inner reserve of vitality that allowed one to battle fatigue and to maintain physical and moral equilibrium. It is therefore unsurprising that someone lacking vigor could be described as *lâche*, as evincing a certain looseness or relaxation of tension that, when used as a substantive, also denoted a coward.[8] On the other hand, expenditures of force through muscular effort, nervous tension, and sexual or gustatory excess threatened to deplete the body's store of energy, thus weakening the organism to dangerous levels. In his surprisingly candid diary, the philosopher Henri-Frédéric Amiel equated manliness with physical robustness in terms of the capacity for resistance that was lacking in more refined social circles: "The stronger one is, the less sensitive he is to all that torments, agitates, worries and upsets worldly people. Robustness is a suit of armour and consequently a source of freedom. Vulnerability is a hard servitude. *Vae debilibus!* Woe to the weaklings!"[9] Among physiologists and health reformers concerned with physical and mental fatigue, the maximization of force and the dream of an inexhaustible body remained ideals well into the twentieth century, and formed the background to the hygienic movement that gathered momentum during the 1890s.[10] As Gilbert Andrieu observes, the "utility of force . . . finds itself in all the preoccupations of the republican man, the secularist and moralist, who sees the roots of progress in the development of force and its control through willpower."[11]

For those who eschewed the "art of living" that attention to hygiene and dietetics implied, the world of patent medicines and dubious devices promised quick and easy measures for the recuperation of force. Le Vin Désiles, for instance, was a popular "regenerating tonic" that seemed perfect for all ailments, and while it promised some benefits for women (as did most products), men clearly formed its target group. An intriguing blend of quinine, coca, kola, cocoa, lime phosphate, iodo-tannic solution, and an unnamed "special" ingredient, this product promised to restore to men the "force, vigor, and health" that had been

Fig. 16. Advertisement for Herculex, *Le Petit Journal,* November 1902, 375.

sapped away due to the "muscular or nervous weakness caused by fatigue, long nights, [and] study."[12] The list of such questionable remedies and even more questionable devices is extensive and worthy of a study in its own right. "Do you lack vigor?" inquired one especially provocative advertisement (Fig. 16): "Do you feel the need for renewed force? Have the abuses of youth or the excesses of adulthood left an imprint on you, such as: spermatorrhea, kidney problems, seminal losses, nervousness, impotence, varicoceles, atrophy of the organs?" If so, then "Dr. Sanden's 'Herculex' electric belt" could be the answer, allowing the wearer to be rejuvenated overnight while "a real current of life and force [penetrates] the weakened organs, curing them while you sleep." In promoting this veritable "fountain of youth for men," the Herculex ad skillfully invoked French anxieties about depopulation and physical decline through its explicit emphasis on muscular and sexual potency—in the image accompanying the text, a rejuvenated nude man hefts a baby boy (presumably the fruit of his reinvigorated loins) while electric sparks fly from his Herculex-clad waist.[13]

Regaining energy was also a central component of the self-help medical manuals of the time. Of course, maximizing physical vitality and well-being had always been the aim of such literature; but around 1900, publishers began to emphasize the virtues of force more explicitly by incorporating vivid buzzwords obviously aimed at tapping into (if not creating) an anxious new market. Manuals with fairly descriptive and neutral titles remained, but they were now joined on the shelf by more ominous appeals to the imperiled customer forced into a defensive posture. A spate of "how to" manuals published in 1900 proclaimed this emphasis on corporeal defense, such as *Comment on se défend contre la neurasthénie*, *Comment on se défend des maladies*, and *Comment on défend ses organes intimes*. The world had become a dangerous place, it seems, requiring one to be kept abreast, as one author suggested, of the *Amis et ennemis du corps humain* (1905). Although the preservation or recuperation of health and manhood may have been subtly woven into older manuals, increasingly, the crisis of masculinity was emphasized. In many cases, male weakness was assumed from the start, not to mention required for book sales, as the rhetoric of defense was complemented by the promise of metamorphosis as suggested by books like *Comment devenir énergique?* (1901), *Comment devenir fort* (1902), *Comment on devient beau et fort* (1905), and *Comment on devient robuste* (1909). If the need for robustness was not apparent enough in these titles, a manual entitled *La Santé virile par l'hygiène* (1901) made this imperative more explicit. Finally, where both men and women were the target audience, the various benefits of hygiene were often gendered into the complementary categories of manly force and feminine beauty, as in *L'Art de conserver la santé et de vivre longtemps. Forces viriles. Beautés féminines* (1907) and *Force et beauté pour tous* (1908).

In these texts, diet and digestion were often cited as domains where force could be easily depleted. "Someone once thought it was good to define a man as a brain served by organs. He should have said the opposite: it is the organs of vegetative life whose functioning dominates the rest."[14] Even though Dr. F. Aumont made this claim in 1908, similar affirmations of the relationship between digestion and personal identity appeared frequently in medical literature. Despite the profusion of such claims among doctors, gastronomes, and eaters of every stripe, however, in the history of the body, matters pertaining to the stomach, intestines, and other viscera rank among the least explored aspects of corporeal experience. Of course, to some extent the influence of dietetic knowledge over culinary practice had waned in the modern period as gastronomy sanctioned the experience of moderate gustatory pleasure without direct reference to health matters (and thus contrasted the gastronome's self-restraint to the gourmand's coarser appetites).[15] Yet this relative detachment of dietetics and cuisine did not mean that people were any less concerned about the relationship between personal well-being and the food they ate. Rather, throughout the nineteenth century, the nature, quality, and quantity of what one consumed played a central role in physical and moral health. Dietetics thus continued to serve as a critical site for self-fashioning. As we have seen, the science of puericulture supplied mothers with medical advice on diets that would promote conception and produce healthy children, and was even cited as a means of determining the sex of the fetus. In fact, advice manuals were filled with recommendations for how to conceive sons. In most cases, it was argued that the sex of the stronger partner determined the sex of the child. The health of the sperm and egg depended upon the amount of nitrogen (*azote*) that resided in each. Women wishing for a son were advised to follow a regimen rich in nitrogenous foods, with generous helpings of meat, and regular exercise. Prospective fathers received the opposite advice. For them, white meat, vegetables, and longer periods of rest were essential.[16] And procreation, if not definitely proven to be more readily facilitated by a vegetarian diet, certainly wasn't being assisted through meat eating, particularly if one accepted the rather circumstantial evidence that the declining French birthrate was paralleled by a rise in meat consumption.[17]

Matters of digestion were also directly associated with the strengths and weaknesses of the self, particularly in terms of morality. In the medieval and early modern periods, the dominance of humoral physiology made it possible for Western medicine to draw close connections between digestion and the moral complexion of the person, and such liaisons were often noted well into the nineteenth century. "The serpent is in man," Victor Hugo proclaimed. "It is the intestine. The belly is a heavy burden; it disturbs the equilibrium between the soul and the body. . . . It is the mother of vices. The Colon is King."[18] A similar perspective was offered by Anthèlme Brillat-Savarin, the master of early nineteenth-century gastronomy, who asserted: "Digestion is of all the bodily operations the one which has the greatest influence on the moral state of the individual. This assertion will astonish nobody, and cannot be contradicted." So convinced was Brillat-Savarin of this fact that he even proposed classifying the entire civilized world into the three categories of the regulars, the constipated, and the diarrhetic. Men of letters, he mused, could easily have their works explained in terms of the state of their bowels, for whereas writers of comic pieces counted among the most regular of men, tragedies obviously sprang from constipated bowels, and pastoral works from diarrhetic ones. Here the physiologist of taste offered a rather unique physiology of letters, in which "the most tearful poet is separated from the funniest by no more than a certain degree of intestinal activity."[19]

The management of one's bodily economy was central to modern hygienic literature, which drew attention not only to what one ate but to how one ate it. Despite their widespread popularity, stimulants like coffee, tea, and tobacco have always been discouraged by physicians as contributing to digestive fatigue and nervousness, and by the end of the nineteenth century, the effects of alcohol were almost universally condemned. Ailments like indigestion (or dyspepsia) sprang from unhealthy eating habits, from irregular mealtimes and hasty eating to incomplete chewing, all of which placed stress on the stomach and intestines, especially when coupled with the ingestion of stimulants. Like neurasthenia, dyspepsia was seen mainly as a scourge of the bourgeois professional and yet another symptom of modernity's corrosive effects on the male body. Dr Samuel Tissot had indicated in the eighteenth century how poorly the man of letters digested his food and made similar observations about the rich diet of social elites.[20] A century later, the quintessential dyspeptic was, as one doctor observed, "a man overtaxed by daily pursuits, constant preoccupations. . . . Journalists, commercial employees, doctors, [and] all busy men are tributaries of dyspepsia."[21] As indigestion and nervousness were viewed as twin complaints of white-collar man, some physicians posited a causal relation between the two. In fact, intestinal complaints were considered a virtually universal feature of nervous exhaustion, so common in fact that physicians like Frantz Glénard and Charles Bouchard were convinced that neurasthenia was itself an effect of more fundamental gastrointestinal disorders. That experts on neurasthenia usually cited Glénard and Bouchard only to dispute their findings did not deter the makers of nostrums and purgatives from capitalizing on the belief that most ailments could be traced to the colon.[22]

Overeating, or *suralimentation*, represented one of the major problems faced by the bourgeoisie, and was often linked to the onset of neurasthenia and morbid emotivity. Like many of his colleagues, Charles Féré recommended that it be "the object of very strict surveillance."[23] Whereas a good appetite had once signified health, by the fin de siècle, it was becoming hard to distinguish the physiological drive of hunger from the caprice of mere appetite, no doubt fired by the expanding array of seductive dishes. "We have wrongly been enraptured with the gluttonous and unruly appetite that, on the contrary, should have awakened apprehensions," observed one author. "It only rarely corresponds to a real need."[24] The great educator of the will, Jules Payot, who passed on many dietary prescriptions to his readers, discouraged the drinking of coffee and alcohol, which he regarded as dangerous stimulants. Like many of his colleagues, Payot conveyed concerns that were at once physiological and moral. Viewing cafés and brasseries as sites of immorality and loose women, Payot discouraged young men from cavorting in such locales with lazy bon vivants. Observing that young men "eat in restaurants two or three times more meat than they need," Payot also concluded that "we eat too much, and too much meat above all." So greatly did the digestive process fatigue the organism that much of the energy acquired through the digestion of food went right back into digestion itself. Rather than being masters of themselves, gluttons were slaves at once to their sensual appetites and to their own viscera: "Isn't it clear that men who eat too much are pure animals reduced to the hardly honorable role of servants of their digestive tract?"[25]

Even more dire consequences awaited the man who could not control his appetite, a fate that no amount of exercise could prevent. "The man who eats too much for his digestive capacities is without a doubt doomed to autointoxication; because if he can (in a strict sense) burn his excess fat, sugar, and *albuminose* through exercise, sport, and oxidants, he can do nothing of this sort against the *toxins* with which he is saturated."[26] While invoking age-old preoccupations about intestinal cleanliness, the hygienic surge inspired by microbiology encouraged widespread concerns at the fin de siècle with personal cleanliness and a fashionable attention to the *dépuration* (purification) of one's internal organs. They also provided elites with yet another way of distinguishing themselves from the vile-smelling populace, this time through the careful cleansing of one's most private areas.[27] Proper hygiene became a veritable obsession of the bourgeoisie, especially when it came to washing away alimentary impurities. Charles Bouchard's theory of intestinal autointoxication achieved a remarkable currency during this time, dovetailing with findings being made by physicians across the Western world. It was through widespread concerns about autointoxication that anxieties regarding modernity became refracted through the body's excretory system. While some moral reformers criticized the extensive nature of this dietary preoccupation, charging that for every patient cured by such prescriptions, a hundred more were driven into some degree of hypochondria, no one could ignore this widespread obsession with the vagaries of digestion.[28]

Many of these concerns came together in the most famous decadent novel of the period, J.-K. Huysmans's *À rebours* (1884). By most accounts, the novel's protagonist, Duc Jean des Esseintes, stands as the epitome of the decadent sensibility that pervaded many elite circles during the 1880s, and his immersion in the unnatural has often been treated with reference to his sexual "inversions." Yet it is crucial to recall that sensual experimentation is not the end point of Des Esseintes's flight from the natural, for ultimately it is a doctor who shows him just how far one can go in his quest to live against nature. With Des Esseintes's stomach so weakened that it cannot bear to ingest food taken orally, the physician prescribes a special enema that shoots concoctions of peptone and liquefied food directly into his colon, astoundingly transforming his anus into a mouth. This is the penultimate moment of the novel, for Des Esseintes "could not help congratulating himself on the event, which was the coping stone, the crowning triumph, in a sort, of the life he had contrived for himself; his predilection for the artificial had now, and that without any initiative on his part, attained its supreme fulfillment! A man could hardly go farther; nourishment thus absorbed was surely the last aberration from the natural that could be committed."[29] Fascinated by this unexpected turn, Des Esseintes begins to experiment with his own recipes for his anally administered meals, just as he had previously done with exotic fragrances. The stomach problems from which Des Esseintes suffers, including dyspepsia, constipation, and loss of appetite, attest vividly to the nervous exhaustion that has rendered him "effeminate"; yet the correction of these problems also signals the end of his decadent retreat from the world. Once he is again able to take food orally, his doctor insists that he return to the city and to a more normal life.

Naomi Schor suggests that Des Esseintes's inverted nourishment is a displaced form of sexuality, paralleling the sexual inversion of the decadent male.[30] While this interpretation has merit, we must also consider that if this aristocrat finds anality to be the supreme form of decadence, many bourgeois were using enemas and laxatives as almost daily components of personal hygiene.[31] The theory of autointoxication built upon older ideas about the relationship between the bowels and the mind and in many respects exacerbated anxieties that were already in place.[32] Explaining that *dépuratifs* were useful for expelling morbid humors in the blood from the body and arresting the effects of infectious germs, one physician recommended purging oneself once or twice a year, "primarily in accordance with changes in the seasons."[33] According to Henri Parville, a medical columnist for the high-brow *Annales politiques et littéraires*, his readers undertook a spring cleaning of a very intimate nature in April. As holiday celebrations throughout the winter often resulted in overeating and fatigue of the digestive tract, many felt compelled to purge their intestines of toxins soon after the weather turned warm. "We tell ourselves: Let's clean," Parville quipped. During this season "each person testifies to his own predilection, this one for *limonades*, that one for soda or magnesium salts. . . . There are [purgatives] for every taste and every income."[34] "Force and beauty" were not only the benefits

22 février 1890   L'ILLUSTRATION   N° 2453 — 175

Fig. 17. Advertisement for Purgatif Géraudel, *L'Illustration,* 22 February 1890, *annonces,* 175.

promised by the Purgatif Géraudel, for instance, but the hygienic aim of men and women throughout the Belle Epoque (Fig. 17).[35]

As the cleansing of filth from the body remained at the center of this respectable attention to intestinal purity, the proliferation of digestive advice and practices among the bourgeoisie may even have enhanced the power of scatological imagery to scandalize its targets. Despite the fact that the use of excremental representations invoked older conventions of invective with roots deep in folk tradition, one can see evidence in the numerous caricatures of Zola that anxieties about digestion and feces spilled over into the political realm. In his study of the popular sensibilities that circulated in the bawdy works of Rabelais, Mikhail Bakhtin demonstrates how the grotesque body of premodern Europe provoked an ambivalence about bodily functions that was never manifested as a simple rejection. Indeed, the grotesque body was treated as unfinished and as always overflowing its boundaries, thus continually integrating the "higher" functions with the "lower material bodily strata" where digestive, excretory, sexual, and reproductive functions are based. Bakhtin notes that this conception of a body creatively engaged with natural cycles of decay and regeneration became gradually marginalized during the modern era, to be replaced by an image of the body as a closed surface.[36]

The ambiguous premodern status of fecal matters would be lost under bourgeois conceptions of the body, thus allowing excremental imagery to stand as unequivocal strategies of debasement. "The ruling classes were obsessed with excretion," Alain Corbin explains. "Fecal matter was an irrefutable product of physiology that the bourgeois strove to deny. Its implacable recurrence haunted the imagination." Such personal repugnance was always mediated by the hierarchizing processes of distinction and displacement, for the bourgeois typically "projected onto the poor what he was trying to repress in himself. His image of the masses was constructed in terms of filth."[37] In middle-class conceptions of the body, the boundary between self and society cut right through the organism itself, transforming the walls of the digestive tract into yet another surface that required regular maintenance and surveillance. One medical journalist, Émile Gautier, highlighted the intestine as "the dangerous zone of our organism, the real chink in our armor," where the toxins of the outside world threatened bodily integrity from the inside. Here the metaphorical identification of criminals as dangerous "microbes" in the social body was reproduced in the personal microcosm. Gautier revealed that "excrement is the preferred milieu" of all of the microorganisms that enter the body through food, thus rendering it "the seat of abominable putrid fermentations." What we need is a counterweight to these pathogens, he concluded, "a police force composed of good microbes capable of indefinitely opposing the multiplication of the enemy with fresh troops." Praising the recent discovery of *Bacillus bulgaricus* (the "good microbes" whose presence in yogurt seemed to explain why the Bulgarians, who consumed vast amounts, enjoyed such longevity), Gautier saw in Dr. Chevretin's yogurt pills all the benefits of this friendly bacteria, without all the yogurt. Thanks to this product, Gautier concluded, the "liberty of the stomach—the most precious of all liberties—is guaranteed."[38]

"A Good Cock is Never Fat"

While dyspepsia, neurasthenia, and autointoxication sowed their damage on the inside of the body, obesity was the most spectacular consequence of overeating, an affliction that, although it affected both men and women, had more dire gender consequences for the former. In *Fat History: Bodies and Beauty in the Modern West*, the social historian Peter Stearns explores the relationship between diet and social life and provides some clues for thinking about the possible connections between obesity and masculine identity. Stearns traces parallel developments in dieting and body images in France and the United States, pointing out that beginning in the 1890s, each country copied the other when it came to denigrating obesity and obsessing over weight loss. What makes this comparative study so compelling is its focus on two Western countries that today represent polar opposites, with America reputed to have the most obese people in the world and France boasting the thinnest population of all Western countries. Stearns repeatedly makes the point that men suffered as well as women from the growing contempt for obesity at the turn of the century, but he does not explore this development in terms of gender identities. This is most evident in his assertion that, unlike Americans, the French were not primarily compelled to diet through moral imperatives resulting from a relaxation of religious rules. Rather, he writes, in France, "there was no full link between overweight and combating the evils of a consumer society. Overweight was a health problem or a fashion problem to be addressed in those terms."[39] Stearns uses the term "moral" in its restricted sense, referring to traditional ethical constraints kept in place by religious injunctions toward self-sacrifice, the very thing that was quickly declining in American life by century's end. In America, dieting thus became a moral counterweight to consumer indulgence as new areas of discipline were created to compensate for the loosening bonds of religion. The body became the site of these new disciplinary measures: "A good body, defined now by self-restraint, was a vital sign of moral quality."[40]

"Why were the obese so hard to treat?" Stearns asks of the French scene: "Because [in the eyes of contemporaries] they were often 'nervous, impulsive, unstable, weak-willed.'"[41] It is surprising that Stearns glides so quickly over what the French considered to be at the heart of obesity, for in so doing he passes up an opportunity to explore the complexity of obesity as a gender issue. Not only were such traits as nervousness, impulsiveness, and a lack of willpower "moral" attributes, at least in the broad sense of the term, but, as we have seen in Chapter 3, they were also explicitly gendered qualities that meant different things for men and for women. We have seen how physicians had emphasized the amorphousness of female psychology, arguing that an inherent instability rendered women especially prone to nervousness and more subject than men to the demands of the flesh. This is not to say that women were not often implored to perform feats of self-denial that might attest to their solid moral standing—indeed, numerous examples of female self-abnegation in the nineteenth century illustrate this fact. Rather, these gendered medical assumptions in a sense provided women with a moral safety net when they erred. Although unfortunate and perhaps even embarrassing, lapses of the female will ultimately testified to what most men considered the natural weakness of women, which meant that nervous, weak-willed women were still safely within the parameters of their sex. The fate of the so-called "fasting girls" in the hands of nineteenth-century physicians vividly illustrates this point. By diagnosing them as anorectics, doctors were able to explain the female refusal of food by reference to a irrational compulsion rather than conscious design, thereby transforming what might have been viewed as an act of will into a simple subordination to a fixed idea.[42] There is thus a gender dimension to the issue of obesity and weight loss that is implicit but undeveloped in Stearns's work. When not reduced to a hereditary or glandular problem, the fact of obese individuals attested to a failure of the will, suggesting a person's inability to overcome the demands of the flesh: "What compounds the difficulty of treatment," noted one physician, "is that nearly all fat people suffer from a veritable intellectual apathy; among them the force of will has diminished considerably."[43] For all of the scorn heaped upon her, a weak-willed woman still qualified as feminine (despite her straying away from conventions of female beauty), while a weak-willed man was no man at all, at least not in any normative sense.

We have already seen how "educating the will" continued the long cultural process whereby a sense of a discrete individuality was being carved out by members of the bourgeoisie, allowing them at once to distance themselves from their own bodily functions while displacing anxiety about those functions onto other social groups. Scholars have only recently begun to explore diet and the management of appetite as providing an important arena for the construction of such an identity.[44] We have seen above how overeating was discouraged on medical grounds, but there are social dimensions to these prescriptions that cannot be ignored. The sociologist Stephen Mennell claims that a veritable "civilizing of appetite" had been under way at least since the mid eighteenth century, when instances of extreme gluttony were increasingly described as throwbacks to earlier manners. With the rising bourgeoisie aping the aristocracy at every step, Mennell argues, new practices of social distinction were installed at the level of refined eating habits rather than in the quantity of food consumed. One effect of these new practices was a growing contempt for gluttony and the physical excess it sometimes wrought. This seems to have been the case with King Louis XVI, whose excesses at the table were noted with surprise and even contempt, whereas less than a century before, the gluttony of Louis XIV and his court had been considered more or less acceptable.[45] Such themes came to a head on the eve of the French Revolution, where references to the fatness of the "pig-king" were often coupled with revelations about his sexual impotence, providing early evidence of a growing distance between obesity and emerging ideas of manhood.[46]

A more pronounced shift toward thinner bodies took place around the 1890s and coincided with growing concerns about pathologies of the will and the increasing sedentariness of the nation's elite. The shameful victory of appetite over self-control was inscribed in the fat man's belly, which signified the intersection of modernity's material abundance and sensual pleasures with the physical decline of men. The fact that most physicians described the accumulation of fat as an "invasion" (*envahissement*) suggested the penetration of the body proper by a kind of foreign substance, even if that substance too was part of the body.[47] As we shall see below, there was an inverse relationship between obesity and manliness, and not even Napoleon himself was immune. The hygiene reformer Georges Hébert contended that Napoleon's career went downhill from the first signs of weight gain in 1806 through 1809, when "he was frankly obese."[48] Nevertheless, one should not conclude that the fat man found his gendered opposite in the thin man. Rather, physical puniness suggested that same muscular atrophy that was concealed beneath the fat man's bulk, which is why the qualities attributed to the obese bore a more than passing resemblance to the neurasthenic, the epitome of failed (rather than simply deviant) manhood at the fin de siècle. Insofar as both were marked by sexual impotence, muscular weakness, and diseases of the will, the fat man and the gaunt neurasthenic were considered weaklings far removed from the normative masculine standards of the day. While neither of these male figures were pathologized to the same extent as criminals, sexual deviants, homosexuals, and the insane, the fact that homosexuals and Jews could be characterized either by their puniness or their flabbiness revealed how these physical traits could slip between the normal and the pathology. However they were conceptualized, all these figures stood outside of the vaguely defined sphere of heroic male volition and thus risked slipping into vice of every sort.

Although fat people had often provided aesthetic fodder for caricaturists throughout the modern period, one does not encounter many self-help manuals devoted to weight loss before the 1890s, after which obesity became a "disease" that threatened to diminish the force of men and the charms of women.[49] Four arguments allowed physicians to successfully gender the fat man as feminine in the eyes of contemporaries, all of which sketched sharp contrasts to what was considered normative masculine behavior. First, physicians drew close connections between genital activity and digestive processes, and commonly suggested that fat men were sexually inadequate. Second, in an attempt to dispel the perceived equivalence between corporeal bulk and manly strength, physicians emphasized repeatedly that a large body often concealed an inner weakness, both in terms of the energy burned off and the body's capacity for physical force. Third, they invoked widespread anxieties about pathologies of male volition to suggest that fat men lacked willpower and initiative. Finally, there was a colloquial sense, supported more often by cultural stereotypes than by medical knowledge, that obesity was somehow connected to Jewishness and homosexuality, both of which represented styles of manhood far removed from the norm.

Insofar as they envisioned the body as an inner economy where the excessive expenditure of energy in one area threatened to diminish it in other parts, physicians posited a relationship between digestion and genital activity that has often been overlooked in histories of sexuality. Under normal circumstances the functions of the stomach do not provoke a loss of equilibrium, an 1852 text on impotence noted, although extremely obese people sometimes find it functionally difficult to copulate and in order to be successful must resort to sexual positions normally only adopted by libertines. Yet in cases of overeating, this physician observed, the stomach draws upon forces from throughout the body to compensate for this overexcitation. "Everyone knows that after a large meal, especially if one has imbibed spirituous liqueurs, the genital forces are far from responding to the ardors of desire."[50] So widespread was this belief that even Brillat-Savarin counseled his readers against undertaking sexual activity or even intellectual pursuits in the aftermath of a good meal.[51]

Concerns about the intersection of digestion and sexuality were easily transferred to the issue of obesity. When it came to matters of nutrition and digestion, one could not hope for a more authoritative guide than Charles Bouchard, whose take on obesity was nevertheless somewhat surprising, insofar as he insisted that neither overeating nor lack of exercise could be isolated as dominant causes of the disorder. On the contrary, in his writings, genital factors played an especially prominent role. Not only are women twice as disposed to obesity as men, Bouchard explained, but more than three-quarters of obese women become obese after pregnancy, that is, after "one of the acts of the genital life." An inverse development takes place among men, he noted, upon whom "genital activity has a slenderizing effect; on the contrary chastity or castration engender obesity."[52] The *Dictionnaire encyclopédique des sciences médicales* came to a similar conclusion about the relationship between virility and obesity: "Among obese men, the sexual instinct is in general barely developed; some are absolutely impotent." Like some of his colleagues, the author had recourse to an old French proverb to illustrate his point: "a good cock, they say, is never fat."[53] Another physician even observed the complete absence of spermatozoa in the semen of certain fat men, thus ruling out any possibility of conception.[54] Others contended that while fat men could conceive children, they would not be able to engender sons.[55] Not only did body weight become a more or less direct expression of one's capacity to procreate, but fat men came off as less virile than thin men, either by choice or by accident. Amid widespread natalist discourses and anxieties about depopulation, fat men visibly embodied their helplessness in the face of a national crisis.

This opinion was by no means unanimous, however, for physicians like Adrien Proust and Albert Mathieu found evidence that sexual excess could just as easily lead to obesity as to slenderness.[56] Nevertheless, their description of the classic obese weakling was explicitly gendered: "Weak, anemic, and plethoric fat people," they wrote, "are pale, fatigued, lifeless. . . . they are apathetic, drowsy, without energy and without courage." Significantly, this form of obesity was to be found most often among children and young people, and especially among girls.[57] Along with Bouchard, Proust and Mathieu also recognized a direct relationship between obesity and nervous disorders that suggested the femininity of overweight people. Bouchard, too, had noticed that hysteria was frequently accompanied by instances of monstrous obesity: "Given the predominant role that the nervous system plays in all nutritional changes," he wrote, "one should count on a close relationship between certain nervous disorders and obesity."[58] Such observations convinced many physicians of the need to treat the nerves as an indirect means of curing obesity and other digestive problems, and they often recommended conventional therapies such as hydrotherapy.[59]

Fat men were charged not only with being unable to engender children but with lacking the capacity for muscular force. Traditional popular beliefs were perhaps the most formidable obstacle for the physicians to overcome in the pathologization of obesity, especially since fat had once seemed synonymous with strength and well-being. In premodern popular culture, Mikhail Bakhtin notes, the grotesque body was treated as unfinished and always overflowing its boundaries, thus continually integrating the "higher" functions with the "lower material bodily strata" where digestive, excretory, sexual, and reproductive functions reside. Obesity signified a healthy abundance that would by the modern period become denigrated as the ideal body was gradually depicted as closed and the lower strata isolated from conceptions of the whole.[60] The residue of this ideal lingered on in juxtapositions of bulky officers and shriveled intellectuals during the Affair. Medical opinion militated explicitly against such conventions, suggesting that what had been ordinarily considered a sign of vitality, potency, and force was in fact evidence of weakness and sterility. "Many men who seem vigorous exist only in their stomachs," explained the author of *La Santé virile par l'hygiène:* "the little real energy they have is concentrated there . . . they are certainly not as strong as they seem."[61] Another physician suggested close attention to the words typically used to describe fat men: "Let's ask these 'strong'—read 'bloated'—individuals, whom the vulgar believe enjoy perfect health, to perform some physical labor and our opinion will be *faite de coup.*"[62] The joys of frivolity and excess that Bakhtin found in the grotesque body no longer played a central role in a bourgeois culture where bodily strength was subordinated to productivity and the work ethic. No doubt part of the problem had to do with appearance, and Peter Stearns has noted cases in which aesthetics played a central role in the growing French disgust with obesity. Yet when it came to men, physical force rather than health or beauty was the primary consideration. It was not that obese men were simply unhealthy, but that they lacked the strength and productive power that were frequently expected of "true" men.[63]

As a crucial aspect of the kind of bodily control that signified masculine identity, willpower was seen as woefully lacking in most fat people. In the medical literature on obesity, one finds repeated references to the lack of will and "intellectual apathy" manifested by the obese, qualities that posed significant obstacles to treatment. The hygiene reformer Philippe Tissié regretted that so many of the obese lacked the "force of character" needed to lose weight: "for them their enemy is their own stomach."[64] Proust and Mathieu invoked the importance of will and perseverence as part of a manly triumph over the seductive allure of gustatory delights. "In order to stop gaining weight and to shed one's pounds," they wrote, "one must first of all possess great force of character. One must resist the temptations of the table, resist seduction and the bad habits one has acquired."[65]

This fantasy about the manly encounter with seductive food not only dovetails with broader anxieties about the sensual snares of modernity but invokes some of the ways in which the dining experience had been described in the nineteenth century: as a woman to be taken or an enemy to be overcome.[66] Thanks to medical intervention, the masculine credentials that were once confirmed through the gourmand's symbolic conquests could similarly be affirmed through the gastronomical chastity of *l'homme à régime.*

A variety of obesity treatments were available to the French during this period, from thyroid pills, massage, and exercise to a wide selection of dietary regimes. In fact, by 1912, obese people were offered at least twenty different weight-loss diets from several countries. A number of French spas had been identified as featuring waters whose laxative properties were considered especially conducive to weight loss; and the undisputed capital of obesity treatment was the sanatorium at Brides (Savoie), where taking the waters was complemented by a severe regime that reportedly produced the most favorable results.[67] A medical consultant at Brides, Dr Laissus, explained the various therapeutic measures practiced at the spa, which ranged from hot and warm baths in running water to massage, dietary restrictions, and the so-called "light bath" (*bain de lumière*). In the latter technique, the patient was hermetically sealed in a box whose interior was lined with up to eighty electric light bulbs. With only his head emerging from a hole in the top, the patient's body was subjected to temperatures of between fifty-five and sixty degrees Celsius for up to twelve minutes, after which he or she was removed from the box and wrapped in blankets before being ushered off to the shower. Through such practices, Laissus promised, most patients could expect to lose between twelve and twenty pounds in about three weeks.[68]

The cure that Laissus illustrated through a series of notable case studies suggested an interplay between doctor and patient that, despite its insistence on total submission to medical authority, nevertheless congratulated the male patient's ability to follow orders fully. Female patients, it was suggested, might require greater intervention. This was also the case in the United States, where in the eyes of physicians, male dieting confirmed a man's willpower, while female dieting reinforced the need for expert intervention.[69] Although this affirmation of the male patient did not exactly confirm free agency, it did attest to the exercise of the will in a manner that would allow for the conquest of obesity and the recovery of manhood. It is therefore striking that in his two case studies of male curists, Laissus selected men who could not have been considered utter weaklings before arriving at Brides. For example, Mr C . . . was a big eater and drinker who had steadily gained weight after performing his military service. Yet it was because he was "full of confidence and animated by a great desire to make a serious cure" that he was able to lose more than twenty-seven kilograms in less than two months. In order to explain this success, Laissus observed, "it is enough to show that he had willpower and that the doctor had much vigor [*fermeté*]." A similar scenario was illustrated in the case of Mr D . . . , who, despite being strong and muscular, "confessed readily that he had an enormous appetite and that he could not moderate it." Central to this patient's success was the "force of character" that allowed him to keep to a strict dietary regimen even after leaving the spa. When he returned the following season, he had become considerably more slender, so much so that the doctor hardly recognized him.[70]

The adolescent Miss B . . . was a very different case. This unfortunate fifteen-year-old, who weighed more than 125 kilograms, was "a formless mass nearly incapable of moving" and did not demonstrate much force of character. Initially believing that his firm instructions had made an impression on her, Laissus was later surprised to find steadfast opposition to his insistence that she reform her eating habits. "I realized that I would have difficulty with this capricious child," lamented the doctor, "and that I would need to double my energy and surveillance in order to triumph over this invincible apathy." After investing a great deal of personal attention in this case, Laissus eventually triumphed over his patient, who adhered to the prescribed dietary and exercise regimen with only occasional lapses.[71] Unlike that of the male patients, whose willpower seemed to complement the firmness of the physician, Miss B . . .'s participation in her own cure was barely acknowledged, affirming at once the perceived weakness of female volition and the physician's commendable ability to impose his own will on such recalcitrant patients.

While medical literature was not always explicit about the association between obesity and male weakness, in the early twentieth century, proponents of physical culture did not mince words in their wholesale assault upon the fat man. As we shall see in Chapter 6, experts concerned about the acquisition of muscular force were especially critical of the "soft" lifestyles led by many bourgeois men, and frequently saw flabbiness as evidence of such softness. Edmond Desbonnet, the period's best-known proponent of physical culture, promised a cure for obesity, stomach ailments, and neurasthenia in his chain of bodybuilding centers. In such circles, physique was a sheer matter of willpower and proper lifestyle, and little kindness was shown to those with a hereditary predisposition to obesity.

Among such individuals, "the aptitude to fatten is developed by the hygienic faults of the subject. . . . It is less the inevitable result of a temperament than the unhealthy administration of that temperament."[72] Hearkening back to Greek models of the ideal male body, physical culturists emphasized wide chests and slender waists that attested to strength as well as beauty, and called attention to the abdominal muscles as being central to a manly bearing. Fat men thus lacked beauty as well as willpower. "It is a waste for those men to live on the fifth floor," noted one expert: "If by chance they drag their fat to the top of their house, they breath noisily, their hearts palpitate, they are worn out, [and] they collapse into a chair; you would think they were about to die."[73] For the sake of the "regeneration of the race," which was one of the explicit aims of Desbonnet's magazine *La Santé par les sports*, it was imperative that the public stop confusing physical bulk (*grosseur*) with muscular force. By being more discerning in their choice of husbands, women might avoid procreating with a "ridiculous and horrible" fat man.[74] Of course, during the prewar years, the rhetoric of bodily force was no doubt more pervasive than the reality of an iron-pumping population; yet it is nevertheless evident that the ugly, weak, and perhaps impotent fat man was quickly becoming an object of ridicule. "A fat belly is synonymous with physical degradation,"[75] noted one physical culturist, while another put the matter quite baldly: "To be obese is to be disgraceful" (Fig. 18).[76]

Alongside these condemnations of how obesity afflicted "normal" men, it is worth noting how the cultural tendency to associate overweight with effeminacy also led to the notion that Jews and homosexuals were especially prone to this disorder. While in the eyes of some physicians acquisitiveness, base appetites, and sedentariness rendered Jews much more susceptible to obesity, anti-Semites were quick to note how the Jews had figuratively grown fat through their parasitical draining of the French body. "It was to fatten [*engraisser*] the Jews," Drumont alleged in *La France juive*, "that our soldiers succumbed, under the Republic, to typhoid fever in Tunisia."[77] Jewish obesity thus implied a voracious appetite that conflated the conventional ridicule of bourgeois gluttony with more fantasmatic anxieties about the vampiric drainage of men and nations. Homosexuals, on the other hand, were a group whose bodies were seen as bearing the softness that allegedly corresponded to their moral state. Physicians generally contended that obesity created men whose body shapes were "rounded, nearly feminine,"[78] so it is not surprisingly to find associations between obesity and men who displayed other "feminine" characteristics. In Paris, for example, the much

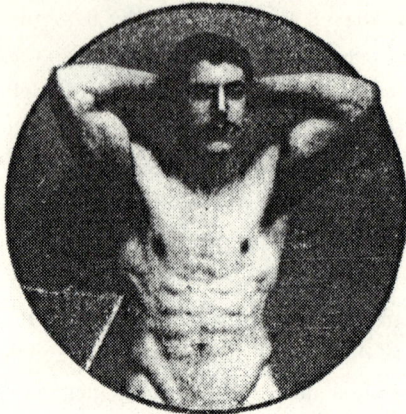

La Beauté, c'est la Santé.   La Laideur, c'est la Maladie.

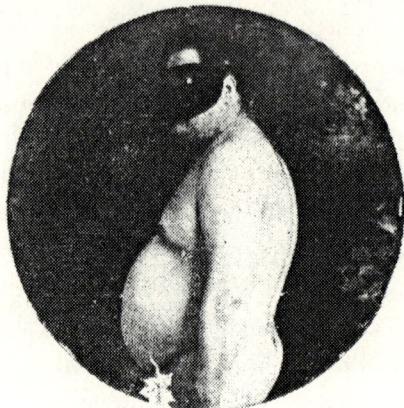

Fig. 18. Unsigned, "Comme quoi il est prouvé que la Beauté est un gage de Santé," *Santé par les sports*, 8 April 1913, 6. By permission of the Bibliothèque nationale de France.

publicized trial of Oscar Wilde generated a number of comments about the flabbiness of this "fat boy" that were obviously meant to confirm his gender transgression by citing his bodily signs.[79] Responding to a literary critic who described him as "almost feminine," moreover, Marcel Proust engaged directly with the perceived tension between virility and obesity: "The men who have acted as my seconds in duels will tell you if I have the flabbiness of the effeminate."[80] Some physicians were quite explicit about the association of obesity and homosexuality. Dr Émile Laurent reinforced the feminizing implications of obesity's connection with impotence by arguing that homosexuals were often marked by both, thus rendering them unfit either for marriage or military service. Afflicted in this manner, he claimed, such individuals were "in physical terms, hardly men at all."[81] Although the meaning of obesity varied from group to group, flabbiness in the Jew and the homosexual conjured up the same images of softness, looseness, and a lack of willpower that were identified in other fat men.

Zola's Body

Like other physical features that were capable of being caricatured, references to obesity appeared frequently in the literature of the Dreyfus Affair. Just as analyzing the comportment of Dreyfus seemed to reveal volumes about his soul, so too did the physiques of one's enemies provide fodder for sometimes scathing critiques, many of which concerned issues of diet and body shape. Joseph Reinach, for instance, remembered the "fat round man" who presided over the Esterhazy trial, Alexandre Délagorgue, whose appearance had "the florid hue of the gourmand."[82] During the Rennes trial, Maurice Barrès relished describing Dreyfus's lawyer, Fernand Labori, as "this fat boy" whose courtroom demeanor "never thrilled me except through the physical sight of his labors, and all the weight of his eloquence weighed upon the public in the same manner that his corpulence and his ardor weighed upon the floorboards that he bent."[83] Even when obesity itself was not at issue, one could easily cite abnormal eating habits as symptoms of mental disorder, as in the case of Esterhazy, who, as Reinach contended, "supported himself with alcohol, he ate too much, devouring his food."[84] As far as polemical strategy was concerned, all aspects of a man's moral and physical life were fair game.

In light of Zola's well-known physique and the gathering contempt for male obesity, it is safe to say that designating him the "belly of Paris" was no idle metaphor. Indeed, the novelist had since the 1870s been a frequent guest at the celebrated banquets of the literary brothers Jules and Edmond Goncourt and on more than one occasion had surprised his hosts with his culinary discernment and formidable appetite. In 1876, Jules de Goncourt observed "a Zola I never knew before, a Zola who was a glutton [*gueulard*], a gourmand, and a gourmet, a Zola spending all his money on food [*choses de la gueule*], running to food merchants and grocers of great renown, gorging himself on the best." In this, the heyday of modern French cuisine, even renowned gastronomes like the Goncourts were taken aback by Zola's obsession with food: "I fully understand the caprice of the stomach's imagination that compels one, every now and then, to have a fine, delicate, and original dinner, but to do so every day strikes me as intolerable."[85] Zola's reputation for gluttony and obesity was made quite clear in the wider culture, where the novelist's girth was often offered as evidence that he had become complacent about his literary success.

The novelist's immense appetite and refined tastes formed just one part of a well-known study of Zola carried out by Dr. Édouard Toulouse, a physician who ambitiously planned a multivolume series exploring the bodies and minds of famous intellectuals. Taking such a celebrated figure as a subject ensured that Toulouse's study would not be consigned to the commercial oblivion that awaited more specialized medical texts. On the contrary, his book attracted a readership among those who were at once familiar with the novelist's writings and interested in matters of health.[86] We have seen in Chapter 2 how some opponents seized upon the more negative conclusions that Toulouse drew about Zola's health, particularly his observations about the novelist's nervous temperament and his ranking of Zola among the "superior degenerates" who are often great culture heroes.[87] Yet the issue of Zola's obesity provided an important counterpoint to whatever unflattering effects such a diagnosis may have entailed, and it thus renders the impact of Toulouse's book ambiguous at best.

As Toulouse revealed in his case history of the novelist, Zola's obesity began at a fairly early age and increased as he grew older and more successful. In time, he began to experience physical difficulties that compelled him to rethink his daily regimen: "He was winded by the least physical effort." When Zola decided to start dieting in 1887 he weighed 192 pounds and his belly measured 1.14 meters around.[88] He began to regulate his eating and took up cycling every day. By the time of the Affair, he had dropped nearly twenty pounds, but still manifested a certain roundness reminiscent of his old self. Toulouse paid special attention to the novelist's nervous character, which in many circles would have suggested a psychological disposition more commonly found among women. Nevertheless, Toulouse countered the potentially negative effects of his appraisal by emphasizing qualities that would be easily construed as evidence of manliness. Zola was "Robust, energetic, tenacious, combative, composed and very reasonable despite his nervous troubles and some morbid thoughts."[89] Toulouse was particularly impressed by Zola's willpower, his "tenacity, his persistence in effort. We find this quality in everything he does. If a difficulty arises when he is working, he does not stop, he does not get up in order to divert his mind; on the contrary he remains at his desk, working intently on the obstacle and only breathing easy once he is free of it." This capacity to devote himself single-mindedly to his goal was the motor force behind Zola's professional success, and it "appeared also in his private life, for example, in his struggle against obesity. He is the man of combat who is impassioned and sustained by combat."[90]

Ironically, Zola himself had often expressed doubts about his capacity for self-mastery, and once confided to Goncourt that his own work habits owed more to nervous compulsion than to inner strength: "[Y]ou should not think that I have willpower, I am by nature the weakest being and the least capable of *entraînement*. In me the will is replaced by *l'idée fixe,—l'idée fixe* that makes me ill if I do not submit to its obsession."[91] On the one hand, this self-revelation accords well with Toulouse's general finding that Zola was at heart "truly a neuropath" who displayed traits of "nervous disequilibrium, [and] a really morbid exaggerated emotivity."[92] On the other hand, Toulouse made every effort to salvage the novelist's sense of manly self-control, which might have been forfeited by dwelling on nervous disorders, and underscored Zola's struggle against obesity as one aspect of his essentially robust nature, which made him a "man of combat" despite his condition as a "superior degenerate." It was perhaps for this reason that Zola remained quite pleased by the findings of Toulouse and thanked the doctor for presenting an analysis that showed such "great care for the truth while maintaining balance and a great deal of tact." Zola was especially pleased that revelations of his daily struggle for artistic creation might finally put to rest the old myths about him being a mere "beast of burden" (*boeuf de labeur*) who labored only for money. "Thank you for having studied and labeled my dirty laundry. I believe that I have benefited from it."[93]

Zola's heroic weight-loss through strict dieting was for Toulouse evidence of a strong will in action, a belief echoed by other contemporaries. In his 1903 memoirs of the Société des gens de lettres, of which Zola was president four times, the novelist Albert Cim eulogized Zola's "iron will," as shown by his notable weight loss. This was a transformation that "only the most energetic will could impose," declared Cim. "Haven't we gone so far as to claim that if, as big, heavy, and obese as he [Zola] was for thirty years, he became thin and slender at fifty, it was only *because he wanted it*, because he applied himself, tenaciously, to make himself diet? [emphasis in original]"[94] John Grand-Carteret, an amateur cultural critic who had written several books on caricature and the graphic arts at the height of the Dreyfus Affair, also extolled Zola's willpower. Ruminating on the difference between the fat Zola and the thin Zola, Grand-Carteret applauded the novelist's decision to confront his "disgraceful proportions" by exercising and controlling his appetite. Like Séverine, he too saw Zola's role in the Affair as a heroic struggle against injustice and the forces of tradition, and he noted that the novelist's timing could not have been better, "[B]efore hurling himself headlong into the struggle, Zola wanted first to obtain a victory over himself." Grand-Carteret saw in this physical reform something for others to emulate, a veritable conquest of the flesh that epitomized the manly will in action: "Whoever wants to go to war against human cowardice should first triumph over his own troubles. It was with this goal in mind . . . that Zola proclaimed, through his outward appearance, the rejuvenation and transformation of his person."[95] Grand-Carteret thus echoed a sentiment shared by many Dreyfusards of his day: the struggle against military lies and religious superstition required a manly stance best exemplified by Zola. The novelist's conquest of his own body was a beacon for those who also struggled for the light of Truth against the darkness of the flesh.

By the early twentieth century, male obesity signaled a lack of willpower that was out of step with the gender trends of the day. Insofar as demonstrations of heroic volition were considered essential to the body politics of the Affair, it is easy to see why Dreyfusards would exploit the masculine significance of Zola's diet and exercise regime. To the extent that the turn of the century was a transitional period in French attitudes toward weight, however, one does not encounter unanimous opinions about slenderness and obesity at this time. For instance, it was also during this period that the Michelin tire company introduced Bibendum, the jolly promotional figure whose impressive girth suggested the comfortable prosperity of those able to afford one of the new automobiles. Anti-Dreyfusard polemic, moreover, sometimes contrasted the robust corpulence of generals with the anemic slenderness of intellectuals (Fig. 4), thus revealing the persistence of older associations of bodily bulk with physical strength. Nevertheless, others challenged the idea that such bodies were reliable indices of prosperity or health: "We freely admit that a florid hue, a full body, augurs well; [yet] the 'healthy look' denotes in principle one thing: congestion."[96] While there is a certain cultural unevenness in responses to medical prescriptions about weight loss, it is nevertheless certain that the path toward a greater emphasis on body size was reinforced around 1900 by related obsessions with diet, digestion, and exercise.

CHAPTER SIX

The New Man and the Culture of Force

When the socialist Urbain Gohier learned in 1898 that he was being sued by two anti-Dreyfusard politicians for their portrayal in his scandalous book, *L'Armée contre la nation*,[1] he met with a friend to brainstorm legal strategies. They finally agreed that Gohier should seek counsel, and his friend telephoned a young lawyer of his acquaintance, who was also an admirer of Gohier's antimilitarist writings. Asked if he would represent Gohier, however, the young man's initial enthusiasm quickly faded.

> —Oh! là là! What are you saying? Don't play this terrible trick on me! To say that I admire Gohier is nothing. I love him. I praise him everywhere. If he needs some service, I am there for him. But not that, not that. First, I am not a deputy. For those things one is as good as condemned without a political lawyer. And then I tell you, because I cannot hide it: I am for force against thought.
> —What?
> —I said that *I am for force against thought.*
> —You?
> —Yes. One must be of one's time.

Soon after Georges Clemenceau learned of this exchange, he related it to the readers of *Aurore*. "Finally we have found a young man who, by simple probity of the soul, ingeniously summed up his epoch in one concise formula." Clemenceau's response well expressed the prevailing Dreyfusard view of *la force*, an often maligned concept that suggested the triumph of brutal domination over reasoned argument and justice. A catchword of social Darwinism, force also signified the energy that had to be expended in the struggle for life, as well as the violence of the crowd or of the thugs who were sometimes hired to disrupt Dreyfusard meetings and to harass prominent Dreyfusards on the streets or at their homes.[2] An attack on the president of the republic at a racetrack and Paul Déroulède's failed attempt at a coup were further evidence of how brutal force could become. The canes menacingly brandished by neoroyalist shock troops, the *camelots du roi*, were a constant reminder of force's tendency to slip into cruder forms of expression. Predicting the eventual victory of the Dreyfusard cause, Clemenceau responded with the recommendation that "young men who are still 'for force against thought' should hasten to profit from the moment." The time was coming, Clemenceau assured his readers, when the defenders of thought would put an end to the reign of force.[3]

Despite the creation of a pro-Dreyfusard cabinet, the retrial and pardon of Dreyfus in 1899, and the rise of radical republicans to power three years later, Clemenceau's prediction was only partly accurate. What this lawyer meant in claiming to prefer "force" is unclear. But in the years that followed, many more young men would sing the praises of force rather than thought, and in their minds the word did not necessarily denote the brutal circumvention of the law. Rather, force, energy, and action were asserted as cultural values intimately related to the idea of order, at once within a person (as in the subjugation of unruly passions) and in society. As such, they indicated physical strength that could serve as the bedrock of character and national regeneration. Astute observers sensed this shift in attitudes, especially among the young, as early as 1899, and commented that the new generation seemed "very sensitive to the urgency of action and its virile beauty."[4] In some respects, this did not differ fundamentally from what had concerned the Dreyfusards all along: in their own way they, too, celebrated force, insofar as they sang the praises of health, willpower, character, and courage. Yet after 1900, with the growing interest in sports and increasing anxieties about the status of French manhood, the celebration of force increasingly presupposed muscularity and action, which had become virtually antithetical to the celebration of intellect. For many people, force had become a fact of life, and after the Affair, Clemenceau himself admitted that "the world is given over to force; to conflicts, to struggles of interests."[5] By the time he became premier a few years later (with Colonel Picquart as his minister of war), Clemenceau endorsed the use of force by calling on the army to break up strikes and to arrest prominent labor leaders. The evaporation of the unity and manly potential of the *bloc des gauches,* clearly signaled by this betrayal of its leftist constituency, seemed confirmed once Picquart had been made into the tool of Clemenceau. As a profoundly disillusioned Joseph Reinach saw things, Picquart was "no longer the same man." Since as minister of war, he now willingly deferred to Clemenceau, this onetime exemplar of Dreyfusard manhood had been reduced to a feminized creature: "A single man has influence over him . . . Clemenceau; he was dominated, as a woman would be, by this hard juggler of ideas; he succumbed to the contagion of this desiccated intelligence, this energy-depleting mind [*de cet esprit tarisseur de sources*]."⁶

Whereas earlier chapters have analyzed the issues that allowed contemporary anxieties about masculinity to be refracted through the polemics of the Dreyfus Affair, Chapter 6 appraises the impact that such anxieties had on French culture from the "victory" of the Dreyfusards to the eve of World War I. It is well established that the radical right deplored *la révolution dreyfusienne* as the rise to power of a gang of effeminate and opportunistic weaklings; yet such attacks upon the virility of *les intellectuels* have generally not been considered beyond the scope of rightist and "prefascist" political discourses. Rather than presenting a detailed examination of this complex and eventful period, a task that would no doubt require a book in its own right, this chapter considers the cultural legacy of "the intellectual" from the broader perspective of an emerging culture of muscular force. The Dreyfusards had hoped to transcend the problematic gender implications of their professions by asserting the virile nature of their bodies and deeds, but the substantive *intellectuel* was by 1914 still being counterposed in popular usage to *manuel*, thus distancing Dreyfusards from the virtues of muscular force and action that were increasingly lauded throughout French culture. Many young Frenchmen considered "Herculean force" a more desirable attribute than intellect.⁷ After presenting an overview of the concept of force and its various manifestations around 1900, this chapter considers how the physical culture movement mounted the period's most explicit gender critique of men who privileged mind over muscles. It shows that by emphasizing the muscular body as the ground of manhood, physical culture helped to usher in a new age of body consciousness among Frenchmen. The last section of the chapter shows how the related cultures of physical and political force converged on the eve of World War I among the young men of the generation of 1914.

The Culture of Force

In this book, we have considered how the overcerebralized weakling became a favorite target for those sponsoring more muscular conceptions of the ideal male, and that this image played an important role in the gender politics of the Dreyfus Affair. Yet it is important to remember that we have been dealing in representations and ideals rather than sociological facts. After all, physicians, educators, and social critics from across the political spectrum criticized the lack of physical education in the lycées and advocated physical fitness as a path toward national regeneration. The noted chemist Marcellin Berthelot, for instance, served as president of the Ligue nationale de l'éducation physique, with Georges Clemenceau as vice president. The man who had founded this organization, Paschal Grousset, went on to pen several books in support of the pro-Dreyfus campaign. Even within the literary avant-garde, not known for its physically impressive men, one discerns evidence of sporting enthusiasm. After writing for *La Revue blanche*, the wealthy Tristan Bernard eventually launched a cycling review and built France's first indoor velodrome.[8] Of course, endorsing athletics was one thing, but how many enthusiasts put their muscles to the test by pursuing more energetic lifestyles? Several prominent writers did just that. As a young man, for instance, Charles Péguy had successfully lobbied the headmaster of his lycée to permit the older boys to play football, and Zola avidly pursued his daily regimen of dieting and cycling. The novelist Jean Richepin was even eulogized by *La Culture physique* after his death for his commendable activities as a sportsman.[9]

Nevertheless, such men were the exceptions that proved the rule. It is true that men and women of the bourgeoisie availed themselves of the many hygienic treatments offered at the fin de siècle, and that in addition to incorporating conventional medical prescriptions, they proved a responsive market for the seemingly infinite variety of nostrums and tonics offered in magazines and newspapers. Yet these people also recognized a distinction between different kinds of physical exertion that complicated the acceptance of athletics into their lifestyles. Eighteenth-century ideals of physical force were largely structured by the concerns of the nobility, and thus centered on the cultivation of the appearance of physical strength that did not necessarily manifest itself in directly observable demonstrations of muscularity. Of course, aristocratic practices like fencing, riding, and dancing demanded muscular expenditure, but in such circles, an emphasis was placed on achieving control, elegance, and grace rather than on "vulgar" displays of brute or animal force.[10] As with many other noble customs, bourgeois men inherited this ethos, and in their choices of both professional and leisure activities, they cultivated the art of being strong without appearing to expend physical force directly.[11] For them, disciplining the raw power of the animal within (or, in the case of riding, the animal without) testified to the manly exercise of willpower and thus the achievement of grace and ease. Demonstrations of overt force were largely restricted to the popular domain of strongmen who performed feats of physical prowess on the boulevards and in the circus. While they might admire the spectacles of acrobatic strength and agility offered by the popular Cirque Molier, sedentary bourgeois men rarely engaged in leisure activities that demanded raw muscular power.[12] It is easy to see why man-to-man combat with fists and feet (that is, kickboxing, the popular urban practice of *savate* or *chausson*) would have been frequently denigrated for its apparent coarseness and vulgarity. And even when *savate* was appropriated by some elites and rebaptized *la boxe française* in 1854 (and adopted by the army in 1894), elegance and control were cited as the truly distinctive marks of the sport (and as what set it apart from English boxing).[13]

Among bourgeois elites, the explosive potential of unrefined muscular energy was generally subordinated to the dictates of convention and style. Form, in other words, took precedence over force. Nevertheless, claims that bourgeois men were a largely sedentary lot were not unfounded. Few of the bourgeois elites studied by Christophe Charle professed any interest in sports, with bureaucrats representing the group least likely to admit to physical exercise, a finding that corroborates many of the period's assumptions about the physical limitations of functionaries.[14] The acceptance of gymnastics among the bourgeoisie was further hampered by the traditional association of such exercises with the regimentation of the military, and it was only during the 1890s that physical fitness came to be lauded for the hygienic potential it possessed rather than simply for its role in the training of soldiers. Since many agreed that institutionalized neglect of the body and excessive mothering had produced a nation of weaklings, the stage was set for more positive conceptions of physical force that would fulfill therapeutic as well as hygienic ends. Beginning in the late 1880s, the administration of public instruction had made a point of introducing physical exercise into the primary and secondary school curricula in order "to reestablish the equilibrium between intellectual work and bodily exercises."[15] Primary school became a strategic site for the inculcation of the "virile education" that exercise promised, and even before sending their children to school, parents were encouraged to teach them games that would be preparation for more intense sporting activities later in life.[16] As Marcel Spivak observes, however, this transformation proceeded slowly, at first more on the level of mentalities than in terms of methods and application. It would not be until 1905 that sports would occupy a central place in French society and in the everyday lives of city dwellers.[17] By then interest in sport and fitness had become so widely celebrated that Albert Surier's bodybuilding magazine, *La Culture physique*, could boldly declare "criminal" any father who failed to teach his children the basics of physical education—as criminal, in fact, as one who deprived his family of food (Fig. 19). The

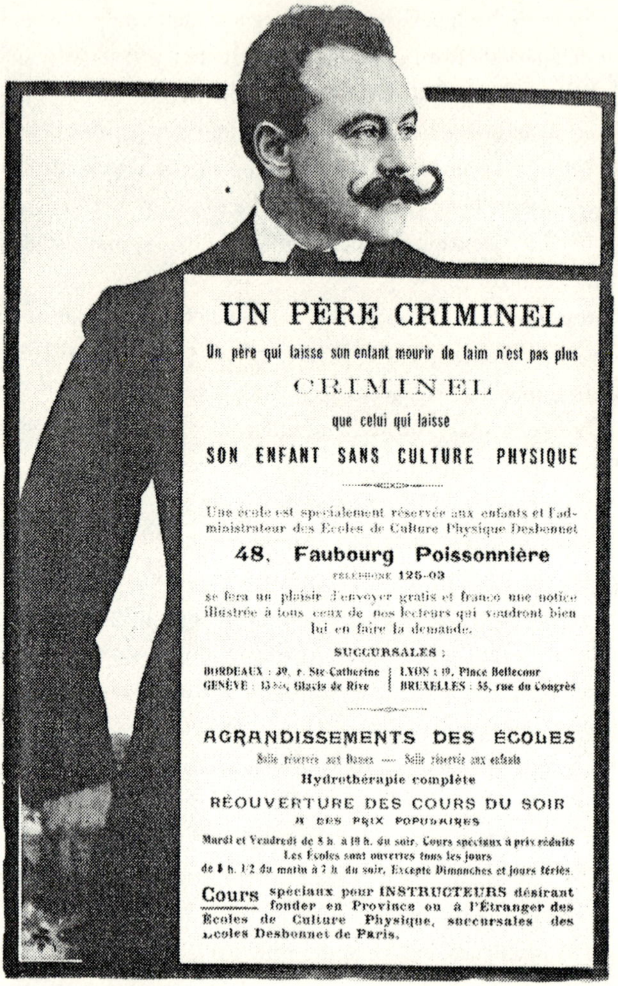

Fig. 19. Advertisement, "Un père criminel," *La Culture physique*
1, no. 79 (15 April 1908). By permission of the Wellcome
Library, London.

gender anxieties of the Dreyfus Affair thus circulated during a transitional period in French views of athletics and physical culture. Despite the rising popularity of athletics, it was still considered gauche in 1904 to write about it in high-
brow reviews and magazines. Doing so required, as one enthusiast declared in
La Revue de Paris, "beaucoup de courage."[18]

Just as Dreyfusards sought to overcome associations of intellectuality with physical weakness, however, defenders of the army tried to refine the idea of force. In the face of antimilitarist critiques during the 1880s and 1890s, they often pointed to the multiple and beneficial forms that force could assume, from the body's physiological energy to the state's ability to struggle against injustice and illegality. Arguments such as these were readily extended to the Affair, where, refusing to see *force* simply as a synonym for brutal imposition, anti-Dreyfusards insisted that it was also the very foundation of manhood and national vitality. In 1898, Father Henri Didon extended his critique of intellectual weaklings by promoting an understanding of force that was synonymous with muscularity and physical vigor. The army, Didon declared, was "material human force in its highest expression," and the military spirit was "a spirit of force and robustness. . . . For a man endowed with such a spirit, the energy of the soul and the will are transfused right in the body, which becomes capable of marvels of endurance, defying labor and braving fatigue."[19] Those who denounced such a spirit misunderstood the true needs of the country: "The madmen! How do they fail to see that force is good in itself, and that, along with willpower and intelligence, it composes an indissoluble trinity?" Men who disputed the virtues of force were merely "*émasculés*, [who,] having lost not only their energy but the very awareness of energy, dare to stand on the pavement of opinion."[20] Significantly, Didon's notion of force did not sanction unbridled brutality but was always subordinate to the maintenance of order. "I love force. I would be lying if I said otherwise. But I love it as the guardian of law."[21]

If French tradition seemed deficient when it came to promoting force and energy in males, many suggested a closer look at how other nations transformed boys into men. With its tradition of character-building team sports, England was the most logical place to begin. The showdown between the two colonial powers at Fashoda in Sudan in 1898 signified a low point of Anglo-French relations, but the subsequent rebuilding of diplomatic contacts between the two countries resulted as well in renewed appreciation for Anglo-Saxon cultural values, and for the measures they took to create virile men in particular. Inspired in part by the efforts of Anglophiles like Pierre de Coubertin, this was encouraged by a much-debated book that appeared around the time of the Dreyfus Affair, Edmond Demolins's *A quoi tient la supériorité des Anglo-Saxons* (To What Is the Superiority of the Anglo-Saxons Due), which brought the problem of educational reform and cross-cultural anxieties to a national forum. The primary goal of French schools, argued Demolins, was "to train soldiers and functionaries [rather] than to develop virile energy, spontaneity, [and] the sentiment of personal valor."[22] Rote learning and cramming for exams produced men who were at best only capable of obeying orders. Like the soldier, the good functionary was marked by "the absence of initiative, the uniformity of feelings and ideas, in a word, everything that robs a man of his personality."[23] Demolins created a French counterpart to the British public schools in the shape of the École des Roches, where three afternoons a week were devoted to sports.[24]

This critique of functionaries was not a new development. Since the early nineteenth century, men had often expressed feelings of shame about the limited independence (and thus loss of honor) that seemed implicit in becoming part of the state bureaucracy, and a century later this lack of initiative continued to be cited as a reason why certain careers ranked low in the hierarchy of prestigious professions.[25] In the eyes of many, *fonctionnarisme* remained one of the nation's "great scourges. . . . the ruin of France" where bureaucrats were likened to Chinese mandarins.[26] They were also cited as evidence of the burgeoning intellectual proletariat described in Chapter 2. Observing how vast numbers applied for a handful of positions in the state bureaucracy (in one case, there were 2,821 candidates for 12 vacancies), one critic predicted that young men would eventually renounce this "bureaucratomania" by looking for "labors more active and worthy of valid citizens."[27] For many critics, turning away from bureaucracy was synonymous with a recuperation of manly initiative, but in light of fin-de-siècle anxieties about mental labor, overcoming *fonctionnarisme* also implied conscientious attention to the body itself. The English monitored developments across the Channel with approval. "Until quite recently," observed one physical culturist in 1901, "the Ministry of Education . . . seems to have been unaware that young France possessed besides a head to be more or less usefully filled, a chest to be broadened and legs and arms to be developed." Fortunately, things were changing for the better, so that in time the French "will be worthy rivals for us in things athletic. . . . who shall say that a friendly rivalry on the football field may not lead to more than friendship on another and grimmer field, if ever unhappily should the need arise?"[28] More good news was noted the following year, when another commentator observed a slow shift in French sensibilities. Of course, the French still seemed overly enamored with strictly intellectual culture, so much so that being "an official in a great city is an almost universal ideal," but fashions were changing in such a way that "the individual Frenchman is paying more and more attention to his physical development." Writers like Max Nordau who pessimistically forecast the irreversible decline of French culture had thus overreacted, for the decadent fashions of the 1890s had

clearly seized a golden opportunity to draw young men back to the fold.[38] This sportive ethos was complemented by the Church's association with the martial tradition: if the radical republic seemed more committed to privileging mind over muscles, among many, Catholicism seemed to lavish more praise upon martyrdom and crusading than on mysticism and learning.[39] Several Catholic writers proved especially concerned about promoting a recovery of manhood, and through the writings of Father Didon, Abbot H. Mocquillon, and F. A. Vuillermet, physical culture and the education of the will were endorsed as part of "the art of making a man."[40] Despite their different political agendas, religious and secular proponents of force were animated by common anxieties about French manhood.

Appeals for the cultivation of force as an indispensable complement to intellectual training came from across the political spectrum, and although conservatives and reactionaries made ample use of sportive values, one cannot relegate this phenomenon to the political right. The Universités populaires that were promoted by left-leaning Dreyfusards to educate the working class also preached the value of physical exercise, encouraging dancing, fencing, Swedish gymnastics, and physical culture.[41] In 1901, the socialist leader Jean Jaurès incorporated bourgeois sportive values into his vision of a healthy proletariat, and four years later, the unified Socialist party formally encouraged athletics to develop the muscles of proletarians, purify their lungs, offer them healthy distractions from their daily toil, and foster camaraderie among them.[42] By 1908, an official workers' sporting union had been established.[43] Shifts in literary tastes simultaneously reflected this trend and provided it with some of its most vivid imagery. It was during this period that the colonial adventure novel came into its own in France, transporting readers to exotic locales where physical courage was essential for conquest, if not survival.[44] In short, force and action continued to be cited as cultural values and manly ideals through World War I. "Fashion has implanted in our time the need to preach energy and to glorify action," commented one observer in 1914; "it is an irresistible current."[45]

In light of the frequent complaint that Jewish men lacked honor and physical prowess, it is not surprising to find that an emphasis on energy and force affected the Jewish community as well. We have seen how some reformers echoed Max Nordau's call for a new "muscle Jew" who enjoyed a more robust physicality, noting that "tradition in its turn does not seem to disdain muscular power. It seizes upon bodily force and praises exercise. It admires the fit suppleness of this rabbi, the biceps of another. . . . It makes little of the emaciated beauties of mystics; it prefers them beefier, more substantial [*plantureuses*]."[46] Nevertheless, the Jewish press did not profile beefcake rabbis of the Belle Époque but focused instead on the practical use of Jewish muscle for adventurous and heroic deeds. A memorable article considered the strange case of the "Jewish Hottentot chief" who had frustrated German colonial projects in Africa. This Jew, Abraham Morris, had served in many British regiments and fought valiantly in the Boer War, but disappeared after gambling his money away, resurfacing later as a Hottentot chief. Surprisingly, no explanation was given as to how Morris actually *became* a Hottentot chief, but to this author the story proved "that the Jew can possess the taste for adventures and efforts that his enemies like so much to deny."[47]

There is no reason to suppose that young Jews were unmoved by the period's calls for force, even if Jewish magazines usually only discussed youth in order to bemoan their waning religious fervor. In 1901, Nordau claimed that educated youths had applauded his call for a muscular Judaism, though at present most Jews had not yet modified their lifestyles.[48] At the very least we know that some Jewish fathers deliberately sought to complement their sons' intellectual abilities by encouraging them to exercise their bodies. Having been long removed from his children's lives, Alfred Dreyfus insisted after his release that his son Pierre accompany him on mountain hikes in Switzerland so that the boy's sedentary proclivities would be countered by a more robust body. In other cases, physical fitness became a simple matter of self-defense. Acknowledging that many Jews quaked with fear in the face of persecution, one writer called for Zionist gymnastic societies that would make them stronger and more courageous, "to teach our people how they should meet the enemy."[49] After the Dreyfus Affair, Joseph Reinach, still a reviled figure in Paris, wanted to spare his slight son, Ado, the kind of persecution he had once himself faced as an intellectually talented youth at the prestigious Lycée Condorcet. Anticipating correctly that Ado would become more of a target due to his father's Dreyfusard past, Reinach arranged to have his son taught English boxing to ward off bullies (boxing was not enough, however, and Reinach secretly hired a security guard to discretely follow Ado around).[50] Self-defense was also on the mind of the poet Edmond Fleg, who responded to the resurgence of anti-Semitism around 1909 by encouraging several Jewish students to take lessons with him in fencing and shooting.[51] Considering the rhetoric of vitality that ran throughout the Jewish press, it is difficult to conclude that these were isolated cases. By 1924, we even see the creation of a Jewish branch of the scouting movement, the Éclaireurs israélites, to stand alongside its secular and Protestant counterparts.[52]

Affirmations of Jewish energy were often illustrated by reports from agricultural colonies, especially those in Uganda, Argentina, and Palestine, where Herzl had tried to secure tracts of land for Jewish settlement. That this project was part of a broader Zionist aim to recuperate Jewish manhood by mimicking the expansionist policies of gentile nations (thus elevating Israel to statehood) has been argued by a number of scholars.[53] Despite their general distrust of Zionism, even assimilated Jews in France acknowledged the beneficial effects that such projects could have on images of Jewish manhood. Against the belief that Jews were unfit for manual labor, here was proof that they too could be as hardy as peasants; in the face of accusations of cowardice, here was evidence that they could indeed court danger and embark on adventures. Obviously inspired by Rooseveltian thinking, Hippolyte Prague applauded how a taste for "the strenuous life" (*la vie intense*) had compelled a group of Moroccan Jews to emigrate to Peru, thus attesting to the courage and vitality that was not always apparent in the Jewish physique. "Under its feeble appearance [and] its sickly look, which bear the stigmata of a long history of trials, Israel has all the vitality of a wrestler, thus justifying the etymology of the name Jacob, received when he gained the upper hand over the mysterious being who had provoked him to single combat."[54] Growing numbers of Jews in Palestine were further evidence of this taste for adventure, and, as acculturated French Jews acquired a growing appreciation for Zionism during the prewar years, even Prague admitted that Herzl's movement was largely responsible for the "regeneration of Palestine" being witnessed in 1909.[55]

If these cases illustrate the extent to which *la force* became pervasive during the prewar years, they also suggest the difficulty of disentangling physical and political understandings of this concept. Whether aimed at the health of the bourgeoisie, the proletariat, or the nation as a whole, appeals for the cultivation of force were deeply embedded in social and political discourses. It is well documented that the most notorious celebrations of violence erupted at the fringes of political life, particularly among the "prefascist" thinkers of revolutionary syndicalism and the Action française. Georges Sorel's *Réflexions sur la violence*, a crucial ingredient in the development of radical rightist thought, prescribed physical force as a form of social therapy. Bemoaning the weakened state of the French bourgeoisie, which was for him epitomized by the ascent of Dreyfusards to political power, Sorel looked to America for the manly values that could revitalize French society. For Sorel, American identity, expressing itself in commercial endeavors, westward expansion, and even the lynch mob, revolved around viewing life as an endless struggle rather than the complacent enjoyment of pleasures.[56] Unlike in France, where functionaries reigned supreme, in America, the aspirations of men were dominated by capitalism: "[W]e should bear in mind this similarity between the capitalist type and the warrior type; it is for very good reasons that the men who directed gigantic enterprises were named *captains of industry*. This type is still found today in all its purity in the United States: there are found the indomitable energy, the audacity based on a just appreciation of its strength, the cold calculation of interests, which are the qualities of great generals and great capitalists."[57] Sorel maintained that the inevitability of the class warfare that Marx foretold was only possible when the bourgeoisie had achieved this state of energy, which is why he hoped for a regeneration of the French middle class. If the bourgeoisie refused to adopt a more aggressive attitude toward the working class, then Sorel prescribed proletarian violence as a form of therapy. Forcing the bourgeoisie to act would rouse it from its pacifistic slumber and compel it toward action. In other words, such therapeutic violence had the effect of virilizing effeminate men, thus preparing the way for a contest between two equal and worthy opponents.[58]

The arch-Sorelian Édouard Berth pressed his master's conclusions even further in his prewar essays, several of which were later published as *Les Méfaits des intellectuels*. In his work, Dreyfusard intellectuals were marked by limitations that also characterized the cerebral bourgeoisie generally: an inability to fight and to perform manual labor, and an inability to understand either warfare or labor. "At the Cercle Proudhon . . . we have every reason to attack this type of caste, the Intellectuals."[59] Idealizing a "warrior state" marked by heroic values rather than the abstract humanitarianism of the Third Republic, Berth perceived why "our lay clerics" were so opposed to such an idea. Despising military men as brutes, they rejected the belief that "the warrior should be the ideal of virile dignity; all these wimps [*femmelins*], by virtue of their basic effeminacy [*féminisme*] and impotence, detest a priori what they feel unable to possess or acquire: force, loyalty, rectitude, a soldier's sentiment of honor." A deficit of masculinity seemed to reside at the heart of intellect itself, revealing why thinking men often used martial values as a form of compensation. Such, Berth contended, was the nature of intelligence, "that born courtesan, who, feeling weak and dispossessed, in order to feel strong needs to support herself, like a woman on the arm of a man, on a virile power, in a word, on the Sword."[60] Similar views were expressed by Daniel Halévy, whose vision of the future in *Histoire de quatre ans, 1997–2001* (1903) was marked by Sorelian concerns about the degenerative effects of material well-being and the morally redemptive potential of manual labor and combat, values that posed a stark contrast to the intellectualized culture of the bour-geoisie.[61]

Finally, whether expressed through fantasy or outright violence, the value of physical force was praised even within the respectable bourgeoisie, at once as the ultimate foundation of male sexual difference and as a political weapon against dangerous feminists. In *Idols of Perversity*, Bram Dijkstra recounts numerous cases where artists of the period projected fantasies of dead or dying women and raised the specter of "therapeutic rape" as a means of controlling, through fantasy, women who threatened to stray from their conventional roles.[62] Similar ten-dencies appeared in literature, where Annelise Maugue reveals a strand of vio-lently misogynist sentiment among fin-de-siècle novelists. If there was indeed to be a war of the sexes, as some predicted, the victory would be, Albert Cim boasted, "on the side of biceps."[63] Women would be fatally vanquished, warned Roger Dembrun, for "we know how important physical force is in the struggle for life." The recuperation of manhood, which was in this case to be achieved through the forceful control of women, called for a move away from the refine-ments of modernity to the crudeness of the caveman. Maugue admits that this violence was ultimately more verbal than physical: "[O]ne does not see mascu-line commandos forcefully forbid the holding of feminist meetings, sack the of-fices of *La Fronde*, or lynch the most visible militants." Nevertheless, she rightly argues, the effectiveness of such a persistently menacing discourse must not be underestimated, for "the violence of the word already presses its weight."[64] In short, one cannot entirely disentangle these competing definitions of force. The same biceps that signified manly vitality could also be used to defend the nation or to bash undesirables into submission.

"Today the Brain has Killed the Muscle"

So declared Georges Rouhet, medical doctor and outspoken advocate of phys-ical culture.[65] If force had become a manly virtue during the prewar years, no one proclaimed this belief more loudly than Rouhet and his colleagues at *La Cul-ture physique*, the magazine founded to disseminate the ideas of the bodybuild-ing guru Edmond Desbonnet. A look at physical culture is significant for our purposes, mainly because its challenge to the sedentary cerebral lifestyle became more shrill around the time that the Dreyfusards achieved political power. From the development of a body-based gender identity to quasi-eugenic concerns about racial and military fitness, physical culture appealed to men on the level of personal fantasy as well as patriotism. Whereas exercise in the schools or the army was compulsory, commercialized physical culture responded to the logic of supply and demand, revealing how many men and women were willing to pay for the improvement of their bodies. By claiming that their methods provided men with the strength that would enable them to participate in any sport, the proponents of physical culture situated themselves at the crossroads of a variety of athletic activities and thus synthesized concepts from across the fitness world. If medical writers often remained somewhat circumspect about fostering virility in their readers, many physical culturists not only proclaimed loudly that their methods offered the surest path to manhood but cited numerous contemporary examples of men who failed to measure up. Most important, through the methodical reconstruction of the body, physical culture promised to accomplish what Dreyfusards tried to achieve through rhetoric: the transformation of enfeebled brain workers into robust, healthy men.

Despite the undeniable interest in exercise and athletics during this period, the fitness movement was largely divided into two competing camps. On the one hand, there were physiologically minded reformers who promoted gymnastics at the level of primary and secondary school, as well as through voluntary organizations in Paris and the provinces; on the other, there were commercial reformers who enticed men and women to undertake private training at a range of bodybuilding centers. In very general terms, the tension between these approaches reflected competing conceptions of the location and value of physical force. Even though physiological reformers like Philippe Tissié, Georges Hébert, and Georges Demenÿ encouraged the development of muscular power, their emphasis was on the lungs and proper respiration (muscles were a secondary concern). Though sometimes disagreeing about the usefulness of various gymnastic styles, they shared a physiological vision that was restricted by their scientific concern with the limits of the "normal" man and his usefulness to society, not with those who aspired to break records.[66] As Demenÿ had proposed, proper physical education should aim only to restore "a salutary equilibrium among the functions of an organism."[67] Entrepreneurial reformers like Edmond Desbonnet, however, expressed a more exalted vision, one that reveled in feats of muscular prowess and sought to transcend the bodily limits set by physiologists. This vision was reminiscent of the spectacles of the circus and a range of other activities where the male emerged victorious from his struggle with the world and with himself.[68] That such a vision would ultimately prove more chauvinistic and even racist in its focus on the vitality of French bodies demonstrates the many uses to which the culture of force could be put. Physical culturists not only sought to strengthen the body as a means of sustaining manliness in the face of modernity's corrupting influences, they also embraced the exhilaration of speed and the fantasies of bodily transcendence that were rife at the dawn of the twentieth century.

Proponents of these competing approaches had reached a truce of sorts during the prewar years, with champions of sports admitting that gymnastics could indeed be useful for athletic training. Nevertheless, disagreements remained about the personal and social benefits of fitness. "All the physiologists have applauded this general movement," conceded the physician Alfred Binet, "they have seen in it a means of regenerating the race; patriots are moved by it, they have been persuaded that this intensive physical culture will give us better soldiers." Nevertheless Binet and others warned the public against confusing muscularity with physical health, a confusion that seemed to be growing.[69] Modern life had indeed removed people from "normal and natural conditions," observed Georges Demenÿ, and the increasing reliance on mental labor "at the expense of muscular activity" made it easy to distinguish an athlete from a bureaucrat, whom he described as a "sedentary man" whose muscular weakness ranked alongside that of women and children.[70] Demenÿ nevertheless warned that the "culture of force for the sake of force is an infantile thing when it does not become immoral and unhealthy. . . . Physical education should be understood as a complement to intellectual and moral education, but it should not be cultivated exclusively."[71] As another reformer put it, the French must strike "a just balance between mental work and muscular work."[72] Many agreed with Pierre de Coubertin that by strengthening willpower, athletics cultivated a virtue that "impregnates sport and transforms it into a marvelous instrument of 'virilization'";[73] others recommended a more moderate and restrained approach to physical exercise. Equally concerned about maximizing willpower, Philippe Tissié warned that sporting activities could have the opposite effect if they became a obsession, a disorder that he had termed "ludomania" in the late 1890s. A decade later, physicians like Binet reiterated such warnings, this time alleging a real decline in mental qualities. "In the *collèges* and *lycées* where the sportive life is adopted with the most fervor," Binet observed, "the level of studies is diminished. . . . too much physical exercise harms intellectual development."[74] Finally, although admitting that "physical exercise has never been more necessary than in our epoch of the strenuous life," even Catholic critics like Vuillermet warned against "crudely confusing health and muscular force."[75]

Edmond Desbonnet was not deterred by these criticisms. Like the world-famous strongman Eugen Sandow, Desbonnet was a student of Professor Louis Attila (Ludwig Durlacher) and believed that physical culture was the key to rejuvenating the nation. He hailed from northern France, and he had opened two exercise studios in Lille (in 1888 and 1895) and sponsored several French and Belgian athletic contests before opening his Paris studio in 1899 at 48 rue du Faubourg-Poissonnière (ninth arrondissement). After he founded *La Culture physique* in 1904 with a fellow enthusiast, Albert Surier, Desbonnet's industry rapidly expanded, despite the fire it sometimes drew, so that by 1911, it became necessary to found a separate review for the publication of strictly hygienic literature. *La Santé par les sports*, whose subtitle, "Organ for the regeneration of the race," clearly spelled out the ambitions adopted by physical culture. Desbonnet would thereafter devote himself to the new review, while Surier remained editor of *La Culture physique*.[76]

Desbonnet outlined his fitness philosophy and method in *La Force physique* (1901), taking aim at men who were trapped in a world of mental work and physical decrepitude. Encouraging young men to enter into industry, commerce, agriculture, and "to populate our colonies," Desbonnet promised a way out of "the *fonctionnarisme* in which they are already too encumbered, but the task is difficult. Why? Because they lack the most important thing: *energy*, and energy is only acquired through a vigorous physical education." Obesity was perhaps the most obvious symptom of the bureaucrat's lack of energy, and signified a physical degradation that resulted from sedentariness, laziness, and a lack of will in a world of plenty. Desbonnet denounced the laziness of fat men who bleated that "'There is nothing to be done, it's my nature to be like that.' . . . If three-quarters of these obese men achieve no results in their training, the only cause is their lack of energy." A vast gulf separated the soldier from the fat functionary, Desbonnet claimed. "In an active army of 50,000 men, we do not encounter a single fat man, but we know that twenty-five out of fifty individuals become obese through idleness and abundance." Like many of his contemporaries, Desbonnet averred that the creation of vigorous young men required action, but for him action could only emerge through "*forces*, and *forces* are created through *physical culture*."[77]

Physical culturists launched a frontal assault on men who allowed their bodies to atrophy or to be "invaded" by fat. Puny or obese, these were weaklings whose physical decay testified to their inability to withstand the abundance, temptations, and conveniences of modernity. These were also largely sedentary types who believed that "physical exercise is prejudicial to mental work," with each possessing "a strong tendency to consider himself as *intellectuel*."[78] In his depiction of the enfeebled modern man, Georges Rouhet conjured a grotesque image that could have been torn from the pages of *Psst . . . !* "What should we think of a 'civilization' that promises us, in the near future, a race of dwarfs with flabby and undefined muscles, thin limbs, the faces of inferior anthropoids, with big hydrocephalus heads?"[79] The only excuse that these *intellectuels* could have for their weakness, observed another writer, was having spent so many years in a "depressing and stupid" scholarly regime that left them timid, weak, and cowardly.[80] Only the English had managed to balance study with exercise, it was claimed, thus making "les intellectuels anglais" superior to all others: "they are not only dreamers and speculators, but they are also men of action."[81] In order to cope with modern conveniences that encouraged men to be lazy, manhood had to be reformed at the level of daily habits and lifestyle: "avoid taking the streetcar, do not retreat before staircases, go look for information yourself, that will make you act. . . . Carry your own valise to the train station, your own luggage to your driver, if your collar stud rolls under your chest of drawers, go down quickly on your stomach and do not resort to your cane to retrieve it."[82] For those who required more formal training, an advertisement for the Desbonnet schools hailed them directly: "To the intellectuals.—For a man overtaxed by mental labor, it is important to seek out exercises that do not require the use of the brain. Muscular labor can be automatic at the Écoles du Professeur Desbonnet" (Fig. 20).[83]

The men who seemed to thrive during the 1890s—functionaries, *intellectuels*, and dandies—were all combined in a single category of decadent and weak men. Physical culturists issued shrill warnings to these weaklings, demanding that they take a serious look at what they had become. "It is to you fin-de-siècle young men that I address myself, a generation of playboys and pleasure-seekers, anemic and neurasthenic, bereft of both will and courage; to you, the impotent and the tubercular, who lie about in your scrawny carcasses in café-concerts and fashionable brasseries."[84] To this author, the hygiene reformer and law professor Louis Bally, contemporary men seemed quite unsubstantial, their manliness a mere façade constructed from the deceptive accessories of fashion. "I know that more than one of my readers will shrug their shoulders, but what does the contempt of such fake shoulders matter to me, [made as they are] of cotton and padding, the creations of our modern tailors!"[85] The writer Albert Surier responded to such appeals and was so impressed that he founded the magazine *La*

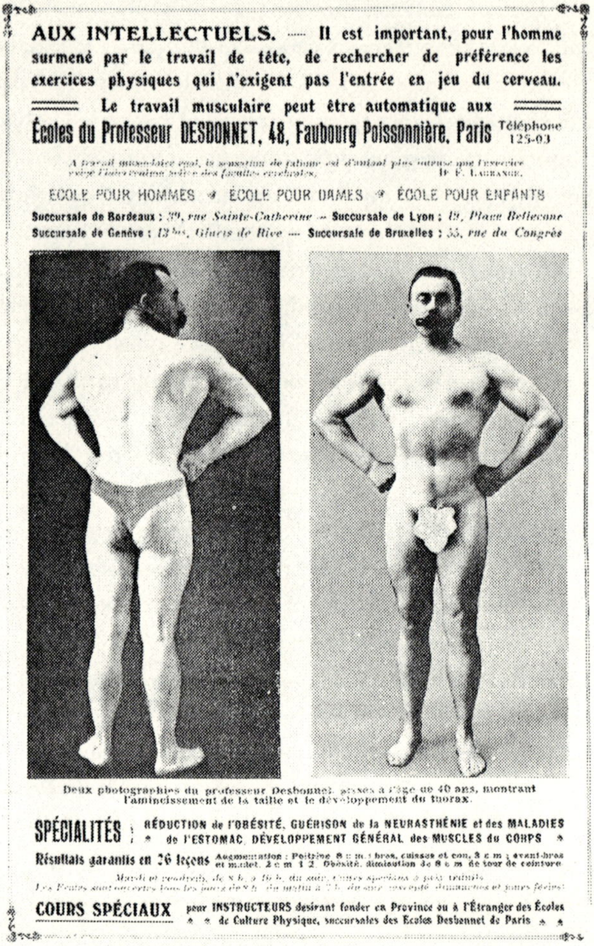

AUX INTELLECTUELS. —— Il est important, pour l'homme surmené par le travail de tête, de rechercher de préférence les exercices physiques qui n'exigent pas l'entrée en jeu du cerveau.
—— Le travail musculaire peut être automatique aux ——
Écoles du Professeur DESBONNET, 48, Faubourg Poissonnière, Paris Téléphone 125-03

A travail musculaire egal, la sensation de fatigue est d'autant plus intense que l'exercice exige l'intervention active des facultés cérébrales.   Dᴿ F. LAGRANGE.

ÉCOLE POUR HOMMES ⚜ ÉCOLE POUR DAMES ⚜ ÉCOLE POUR ENFANTS
Succursale de Bordeaux : 39, rue Sainte-Catherine — Succursale de Lyon : 19, Place Bellecour
Succursale de Genève : 13 bis, Quais de Rive —— Succursale de Bruxelles : 55, rue du Congrès

Deux photographies du professeur Desbonnet, prises à l'âge de 40 ans, montrant l'amincissement de la taille et le développement du thorax.

SPÉCIALITÉS : RÉDUCTION de l'OBÉSITÉ, GUÉRISON de la NEURASTHÉNIE et des MALADIES de l'ESTOMAC. DÉVELOPPEMENT GÉNÉRAL des MUSCLES du CORPS ⚜

Résultats garantis en 36 leçons Augmentation : Poitrine 8 c m ; bras, cuisses et cou, 3 c m ; avant-bras et mollet, 2 c m 1 2. Obésité, diminution de 8 c m de tour de ceinture

Mardi et vendredi, de 8 h. à 10 h. du soir, cours spéciaux à prix réduits.
Les Écoles sont ouvertes tous les jours, de 8 h. du matin à 7 h. du soir, excepté dimanches et jours fériés.

COURS SPÉCIAUX pour INSTRUCTEURS désirant fonder en Province ou à l'Étranger des Écoles ⚜ ⚜ de Culture Physique, succursales des Écoles Desbonnet de Paris ⚜ ⚜

Fig. 20. Advertisement, "Aux intellectuels," *La Culture physique* 1, no. 94 (1 December 1908). By permission of the Wellcome Library, London.

Culture physique, which served for years as the primary organ for the dissemination of Desbonnet's message. Greatly moved by Desbonnet's *La Force physique*, Surier decided to meet the man at his center in 1902. Here Surier acquired first-hand knowledge of just how clothing could conceal a man's actual weaknesses. Gazing at the numerous photos of bodybuilders that graced the walls of the center, Surier at first deluded himself into drawing "not unfavorable comparisons . . .

between my anatomy and those of the athletes." After being asked to undress in preparation for exercise, he encountered a deeper, more embarrassing truth. "Where, then, were my muscles, my shoulders, my thighs, my calves? . . . The pitiless mirror scrupulously sent back to me the exact image of my own puniness."[86]

Such observations appeared frequently in the literature of physical culture and signaled a change in attitudes toward the male body that paralleled developments in female bodies. The V-shaped male torso so idealized in the West had for centuries stood as a model of male body shape, but for much of the modern era, men were rarely called upon to approximate this ideal in their own bodies, at least not without some assistance. Ever since the early nineteenth century, male fashion had served the purpose of enhancing impressions of muscularity and youthfulness through the careful placement of padding and, at times, corsetry, thus concealing the idiosyncrasies of the actual body behind a façade of aestheticized uniformity.[87] In cultural terms this posed few problems, for images of the male nude—the longtime standard for nude paintings—had since the early nineteenth century virtually disappeared from the art world. In 1858, Théophile Gautier complained about fashion's tendency to efface the male body, functioning as "a sort of skin that no man will shed under any pretext. It sticks to him like the pelt of an animal, so that nowadays the real form of the body has fallen into oblivion."[88] It was perhaps no coincidence that a renewed artistic appreciation for the unclad male body would emerge around the same time that bodybuilders began imploring men to look for proof of manhood beneath the veneer of fashion. Like the gradual demise of the corset as a necessary accouterment of women's fashion, this was a mixed blessing. Admittedly, the bourgeois body had been physically constrained and concealed behind the artifices of fashion, but whatever "liberation" that body experienced was subtly undercut by an associated shift in the point of application of personal discipline. The self who had once been responsible for the tasteful selection and display of fashions that projected both beauty and morality was now expected to pull off this performance through the direct control of the body, without the assistance of props, pads, or prostheses. In time women would be implored to exercise so as to enjoy "nature's muscle corset" which, when "properly disciplined to perform its function," will "hold protruding shoulder blades down flat on the ribs more effectively and permanently than any Parisian corset decreed by fashion."[89] The body still remained the bearer of social, gender, racial, and moral significance, but now its morphology was to be held in check through acts of will and the cumulative effect of healthy habits.

As in most hygienic literature, especially that devoted to weaknesses of volition, physical culture instilled in its practitioners an agonistic relationship to the self, and fostered particular hostility toward those aspects deemed weak or effeminate. As the lawyer and bodybuilding enthusiast Richard Andrieu explained, every man has within him two men locked in combat, the hero and "the idler, the voluptuary, the gourmand." "Therefore, young men, at the beginning of your lives as men you should make yourselves masters of your . . . of our instincts toward laziness and well-being, you must grab hold of the fat man and subdue him." Hence the need for a daily exercise regimen, to be "mercilessly quotidian" in one's attention to an athletic program, "to attack directly the Sancho Panza who is within you."[90]

Much of the reflexivity encouraged by physical culture was heavily dependent upon visuality, thus fostering an endless chain of comparisons and contrasts that bridged the gap between identity and desire. The first few issues of *La Culture physique* emphasized the physical icons of manhood captured in classical sculpture, and readers were encouraged to take note of how far their own lives had deviated from those of the virile men of times past. Nevertheless, within a few years, the magazine emphasized the importance of living models of force, immortalized for popular consumption through photography. The snapshots of athletes that adorned the walls of physical culture schools were also fetish goods avidly collected by Desbonnet's clientele, offering them ample opportunity to compare their own physiques to those of the world's strongest men. It was perhaps even more thrilling to have unmediated access to the superior body of your own teacher. The instructor Georges Rouhet exercised a charismatic authority over both his students and readers, and was never at a loss for vivid descriptions of the weaknesses of modern men. One of Rouhet's admiring students poured out his praise in verse and sent it to *La Culture physique*. Having searched throughout France for men with "virile elegance," this student found only "skeptical minds / In stunted, emaciated, and consumptive bodies; / No muscles—some nerves. . . . . Alas, the nerves of women." In the masterful hands of Rouhet, such soft beings would be expertly crafted into real men:

> His voice can in turns hold us under its charm
> And make us pale with its manly sound.
> He knows how to train us in all the powerful games,
> To fashion our flesh and straighten our torsos,
> To enlarge our lungs and increase our forces tenfold.
> A thinker inspired by an audacious dream,

He wants to regenerate, through his precious art,
The weak, puny, and wretched beings that we are,
To make us beautiful and strong, to make men of us.[91]

These lines underscore the concern with metamorphosis that preoccupied many men of the Belle Époque, and suggest that one man, at least, had found his perfect guru. Yet in time even the need for a teacher was considered unnecessary. By 1911, one could, after filling out a questionnaire and signing up for a particular exercise program, exercise at home through correspondence (gone was the medical examination that had once been compulsory for admission to the Desbonnet centers).[92]

Exercising alone encouraged this reflexive attitude even more. Desbonnet had always recommended that, when at home, his students practice shirtless in front of a mirror so that they could "follow every contraction of the muscles and avoid any inaccuracy in the execution of different exercises."[93] Yet the mirror encouraged men to do more than simply perfect their technique: it fostered a focus on visuality through which desire and identity merged, thus encouraging men to ground their sense of manhood more firmly in their unclothed musculature. Photography was an important component of this visual culture, allowing for before and after shots, as well as the fixing of personal identity by reference to the naked body itself. As collectors of bodybuilding images, readers of *La Culture physique* were invited to enter contests by submitting pictures of themselves along with their measurements to the magazine, which would judge the entries and publish the images of the winners. This was an attractive new means for self-actualization, for whereas mass-produced calling card-sized photos of famous athletes had been available since the mid 1860s, here was an opportunity for young men to appear alongside famous sporting celebrities.[94] Photographers and photographic suppliers were aware of this tendency toward self-display and through regular advertisements appealed to potential customers in the pages of *La Culture physique*. Anticipating that most of his bodybuilding clients would probably be neophytes, for example, one photographer assured potential models that he specialized in working with amateurs.[95]

If visuality was central to physical culture, men were not the only ones looking. It was taken for granted that female desire would naturally gravitate toward the beautiful male specimen, an assumption clearly illustrated in a 1906 poster depicting a fashionable woman ogling a well-built man.[96] Yet despite frequent claims as to what women instinctually desired, in other cases women had to be schooled in reading male bodies for evidence of moral and physical worth, particularly when it came to reproducing the race. In addition to being warned against procreating with fat men, women were taught to observe the posture of prospective mates as a means of telling real men from weaklings. A man with good posture "proves the influence of the will over the plasticity of the human body" and exudes "an air of confidence" that makes him a promising candidate for marriage: "Young ladies, choose your husbands from those who hold themselves upright." Men who slouched or who had rounded backs could never win the respect of women, for, in addition to suffering from indigestion, appendicitis, constipation, melancholy, neurasthenia, and a general disgust with life, they came across as men who had been "vanquished by life, vanquished in the social struggle and oppressed in their *foyer.* How indeed could a woman regard him as her master? . . . This is not a man in every sense of the word, and woman's instinct is to feel a certain contempt for him. Not being able to dominate, he becomes a slave."[97] Nor should women prevent their husbands from engaging in physical culture when they became obese, for by doing so they risked stripping ten years or more from their partners' lives during their most productive years. "You women who see your husbands gain weight, make them do physical culture at least twice a week."[98]

Disapproving of violent exercises that could harm the body, critics of bodybuilding also looked with scorn upon its strong visual component. "That the imbecile who is incapable of reflecting . . . contemplates his athletic muscles with pride, we see no difficulty with that," observed Jules Payot. "But to recommend such a life to our future doctors, lawyers, savants, [and] litterateurs is nonsense."[99] Neither Desbonnet nor his colleagues, however, envisioned muscular development as an end in itself, but recommended that students aim for something "that can be useful for you." While acknowledging that it might be "pretty" to march gracefully and in unison with others in military parades, Desbonnet warned that such displays "make neither men nor, above all, soldiers." Preparation for military service had always been an aim of physical culture, and was often stated explicitly in promotional literature for the Desbonnet centers. Yet few reformers recommended physical culture only for the preparation of soldiers, but for instilling in any man the moral and physical qualities associated with the military. Like many of his colleagues, whether physiologically or commercially inclined, Desbonnet broke down the barrier between military and civilian fitness by suggesting that soldierly virtues like force, suppleness, agility, self-confidence, and the ability to withstand fatigue could be useful in everyday life. "Now today everyone should be a soldier, and being a soldier is not a matter of pageantry but of being able to resist fatigue and privations."[100]

The kind of manliness fostered through physical culture thus maintained a close connection to military ideals, whether or not these men would actually face battle. Like many of his contemporaries, Albert Surier was not convinced that the strong should be the ones to fight in wars. Surier recommended physical culture as a means of improving the race and thus of rehabilitating the nation's weaker elements, but nevertheless claimed that in warfare "it would be more intelligent to sacrifice the weaklings, those who could be called human waste [*les déchets humains*]." In this manner, warfare would prove "a logical selection, a brutal elimination of the less resistant. Contemporary warfare is artificial selection [*une sélection à rebours*]."[101] Preserving the strongest elements of the race remained a preoccupation of physical culture, and it is not surprising to note its flirtation with eugenic ideas. When Surier himself looked to the future, he longed for the eradication of society's weakest elements. "No one today has the right to be weak. The emaciated race of 'copurchics' who, under a conquering breastplate [*un plastron conquérant*], conceal a hollowed-out thorax, is going to disappear little by little; these poor beings, unhealthy flowers of late-night restaurants, are going to die out and pass into the realm of legends and freaks."[102] Here, too, entrepreneurial and physiological health reformers seemed to agree. "The present generation is born fatigued," Philippe Tissié declared, "it is the enervated product of a whole century of convulsions. After the great commotions of the first Revolution came the great wars of the first Empire, which, in overthrowing Europe, carried away from each nation, and above all from our own, the best blood of its subjects. Only the weaklings remained at home, where they procreated. . . . Cerebral fathers will give life to babies conceived in maternal nervousness, made of violent emotions."[103] As we have seen, physical weakness and maternal tenderness were thought to be a dangerous combination, and the legion of French *intellectuels* were considered the fruit of such unwholesome unions.

Whether or not a man would be tested in the field of battle, maximizing fighting skills remained one of the more practical benefits of physical culture, and acquired more urgency once the rise of violent street gangs (the so-called *apaches*) after 1905 made city life increasingly dangerous.[104] This entailed a break with more conventional bourgeois fighting styles. Of course, willingness to defend one's honor through dueling was de rigueur for any respectable man, but the duel's highly formalized conventions (not to mention the fact that in France skill was often less important than the public demonstration of courage) diminished its usefulness on the streets. Not only was it prohibited to carry weapons during the Belle Époque, but working-class *apaches* were hardly bound by the gentlemanly conventions of the duel. Defending oneself on the streets required different techniques, and physical culturists encouraged men to acquire these skills. Here the bourgeois tendency to avoid crudely physical confrontations proved a liability. As one commentator explained, "the advances of civilization have helped to develop in the 'brave men' of the middle class a growing fear of all that resembles brutality, struggle . . . in a word, the fear of blows." That street thugs had evidently not been instilled with this fear made the acquisition of self-defense techniques even more important.[105]

Self-defense allowed well-trained, muscular men to prove their virility in practical ways. Indeed, although the drama of the physically fit body was no doubt impressive, there was a world of difference between lighting one's cigar with a toppled lamppost when ruffians were long gone and confronting the same hoodlums face-to-face. Of particular interest was the Japanese martial art jiujitsu, which offered an example of force that challenged the stereotypes of the physically weak Asian man. The arrival in Paris of Ré-Nié, the only European teacher of jiujitsu, caused quite a sensation, especially when in 1905 he defeated the noted fencer, boxer, and bodybuilder Georges Dubois in twenty-six seconds (the actual engagement lasted all of six seconds). As one stunned journalist put it, "The representative of the French method [of boxing] did not even *exist* before the representative of jiujitsu."[106] Through the training center that Ré-Nié soon established, jiujitsu represented a perfect opportunity for weaker men to defend themselves against attacks by street thugs, becoming so popular that the chief of police even enrolled seven of his men in the program.[107] Jiujitsu was touted as a marvelous way to give men confidence in the streets. "*Messieurs les apaches* had better abandon their activities, because it seems that after twenty or thirty lessons in jiujitsu, a man with below average muscular force easily throws a colossus like [the wrestler Paul] Pons or Apollo [Louis Uni] to the ground."[108] The effects of these techniques on one's opponent, "*un apache*, some evildoer," were described in delicious detail: "If your aggressor throws a fist at you, jiujitsu possesses the infallible means to fracture his forearm; if he kicks, the leg is broken; if he grabs you around the body, he is dead." All men (not to mention a fair number of women) could benefit from such skills, whether on the street or the battlefield: "[O]n the day that the French soldier is initiated into the secrets of jiujitsu, no one will be able to withstand him."[109]

Among many the need to defend oneself on the street, and perhaps on the field of battle, vindicated the controlled use of force as a tool of the civilized, thus breaking down the barrier that some tried to build between force and thought. "So long as men are not civilized enough to substitute the laws of right and reason for those of force," observed one of jiujitsu's proponents, "those on the side of right must use force to make right triumph. And so long as there are in our streets dangerous prowlers to beat, strangle, or stab peaceful passers-by, it will be good that honest men are in a position to defend their lives, without counting too much on the police."[110] Street thugs were only enraged by signs of timidity or by verbal appeals to reason, another writer observed, leading him to conclude that "immediate and even somewhat swift corrections are the only way to moralize brutal men."[111] French boxing was eminently practical in this regard, for "it allows one to face an adversary who, by attacking unexpectedly, does not leave you time to use weapons other than your feet and hands. A well-placed punch can thus shake off your adversary: Better to kill the devil than be killed by him."[112]

Having positioned itself as the prerequisite of all athletic achievement and manly robustness, physical culture self-consciously declared itself a school of virility through the cultivation of force. Among men crippled by an overly cerebral world, the path back to manhood would necessarily pass through the body itself, where the recuperation of physical force promised to restore the virile virtues of energy, initiative, willpower, and courage. Explicitly contrasted to the physical and moral decadence that was often associated with the 1890s, the culture of force encouraged its adherents to see themselves as new men. It is therefore not surprising that calls for physical vitality would be picked up most avidly by the younger generation, who saw themselves as distinct from their elders in every way.

Young Men and New Men

In the immediate prewar years, all of the factors that contributed to the weakening of French manhood were bundled together and condemned, particularly when it came to discussions about the proper method of transforming boys into the right kind of men. Despite the generational rhetoric articulated among some young men, no age group enjoyed a monopoly on the culture of force. In fact, most had become aware of a common set of problems. According to Paul Leroy-Beaulieu, maternal tenderness and domesticity accounted for the Frenchman's distance from the ideology of adventure: "The children of our families, one or two in number, surrounded with indulgent tenderness, with debilitating care, are inclined to a passive and sedentary life and only exceptionally manifest the spirit of enterprise and adventure, of endurance and perseverance that characterized their ancient ancestors and that the sons of prolific German families possess today."[113] Even those who celebrated the disinterestedness of intellectuals acknowledged the national benefits of the glorification of energy and action. This was "a useful warning against the softening through well-being that is invading us, in an epoch where the solicitude of mothers, who always remain *mamans*, overwhelms what few children we have with a precocious comfort they have done nothing to acquire and of which they make a necessity."[114] Sportive nationalism was, as Robert Nye observes, "a profoundly compensatory movement" that "took the place of an unrealizable military revenge on Germany, while helping to convince the French that they had not fallen into an irremediable moral and physical decadence."[115]

During this time, education became even more of an issue, and despite the steps the state had taken to encourage physical education in primary and secondary schools, many contended that it did not go far enough. Once again, schools came under fire for their failure to transform boys into men. The intellectual and moral education of the nation's youth would always be incomplete, declared Dr. Paul Audollent, unless secondary schools began to recognize that the strengthening of the body was essential for intellectual and moral development. Without physical education, he insisted, "you cannot make men [*sic*] in the broadest and most noble sense of the word."[116] "It is in order to make men that we have multiplied the schools at the price of the greatest financial sacrifices," commented Vuillermet; yet while these efforts enlarged the domain of science, no science could fashion men. "Without a doubt we have made cultured men [and] career men of them, but we forgot to make them men of character. . . . We have done everything to fashion *intellectuels* and *bacheliers*, and have done nothing or almost nothing to prepare young men for the struggles of life. What we lack is not instruction, but *éducation*."[117] Here too the Anglo-Saxon model seemed worth emulating. After a brief teaching stint at the American University of Beirut, a Parisian professor of commerce (who also wrote poetry and travel literature) returned home brimming with praise for how American schools had successfully cultivated men. Reflecting on his own country provoked some sadness, for while "France has many intellects, she has few men!"[118]

These developments suggest a dramatic shift in the styles of manhood that were observed and celebrated during these years, as well as the decline of mental labor as a vocation for young men. At least this is what many observed during the prewar years. "Today the taste for sports is quite widespread among young people," Alfred Binet observed in 1909, "it is even one of the curious signs of our time, and the happiest." Gone were the bookish and frail young men of previous decades: "[T]he sickly little schoolboy, with glasses, the boy who, in days of old, was good at school [*le fort en thème*] has nearly become a myth; in every case, he is much less esteemed, imitated, envied."[119] Writing the following year about the athletic renaissance that had rejuvenated France in recent years, Jean Daçay explicitly contrasted his own day with previous decades when "university-ism was king" and decadent literary schools conquered young minds. Back then the international reputation of French manhood was at its lowest. "Those were the days. The Frenchman was everywhere said to be a domestic being, with a first-rate education, but without virility and without initiative." The explosion of sports of every sort testified to a veritable sea change in public opinion and a recuperation of the Frenchman's international image. With the *baccalauréat*, that "fetish of French education," now considered more of a formality than a sign of prestige, "commerce, industry, agricultural and colonial exploitations curry greater favor every day, [while] *les grandes écoles* see their recruitments curtailed year by year." Since book learning was being complemented by a vigorous physical culture, young Frenchmen now enjoyed a truly "virile education" that taught them "the spirit of initiative, the will to act, a feeling for the realities that can be conquered and the perseverence to succeed."[120]

Numerous surveys of young men during the prewar years illustrated this claim that force had become more important than thought in the lives of bourgeois youths. This certainly seemed true of the literary circles polled by Émile Henriot, where many young writers professed their love of "energy, action, force, robustness and virility.[121] Similar sentiments were expressed in Étienne Rey's *La Renaissance de l'orgueil français*, which cited the Dreyfus Affair as the real turning point in national rejuvenation.[122] These ideas were central to the famous survey conducted by Agathon (Henri Massis and Alfred de Tarde), *Les Jeunes Gens d'aujourd'hui*, where it was claimed that sizable segments of the emerging intellectual elite had found in athletics a source of virility they would never find in books. Unlike men of the 1890s, whose idealism had "exalted pure intelligence to the detriment of force," sports and a taste for action figured prominently on the list of qualities that distinguished these young men from their elders.[123] Georges Rozet, a regular contributor to *La Culture physique*, saw in sports something integral to the self-identity of young men. In previous decades, he explained, young provincial boys had used to form literary and dramatic societies, often with magazines with very small circulations, but were usually discouraged when they compared their works to the superior products of their elders. With sports, however, these young men felt more competent in their activities and carved out a niche where they could even be superior to their elders. It gave them a definite sense of identity, of being: "Through sport . . . young sportsmen feel that they 'exist.'"[124] The men of the 1890s were not merely over the hill in neglecting their bodies, Agathon's respondents suggested; even in their prime, they had failed to embrace the virile qualities now embodied in their sons.

Through athletics, it was said, young men had crafted themselves into men of action where virility was founded mainly on physical force rather than thought. According to one observer, the new generation represented "an active elite, entirely different from the intellectual elite, and that will have more prestige than it. . . . They have young blood and muscles."[125] Hardly devoid of intelligence, these robust young men were "less enamored with intelligence" and thus more likely to read *L'Auto* than *La Revue des deux mondes*. Without Desbonnet or his method of physical culture being explicitly cited, the new generation clearly subscribed to the idea that male identity should be grounded in firm musculature, and they thus found joy in the spectacle and sensation of their youthful bodies. "They take pride in their bodies, in their vigorous muscles and skillful actions," observed Henry du Roure. "Seeing them at their exercises, agile, supple, overflowing with physical life, one thinks of horses galloping in the meadow." Since these young men experienced what would have been for others a fantasy of adventure and escape from the mundane, du Roure contended, more bookish types could not resist being enthralled and jealous of such specimens of vibrant manhood. "We understand the type of fascination that these barbarous young men exert over men of study and solitary labor. This is joyful effort opposed to painful research, a carefree attitude to the anguish of the mind, the great sun to nights under a lamp, *la joie de vivre* to the sadness of thinking."[126] For the new men of France, there would be no turning back to older intellectual ideals, a conviction aptly summed up in Ernest Psichari's rhetorical question: "Hasn't the noble word 'intellectual' become among them the worst of insults?"[127]

This chapter has charted how an emphasis on muscular force provided the French with a potent discourse for the recuperation of manhood. Many who had become disillusioned with the bourgeoisie looked, with Georges Rozet, to "a race of young men, more physically muscular and morally robust, to teach it temperance and the ardor of labor."[128] Yet had the Frenchman of old ever been as enfeebled as young men alleged, and had he truly been transformed into a virile athlete? That such surveys exaggerated the uniqueness of the action, patriotism, and virility exemplified by contemporary youth was observed by many commentators and is generally accepted among historians. Yet while critics of youthful arrogance often bristled at the apparent glorification of "action for action's sake," they rarely disputed the basic issues that young men identified as obstacles to French vitality. In fact, much of this book provides ample support for Georges Le Cardonnel's irritated response to Agathon: not only had the men of the 1890s been equally concerned about action, willpower, nationalism, and the negative consequences of intellectualism, but the recent interest in athletics and muscular force was hardly the exclusive preserve of the young.[129] As Robert Nye rightly observes, recapturing physical and moral energy was a widespread dream of the Belle Époque, but one that seemed more urgent and vital when coupled with generational tensions: "In adopting the language of hygiene, energy, and spiritual action, the prewar generation was simply bringing an important theme in the ideology of the positivist Republic to its logical fulfillment. . . . But they used it in a manner that made it pulse with the excitement of a great crusade and promised a regeneration of the French nation that would transform it in body and soul."[130]

For our purposes, the fact that the Dreyfus Affair was cited frequently as the real crossroads of French energy is perhaps the most relevant consequence of this generational crisis. Observing that spokesmen for the young generation often cited the Dreyfus Affair as a catalyst for the youthful cultivation of energy, Le Cardonnel reiterated Péguy's insistence that, far from being opposed to manliness and national vitality, the Dreyfusards had in fact been "heroes" at a time when the nation needed heroism the most.[131] Others, however, saw in the pretensions of youth an opportunity to settle old scores. The conservative writer Hugues Le Roux reveled in how completely *la culture de la force* seemed to have penetrated a new generation of young men who refused to develop their minds at the expense of their muscles. Their republican professors, Le Roux charged, had acted in a manner similar to the *clercs* of the time of Charlemagne; they, too, had struggled against men of arms who preferred to *make* history rather than merely write about it. The Dreyfus Affair was for him the most obvious referent for this struggle between thinking men and men of action. Overly cerebral and alienated from reality, Dreyfusard intellectuals had been enemies of force: "They invented, unfortunately, the word 'intellectual' to oppose it to 'man of action.'" In this respect, they had manifested along with traditional Catholics a "disdain for the body" that no longer commanded the allegiance of young men, whose wholehearted embrace of physical force had produced a nerves of steel. An American track and field coach had assured Le Roux of this in a manner that was most flattering to French national pride. "These Germans," the coach averred, "have neither the muscles of our young Anglo-Saxons nor the nervous systems of you Frenchmen. . . . What magnificent powers of energy have accumulated in your race! . . . Thanks to the nervous system you have inherited from your elders, the day will come when you . . . will be unbeatable."[132]

An Affair to Remember

In March 1914, the fashionable magazine *L'Illustration* reported a remarkable transformation at the École normale supérieure, one of the venerable *grandes écoles* that had been closely associated with the production of the intellectual elite for more than a century. In days of old, this prestigious school had been a "pedagogic seminary" that produced "distinguished and frail *universitaires*, bespectacled philosophers, and valetudinarian mathematicians." The 1913 law that increased compulsory military service to five years, however, had transformed it into "our third special military school" alongside Saint-Cyr and the École polytechnique. The rigorous training in weaponry, maneuvers, and geography that now made the school seem more like a barracks was laudable, the writer concluded, for it stood as proof that, contrary to the relative disinterest in physical and military matters of previous years, "another spirit animates our intellectual youth."[1] If readers demanded confirmation of Agathon's earlier claims about the young men of the day, these developments at the rue d'Ulm may have proved quite persuasive. Even among *les intellectuels*, it seemed, mental endeavors were being more conscientiously balanced by rigorous physical exercise and military preparation, even in a school whose students had once marched eagerly under Dreyfusard colors. The large number of *normalien* casualties in the Great War suggested that such changes had been anything but superficial.[2]

It was as if the advice made years earlier by the Catholic poet Victor de Laprade had finally been heeded. "We must have more male saviors / In the frightful storm in which we find ourselves / We have had too many dreamers / Be men!"[3] For all intents and purposes, something seemed to have changed in the very manner in which males endeavored to "be men" in France, at least in terms of cultural representations. Whatever ontological status was accorded the state of "being" a man, however, was undermined by the complex, never-ending task of "becoming" one. When the Catholic writer F. A. Vuillermet decided to write a book about manhood, for example, he gave it a title that, in addition to its obvious reference to Laprade, unwittingly conveyed the paradox of masculine identity during this period: *Soyez des hommes! À la conquête de la virilité* (Be Men! To-

ward the Conquest of Virility). Vuillermet was, of course, no social construc-
tionist, but the notion that masculinity was something that had to be *conquered*
suggested how contemporary observers sensed, despite frequent references to
the naturalness of gender identity, that there was something necessarily contingent and constructed about masculinity. Even when men could agree on a stable
definition of the term, manhood was neither something that could be taken for
granted nor a set of character traits guaranteed by possession of a male anatomy.
Rather, as the very process of "conquest" implied, it was viewed as the result of
repeated effort and constant vigilance. At the same time, the very contingency
of masculine identity rendered it especially vulnerable and thus something that
could be itself overcome, or "conquered," by the tide of femininity and decadence that seemed to be rising everywhere at the turn of the century: in pornographic literature and prostitution, in schools and elite culture, in the declining
birthrate and the modest rise of feminist politics. Subtle concessions to the constructed nature of gender, however, hardly diminished the cultural drive to craft
"real" men. As we have seen, it was when the vulnerability of normative manhood was being repeatedly underscored that new efforts were made to conquer
virility through sports, dieting, and physical culture. Writing about the rebirth
of French pride in 1912, Étienne Rey added his voice to the chorus that demanded that French manhood ground itself in more robust pursuits: "More than
ever before we live under the reign of Force, and France will cease to exist if
she should only be the delicate flower of Latin culture."[4] By 1913 even the health
reformer Georges Hébert, who had criticized physical culture's potential for excess, concurred nevertheless that new men must be made: "Be strong! Weaklings
are either useless or cowards."[5]

For Laprade and many others at the turn of the century, manhood required
abandoning contemplation in favor of action; in a culture of force, "dreamers"
do not qualify as "men." During the final decades of the nineteenth century,
doubts about the masculinity of men engaged in sedentary and cerebral pursuits
had been emerging throughout Western culture, but not at the same pace or with
the same degree of intensity. In Britain, Australia, and the United States, for instance, physical exercise, muscularity, and team sports had been vigorously proposed since the 1870s as necessary elements of embodied masculinity, if not as
correctives to the feminizing influence of motherly love and muscular weakness.
As a consequence, in these countries, weak, bookish, sedentary young men were
increasingly denounced as sissies or worse.[6] Although the developments outlined
in this book were not unique to France, the gender conventions that were al-

ready in place and the manner in which changes unfolded reflect the specificities of the French experience. That this process took place later in France, often with an admiring eye to these Anglo-Saxon counterparts, reveals the more durable attachment between intellectuality and manhood for the bourgeoisie, which had only come to preeminence with the consolidation of the Third Republic and was just beginning to reap the benefits of a more meritocratic educational system. On the other hand, the emerging critique of the intellectual male, however belatedly it occurred, also reveals a lingering tension at the heart of French conceptions of manhood, especially when compared to gender conventions upheld by other nations. The persistent tendency of French rightists to condemn both leftist intellectuals and the bourgeoisie as flabby, weak, and effeminate clearly illustrates the persistence of this tension in a society where, during the 1950s, many people happily characterized themselves as *intellectuel.* To say that French culture has a more positive view of intellectuals than, say, American or Australian culture, would, generally speaking, be correct. It would nevertheless be simplistic, however, to allow such cultural prestige to mask the ambivalent relationship that exists in French culture between intellectuality and masculine identity.

Misgivings about the reputation of French manhood on the international stage did not depend upon the conflicts of the Dreyfus Affair in order to be fully articulated. As stated in Chapter 2, Dreyfusard intellectuals had inherited and tried to negotiate with a pejorative definition of the man of thought that, albeit several centuries old, had been steadily gaining ground in France since the 1880s. There is thus every reason to believe that the decline of the intellectual male as an emblem of French manhood would have taken place without the tensions generated by the Dreyfus Affair, but it is unlikely that it would have proceeded in the same manner. As we have seen, the emergence of a group of men who embraced this designation in the name of the national interest allowed hitherto localized critiques of overly cerebral and physically weak bourgeois males to rise to public consciousness. By juxtaposing competing definitions of masculinity, the scandal provoked by the Dreyfusards' critique of the military may have even accelerated these developments.

If the Dreyfus Affair constituted an arena for the contest of masculinities, it also played a part in the formation of twentieth-century French views on manhood and politics. Many scholars point to the Dreyfus Affair as a significant turning point in European political and racial attitudes, and have thus rightly identified it as a pivotal development that, despite the particularities of its fin-de-siècle context, ultimately points beyond itself. That the debates and divisions of the Affair were not put to rest with the 1899 pardon or the 1906 rehabilitation of Dreyfus demonstrates the continuing relevance of the Affair for debates about race, gender, and nation well beyond World War I. The alarming rise and triumph of fascist politics during the 1920s and 1930 prompted many intellectuals to search for the political origins of fascism in the Dreyfus Affair, the violence of which, in the words of Hannah Arendt, "foreshadowed future developments, so that the main actors of the Affair sometimes seem to be staging a huge dress rehearsal for a performance that had to be put off for more than three decades."[7] Historians, too, have often been unable to write about the Affair without alluding to its ominous long-term effects. "With hindsight it is easy to be perceptive," confess Jean-Marie Mayeur and Madeleine Reberioux: "the cult of the soil, the mystique of race, the power of the military, all in the name of national order—these words mean something to us, these images are outlined on the horizon behind us. Dreyfusism undoubtedly deserves to be an eternal ideal. As for anti-Dreyfusism, it was certainly a sign for the future, but no one fully recognized it."[8] Viewing the Dreyfus Affair in teleological terms has consequences for how we assess the aims and motivations of its main actors: anti-Dreyfusards emerge not merely as anti-Semites but as veritable protofascists helping to usher in the age of total war and mass extermination. While a claim such as this cannot be categorically denied, it prefigures the manner in which we perceive those who struggled against this movement. With their enemies roundly condemned as protofascists, the Dreyfusards come off as everything they always claimed to be: selfless, unproblematic defenders of human rights, veritable antifascists *avant la lettre*.

Such a perspective has no doubt contributed to what might be seen as the political mythology of the heroism of liberal and leftist intellectuals. For much of the twentieth century, inquiries into intellectuals reflect a similar view, from Karl Mannheim's "free-floating intelligentsia" to Jean-Paul Sartre's attempt to embody the "total" intellectual. That the Dreyfus Affair provided a matrix for such a heroic person is now part of the lore of the modern intellectual, a body of thought that has retained its currency in certain circles. Bernard-Henri Lévy, for instance, sustains this association between intellectuals and heroism when he writes passionately about how, lining up against the forces of racism was "the other France. . . . It stood for courage and honor and the fight for justice and truth, which was already on the march. High-minded, indomitable, democratic Frenchmen took Dreyfus's part and rebelled against what they took to be an outrage." In Lévy's view, Dreyfusards were not merely courageous in their opposition to official and popular views of Dreyfus but represented courage itself in embarking, like other intellectuals in his 1991 book *Les Aventures de la liberté: Une Histoire subjective des intellectuels*, on their "adventures on the freedom road."[9]

In Lévy's view, the engaged intellectual is validated by his participation in the ideology of adventure. Yet the alleged manliness of such intellectuals was no less controversial during the interwar years than it had been during the Affair, and in the hands of fascist writers, the figure of the intellectual was challenged as much because of his alleged physical inferiority as for his divergent political views. Although scholars like Zeev Sternhell list virility among the many qualities that characterized the future order envisioned by fascists, Barbara Spackman rightly observes that such qualities (like youth, duty, sacrifice, strength, obedience, sexuality, and war) were in fact all "inflections of the term 'virility.'"[10] Klaus Theweleit, George Mosse, and others have revealed how important assertions of virility were for German fascism, and how these claims were positioned in relation to women, Jews, homosexuals, and other "pathological" types. That the intellectual and the cerebral, sedentary bourgeois would be singled out as pathetic modern countertypes to the fascist fantasy of manliness illustrates quite well the resonance of fin-de-siècle gender tensions well into the twentieth century.[11] Just as the political and racial tensions of the Dreyfus Affair arguably set the stage for future developments, so, too, did the contest of masculinities that it articulated and facilitated.

Nor did these tensions abate with the end of World War II, even in France itself, where the resurgence of rightist politics since 1945 featured a corresponding reassertion of old gender typologies, especially as many tried to reconstruct French manhood in the wake of the defeat and occupation.[12] This made it possible for the Poujadists of the 1950s to condemn leftist intellectuals for their "corporeal mediocrity," as Roland Barthes put it, in contrast to the Poujadists themselves, who labored with their hands.[13] In the early 1960s, Gilles Parrault celebrated the virtues of fascism by way of an explicit contrast with the kind of men we have encountered already in this book. "On one side, force and beauty, purity; on the other, the obese ones and skinny ones, the aperitif drinkers, men who are vile and impure. . . . For those who *live* the fascist glory cannot help but profoundly despise, and despise *physically*, those who stagnate in the somber valleys of life, the old ones, the ugly ones, the ones who would never march thirty kilometers at a stretch, who would never jump with a parachute, the ones who think, gossip, and have it easy—the subhumans."[14]

If rightists transformed intellectuals into effeminates, however, liberal and socialist intellectuals countered such claims with strategies of their own. As a number of recent studies of political discourses reveal, throughout the twentieth century, stereotypes about gender and sexuality have abounded in discourses that are for and against fascism. While we know that German and Italian fascists issued obsessive calls for virility and violent condemnations of the "effeminacy" of Jews, homosexuals, intellectuals, and the decadent bourgeoisie, we also know that socialists and liberals have often explained fascism by reference to the deficient manliness or "unnatural" sexual preferences of fascist men and the crowds they inspired. Pointing to the real or repressed homosexuality of fascists as the dark underbelly of their "tough guy" personae has been a favorite way for nonfascist intellectuals to demonstrate how far they stand from such "perverse" political and sexual practices, thus asserting the normality, if not the virility, of those who would challenge authoritarianism.[15] In such discourses, healthy heterosexuality and "true" manhood seem to be assured through the battle against fascism, even if that battle is waged only with a pen and miles away from the action.

Given the tendency of antifascist literature to denounce both fascists and collaborators as effeminate, if not homosexual, David Carroll warns against concluding "that 'the masculine' is *in its essence* already fascist or prefascist, and that 'the feminine' is thus privileged as the antifascist principle or force par excellence."[16] This is good advice. Of course the styles of masculinity celebrated by fascists and antifascists differed in some respects; yet insofar as both emphasized courage, action, struggle, and sacrifice, their views of what counted as "manly" were no more antithetical than those which circulated during the Dreyfus Affair. Here the distinction between the fascist and nonfascist male must surely be problematized, for as Barbara Spackman observes, fascism "as a discursive regime is . . . merely a particularly feverish example of a more general formulation."[17] It is rather more sensible to submit that, like the Dreyfus Affair, fascism raised issues and provoked tensions that placed masculinity itself at stake by pitting different kinds of men against one another. One might even maintain that by resurrecting the tension between force and reason, fascism represented one more conflict between men of thought and men of action, here featured in the form of sedentary bourgeois and heroic soldier-athletes. To wonder whether one or the other style of masculinity had more of a hand in the rise of fascism misses the point. Whereas in earlier decades, historians had confidently plotted the long-term development of totalitarian and racist thought by way of the most explicit instances of nationalist and anti-Semitic ideology, many scholars today dispute narratives that depict such developments as simple deviations from Western liberal humanism. If we accept Zygmunt Bauman's view that fascism and the Holocaust were integrally bound up with the processes of modernity, we also need to admit that it took both kinds of men to initiate and maintain the fascist machine.[18]

Although more work is needed on these matters, it is evident that the tensions explored in this book extend beyond the scope of French culture and fascism. After all, the crisis of French manhood was a particular expression of a broader Western cultural tendency to stress the importance of physicality as a means of avoiding the feminizing pitfalls of modernity. Our contemporary crisis of masculinity appears to have roots extending at least as far back as the fin de siècle, when "crisis" emerged as a more or less permanent state of affairs.

Notes

Introduction: The Body Politics of the Dreyfus Affair

1. Le Moine, "Le Juif," *La Croix*, 3 November 1894, 1.

2. Unsigned, "Traitre," *La Croix*, 23 February 1898, 4.

3. Bertrand Taithe, *Defeated Flesh: Welfare, Warfare, and the Making of Modern France* (Manchester: Manchester University Press, 1999); Eugen Weber, *France, Fin de Siècle* (Cambridge, Mass.: Belknap Press, 1986), 105–29; Robert A. Nye, *Crime, Madness, and Politics in Modern France: The Medical Concept of National Decline* (Princeton, N.J.: Princeton University Press, 1984).

4. Émile Zola, "The Syndicate," in *The Dreyfus Affair: "J'accuse" and Other Writings*, ed. Alain Pagès (New Haven, Conn.: Yale University Press, 1996), 19.

5. André de Séipse [André Suarès], *Lettre III sur la soi-disant Ligue de la patrie* (Paris, 1899), 15–16.

6. T. J. Jackson Lears, "American Advertising and the Reconstruction of the Body, 1880–1930," in *Fitness in American Culture: Images of Health, Sport, and the Body, 1830–1940*, ed. Kathryn Grover (Amherst: University of Massachusetts Press, 1989), 63.

7. The following works are notable for breaking with conventional approaches to the Dreyfus Affair: Norman L. Kleeblatt, ed., *The Dreyfus Affair: Art, Truth, and Justice* (Berkeley: University of California Press, 1987), Christophe Charle, *Naissance des "intellectuels," 1890–1900* (Paris: Minuit, 1990); Richard Griffiths, *The Use of Abuse: The Polemics of the Dreyfus Affair and Its Aftermath* (London: Berg, 1991); and Venita Datta, *Birth of a National Icon: The Literary Avant-Garde and the Emergence of the Modern Intellectual* (Albany: State University of New York Press, 1999). As this book will reveal, my own understanding of the cultural politics of intellectual life has been greatly enhanced by these pioneering studies.

8. Edward Berenson, *The Trial of Madame Caillaux* (Berkeley: University of California Press, 1992); Ruth Harris, *Murders and Madness: Medicine, Law, and Society in the Fin de Siècle* (Oxford: Clarendon Press, 1989); Robert A. Nye, *Masculinity and Male Codes of Honor in Modern France* (New York: Oxford University Press, 1993); Daniel Pick, *Faces of Degeneration: A European Disorder, c. 1848–c. 1918* (New York: Cambridge University Press, 1989); and Ann-Louise Shapiro, *Breaking the Codes: Female Criminality in Fin-de-Siècle Paris* (Stanford, Calif.: Stanford University Press, 1996).

9. Here too there are notable exceptions, but studies of the Dreyfus Affair that consider the role of sexual stereotypes about Jews accord more attention to right-wing circles, where anti-Semitic imagery was generally more intense, thus exposing so-called "philo-Semitic" discourses to less scrutiny. See Pierre Birnbaum, *Anti-Semitism in France: A Political History from Léon Blum to the Present*, trans. Miriam Kochan (Oxford: Blackwell,

1992), 147–77, and Stephen Wilson, *Ideology and Experience: Antisemitism in France at the Time of the Dreyfus Affair* (Rutherford, N.J,: Fairleigh Dickinson University Press, 1982). Among Sander Gilman's many books on anti-Semitism in Western culture and medicine, see *Jewish Self-Hatred: Anti-Semitism and the Hidden Language of the Jews* (Baltimore: Johns Hopkins University Press, 1986), *The Jew's Body* (New York: Routledge, 1993); *Freud, Race, and Gender* (Princeton, N.J.: Princeton University Press, 1993), and *Franz Kafka, The Jewish Patient* (New York: Routledge, 1995).

10. See, e.g., Roger Chartier, *Cultural Origins of the French Revolution* (Durham, N.C.: Duke University Press, 1991); Robert Darnton, *The Forbidden Best-Sellers of Pre-Revolutionary France* (London: HarperCollins, 1996); Lynn Hunt, *The Family Romance of the French Revolution* (Berkeley: University of California Press, 1993); Dorinda Outram, *The Body and the French Revolution: Sex, Class, and Political Culture* (New Haven, Conn.: Yale University Press, 1989); and Antoine de Baecque, *The Body Politic: Corporeal Metaphor in Revolutionary France, 1770–1800* (Stanford, Calif.: Stanford University Press, 1997).

11. Robert L. Hoffman, *More Than a Trial: The Struggle over Captain Dreyfus* (New York: Free Press, 1980), 152.

12. Hannah Arendt, *The Origins of Totalitarianism* (San Diego: Harcourt Brace, 1976); Robert S. Wistrich, "Three Dreyfusard Heroes: Lazare, Zola, Clémenceau," in *Les Intellectuels face à l'affaire Dreyfus alors et aujourd'hui*, ed. Roselyne Koren and Dan Michman (Paris: L'Harmattan, 1998), 13–41.

13. Zygmunt Bauman, *Modernity and the Holocaust* (Ithaca, N.Y.: Cornell University Press, 1989), 5.

14. Rita Felski, *The Gender of Modernity* (Cambridge, Mass,: Harvard University Press, 1995), 4–5.

15. Scholars in gender studies are sometimes skeptical about whether a "crisis of masculinity" actually occurred during this time, often citing the persistence of patriarchal social relationships and the continued subordination of women. Yet because gender is as much about identification as it is about social position, a crisis of gender identity is not easily reducible to shifting social structures. For instance, if we concede that the construction of personal and group identity proceeds through exclusion, disavowal, contestation, and redefinition, one can agree with Steven Angelides that sexual identity, "indeed all identity, is therefore in a state of perpetual crisis: an inability to complete, and the compulsion to repeat, the forever unstable and shifting norms and boundaries of identity. This is *the crisis of identity which is identity itself*." Clearly, however, perceptions of crisis are felt more keenly during certain historical periods, where insistent proclamations of crisis fulfill a number of discursive functions. In other words, what is at stake is less the "reality" of crisis than the effects that flow from endless talk about crisis. Sally Robinson describes the importance of taking the discourse of gender crisis seriously: "Announcements of crisis, both direct and indirect, are *performative*, in the sense that naming a situation a crisis puts into play a set of discursive conventions and tropes that condition the meanings that event will have. A crisis is 'real' when its rhetorical strategies can be discerned and its effects charted." Whether we acknowledge a real diminishment of male power and privilege during the fin de siècle is thus less important than examining how the rhetoric of crisis creates a sense of trauma and "performs the cultural work of centering attention on dominant masculinity." See Steven Angelides, *A History of Bisexuality* (Chicago: University of Chicago Press, 2001), 193; Sally Robinson, *Marked Men: White Masculinity in Crisis* (New York: Columbia University Press, 2000), 10, 11.

16. Pick, *Faces of Degeneration*, 73.

17. Annelise Maugue, *L'Identité masculine en crise au tournant du siècle, 1871–1914* (Paris: Rivages, 1987), 7.

18. Pascal Ory and Jean-François Sirinelli, *Les Intellectuels en France, de l'affaire Dreyfus à nos jours* (Paris: Armand Colin, 1986), 8–10.

19. Datta, *Birth of a National Icon.*

20. Jeremy Jennings, "Introduction: Mandarins and Samurais: The Intellectual in Modern France," in *Intellectuals in Twentieth-Century France: Mandarins and Samurais*, ed. id. (New York: St. Martin's Press, 1993), 12. Well into the 1950s, many French people professionally as diverse as doctors, lawyers, engineers, army officers, teachers, booksellers, typists, and insurance clerks preferred to describe themselves as *intellectuels*. Cf. Theodore Zeldin, *A History of French Passions, 1848–1945*, vol. 2: *Intellect, Taste and Anxiety* (1977; Oxford: Clarendon Press, 1993), 1121.

21. Michael Nerlich, *Ideology of Adventure: Studies in Modern Consciousness, 1100–1750*, trans. Wlad Godzich (Minneapolis: University of Minnesota Press, 1987).

22. John M. Hoberman, "Otto Weininger and the Critique of Jewish Masculinity," in *Jews and Gender: Responses to Otto Weininger*, ed. Nancy A. Harrowitz and Barbara Hyams (Philadelphia: Temple University Press, 1995), 145.

23. On the modern masculine stereotype, see George Mosse, *The Image of Man: The Creation of Modern Masculinity* (New York: Oxford University Press, 1996). Among intellectual communities in the West, verbal sparring was often cast in strictly martial terms, perhaps as a compensatory gesture. See Walter Ong, *Fighting for Life: Contest, Sexuality, and Consciousness* (Amherst: University of Massachusetts Press, 1989), 119–48, and Dena Goodman, *The Republic of Letters: A Cultural History of the French Enlightenment* (Ithaca, N.Y.: Cornell University Press, 1994). On businessmen employing martial language as a compensatory strategy, see Peter N. Stearns, *Be a Man! Males in Modern Society*, 2d ed. (New York: Holmes & Meier, 1990), 112. On the revival of medievalism and the martial ideal in late-nineteenth-century America, see T. J. Jackson Lears, *No Place of Grace: Antimodernism and the Transformation of American Culture, 1880–1920* (New York: Pantheon Books, 1981).

24. Edmond Goblot, *La Barrière et le niveau: Étude sociologique sur la bourgeoisie française moderne* (1925; reprint, Paris: Presses universitaires de France, 1967), 35, 26.

25. Pierre Bourdieu, *Distinction: A Social Critique of the Judgement of Taste*, trans. Richard Nice (Cambridge, Mass.: Harvard University Press, 1984), 100. For more on the habitus and the body, see Pierre Bourdieu, *The Logic of Practice*, trans. Richard Nice (Stanford, Calif.: Stanford University Press, 1990), 66–79.

26. See also Anne C. Vila's attempt to "re-somatize" the eighteenth century in *Enlightenment and Pathology: Sensibility in the Literature and Medicine of Eighteenth-Century France* (Baltimore: Johns Hopkins University Press, 1998).

ONE: Masculine Performances

1. Martin Johnson, *The Dreyfus Affair: Honour and Politics in the Belle Époque* (New York: St. Martin's Press, 1999), 32–36; Jean-Denis Bredin, *The Affair: The Case of Alfred Dreyfus*, trans. Jeffrey Mehlman (New York: George Braziller, 1986), 3–8.

2. Bredin, *Affair*, 3–8.

3. Eric Cahm, *The Dreyfus Affair in French Society and Politics* (London: Longman, 1996), 16–19.

4. Joseph Reinach, *Histoire de l'affaire Dreyfus* (Paris: Éditions de la Revue blanche, 1901–11), vol. 1: *Le Procès de 1894*, 502–3.

5. Unsigned, "L'Exécution: Dégradation d'Alfred Dreyfus," *La Lanterne*, 7 January 1895, 1.

6. Thomas Grimm, "L'Expiation," *Le Petit Journal*, 6 January 1895, 1.

7. Unsigned, "Le Général Mercier, ministre de la guerre," *Paris-Journal*, 6 January 1895, 1.

8. Unsigned, "La Dégradation du traître Dreyfus," *Le Petit Parisien*, 6 January 1895, 1.

9. Maurice Paléologue, *My Secret Diary of the Dreyfus Case*, trans. Eric Mosbacher (London: Secker & Warburg, 1957), 42.

10. Vanessa R. Schwartz, *Spectacular Realities: Early Mass Culture in Fin-de-Siècle France* (Berkeley: University of California Press, 1998); Rae Beth Gordon, *Why the French Love Jerry Lewis: From Cabaret to Early Cinema* (Stanford, Calif.: Stanford University Press, 2001).

11. Cf. Jonas Barish, *The Antitheatrical Prejudice* (Berkeley: University of California Press, 1981); Marvin Carlson, "The Resistance to Theatricality," *SubStance* 31 (2002): 238–250.

12. Jan Goldstein, "'Moral Contagion': A Professional Ideology of Medicine and Psychiatry in Eighteenth- and Nineteenth-Century France," in *Professions and the French State, 1700–1900*, ed. Gerald L. Geison (Philadelphia: University of Pennsylvania Press, 1984), 207–8.

13. Katherine Fischer Taylor, *In the Theater of Criminal Justice: The Palais de Justice in Second Empire Paris* (Princeton, N.J.: Princeton University Press, 1993), 27, 28, 40, 42, 53.

14. Ibid., 47–48.

15. Joseph Reinach, *Histoire de l'affaire Dreyfus*, vol. 1: *Le Procès de 1894*, 491.

16. G., "L'Attitude de Dreyfus au Conseil de guerre de 1894," *Le Gaulois*, 7 August 1899, 1.

17. Ch[arles]. D[upuy]., "La Moustache de Dreyfus," *La Gazette de France*, 9 August 1899, 1.

18. De Vandières, "L'Actualité: La Dégradation," *Gil Blas*, 7 January 1895, 2.

19. *La Petite République*, 7 January 1895, 2.

20. Anne Vincent-Buffault, *A History of Tears: Sensibility and Sentimentality in France* (London: Macmillan, 1991), 204.

21. Edward Berenson, *The Trial of Madame Caillaux* (Berkeley: University of California Press, 1992).

22. Jean Ajalbert, *Gil Blas*, 6 January 1895. See Michel Drouin, *L'Affaire Dreyfus de A à Z* (Paris: Flammarion, 1994), 38.

23. Shapiro, *Breaking the Codes*, 138.

24. Dorinda Outram, *The Body and the French Revolution: Sex, Class, and Political Culture* (New Haven, Conn.: Yale University Press, 1989), 68–89.

25. Michael Burns, *Dreyfus: A Family Affair* (New York: HarperCollins, 1991).

26. Peter N. Stearns, *American Cool: Constructing a Twentieth-Century Emotional Style* (New York: New York University Press, 1994).

27. Burns, *Dreyfus*, 64, 69, 71, 121.

28. Ibid.

29. Paléologue, *My Secret Diary*.

30. Léo Marchès, "La Dégradation du capitaine Dreyfus," *Le Siècle*, 6 January 1895, 2.

31. Unsigned, "Dégradation du traître," *La Croix*, 6 January 1895, 2.

32. Édouard Conte, "La Dégradation du capitaine Dreyfus," *Echo de Paris*, 7 January 1895, 2.

33. André de Boisandré, "L'Exécution de Dreyfus," *La Libre Parole*, 6 January 1895, 1.

34. Unsigned, "La Dégradation du traitre Dreyfus," *Le Petit Parisien*, 6 January 1895, 2.

35. M.D., "Après la dégradation," *Gil Bas*, 7 January 1895, 3.

36. Gaston Méry, "La Dégradation de Dreyfus," *La Libre Parole*, 6 January 1895, 2.

37. This file, held by the Centre des archives d'outre-mer, commented on the stiffness of Dreyfus's left arm, his baldness, and a few scars, but reported nothing that would have connected his bodily signs to criminal behavior.

38. Thomas Grimm, "L'Expiation," *Le Petit Journal*, 6 January 1895, 1.

39. Unsigned, "L'Exécution," *La Lanterne*, 7 January 1895, 1.

40. Robert A. Nye, *Masculinity and Male Codes of Honor in Modern France* (New York: Oxford University Press, 1993), 107–8.

41. Michael Anton Budd, *The Sculpture Machine: Physical Culture and Body Politics in the Age of Empire* (New York: New York University Press, 1997), 15.

42. Général Thoumas, *Le Livre du soldat: Vertus guerrières* (Paris: Berger-Levrault, 1891), 331.

43. Édouard Drumont, *La France juive* (1886; Paris: Flammarion, 1912), 1: 11.

44. Daniel Boyarin, *Unheroic Conduct: The Rise of Heterosexuality and the Invention of the Jewish Man* (Berkeley: University of California Press, 1997), 72, 81.

45. Jews were well represented in the French officer corps; in 1895, there were 10 generals, 9 colonels, 9 lieutenant-colonels, 46 majors, 90 captains, 89 lieutenants, and 104 NCOs. Reuben Ainsztein, *Jewish Resistance in Nazi-Occupied Eastern Europe* (London: Paul Elek, 1974), 92.

46. See, e.g., Zygmunt Bauman, "Exit Visas and Entry Tickets: Paradoxes of Jewish Assimilation," *Telos* 77 (Fall 1988): 45–77.

47. Abbé Henri Grégoire, *Essai sur la régénération physique, morale et politique des juifs: Ouvrage couronné par la Société royale des sciences et des arts de Metz, le 23 août 1788* (Metz: Devilly, 1789; reprint, Paris: Stock, 1988), 57–64, 163, 168, 175.

48. Ibid., 58, 175. On the representation of Jewishness in the pre-Zionist writings of Max Nordau, see Jay Geller, "The Conventional Lies and Paradoxes of Jewish Assimilation: Max Nordau's Pre-Zionist Answer to the Jewish Question," *Jewish Social Studies* 1 (Spring 1995): 129–60. See also Robert S. Wistrich, "Max Nordau and the Dreyfus Affair," *Journal of Israeli History* 16 (1995): 1–17.

49. There is now a wide body of scholarship on the role of gender before and during the French Revolution. See, e.g., Joan B. Landes, *Women and the Public Sphere in the Age of the French Revolution* (Ithaca, N.Y.: Cornell University Press, 1988); Lynn Hunt, *The Family Romance of the French Revolution* (Berkeley: University of California Press, 1993); and Antoine de Baecque, *The Body Politic: Corporeal Metaphor in Revolutionary France, 1750–1800* (Stanford, Calif.: Stanford University Press, 1997).

50. Bauman, "Exit Visas and Entry Tickets," 52.

51. Sander Gilman, *Making the Body Beautiful: A Cultural History of Aesthetic Surgery* (Princeton, N.J.: Princeton University Press, 1999), 22.

52. Simon Schwarzfuchs, *Napoleon, the Jews, and the Sanhedrin* (London: Routledge & Kegan Paul, 1979), 127. See also Paula E. Hyman, *The Jews of Modern France* (Berkeley: University of California Press, 1998), 47.

53. André de Boisandré, *Napoléon antisémite* (Paris: Librairie antisémite, 1900), 20–21.

54. See John M. Efron, "Images of the Jewish Body: Three Medical Views from the Jewish Enlightenment," *Bulletin for the History of Medicine* 69 (1995): 349–66. Gender performance and assimilation to gentile culture were therefore closely related (if not synonymous) activities that were expected of Jewish men. So pervasive had this assimilationist drive become in France that it served to separate the nation's various Jewish communities, with acculturated Jews from Paris and the Bordeaux region drawing stark contrasts between themselves and those from traditional communities in the eastern provinces near Strasbourg, who were often derisively dismissed as "Germans." At the end of the nineteenth century, this tension between assimilated and unassimilated Jews became even more marked amid the massive migration of Jews from eastern Europe into France. Being recognized as an acculturated *israélite* rather than as a traditionalist *juif* was upheld as a cultural ideal, and in the eyes of many assimilated Jews being called the latter constituted an insult.

55. Dr F. Devay, *Du danger des mariages consanguins* (Paris: V. Masson, 1857), cited in Jean-Paul Aron and Roger Kempf, *La Bourgeoisie, le sexe et l'honneur* (Paris: Éditions complexe, 1984), 271.

56. Anatole Leroy-Beaulieu, *Israel Among the Nations: A Study of the Jews and Anti-Semitism*, trans. Frances Hellman (New York: G. P. Putnam's Sons, 1904), 178–79.

57. Ibid., 164, 164, 150.

58. Stephen Wilson, *Ideology and Experience: Antisemitism in France at the Time of the Dreyfus Affair* (Rutherford, N.J.: Fairleigh Dickinson University Press, 1982), 588.

59. Leroy-Beaulieu, *Israel Among the Nations*, 163–64, 165, 168, 169. On Jews and nervousness, see also Edward Shorter, *From the Mind into the Body: The Cultural Origins of Psychosomatic Symptoms* (New York: Free Press, 1994), 95–108.

60. Susan Kassouf, "The Shared Pain of the Golden Vein: The Discursive Proximity of Jewish and Scholarly Diseases in the Late Eighteenth Century," *Eighteenth-Century Studies* 32, no. 1 (1998): 101.

61. Émile Zola, "A Plea for the Jews," in id., *The Dreyfus Affair: "J'accuse" and Other Writings*, trans. Eleanor Levieux (New Haven, Conn.: Yale University Press, 1996), 3–5.

62. Linda Nochlin, "Degas and the Dreyfus Affair: A Portrait of the Artist as an Anti-Semite," in *The Dreyfus Affair: Art, Truth, and Justice*, ed. Norman Kleeblatt (Berkeley: University of California Press, 1987), 103, 111.

63. Zygmunt Bauman, "Allosemitism: Premodern, Modern, Postmodern," in *Modernity, Culture and "the Jew,"* ed. Bryan Cheyette and Laura Marcus (Cambridge, UK: Polity Press; Stanford, Calif.: Stanford University Press, 1998), 143–56.

64. Auguste-Frédéric-Louis de Marmont, *De l'esprit des institutions militaires* (Paris: Librairie militaire, 1845), 184.

65. Dominique Maingueneau, *Les Livres d'école de la republique, 1870–1914* (Paris: Le Sycomore, 1979), 101–17; Paul B. Miller, *From Revolutionaries to Citizens: Antimilitarism in France, 1870–1914* (Durham, N.C.: Duke University Press, 2002), ch. 1.

66. *Le Livre du gradé à l'usage des élèves caporaux, caporaux et sous-officiers d'infanterie* (Toulouse, 1893), quoted in Theodore Zeldin, *A History of French Passions*, vol. 2: *Intellect, Taste and Anxiety* (1977; reprint, Oxford: Clarendon Press, 1993), 881.

67. Stéphen Coubé, *L'Âme du soldat* (Paris: Victor Retaux, 1899), 20.

68. Augustin Hamon, "Les Professionels militaires," *Mercure de France* 9 (September 1893), 63–67.

69. Eugen Weber, *Peasants into Frenchmen: The Modernization of Rural France, 1870–1914* (Stanford, Calif.: Stanford University Press, 1976), 294–99.

70. Adrien Proust and Gilbert Ballet, *L'Hygiène du neurasthénique* (Paris: Masson, 1897), 12.

71. Alain Flambart, "L'Hystérie masculine en France à travers la littérature médicale" (doctoral diss., Faculté de Médecine, Université de Caen, 1981), 59. "Hysteria itself is observed today in the barracks!" claimed A. Corre in his *Aperçu général de la criminalité militaire en France* (Lyon: A. Storck, 1891), 32.

72. William Serman, *Les Officiers français dans la nation (1848–1914)* (Paris: Aubier Montaigne, 1982), 214.

73. Peter N. Stearns, *Be a Man! Males in Modern Society*, 2d ed. (New York: Holmes & Meier, 1990), 126.

74. See Lieutenant Guennebaud, *La Vie à la caserne au point de vue social* (Saint-Brieuc: Imprimerie René Prud'homme, 1906).

75. Carolyn J. Dean, *The Frail Social Body: Pornography, Homosexuality, and Other Fantasies in Interwar France* (Berkeley: University of California Press, 2000), 118–20.

76. Corre, *Aperçu général de la criminalité militaire en France*, 31.

77. Rudi C. Bleys, *The Geography of Perversity: Male-to-Male Sexual Behavior Outside the West and the Ethnographic Imagination, 1759–1918* (New York: New York University Press, 1995), 148–49. In medical texts, soldiers often figured among the social types most likely to succumb to the lure of same-sex attraction. See Dr J. Chevalier, *Une Maladie de la personnalité: L'Inversion sexuelle* (Paris: G. Masson, 1893), 215.

78. Dr L. Thoinot, *Attentats aux moeurs et perversions du sens génital* (Paris: Octave Doin, 1898), 313.

79. F. Carlier, *Les Deux Prostitutions* (Paris: E. Dentu, 1887), 283.

80. Ibid., 415n.

81. Pierre Delcourt, *Le Vice à Paris* (Paris: Alphonse Piaget, 1887), 283, 286.

82. John Grand-Carteret, *Derrière "lui" (homosexualité en Allemagne)* (Paris: E. Bernard, 1907; reprint, Lille: Cahiers Gai-Kitsch, 1992).

83. See *Le Petit Bleu*, 10 August 1899, 1. For a discussion of how homosexual imagery became bound up in discussions of the Affair, see Jean-Bernard, *Le Procès de Rennes 1899* (Paris: Alphonse Lemerre, 1900), 5–6.

84. Carlier, *Deux Prostitutions*, 462.

85. Joseph Davy, "La Vie privée d'Alfred Dreyfus," in *L'Affaire Dreyfus*, ed. Michel Winock (Paris: Seuil, 1998), 95.

86. Nicholas Dobelbower, "Petits bleus et Billets doux: Dangerous Correspondence(s) of the Dreyfus Affair," in *Intolérance et indignation: L'Affaire Dreyfus*, ed. Jean-Max Guieu (Paris: Fischbacher, 2000), 130–40.

87. Dean, *Frail Social Body*, 143n.

88. Unsigned, "Portrait du traître Dreyfus," *La Croix supplément*, 11 December 1894, 2.

89. Founded in 1880, the École supérieure de guerre was modeled on the Berlin military academy, thus enhancing its reputation as a "foreign" institution. See Jérôme Hélie, "L'Arche sainte fracturée," in *La France de l'affaire Dreyfus*, ed. Pierre Birnbaum (Paris: Gallimard, 1994), 233–35.

90. G., "L'Attitude de Dreyfus au Conseil de guerre de 1894," *Le Gaulois*, 7 August 1899, 1.

91. Thomas Grimm, "L'Expiation," *Le Petit Journal*, 6 January 1895, 1.

92. Édouard Drumont, "Le Cas de Dreyfus," *La Libre Parole*, 10 August 1899, 1.

93. F. Bellay, "Le Procès du Traitre," *L'Intransigeant*, 9 August 1899, 1.

94. Drumont, "Cas de Dreyfus," 1.

95. Maurice Barrès, *Ce que j'ai vu à Rennes* (Paris: Sansot, 1904), 10–11.

96. Unsigned, "Devant le conseil de guerre," *Le Matin*, 8 August 1899, 1.

97. Joseph Cornély, *Notes sur l'affaire Dreyfus* (Paris: Société française d'éditions d'art, 1899), 530.

98. Joseph Reinach, *Histoire de l'affaire Dreyfus*, vol. 5: *Rennes*, 281.

99. Henri Varennes, "Dreyfus devant ses juges." *L'Aurore*, 8 August 1899, 1; Joseph Reinach, "Classiques et romantiques," *Le Siècle*, 8 August 1899, 1.

100. Joseph Reinach, *Histoire de l'affaire Dreyfus*, vol. 5: *Rennes*, 296.

101. Roger Gatineau, "Le Procès Dreyfus," *La Petite République*, 14 August 1899, 2.

102. Unsigned, "Les Deux Dossiers," *Le Matin*, 10 August 1899, 2.

103. H. Villemar, *Dreyfus intime* (Paris: Stock, 1898), 75.

104. Nye, *Masculinity and Male Codes of Honor*, 207–8.

105. Leroy-Beaulieu, *Israel Among the Nations*, 202n.

106. Max Nordau, "Discours prononcé par M. le Dr Max Nordau," in Dr Théodore Herzl and Dr Max Nordau, *Discours prononcés au IIe congrès sioniste de Bâle*, trans. Jacques Bahar (Paris: Aux bureaux du Flambeau, 1899), 24–28.

107. Michael R. Marrus, *The Politics of Assimilation: A Study of the French Jewish Community at the Time of the Dreyfus Affair* (Oxford: Clarendon Press, 1971), 205.

108. Jean Ajalbert, *Sous le sabre* (Paris: Éditions de La Revue blanche, 1898), 221.

109. Pierre Birnbaum, "La Citoyenneté en péril: Les Juifs entre intégration et résistance," in *La France de l'affaire Dreyfus*, ed. Pierre Birnbaum (Paris: Gallimard, 1994), 514.

110. Prague, "Causerie," *Archives israélites* 50 (1 August 1889): 241.

111. *Archives israélites* 50 (27 June 1889): 208; Dr Paul Salmon, "Le Sanitorium israélite de Nice," *Univers israélite*, 16 February 1900, 693–94.

112. See Nye, *Masculinity and Male Codes of Honor*, 206, 209–10. See also L[ouis]. L[évy]., "Les Vertus militaires de juifs," *Univers israélite*, 5 February 1897, 632–34; id., "Le Soldat juif," *Univers israélite*, 7 May 1897, 204–6; R.T., "Le Duel et les juifs," *Univers israélite*, 26 November 1897, 293–96.

113. Pierre Birnbaum, *Anti-Semitism in France: A Political History from Léon Blum to the Present*, trans. Miriam Kochan (Oxford: Blackwell, 1992), 166–67.

114. T. J. Jackson Lears, "From Salvation to Self-Realization: Advertising and the Therapeutic Roots of the Consumer Culture, 1880–1930," in *The Culture of Consumption: Critical Essays in American History, 1880–1980*, ed. Richard Wighton and T. J. Jackson Lears (New York: Pantheon Books, 1983).

115. Hippolyte Prague, "Propos de Tischri: La Cure spirituelle," *Archives israélites* 50 (26 September 1889): 310–11.

116. Hippolyte Prague, "Questions du jour: Les Israélites hors de chez eux," *Archives israélites* 50 (20 August 1889): 278.

117. Maurice Bloch, "Les Vertus militaires des juifs," *Archives israélites* 58 (4 February 1897): 35.

118. Ibid.

119. L[ouis]. L[évy]., "Le Soldat juif," *Univers israélite*, 7 May 1897, 206.

120. Anonymous, "L'Héroïsme juif," *Archives israélites* 59 (1 September 1898): 285.

121. Hippolyte Prague, "Un Héros juif: Salomon Braun," *Archives israélites* 60 (4 November 1899): 359–60; Anonymous, "Variétés: L'Héroïsme d'un soldat juif," *Archives israélites* 61 (13 September 1900): 902.

122. Raou., "De face et de profile: I. M. Zadoc Kahn," *Univers israélite*, 18 November 1898, 269–70.

123. Louis Lévy, "M. Max Nordau et le Sionisme (deuxième article)," *Univers israélite*, 31 March 1899, 42–43. This term, *la femmelette*, also had definite homosexual connotations, which Lévy would have surely disavowed. See Vernon A. Rosario, *The Erotic Imagination: French Histories of Perversity* (New York: Oxford University Press, 1997), 87.

124. Hippolyte Prague, "Contre la décadence," *Archives israélites* 58 (21 January 1897): 17–19.

125. Mathieu Wolff, "Soyez forts!" *Univers israélite*, 15 December 1899, 398–400.

126. Zadig, "L'Attitude de Dreyfus," *Archives israélites* 60 (17 August 1899): 264.

PART II: Dreyfusard Fantasies

1. Richard Griffiths, *The Use of Abuse: The Polemics of the Dreyfus Affair and Its Aftermath* (New York: Berg, 1991), 4–5.

TWO: Sanctifying Dreyfus

1. Unsigned, "Au dépot: Dreyfus à l'anthropométrie et à la prison," *L'Eclair*, 7 January 1895, 2.

2. Joseph Reinach, *L'Affaire Dreyfus: La Voix de l'île* (Paris: Stock, 1898), 6.

3. Mark H. Gebler, "What Is Literary Antisemitism?" *Jewish Social Studies* 47 (Winter 1985): 1–20; Anna Sapir Abulafia, "Bodies in the Jewish-Christian Debate," in *Framing Medieval Bodies*, ed. Sarah Kay and Miri Rubin (Manchester: Manchester University Press, 1994), 123–37.

4. Richard Griffiths, *The Use of Abuse: The Polemics of the Dreyfus Affair and Its Aftermath* (New York: Berg, 1991), 96–99. Griffiths also maintains that the surprisingly widespread appearance of religious imagery in Dreyfusard polemic testifies more to the enduring legacy of such symbols in a predominantly Catholic country than to the existence of any sincere religious sentiment among these intellectuals.

5. G., "L'Attitude de Dreyfus au Conseil de guerre de 1894," *Le Gaulois*, 7 August 1899, 1. See also Thomas Grimm, "L'Expiation," *Le Petit Journal*, 6 January 1895, 1.

6. Ferdinand Brunetière, "Après le procès," *La Revue des deux mondes*, 15 March 1898, 428–46.

7. See, e.g., Jean Ajalbert, *Sous le sabre* (Paris: Éditions de La Revue blanche, 1898), 3.

8. Christophe Charle, *Naissance des "intellectuels," 1880–1900* (Paris: Minuit, 1990).

9. Geneviève Idt, "L'Intellectuel' avant l'affaire Dreyfus," *Cahiers de lexicologie* 15 (April 1968): 35–46.

10. Edmond Goblot, *La Barrière et le niveau: Étude sociologique sur la bourgeoisie française moderne* (1925; reprint, Paris: Presses universitaires de France, 1967), 32–33.

11. Peter N. Stearns, *Be a Man! Males in Modern Society*, 2d ed. (New York: Holmes & Meier, 1990), 112.

12. John Grand-Carteret, *L'Affaire et l'image: 266 caricatures françaises et étrangères* (Paris: Flammarion, 1898), 10.

13. Steven Shapin, "The Philosopher and the Chicken: On the Dietetics of Disembodied Knowledge," in *Science Incarnate: Historical Embodiments of Natural Knowledge*, ed. Christopher Lawrence and Steven Shapin (Chicago: University of Chicago Press, 1998), 37.

14. Charle, *Naissance des "intellectuels."*

15. Stearns, *Be a Man!* 132–33.

16. Samuel Tissot, *Essai sur les maladies des gens du monde* (Paris: P.-F. Didot le jeune, 1771).

17. Anne C. Vila, *Enlightenment and Pathology: Sensibility in the Literature and Medicine of Eighteenth-Century France* (Baltimore: Johns Hopkins University Press, 1998), 95–97.

18. J. H. Réveillé-Parise, *Physiologie et hygiène des hommes livrés aux travaux de l'esprit* (Paris: Baillière, 1881); Aimé Riant, *Hygiène du cabinet de travail* (Paris: Baillière, 1882).

19. On the mounting critique of the bureaucratic male, see Annelise Maugue, *L'Identité masculine en crise au tournant du siècle, 1871–1914* (Paris: Rivages, 1987), 71–74.

20. George Mosse, *The Image of Man: The Creation of Modern Masculinity* (New York: Oxford University Press, 1996), 83.

21. Eugen Weber, "Gymnastics and Sports in *fin-de-siècle* France: Opium of the Classes?" *American Historical Review* 76 (1971): 70–98.

22. Paul Gerbod, "L'État et les activités physiques et sportives des années 1780 aux années 1930," *La Revue historique* 301 (January–June 1999): 320.

23. Jadwiga Szejko, *Influence de l'éducation sur le développement de la neurasthénie* (Lyon: A Rey, 1902), 59.

24. Borel, *Nervosisme ou neurasthénie*, 44.

25. Foveau de Courmelles, *Comment on se défend contre la neurasthénie*, 24. For more on this topic, see my "Neurasthenia and Manhood in Fin-de-Siècle France," in *Cultures of Neurasthenia from Beard to the First World War*, ed. Roy Porter and Marijke Gijswijt-Hofstra (Amsterdam: Rodopi, 2001), and Robert A. Nye, "Degeneration, Neurasthenia and the Culture of Sport in Belle Époque France," *Journal of Contemporary History* 17 (January 1982): 51–68.

26. Angus McLaren, *Trials of Masculinity: Policing Sexual Boundaries, 1870–1930* (Chicago: University of Chicago Press, 1997), 35.

27. This was not a new concern, for the problem of an "excess of educated men" had plagued France since the eighteenth century. Under the July Monarchy, for instance, Louis-Philippe's prefect of the Seine warned him about such potential threats: "The déclassés, the doctors without patients, the architects without buildings, the journalists without journals, the lawyers without clients, all the misunderstood, maladjusted, famished characters who, having found no seat at the banquet, try to overturn the table to get the plates. There are your makers of revolutions, your high-priests of anarchy, your buccaneers of insurrection." Quoted in Alan B. Spitzer, *The French Generation of 1820* (Princeton, N.J.: Princeton University Press, 1987), 225–26.

28. Henry Bérenger, *Les Proletaires intellectuels en France* (Paris: Éditions de La Revue, 1896), 33.

29. Anson Rabinbach, *The Human Motor: Energy, Fatigue, and the Origins of Modernity* (Berkeley: University of California Press, 1990).

30. Henri de Parville, "Psychologie: Travail de tête et travail manuel," *Annales politiques et littéraires*, September 1896, 189–90. See also Riant, *Hygiène du cabinet de travail*, 60.

31. Père Didon, *Influence morale des sports athlétiques* (Paris: J. Mersch, 1897), 19–20.

32. Julien Benda, *La Jeunesse d'un clerc* (1937; reprint, Paris: Gallimard, 1964), 24, 33, 35.

33. Ibid., 69–71.

34. Ibid., 58, 96.

35. René Ghil, "Parole féconde," in *Livre d'hommage des lettres françaises à Émile Zola* (Paris: Société libre d'Édition des Gens de Lettres, 1898), sec. 1, 60.

36. Paul Gerbod, "L'Éthique héroïque en France (1870–1914)," *Revue historique* 268 (July–December 1982): 409–29.

37. Philippe Tissié, *La Fatigue et l'entraînement physical* (Paris: Alcan, 1897), 334, cited in Nye, "Degeneration, Neurasthenia and the Culture of Sport in Belle Époque France," 67n.

38. Gustave Le Bon, *The Psychology of Socialism* (1899; reprint, Wells, Vt.: Fraser Publishing, 1965), 52.

39. Unsigned, "Le Prolétariat intellectuel," *Le Temps*, 25 January 1898, 1.

40. Maurice Barrès, *Scènes et doctrines du nationalisme* (1902; reprint, Paris: Émile-Paul, 1926), 226.

41. Maurice Barrès, *Ce que j'ai vu à Rennes* (Paris: Sansot, 1904), 108.

42. On the purported inverse relationship between brain volume and musculature, see Szejko, *Influence de l'éducation*, 64–67.

43. Pierre Quillard, ed., *Le Monument Henry* (Paris: Stock, 1899), 405–6.

44. Philippe E. Landau, *L'Opinion juive et l'affaire Dreyfus* (Paris: Albin Michel, 1995), 68.

45. Stephen Wilson, *Ideology and Experience: Antisemitism in France at the Time of the Dreyfus Affair* (Rutherford, N.J.: Fairleigh Dickinson University Press, 1982), 609–11; Venita Datta, *Birth of a National Icon: The Literary Avant-Garde and the Emergence of the Modern Intellectual* (Albany: State University of New York Press, 1999).

46. Rabinbach, *Human Motor*, 156. See also Jan Goldstein, "The Wandering Jew and the Problem of Psychiatric Anti-Semitism in Fin-de-Siècle France," *Journal of Contemporary History* 20 (1985): 521–52.

47. Quillard, ed., *Le Monument Henry*, 158, 440, 442, 637.

48. Caran d'Ache, "Page d'histoire: 'Baptême intellectuel,'" *Psst . . . !* 12 February 1898, 3.

49. Georges Clemenceau, "Le 'Syndicat' grandit," in *L'Iniquité* (Paris: Stock, 1899), 142, 143. This article was originally published on 18 January 1898.

50. Paul Brulat, *L'Affaire Dreyfus: Violence et raison* (Paris: Stock, 1898), 152.

51. Ghil, "Parole féconde," 60.

52. Robert A. Nye, *Masculinity and Male Codes of Honor in Modern France* (New York: Oxford University Press, 1993), 206, 209–10.

53. Jean-Marie Mayeur and Madeleine Reberioux, *The Third Republic from Its Origins to the Great War, 1871–1914*, trans. J. R. Foster (Cambridge: Cambridge University Press, 1984), 192.

54. A. Gerschel, *Les Défenseurs de la justice* (Paris: Stock, 1898), n.p.; listed under "les indépendants." Stock identifies Henri de Bruchard as a friend of Octave Mirbeau, but says little more. P.-V. Stock, *Mémorandum d'un éditeur* (Paris: Stock, Delamain et Boutelleau, 1938), 98.

55. Joseph Cornély, *Notes sur l'affaire Dreyfus* (Paris: Société française d'éditions d'art, 1899), 512.

56. "Hommage au bon géant invincible à qui cette consécration sanglante manquait seule pour que ce ne fut pas au figuré qu'on parlât pour lui de combat et de victoire, et qui n'a même plus à envier à la gloire militaire le privilège magnifique des soldats: Donner

son sang." Marcel Proust to Fernand Labori, 15[?] August 1899, in Proust, *Correspondance*, *vol. 1896–1901* (Paris: Plon, 1976), 295.

57. Georges Clemenceau, "Des hommes!" in *Vers la réparation* (Paris: Stock, 1899), 58. This article was originally published on 10 August 1898. The phallic implications of these metaphors of army and Church—the saber and *le goupillon* (aspergillum, or holy water sprinkler)—are fairly obvious. It is worth mentioning that *le sabre et le goupillon* were rivals as well as partners in power, and one Catholic writer even insisted that the saber "is but a toy in comparison with this far more formidable weapon: *le goupillon!*" Le Moine, "Goupillon," *La Croix*, 28 February 1898, 1.

58. Brulat, *L'Affaire Dreyfus: Violence et raison*, 12.

59. Datta, *Birth of a National Icon*, 153.

60. Octave Mirbeau, "Préface: Derrière un grillage," in *Hommage des artistes à Picquart* (Paris, 1899), 1.

61. Joseph Reinach, *Une Conscience: Le Lieutenant-colonel Picquart* (Paris: Stock, 1898), 6, 7.

62. Francis de Pressensé, *Un Héros: Le Colonel Picquart* (Paris: Stock, 1898), xi.

63. Maurice Barrès quoted in John Cerullo, "The Intellectuals and the Imagination of Heroism During the Dreyfus Affair," *Proceedings of the Western Society for French History* 25 (Fall 1997): 191.

64. Barrès, *Ce que j'ai vu à Rennes*, 80.

65. H. Villemar [Hélène Naville], *Essai sur le colonel G. Picquart* (Paris: Stock, 1899), 37.

66. Mirbeau, "Préface: Derrière un grillage," 2.

67. Dr Édouard Toulouse, *Enquête médico-psychologique sur les rapports de la supériorité intellectuelle avec névropathie: Introduction générale: Émile Zola* (Paris: Société d'Éditions scientifiques, 1896). For more on the Toulouse study, see Chapter 5.

68. Unsigned, "M. Zola poursuivi," *Eclair*, 15 January 1898, 2.

69. Saint-Georges de Bouhélier, contribution to "Non! Pour Émile Zola," *L'Essor*, 6 February 1898, 14.

70. Octave Mirbeau, "Un matin, chez Émile Zola," in *Livre d'hommage des lettres françaises à Émile Zola* (Paris: Société libre d'Édition des Gens de Lettres, 1898), 73.

71. Georges Clemenceau, "Le Lieutenant Zola," in *La Honte* (Paris: Stock, 1903), 24. This article was originally published on 25 December 1899.

72. Lucien Victor-Meunier, contribution to *Livre d'hommage des lettres françaises à Émile Zola*, 71.

73. Gerschel, *Les Défenseurs de la justice*, n.p. (first page).

74. Villemar, *Essai sur le colonel G. Picquart*, 7.

75. Frederick Brown, *Zola: A Life* (London: Papermac, 1997), 746. On the enduring theme of sacrifice in twentieth-century French intellectual life, see Allan Stoekl, *Agonies of the Intellectual: Commitment, Subjectivity, and Performativity in the Twentieth-Century French Tradition* (Lincoln: University of Nebraska Press, 1992).

76. See Carolyn Walker Bynum, *Jesus as Mother: Studies in the Spirituality of the High Middle Ages* (Berkeley: University of California Press, 1982).

77. See G. Stanley Hall, *Jesus, the Christ, in the Light of Psychology* (1917), cited in T. J. Jackson Lears, "From Salvation to Self-Realization: Advertising and the Therapeutic Roots of the Consumer Culture, 1880–1930," in *The Culture of Consumption: Critical Essays in American History, 1880–1980*, ed. Richard Wighton and T. J. Jackson Lears (New York: Pantheon Books, 1983), 10.

78. Thomas Hughes's *The Manliness of Christ* (London: Macmillan, 1879), nicely exemplifies this tendency to masculinize Jesus. See also Donald E. Hall, ed., *Muscular Christianity: Embodying the Victorian Age* (Cambridge: Cambridge University Press, 1994). One could conclude that the appropriation of Christ as an archetype of manliness is symptomatic of what Michael Kimmel has described as the raiding of the cultural heritage for emblems capable of supporting new definitions of masculinity. See Michael S. Kimmel, "Consuming Manhood: The Feminization of American Culture and the Recreation of the Male Body, 1832–1920," *Michigan Quarterly Review* 33 (Winter 1994): 7.

79. Edward Berenson, *The Trial of Madame Caillaux* (Berkeley: University of California Press, 1992), 191–92.

80. See Jan Goldstein, "The Hysteria Diagnosis and the Politics of Anticlericalism in Late Nineteenth-Century France," *Journal of Modern History* 54 (June 1982): 209–39; Dr Binet-Sanglé, *La Folie de Jésus: Ses connaissances, ses idées, son délire, ses hallucinations* (Paris: A. Maloine, 1910), vols. 1–4. For a discourse on the beauty of Jesus and his various body parts, see R. P. Philpin de Rivière, *La Physiologie de Christ: Le plus beau des enfants des hommes* (Paris: H. Oudin, 1899), 169–83, 251–70.

81. Ernest Renan, *The Life of Jesus*, trans. J. M. Dent (London: Everyman's Library, 1945).

82. Michael Paul Driskel, *Representing Belief: Religion, Art, and Society in Nineteenth-Century France* (University Park: Pennsylvania State University Press, 1992); Frank Paul Bowman, *Le Christ romantique* (Geneva: Droz, 1973).

83. This was particularly so among Dreyfusards, whose campaign followed stages analogous to the founding of a new faith. "First, there was the epiphany inspired by Zola's intervention; next, the acceptance of a 'priestly' vocation as moral stewards of the sociopolitical order; then, the institutionalization of a new 'church'; and, inevitably, the revolt of heretics against the new orthodoxy." Cerullo, "Religion and the Psychology of Dreyfusard Intellectualism," *Historical Reflections / Réflexions historiques* 24 (Spring 1998): 94.

84. Pressensé, *Héros*, xii–xiii.

85. Armand Charpentier, contribution to "M. Émile Zola et l'opinion," *La Critique* 4, 71 (5 February 1898): 26.

86. Octave Mirbeau, letter to Claude Monet, 22 February 1898, *Correspondance avec Claude Monet* (Tusson: Du Lérot, 1990), 194, quoted in Octave Mirbeau, *L'Affaire Dreyfus*, ed. Pierre Michel and Jean-François Nivet (Paris: Librairie Séguier, 1991), 65n.

87. Caronte, "Ecce homo," *Fischietto*, 8 February 1898, in John Grand-Carteret, *L'Affaire Dreyfus et l'image* (Paris: Flammarion, 1898), 254.

88. Jules Heyne, contribution to *Livre d'hommage des lettres françaises à Émile Zola*, 94.

89. John Grand-Carteret, *Zola en images: 280 illustrations, portraits, caricatures, documents divers* (Paris: Librairie Félix Juven, 1908), 57.

90. Sander Gilman, *Franz Kafka, The Jewish Patient* (New York: Routledge, 1995), 70.

91. This corresponds to the tactics of "displacement" often employed when dealing with Dreyfus. See Jean-Louis Lévy, "Alfred Dreyfus, anti-héros et témoin capital," in Alfred Dreyfus, *Cinq années de ma vie* (Paris: Maspero, 1982), 245–49.

92. Joseph Reinach, *Histoire de l'affaire Dreyfus*, vol. 5: *Rennes*, 206.

93. Maurice Paléologue, *An Intimate Journal of the Dreyfus Case*, trans. Eric Mosbacher (New York: Criterion, 1957), 21.

94. Séverine, *Vers la lumière: Impressions vécues* (Paris: Stock, 1900), 366.

95. Théodore Reinach [Un Intellectuel, pseud.], "Gonse-Pilate," in *Gonse-Pilate et autres histoires* (Paris: Stock, 1899), 43–51. Page nos. hereafter cited parenthetically in the text.

96. Zola, "Letter to M. Félix Faure, President of the Republic ('J'accuse')," in id., *The Dreyfus Affair: "J'accuse" and Other Writings*, trans. Eleanor Levieux (New Haven, Conn.: Yale University Press, 1996), 52.

97. Théodore Reinach, "Juif," in *La Grande Encyclopédie* (Paris: H. Lamirault, 1894), 21: 272–73. Page nos. hereafter cited parenthetically in the text.

98. Michael R. Marrus, *The Politics of Assimilation: A Study of the French Jewish Community at the Time of the Dreyfus Affair* (Oxford: Clarendon Press, 1971), 157–62.

99. Théodore Reinach was revealed as the true author of *Gonse-Pilate* years later by the book's publisher. See Stock, *Mémorandum d'un éditeur*, 242.

100. Louis-Albert Revah, "Les Intellectuels juifs face à l'affaire Dreyfus," *Revue des études juives* 155 (January–June 1996): 202.

101. On the biblical importance of the crowd as the counterpoint of Christ, see Robert G. Hamerton-Kelly, *The Gospel and the Sacred: Poetics of Violence in Mark* (Minneapolis: Fortress Press, 1994), 24, 26.

102. Ch. [Émile] Duclaux, in *Livre d'hommage des lettres françaises à Émile Zola*, 8.

103. Susanna Barrows, *Distorting Mirrors: Visions of the Crowd in Late-Nineteenth-Century France* (New Haven, Conn.: Yale University Press, 1981).

104. Léopold Lacour, "À Zola," in *Livre d'hommage des lettres françaises à Émile Zola*, 66.

105. Dr Léon Marchand, "Une lettre," in *Livre d'hommage des lettres françaises à Émile Zola*, 18.

106. Quoted in Revah, "Intellectuels juifs," 207.

107. Captain Paul Marin, "Lettre à Drumont," in *Esterhazy?* (Paris: Stock, 1898), xiii.

108. Julien Cordier, *Une Bataille pour une idée* (Paris: Stock, 1901), ix.

109. Fernand Hauser, contribution to "M. Émile Zola et l'opinion," 28. See, too, Brulat, *L'Affaire Dreyfus: Violence et raison*, 56, where the tension between Esterhazy (Barrabas) and Zola (Jesus) also appears.

110. On the conceptual connections sometimes made between Jews and crowds, see Peter Hayes, *The People and the Mob: The Ideology of Civil Conflict in Modern Europe* (Westport, Conn.: Praeger, 1992), 16.

THREE: Educating the Will

1. Eric Cahm, "Pour et contre Émile Zola: Les Étudiants de Paris en Janvier 1898," *Bulletin de la Société d'études jaurésiennes*, 1978: 12–15; Nancy Fitch, "Mass Culture, Mass Parliamentary Politics, and Modern Anti-Semitism: The Dreyfus Affair in Rural France," *American Historical Review* 97 (1992): 55–95.

2. Achille Steens, Preface to Léon Escoffier, *Ohé les jeunes!* (Paris, 1898), 3.

3. Jean Lemazurier, *Catéchisme dreyfusard* (Paris, 1898), 15.

4. Paul Brulat, *L'Affaire Dreyfus: Violence et raison* (Paris, 1898), xxiv, 45. On the persistent problems that crowd activity posed for bourgeois republicans, even before the Boulanger crisis, see James R. Lehning, *To Be a Citizen: The Political Culture of the Early French Third Republic* (Ithaca, N.Y.: Cornell University Press, 2001), 58–86.

5. Daniel Pick, *Faces of Degeneration: A European Disorder, c. 1848–c. 1918* (New York: Cambridge University Press, 1989), 223.

6. Andreas Huyssen, *After the Great Divide: Modernism, Mass Culture, Postmodernism* (Bloomington: Indiana University Press, 1986), 52.

7. Susanna Barrows, *Distorting Mirrors: Visions of the Crowd in Late Nineteenth-Century*

France (New Haven, Conn.: Yale University Press, 1981); Robert A. Nye, *The Origins of Crowd Psychology: Gustave Le Bon and the Crisis of Mass Democracy in the Third Republic (London: Sage. 1975).*

8. "The *flâneur* can be born anywhere," noted one writer, "but he can only live in Paris." Un Flâneur, "Le Flâneur à Paris," in *Paris, ou Le Livre des cent-et-un* (Paris: Ladvocat, 1832), 98.

9. In light of how, for much of the nineteenth century, the "doctrine of separate spheres" prescribed for women the "private" domain of domestic pursuits (as opposed to the "public sphere" ideally inhabited by men), an unaccompanied woman on the street (i.e., in "public") risked being taken for a prostitute. Nevertheless this was a normative ideal, and there were numerous ways in which middle-class women challenged this public/private distinction. Cf. Janet Wolff, "The Invisible Flâneuse: Women and the Literature of Modernity," *Theory, Culture, and Society* 2 (1985): 37–46.

10. Antoine Furetière, *Dictionnaire universel* (Lattaye and Rotterdam: Arnaut et Reinier Leers, 1690), vol. 1, s.v. *badaud*, defines the word as "a pejorative nickname that one gives to the inhabitants of Paris."

11. Paul Imbs, *Trésor de la langue française* (Paris: Éditions du CNRS, 1974), 3: 1203.

12. Un Flâneur, "Le Flâneur à Paris," 98. *Les musards* sometimes rivaled *badauds* as countertypes to the *flâneur*, as in Louis Huart, *Physiologie du flâneur* (Paris: Aubert, 1841), 32–34.

13. Ibid., 104.

14. Auguste de Lacroix, "Le Flâneur," in *Les Français peints par eux-mêmes* (Paris: L. Curmer, 1842), 3: 64–72.

15. Priscilla Parkhurst Ferguson, "The *Flâneur* on and off the Streets of Paris," in *The Flâneur, ed.* Keith Tester (New York: Routledge, 1994), 27–28.

16. Alfred Delvau, *Les Dessous de Paris* (Paris, 1860), 121, quoted in Walter Benjamin, *Paris, capital du XIXe siècle*, trans. Jean Lacoste (Paris: Éditions du CERF, 1989), 453.

17. Alfred Delvau claimed that the *flâneur*'s observations of various social strata were not unlike those of a geologist identifying layers in rocks. "If that sort of thing could be done," Benjamin comments, "then, to be sure, life in the big city was not nearly so disquieting as it probably seemed to people." Walter Benjamin, *Charles Baudelaire: A Lyric Poet in the Era of High Capitalism*, trans. Harry Zohn (London: NLB, 1973), 39.

18. Charles Baudelaire, *Journaux intimes* (Paris: Librairie José Corti, 1949), 7.

19. Charles Baudelaire, "Le Peintre de la vie moderne," *Critique d'art* (Paris: Armand Colin, 1965), 1: 449.

20. Ibid.

21. Charles Baudelaire, *Artificial Paradises* (New York: Citadel Press, 1996), 51.

22. Alexandra K. Wettlaufer, "Paradise Regained: The *Flâneur*, the *Badaud*, and the Aesthetics of Artistic Reception in *Le Poème du haschisch*," *Nineteenth-Century French Studies* 24 (Spring–Summer 1996): 388–97. The *badaud* was thus a fragment of the crowd requiring only the mobilizing presence of others for his own actualization. This is why Walter Benjamin points out Baudelaire's mistake in reading Edgar Allen Poe's "The Man of the Crowd" as a negative portrait of the *flâneur*, for "the man of the crowd is no *flâneur*. In him, composure has given way to manic behavior." While the ideal typical *flâneur* wanders willfully and autonomously, the decrepit old man of Poe's tale represents a more pathological social type who cannot stand even his own company. This man of the crowd is propelled by impulse rather than volition, by fear rather than novelty. Yet despite all

this, he is still not entirely passive. This "worst heart of the world" is not merely unreadable, Poe reminds us, but participates actively in its own indecipherability. It "does not permit itself to be read," and therein lies its allure for the *flâneur*, whose vocation is to read the spectacle and transform it into text. Benjamin, "On Some Motifs in Baudelaire," in id., *Illuminations*, trans. Harry Zohn (New York: Schocken Books, 1969), 174. Elsewhere, however, Benjamin, too, reads Poe's story as a straightforward comment on *flânerie*. See Benjamin, *Charles Baudelaire*, 48.

23. Priscilla Parkhurst Ferguson, "The *Flâneur*: Urbanization and Its Discontents," in *Home and Its Dislocations in Nineteenth-Century France*, ed. Suzanne Nash (Albany: State University of New York Press, 1993), 48.

24. Victor Fournel, *Ce qu'on voit dans les rues de Paris* (Paris: Adolphe Delahays, 1858), 263.

25. Ibid., 261.

26. Charles Féré, *La Pathologie des émotions* (Paris: Alcan, 1892).

27. Fournel, *Ce qu'on voit dans les rues de Paris*, 263. For a discussion of the ubiquity of *badauderie* at the turn of the century, see Charles Rearick, *Pleasures of the Belle Époque* (New Haven, Conn.: Yale University Press, 1985).

28. Rita Felski, *The Gender of Modernity* (Cambridge, Mass.: Harvard University Press, 1995), 73.

29. Paul Aubry, *La Contagion du meurtre: Étude d'anthropologie criminelle* (Paris: Alcan, 1894), 2.

30. Ibid., 12. On the role of "soil" and "seed" in contemporary debates about tuberculosis, see David S. Barnes, *The Making of a Social Disease: Tuberculosis in Nineteenth-Century France* (Berkeley: University of California Press, 1995).

31. A. Vigouroux and P. Juquelier, *La Contagion mentale* (Paris: Octave Doin, 1905), 22.

32. Rae Beth Gordon, *Why the French Love Jerry Lewis: From Cabaret to Early Cinema* (Stanford, Calif.: Stanford University Press, 2001), 81, 82.

33. A. Corre, preface to Aubry, *Contagion du meurtre*, xxi.

34. As quoted in Deborah L. Silverman, *Art Nouveau in Fin-de-Siècle France: Politics, Psychology, and Style* (Berkeley: University of California Press, 1989), 87.

35. Ruth Harris, *Murders and Madness: Medicine, Law, and Society in the Fin de Siècle* (Oxford: Clarendon Press, 1989).

36. Gustave Le Bon, *The Crowd* (1895; New York: Viking, 1960), 30.

37. Ibid., 65.

38. Émile Duclaux, *Propos d'un solitaire* (Paris, 1898), 12.

39. Rachel Bowlby, *Just Looking: Consumer Culture in Dreiser, Gissing, and Zola* (London: Methuen, 1985), 29–32.

40. Le Bon, *Crowd*, 118.

41. Maurice Vauthier, *La France et l'affaire Dreyfus* (Paris, 1899), 3.

42. Cf. Henry Ner, *Les Prostitués: Études critiques sur les gens de lettres d'aujourd'hui* (Paris, 1904).

43. Brulat, *L'Affaire Dreyfus: Violence et raison*, 126–27.

44. Francis de Pressensé, *Un Héros: Le Colonel Picquart* (Paris: Stock, 1898), viii–ix.

45. Capitaine de l'Armée active [Capitaine Piétri], *L'Officier et la crise française* (Paris: Stock, 1900), 138.

46. Alfred Binet, "La Suggestibilité au point de vue de la psychologie individuelle," *Annales des sciences psychiques* 9 (1899): 75.

47. A. de Browne, *La Puissance en soi-même par le magnétisme et l'hypnotisme* (Macon: Perroux, 1903), 18–19.

48. Angus McLaren, *The Trials of Masculinity: Policing Sexual Boundaries, 1870–1930* (Chicago: University of Chicago Press, 1997), 86–87; Alain Corbin, *Women for Hire: Prostitution and Sexuality in France After 1850*, trans. Alan Sheridan (Cambridge, Mass.: Harvard University Press, 1990), 118, 168, 174–75.

49. Laurent Tailhade, quoted in John G. Hutton, *Neo-Impressionism and the Search for Solid Ground* (Baton Rouge: Louisiana State University Press, 1994), 55.

50. René Ghil, "Parole féconde," in *Livre d'hommage des lettres françaises à Émile Zola* (Paris: Société libre d'Édition des Gens de Lettres, 1898), sec. 1, 60.

51. Charles Albert, *À M. Émile Zola* (Brussels: Administration, 1898), 4.

52. Rita Felski, *The Gender of Modernity* (Cambridge, Mass.: Harvard University Press, 1995), 73–74.

53. Le Bon, *Crowd*, 102.

54. Colline, *Billets de la province*, 82.

55. Daniel Halévy, *Regards sur l'affaire Dreyfus* (Paris: Éditions de Fallois, 1994), 120–21.

56. Joc Maur, *Le Juif sur l'Ile du Diable, ou Critique de la raison impure* (Bern, 1898), 8.

57. McLaren, *Trials of Masculinity*, 33–34.

58. Jean-Jacques Rousseau, *Émile, or, On Education* (1762), trans. Allan Bloom (New York: Basic Books, 1979), 54.

59. A. Corre, preface to Aubry, *Contagion du meurtre*, xv.

60. Dr Pouillet, *De l'onanisme chez l'homme*, 3d ed. (Paris: Vigot Frères, 1897), 39.

61. Max Nordau, *Degeneration (1892)*, trans. from the 2d German ed., 1895 (Lincoln: University of Nebraska Press, 1993), 39.

62. For more on neurasthenia, see my "Neurasthenia and Manhood in Fin-de-Siècle France," in *Cultures of Neurasthenia from Beard to the First World War*, ed. Roy Porter and Marijke Gijswijt-Hofstra (Amsterdam: Rodopi, 2001), 325–57. Michael R. Finn has persuasively demonstrated the importance of neurasthenia to Marcel Proust's own sense of porosity and creativity. See Michael R. Finn, *Proust, the Body, and Literary Form* (Cambridge: Cambridge University Press, 1999). On the increasingly "permeable" nature of the male body generally during this time, see Carolyn J. Dean, *The Frail Social Body: Pornography, Homosexuality, and Other Fantasies in Interwar France* (Berkeley: University of California Press, 2000).

63. Jules Payot, *L'Éducation de la volonté* (1893; Paris: Alcan, 1912), 59, 136, 214.

64. Anne C. Vila, *Enlightenment and Pathology: Sensibility in the Literature and Medicine of Eighteenth-Century France* (Baltimore: Johns Hopkins University Press, 1998), 248.

65. See the discussion of the "cult of invalidism" in Bram Dijkstra, *Idols of Perversity: Fantasies of Feminine Evil in Fin-de-Siècle Culture* (Oxford: Oxford University Press, 1986), 25–63.

66. Janet Beizer, *Ventriloquized Bodies: Narratives of Hysteria in Nineteenth-Century France* (Ithaca, N.Y.: Cornell University Press, 1994), 41, 47, 81.

67. Norbert Elias, *The Civilizing Process* (1939; reprint, Oxford: Blackwell, 1997). For other studies that consider ways in which hygiene helped to construct the bourgeois self, see Georges Vigarello, *Concepts of Cleanliness: Changing Attitudes in France Since the Middle Ages*, trans. Jean Birrell (Cambridge: Cambridge University Press, 1988), and Alain Corbin, *The Foul and the Fragrant: Odor and the French Social Imagination* (Cambridge, Mass.: Harvard University Press, 1986).

68. Rolland, *Lectures encyclopédiques*, cited in Dominique Maingueneau, *Les Livres d'école de la république, 1870–1914* (Paris: Le Sycomore, 1979), 329.

69. Janet Oppenheim, *"Shattered Nerves": Doctors, Patients, and Depression in Victorian England* (New York: Oxford University Press, 1991), 146–51. For an analysis of similar developments in the United States, see Peter N. Stearns, *American Cool: Constructing a Twentieth-Century Emotional Style* (New York: New York University Press, 1994).

70. Anne Vincent-Buffault, *The History of Tears: Sensibility and Sentimentality in France* (London: Macmillan, 1991), 183, 186.

71. Ibid., 246.

72. Théodule Ribot, *Diseases of the Will*, trans. Merwin-Marie Snell from the 8th French ed. (1888) (Chicago: Open Court, 1894, 64.

73. Ribot, *Diseases of the Will*, 91.

74. Ibid., 65. On the impact of Ribot's study on the work of Marcel Proust, see Finn, *Proust, the Body, and Literary Form*, 45–56.

75. Payot, *Éducation de la volonté*, 189–90, 210.

76. Ibid., 24–25.

77. Ibid., 116–17.

78. Ibid., 203, 212–14.

79. For more on "moral vaccination," see Harris, *Murders and Madness*, 189. See also Paul-Émile Lévy, *L'Éducation rationnelle de la volonté* (Paris: Alcan, 1898).

80. Payot, *Éducation de la volonté*, 111.

81. Jan Goldstein, "The Hysterical Diagnosis and the Politics of Anticlericalism in Late Nineteenth-Century France," *Journal of Modern History* 54 (1982): 209–39.

82. Jann Matlock, *Scenes of Seduction: Prostitution, Hysteria, and Reading Difference in Nineteenth-Century France* (New York: Columbia University Press, 1994), 212.

83. Francis de Pressensé, *L'Idée de patrie* (Paris: P. Ollendorff, 1899), 12.

84. Armand Charpentier, *Les Côtés mystérieux de l'affaire Dreyfus* (Paris: Rieder, 1937), 208; see also Armand Israël, *Les Vérités cachées de l'affaire Dreyfus* (Paris: Albin Michel, 2000), 82.

85. Beizer, *Ventriloquized Bodies*, 62.

86. Dr Gustave Lauth, *Que l'on doit éviter, ce que l'on doit faire dans l'intérêt de sa santé* (Paris: Fischbacher, 1888), 36.

87. Payot, *Éducation de la volonté*, 192–93.

88. Nordau, *Degeneration*, 25–26.

89. Jean Ajalbert, *Sous le sabre* (Paris: Éditions de La Revue blanche, 1898), 166.

90. Georges Clemenceau, "L'Archimensonge," in *L'Iniquité* (Paris: Stock, 1899), 389. This article originally appeared on 5 June 1898.

91. Émile Durkheim, "L'Individualisme et les intellectuels," *La Revue bleue* 10 (1898), 10.

92. Villane, *Opinion publique et l'affaire Dreyfus*, 36.

93. Duclaux, *Propos d'un solitaire*, 8.

94. Albert Réville, *Les Étapes d'un intellectuel: À propos de l'affaire Dreyfus* (Paris: Stock, 1898), 2.

95. Ironically, this often meant the convergence of intellectuals who had for years considered one another to be irredeemably degenerate, a compromise notably illustrated by Max Nordau's decision to support Zola, who had been a primary target of his book *Degeneration*. See Hans-Peter Söder, "Disease and Health as Contexts of Fin-de-Siecle

Modernity: Max Nordau's Theory of Degeneration" (Ph.D. diss., Cornell University, 1991), 82.

96. Manuel Devaldès, contribution to "M. Émile Zola et l'opinion," *La Critique* 4, 71 (5 February 1898): 27.

97. P.-V. Stock, *Mémorandum d'un éditeur* (Paris: Stock, Delamain et Boutelleau, 1938), 25.

98. Julien Benda, "L'Affaire Dreyfus et le principe d'autorité," *Revue blanche* 20 (1899): 195, 196, 206.

99. Escoffier, *Ohé les jeunes!* 12.

100. Armand Charpentier, contribution to "M. Émile Zola et l'opinion," *Critique* 4, 71 (5 February 1898): 27.

101. L. Vérax [Docteur Oyon], *Essai sur la mentalité militaire a propos de l'affaire Dreyfus* (Paris, 1898), 56.

102. Joseph Reinach, *Histoire de l'affaire Dreyfus*, vol. 5: *Rennes*, 292.

103. Ginevra, *Catholique-dreyfusard* (Paris: Société libre d'édition des gens de lettres, 1899), 99.

104. Joseph Cornély, *Notes sur l'affaire Dreyfus* (Paris: Société française d'éditions d'art, 1899), 8.

105. Pressensé, *Héros*, v.

106. Edmond Cattier, in *Livre d'hommage des lettres françaises à Émile Zola*, 45.

107. Lucien Victor-Meunier, contribution to *Livre d'hommage des lettres françaises à Émile Zola*, 70.

108. Charpentier, *Côtés mystérieux*, 208.

109. Jean Doise, *Un secret bien gardé: Histoire militaire de l'affaire Dreyfus* (Paris: Seuil, 1994); Robert Kaplan, "Making Sense of the Rennes Verdict: The Military Dimension of the Dreyfus Affair," Journal of Contemporary History 34 (October 1999), 499–515.

110. Esterhazy, *Les Dessous de l'affaire Dreyfus* (Paris: Fayard, 1898), 4.

111. Quoted in Bredin, *Affair*, 222.

112. Séverine, *Vers la lumière*, 7, 8–9.

113. Jacques Bahar, *Le Traître* (Vincennes: Imprimerie L. Levy, 1898), 13.

114. Joseph Reinach, *Histoire de l'affaire Dreyfus*, 3: 248. Vol. and page nos. hereafter cited parenthetically in the text.

115. Sander Gilman, *The Jew's Body* (New York: Routledge, 1993). For a contemporary anti-Semitic portrait of the Jew, see Édouard Drumont, *La France juive* (1886; Paris: Flammarion, 1912), 1: 35.

116. Robert A. Nye, *Masculinity and Male Codes of Honor in Modern France* (Princeton, N.J.: Princeton University Press, 1993); Kevin McAleer, *Dueling: The Cult of Honor in Fin-de-Siècle Germany* (Princeton, N.J.: Princeton University Press, 1994).

117. Esterhazy, *Dessous de l'affaire Dreyfus*, 226.

118. Charles Péguy, *Notre jeunesse* (1910; reprint, Paris: Gallimard, 1957), 190, 192.

FOUR: Adventures of the Naked Truth

1. Eric Cahm, *The Dreyfus Affair in French Politics and Society* (London: Longman, 1996), 35; Mathieu Dreyfus, *L'Affaire Dreyfus telle que je l'ai vécue* (Paris: Grasset, 1978), 47–73.

2. Willa Z. Silverman, *The Notorious Life of Gyp: Right-Wing Anarchist in Fin-de-Siècle France* (New York: Oxford University Press, 1995).

3. These episodes, reported by Joseph Reinach, were relayed with scorn by Georges Sorel in *La Révolution dreyfusienne* (Paris, 1909), 27.

4. Gaston Mery, "Au jour le jour: Les Listes de protestation," *La Libre Parole*, 21 January 1898, 1.

5. P.-V. Stock, *Mémorandum d'un éditeur* (Paris: Stock, Delamain et Boutelleau, 1938), 217–18.

6. Willa Z. Silverman, "Fin-de-Siècle Amazons: Antidreyfusard Women and the Affair," in *Intolérance et indignation: L'Affaire Dreyfus*, ed. Jean-Max Guieu (Paris: Fischbacher, 2000), 199–200.

7. Steven C. Hause with Anne R. Kenney, *Women's Suffrage and Social Politics in the French Third Republic* (Princeton, N.J.: Princeton University Press, 1984), 32–36. On Marguerite Durand, see Mary Louise Roberts, "Acting Up: The Feminist Theatrics of Marguerite Durand," *French Historical Studies* 19 (Fall 1996), 1103–38. Séverine's many articles on the Dreyfus Affair were later published as *Vers la lumière: Impressions vécues* (Paris: Stock, 1900).

8. Séverine, "L'Accusé," *La Fronde*, 6 February 1898, 1.

9. Beatrice Braud, "Séverine, *écrivain de combat*," *Nineteenth-Century French Studies* 4 (Spring 1976): 404–12. See also Mary Louise Roberts, *Disruptive Acts: The New Woman in Fin-de-Siècle France* (Chicago: University of Chicago Press, 2002), 96.

10. Karen Offen, "Depopulation, Nationalism, and Feminism in Fin-de-Siècle France," *American Historical Review* 89 (*June 1984): 648–76*.

11. Others employed the presence of female Dreyfusards in such terms. Paul Brulat, for one, noted how ironic it was that it was the women of *La Fronde* who set "men the example of valiance!" Paul Brulat, *L'Affaire Dreyfus: Violence et raison* (Paris: Stock, 1898), 29.

12. Françoise Blum, "Itinéraires féministes à la lumière de l'Affaire," in *La Postérité de l'affaire Dreyfus*, ed. Michel Leymarie (Villeneuve d'Ascq: Presses universitaires du Septentrion, 1998), 93–101.

13. Pierre Quillard, ed., *Le Monument Henry* (Paris: Stock, 1899).

14. Veuve Michelet, contribution to *Hommage des artistes à Picquart* (Paris: Société libre d'édition des gens de lettres, 1899), 20.

15. Stock, *Mémorandum d'un éditeur*, 100.

16. Victor Basch, quoted in Helen Rodney, "Séverine," in *L'Affaire Dreyfus de A à Z*, ed. Michel Drouin (Paris: Flammarion, 1994), 284–85.

17. As Geneviève Fraisse writes, "Feminism is the appearance of man in woman or of woman in man," which draws even more attention to the pivotal role of the body in any cultural representation of women's struggles for emancipation. See Fraisse, *Reason's Muse: Sexual Difference and the Birth of Democracy*, trans. Jane Marie Todd (Chicago: University of Chicago Press, 1994), 195. On the public menace of feminism and its links to broader cultural fears about female criminality, see Ann-Louise Shapiro, *Breaking the Codes: Female Criminality in Fin-de-Siècle Paris* (Stanford, Calif.: Stanford University Press, 1996), 179–216.

18. Mlle E. Roch, *Ce que vaut une femme: Traité d'éducation morale et pratique des jeunes filles* (Reims: Dubois-Poplimont, 1888), v.

19. Karen Offen, "Depopulation, Nationalism, and Feminism in Fin-de-Siècle France," *American Historical Review* 89 (June 1984): 648–76.

20. Deborah L. Silverman, *Art Nouveau in Fin-de-Siècle France: Politics, Psychology, and Style* (Berkeley: University of California Press, 1989), 288.

21. Judith F. Stone, "The Republican Brotherhood: Gender and Ideology," in *Gender*

and the Politics of Social Reform in France, 1870–1914, ed. Elinor A. Accampo, Rachel G. Fuchs, and Mary Lynn Stewart (Baltimore: Johns Hopkins University Press, 1995).

22. Jean-Paul Laffitte, "Les Femmes et la république," *La Revue bleue*, 27 May 1893, 659.

23. Ibid., 659–60.

24. Elisabeth Badinter, *The Myth of Motherhood: An Historical View of the Maternal Instinct*, trans. Roger DeGaris (London: Souvenir Press, 1981), 254; Jacques Donzelot, *The Policing of Families*, trans. Robert Hurley (New York: Pantheon Books, 1979).

25. Gustave Droz, *Monsieur, madame et bébé*, 116th ed. (Paris: Havard, 1882), 289–305; Rosemary Lloyd, *The Land of Lost Content: Children and Childhood in Nineteenth-Century French Literature* (New York: Oxford University Press, 1992).

26. Émile Boutroux, "Avant-propos" to *Morale sociale: Leçons professées au Collège libre des sciences sociales*, by Émile Boutroux et al. (Paris: Aclan, 1899), iii, iv.

27. Mary Lynn Stewart, *For Health and Beauty: Physical Culture for French Women* (Baltimore: Johns Hopkins University Press, 2000).

28. Philippe Tissié, *L'Homme de demain: L'Éducation physique en France* (Brussels: Hayez, 1905), 61.

29. One expert wrote that "*lactation* is the continuation of *gestation*, and the mother has not fulfilled her role, I am not afraid to call it her duty, vis-à-vis her child until after she has nourished it with her milk." Dr G. Eustache, *La Puériculture* (Paris: Baillière et fils, 1903), 161.

30. Augusta Moll-Weiss, "Souvenirs d'une jeune maman," *Bébé: Revue d'hygiène et d'éducation de la première enfance* 8 (1 February 1904): 28.

31. This is evident in part through the military metaphors that abounded in pronatalist literature. See Rachel G. Fuchs, "The Right to Life: Paul Strauss and the Politics of Motherhood," in *Gender and the Politics of Social Reform*, ed. Accampo et al., 83–84.

32. Charles Féré, *La Pathologie des émotions* (Paris: Alcan, 1892), 257.

33. Here, too, Michelet served as a touchstone when he condemned parasitical forms of maternal love that aimed to "absorb" rather than awaken life in the child. See Jules Michelet, *Du prêtre, de la femme, de la famille*, 2d ed. (Paris: Comptoir des imprimeurs-unis, 1845), 322.

34. Albert-Émile Sorel, "« La Jeunesse pensive »," *La Revue bleue* 12 (11 November 1899): 534, 536.

35. Jacques Porcher, "La Femme française et le culte de l'enfant," *La Revue bleue*, 24 April 1897, 521.

36. Le Père Didon, *Influence morale des sports athlétiques* (Paris: J. Mersch, 1897), 8.

37. Ibid., 17.

38. Abbot H. Mocquillon, *L'Art de faire un homme: Conseils pratiques d'éducation moderne* (Paris: Librairie Molière, 1906), 90.

39. Urbain Gohier, *Les Prétoriens et la congrégation* (Paris: Éditions de La Revue blanche, 1900), 379–84.

40. Linda L. Clark, *Schooling the Daughters of Marianne: Textbooks and the Socialization of Girls in Modern French Primary Schools* (Albany: State University of New York Press, 1984).

41. A. Piffault, *La Femme de foyer: Éducation ménagère des jeunes filles* (Paris: Librairie Ch. Delagrave, 1908), 19. This was not a new idea. In June 1879, Senator Tastelin contended that "[i]n order to have fine men it is the mother who must be cultivated." See

Maurice Crubellier, *L'Enfance et la jeunesse dans la société française, 1800–1950* (Paris: Armand Colin, 1979), 197.

42. Karen Offen, "Feminism, Antifeminism, and National Family Politics in Early Third Republic France," in *Connecting Spheres: Women in the Western World, 1500 to the Present*, ed. Marilyn Boxer and Jean Quataert (New York: Oxford University Press, 1987).

43. Alfred Fouillée, "La Psychologie des sexes et ses fondamens physiologiques," *Revue des deux mondes*, 15 September 1893, 424.

44. Gustave Le Bon, "La Psychologie des femmes et les effets de leur éducation actuelle," *Revue scientifique (Revue Rose)*, 11 October 1890, 453–55.

45. Joseph Reinach, quoted in "Notes et impressions," *L'Illustration*, no. 91 (12 May 1888): 377.

46. Émile Durkheim, *The Division of Labor in Society* (1893; reprint, New York: Free Press, 1984), 20; Jennifer M. Lehmann, *Durkheim and Women* (Lincoln: University of Nebraska Press, 1994).

47. Offen, "Feminism, Antifeminism, and National Family Politics."

48. Michel Bréal, "À propos de l'enseignement des jeunes filles," *La Revue bleue* 17 (September 1892): 354.

49. One writer assured readers of *L'Illustration* that La Fronde was a "feminine" rather than feminist newspaper. M.N., "Chez les frondeuses," *L'Illustration*, no. 111 (13 January 1898): 60–61.

50. Maurice Barrès, cited in Pug., "Ce que pensent les hommes de la 'Fronde,'" *La Fronde*, 23 December 1897, 1.

51. Pierre Quillard, ed., *Le Monument Henry* (Paris: Stock, 1899), 411.

52. L'Abbé Demnise, *Dreyfus: La Révision* (Paris: A. Pierret, 1899), 13.

53. Jean Psichari, "Appel aux femmes de France," in *Livre d'hommage des lettres françaises à Émile Zola* (Paris: Société libre d'édition des gens de lettres, 1898), 26, 447.

54. For selections from these responses, see Michael Burns, *France and the Dreyfus Affair: A Documentary History* (Boston: Bedford/St. Martin's, 1999), 112–14.

55. Caran d'Ache, "Après 28 ans," *Psst . . . !* 39 (29 October 1898): 3; id., "Réveillon," *Psst . . . !* 48 (31 December 1898): 2; id., "Les Joies du retour," *Psst . . . !* 74 (1 July 1899): 2; id., "Complices," *Psst . . . !* 40 (5 November 1898): 2.

56. Quillard, ed., *Monument Henry*, 485.

57. Datta, *Birth of a National Icon*, 162–63.

58. Séverine, *La Fronde*, 14 January 1898, cited in *Défenseurs de la justice*, n.p.

59. Lynn Hunt, cited in Madelyn Gutwirth, *The Twilight of the Goddesses: Women and Representation in the French Revolutionary Era* (New Brunswick, N.J.: Rutgers University Press, 1992), 256.

60. Maurice Agulhon, *Marianne au pouvoir: L'Imagerie et la symbolique républicaine de 1880 à 1914* (Paris: Flammarion, 1989).

61. See also Marina Warner, *Monuments and Maidens: The Allegory of the Female Form* (New York: Atheneum, 1985).

62. Shapiro, *Breaking the Codes*, 66.

63. Matt K. Matsuda, *The Memory of the Modern* (New York: Oxford University Press, 1996), 113–14.

64. Stéphane Arnoulin, *L'Affaire La Roncière: Une Erreur judiciaire en 1835* (Paris: Librairie Paul Ollendorff, 1899), 365.

65. Bram Dijkstra, *Idols of Perversity: Fantasies of Feminine Evil in Fin-de-Siècle Culture* (Oxford: Oxford University Press, 1986).

66. Tamar Garb, *Bodies of Modernity: Figure and Flesh in Fin-de-Siècle France* (London: Thames & Hudson, 1998), 81–113.

67. See also Garb, *Bodies of Modernity*, for another development of this idea.

68. Warner, *Monuments and Maidens*, 318–20.

69. Marius Vallabrègues, contribution to "Hommage des jeunes écrivains à Émile Zola," *L'Essor*, 6 February 1898, 9.

70. Jules Grandjouan design, reprinted in *L'Affaire Dreyfus et le tournant du siècle (1894–1910)*, ed. Laurent Gervereau and Christophe Prochasson (Paris: Bibliothèque de documentation internationale contemporaine, 1994), 82.

71. Hermann-Paul, "Février 99: La Ligue de la Patrie Française," in *Deux cents dessins* (Paris: Éditions de la Revue blanche, 1900), 42.

72. Ibels, "Après les fameuses révélations de M. Cavaignac," *Le Sifflet* 24 (14 July 1898): 1.

73. John Grand-Carteret, *Zola en images: 280 illustrations, portraits, caricatures, documents divers* (Paris: Librairie Félix Juven, 1908), 57.

74. Tania Modleski, *Feminism Without Women*: Culture and Criticism in a Postfeminist Age (London: Routledge, 1991), 7, cited in Abigail Solomon-Godeau, *Male Trouble: A Crisis in Representation* (London: Thames & Hudson, 1997), 38.

75. Gutwirth, *Twilight of the Goddesses*, 256.

PART THREE: Remaking the Male Body

1. Michael Burns, *Dreyfus: A Family Affair* (New York: HarperCollins, 1991), 240–90.

2. Charles Maurras, "Des héros!" *L'Action française*, 5 May 1908: 1.

3. Édouard Berth, *Les Méfaits des intellectuels* (Paris: Rivière, 1913), 257–58, 268.

4. Léon Daudet, "L'Armée en proie aux juifs," *L'Action française*, 3 April 1908, 1.

5. Henri Vaugeois, "Rien n'est fini," *L'Action française*, 12 July 1909, 1.

FIVE: The Belly of Paris

1. Steven Shapin, "The Philosopher and the Chicken: On the Dietetics of Disembodied Knowledge," in *Science Incarnate: Historical Embodiments of Natural Knowledge*, ed. Christopher Lawrence and Steven Shapin (Chicago: University of Chicago Press, 1998), 22.

2. Séverine, *Vers la lumière: Impressions vécues* (Paris: Stock, 1900), 47–50. On images of Zola in popular culture, see Pierre-Olivier Perl, "Les Caricatures de Zola: Du naturalisme à l'affaire Dreyfus," *Historical Reflections / Réflexions historiques* 24 (Spring 1998): 137–54.

3. Plato, *Timaeus*, in *The Dialogues of Plato*, vol. 2, trans. Benjamin Jowett (New York: Random House, 1937), 49, 51. See also Carolyn Korsmeyer, *Making Sense of Taste: Food and Philosophy* (Ithaca, N.Y.: Cornell University Press, 1999).

4. Michael Schoenfeldt, "Fables of the Belly in Early Modern England," in *The Body in Parts: Fantasies of Corporeality in Early Modern Europe*, ed. David Hillman and Carla Mazzio (New York: Routledge, 1997), 243–61; Rita Felski, *The Gender of Modernity* (Cambridge, Mass.: Harvard University Press, 1995), 79–82.

5. "La Gueule," in *Trésor de la langue française* (Paris: Éditions du CNRS, 1981), 9: 583.

6. Cecilia Hartley, "Letting Ourselves Go: Making Room for the Fat Body in Feminist Scholarship," in *Bodies out of Bounds: Fatness and Transgression*, ed. Jana Evans Braziel and Kathleen LeBesco (Berkeley: University of California Press, 2001), 62.

7. "Force," in *Trésor de la langue française* (Paris: Éditions du CNRS, 1980), 8: 1064–68; Jean-Pierre Yahi, "Duel, savate et boxe française: Une Nouvelle Destinée des coups," in *Aimez-vous les stades? Les Origines historiques des politiques sportives en France (1870–1930)*, ed. Alain Ehrenberg (Paris: Recherches, 1980), 129.

8. Jacqueline Picoche, *Nouveau dictionnaire étymologique du français* (Paris: Hachette-Tchou, 1971), 374; Alain Duchesne and Thierry Leguay, *La Surprise: Dictionnaire des sens cachés* (Paris: Larousse, 1990), 153.

9. Henri-Frédéric Amiel, *Journal intime*, ed. Bernard Gagnebin and Philippe M. Monnier (Lausanne: L'Âge d'homme, 1989), 9: 1236, 10 June 1874.

10. Anson Rabinbach, *The Human Motor: Energy, Fatigue, and the Origins of Modernity* (Berkeley: University of California Press, 1990).

11. Gilbert Andrieu, *L'Homme et la force: Des marchands de la force au culte de la forme (XIXe et XXe siècles)* (Joinville-le-Pont: Actio, 1988), 173.

12. Advertisement, *Le Rire*, 182 (20 April 1898): 11.

13. Advertisement, *Le Petit Journal*, November 1902, 375. As was the case with many cures for male weakness, discretion remained paramount, which is why the makers of the Herculex assured interested men that a free brochure would be sent to them "in a sealed envelope."

14. Dr F. Aumont, *L'Estomac des gens du monde: Neurasthénie digestive* (Paris: n.p., 1908), 26.

15. Jean-Louis Flandrin, "From Dietetics to Gastronomy: The Liberation of the Gourmet," in *Food: A Culinary History from Antiquity to the Present*, ed. Jean-Louis Flandrin and Massimo Montanari, trans. Clarissa Botsford, Arthur Goldhammer, Charles Lambert, Frances M. Lopez-Morillas, and Sylvia Stevens (New York: Columbia University Press 1999), 431–32; Priscilla Parkhurst Ferguson, "A Cultural Field in the Making: Gastronomy in Nineteenth-Century France," in *French Food: On the Table, on the Page, and in French Culture*, ed. Lawrence R. Schehr and Allen S. Weiss (London: Routledge, 2001), 14–15.

16. Laure Adler, *Secrets d'alcôve: Histoire du couple de 1830 à 1930* (Paris: Hachette, 1983), 107.

17. Dr E. Contet, *Le Végétarisme: Étude critique, indications thérapeutiques* (Paris: Baillière, 1902), 96.

18. Victor Hugo quoted in Michaela Sullivan-Fowler, "Doubtful Theories, Drastic Therapies: Autointoxication and Faddism in the Late Nineteenth and Early Twentieth Centuries," *Journal of the History of Medicine and Allied Sciences* 50 (July 1995): 364–90.

19. Jean Anthelme Brillat-Savarin, *The Physiology of Taste, or Meditations on Transcendental Gastronomy*, trans. M. F. K. Fisher (New York: Knopf, 1972), 204–5. This bit of folk wisdom received some confirmation in 1981, when physicians demonstrated the relationship between emotional states and rates of excretion. See James C. Whorton, *Inner Hygiene: Constipation and the Pursuit of Health in Modern Society* (Oxford: Oxford University Press, 2000).

20. Samuel Tissot, *De la santé des gens de lettres* (1768; reprint, Geneva: Slatkine, 1981), 25–26.

21. Dr Fernand Barbary, *Les Misères du corps* (Paris: Société d'éditions scientifiques, 1901), 34–35.

22. Dr Frantz Glénard, *À propos d'un cas de neurasthénie gastrique: Entéronéphroptose traumatique* (Paris: Masson, 1887).

23. Charles Féré, *La Pathologie des émotions* (Paris: Alcan, 1892), 539.

24. E. Detois, *La Santé virile par l'hygiène* (Aurillac: Roux, 1901), 3.

25. Payot, *Éducation de la volonté*, 161, 162.

26. Detois, *Santé virile par l'hygiène*, 6.

27. Alain Corbin, "The Secret of the Individual," in *A History of Private Life: From the Fires of Revolution to the Great War*, ed. Michelle Perrot (Cambridge, Mass,: Belknap Press, 1990), 482.

28. Paul Dubois, *Self-Control and How to Achieve It* [*L'Éducation de soi-même*], trans. Harry Hutcheson Boyd (New York: Funk & Wagnalls, 1909), 230–32.

29. J.-K. Huysmans, *À rebours* (1884), trans. as *Against the Grain* (New York: Dover, 1969), p. 195.

30. Naomi Schor, "Agape and Anorexia: Decadent Fast and Democratic Feast," in *French Food: On the Table, on the Page, and in French Culture*, ed. Lawrence R. Schehr and Allen S. Weiss (London: Routledge, 2001), 93.

31. Dr A. Mollière, *Les Préjugés en diététique et dans les maladies des voies digestives* (Paris, 1913), cited in Theodor Zeldin, *A History of French Passions*, vol. 2: *Intellect, Taste, and Anxiety* (Oxford: Oxford University Press, 1973), 731–32.

32. "[C]onstipation leads to always-dangerous encephalic irritations," Dr J.-P. Beaude asserted in *Dictionnaire de médecine usuelle* (Paris: Didier, 1849), 1: lvi.

33. Dr Cassagnet, "Les Dépuratifs," *L'Hygiène au foyer: Médecine, hygiène et sciences vulgaires* 76 (15 June 1907): 79.

34. Citing the opinion of Claude Bernard, who adamantly opposed the use of purgatives because of the damage they caused to the intestines, Parville counseled his overzealous audience against abusing such remedies, suggesting instead a sensible diet and fresh air to allow the toxins to be naturally expelled from the body and "to burn off excess matter." Henri Parville, "Médecine: Hygiène de saison.—Les purgatifs," *Annales politiques et littéraires*, 2 April 1893, 221.

35. Advertisement, Purgatif Géraudel, *L'Illustration*, no. 2452 (22 February 1890), *annonces*, 175.

36. Mikhail Bakhtin, *Rabelais and His World*, trans. Hélène Iswolsky (Bloomington: Indiana University Press, 1984).

37. Alain Corbin, *The Foul and the Fragrant: Odor and the French Social Imagination* (Cambridge, Mass.: Harvard University Press, 1986), 144.

38. Émile Gautier, "Thérapeutique: Pour ne pas vieillir trop vite," *Annales politiques et littéraires*, 7 July 1907, 17–18. For the association between clean bowels and manly vitality in the United States, see T. J. Jackson Lears, *Fables of Abundance: A Cultural History of Advertising in America* (New York: Basic Books, 1994), 165; on the promotion of yogurt for colonic health, see Whorton, *Inner Hygiene*, 172–80. In the social body, excrement also seemed to be the "preferred milieu" of many other threats to the bourgeoisie, from prostitutes and crowds to pornography and homosexuals. Alfred Le Petit's outrageous caricature of Zola manages to capture many of these anxieties. Viewing Zola through the archaic lens of swine imagery (*cochonnerie*), Le Petit exploited the full sexual and excremental debasement implied in this form of abuse. Depicted as a pig, in this caricature, the novelist so often accused of publishing "filth" was shown sodomizing a man while defe-

cating on top of the tricolor flag. Norman L. Kleeblatt, "MERDE! The Caricatural Attack Against Émile Zola," *Art Journal* 52 (Fall 1993): 55–56.

39. Peter N. Stearns, *Fat History: Bodies and Beauty in the Modern West* (New York: New York University Press, 1997), 167.

40. Ibid., 60.

41. Ibid., 169.

42. Joan Jacobs Brumberg, *Fasting Girls: The Emergence of Anorexia Nervosa as a Modern Disease* (Cambridge, Mass.: Harvard University Press, 1988).

43. Dr G. Rouhet, "De l'obésité," *La Culture physique*, April 1910, 246.

44. Medical self-help literature from the sixteenth and seventeenth centuries offered a variety of practices that, by underscoring the uniqueness of individual physical constitution (as well as the correlation between the body's humoral balance and psychological disposition), encouraged greater introspection and care for the body in its most basic functions. Increased attention to the selection of a diet was crucial for the whole project of self-fashioning. As Michael Schoenfeldt remarks, "That the individual consumer can alter disposition by diet at once empowers that individual and pressures all dietary decisions." Michael Schoenfeldt, "Fables of the Belly in Early Modern England," in *The Body in Parts: Fantasies of Corporeality in Early Modern Europe*, ed. David Hillman and Carla Mazzio (New York: Routledge, 1997), 252.

45. Stephen Mennell, "On the Civilizing of Appetite," in *The Body: Social Process and Cultural Theory*, ed. Mike Featherstone, Mike Hepworth, and Bryan S. Turner (London: Sage, 1991), 126–56. For a more historical description of this process, and one that stresses the importance of youth culture to shifting ideals of body shape, see Keith Walden, "The Road to Fat City: An Interpretation of the Development of Weight Consciousness in Western Society," *Historical Reflections / Réflexions historiques* 12 (Fall 1985): 331–73.

46. Antoine de Baecque, *The Body Politic: Corporeal Metaphor in Revolutionary France, 1770–1800* (Stanford, Calif.: Stanford University Press, 1997); Wendy Gibson, "Attitudes Towards Obesity in Seventeenth-Century France," *Seventeenth Century French Studies* 13 (1991): 213–29. Male corsetry was fairly common in France during the early nineteenth century, but it came to be viewed as pretentious and effeminate by the 1840s. See Philippe Perrot, *Fashioning the Bourgeoisie: A History of Clothing in the Nineteenth Century*, trans. Richard Bienvenu (Princeton, N.J.: Princeton University Press, 1994), 162–63.

47. Jula Kristeva's concept of "abjection" is pertinent here: like other aspects of the body, fat appears as a part of the self that must be disavowed if a sense of subjective wholeness is to be projected. See Julia Kristeva, *Powers of Horror: An Essay on Abjection*, trans. Leon S. Roudiez (New York: Columbia University Press, 1982).

48. Georges Hébert, *La Culture virile et les devoirs physiques de l'officier combattant* (Paris: G. Oudin, 1913), 25.

49. On the importance of presenting an upright silhouette for early-nineteenth-century fashion, see Georges Vigarello, *Le Corps redressé: Histoire d'un pouvoir pédagogique* (1978; reprint, Paris: Armand Colin, 2001), 59–60.

50. Dr Rauland, *Le Livre des époux: Guide pour la guérison de l'impuissance* (Paris: 1852), 96–97.

51. Brillat-Savarin, *Physiology of Taste*, 205.

52. Charles Bouchard, *Leçons sur les maladies par ralentissement de la nutrition* (Paris: Librairie F. Savy, 1890), 118–20.

53. E. Demange, "Obésité," in *Dictionnaire encyclopédique des sciences médicales* (1880), 14: 14.

54. Dr Dheur, *Comment on se défend contre l'obésité* (Paris: Société d'éditions scientifiques, n.d.), 24.

55. Adler, *Secrets d'alcôve*, 106.

56. Adrien Proust and A. Mathieu, *L'Hygiène de l'obèse* (Paris: Masson, 1897), 60.

57. Ibid., 20.

58. Charles Bouchard quoted in ibid., 90.

59. See also Dr M. Leven, *La Névrose: Étude clinique et thérapeutique* (Paris: G. Masson, 1887).

60. Bakhtin, *Rabelais and His World*, trans. Iswolsky.

61. Detois, *Santé virile*, 8.

62. Dr. H. van de Velde, *L'Alimentation des gens bien portants et des malades* (Paris, 1899), 11.

63. Contemporary developments in measuring the amount of energy burned off by the "human motor" provided a scientific means of quantifying just how weak these men could be. In a table detailing the number of calories burned by different body types, one physician showed how the *homme solide* outstripped the *homme faible* at rest and during work. Significantly, according to his table, a weak man at rest scarcely burned more calories than an old woman and was surpassed altogether by a lactating mother. See Van de Velde, *Alimentation*, 16.

64. Philippe Tissié, *La Fatigue et l'entraînement physique* (Paris: Alcan, 1897), 26.

65. Proust and Mathieu, *Hygiène de l'obèse*, 207.

66. Jean-Paul Aron, *Le Mangeur du XIXe siècle* (Paris: Robert Laffont, 1973).

67. Demange, "Obésité," 33.

68. Dr Laissus fils, *Considérations sur la cure de l'obésité* (Paris: A. Maloine, 1909), 10–11. For a earlier work recommending the Brides sanatorium to the obese, see Dr Émile Philbon, *Du traitement de l'obésité aux eaux de Brides (Savoie)* (Paris: V. A. Delahaye, 1876).

69. Hillel Schwartz, *Never Satisfied: A Cultural History of Diets, Fantasies and Fat* (New York: Anchor Books, 1986), 17–18.

70. Proust and Mathieu criticized the thermal milieus, claiming that the "advantage of these cures is that one obtains among the patients a docility that they would no longer have at home. Their drawback is bringing about a rapid thinning through intense methods that cause fatigue. Obese people treated in this manner show a great tendency, once they return home and resume their bad habits, to regain quickly all they had lost." Proust and Mathieu, *Hygiène de l'obèse*, 339.

71. Laissus, *Considérations*, 12–29.

72. Dr J.-E. Ruffier, "L'Obésité et la culture physique," *La Culture physique* 13 (March 1905): 13. See also Dr Ruffier, *Le Traitement de l'obésité par la culture physique* (Paris: Librairie de "Portez-vous bien!" 1912).

73. Gabriel Bonvalot, preface to J. de Lerne, *Comment devenir fort* (Paris: Baillière, 1902), vii.

74. Edmond Desbonnet, "Ne confondons pas grosseur et force," *La Santé par les sports*, 15 May 1912, 337–38.

75. Dr J.-B. Wauquier, "L'Obésité: Gros ventre est synonyme de déchéance physique," *La Santé par les sports*, 8 March 1914, 4.

76. Anonymous, "Comme quoi il est prouvé que la Beauté est un gage de Santé," *La Santé par les sports*, 8 April 1913, 6.

77. Édouard Drumont, *La France juive* (1886; Paris: Flammarion, 1912), 2: 227.

78. Georges Demenÿ, *Les Bases scientifiques de l'éducation physique* (Paris: Alcan, 1902), 17.

79. Venita Datta, *Birth of a National Icon: The Literary Avant-Garde and the Emergence of the Modern Intellectual* (Albany: State University of New York Press, 1999), 128.

80. Marcel Proust quoted in Pierre Birnbaum, *Anti-Semitism in France: A Political History from Léon Blum to the Present*, trans. Miriam Kochan (Oxford: Blackwell, 1992), 167.

81. Dr Émile Laurent, *Les Bisexués* (Paris: Georges Carré, 1894), cited in Carolyn J. Dean, *The Frail Social Body: Pornography, Homosexuality and Other Fantasies in Interwar France* (Berkeley: University of California Press, 2000), 140.

82. Joseph Reinach, *Histoire de l'affaire Dreyfus*, vol. 3: *La Crise* (Paris: Librairie Charpentier et Fasquelle, 1903), 339.

83. Maurice Barrès, *Ce que j'ai vu à Rennes* (Paris: Sansot, 1904), 57, 72. Dreyfusards, of course, had different views. "Big, robust, hardy, violent" is how George[s] Bonnamour describes Labori in *Le Procès Zola: Impressions d'audience* (Paris: A. Pierret, 1898), 201.

84. Reinach, *Histoire de l'affaire Dreyfus*, vol. 3: *La Crise*, 9.

85. Edmond and Jules de Goncourt, *Journal: Mémoires de la vie littéraire* (Paris: Fasquelle, 1959), 2: 1149–50, 15 October 1876.

86. The inaugural issue of *Paris-santé illustré*, a small product-oriented magazine published by the Pharmacie Pigalle (34, Boulevard de Clichy), featured a review of Toulouse's work as a cover story. Against literary doubts about the usefulness of such an enterprise, the author stressed the scientific potential for better understanding the man behind the works. Dr Jehan, "Émile Zola, par le Dr Toulouse," *Paris-santé illustré* 1 (June 1897): 2.

87. For more on the Toulouse study, see Daniel Pick, *Faces of Degeneration: A European Disorder, c. 1848–c. 1918* (Cambridge: Cambridge University Press, 1989).

88. Dr Édouard Toulouse, *Enquête médico-psychologique sur les rapports de la supériorité intellectuelle avec névropathie: Introduction générale: Émile Zola* (Paris: Société d'éditions scientifiques, 1896), 119. Toulouse subscribed to the notion that dramatic changes in body weight could bring about striking changes in personality and even observed that "[s]ome have wanted to cite a difference between the fat Zola and the thin Zola in terms of the literary works produced, and they say that the latter is not as good as the former. Zola has nevertheless experienced neither physical nor psychological weakness since his treatment."

89. Ibid., 266–67.

90. Ibid., 262.

91. Goncourt, *Journal*, 2: 898, 3 June 1872.

92. Toulouse, *Enquête médico-psychologique*, 166.

93. Zola to Toulouse, 15 October 1896, in Zola, *Correspondance* (Montréal: Presses de l'Université de Montréal, 1991), 8: 358.

94. Albert Cim, *Le Dîner des gens de lettres: Souvenirs littéraires* (Paris: Flammarion, 1903), 73–74.

95. John Grand-Carteret, *Zola en images: 280 illustrations* (Paris: Librairie Félix Juven, 1908), 22–23.

96. Detois, *Santé virile*, 9.

SIX: The New Man and the Culture of Force

1. Urbain Gohier, *L'Armée contre la nation* (Paris: Éditions de La Revue blanche, 1898). See also Albert Clemenceau, *"L'Armée contre la nation" devant le jury: L'Acquittement d'Urbain Gohier* (Paris: Publication de l'Aurore, 1898).

2. For example, see Georges Clemenceau, *L'Iniquité* (Paris: Stock, 1899), ii. Gyp was responsible for hiring street thugs for such services. Willa Z. Silverman, "Fin-de-Siècle Amazons: Antidreyfusard Women and the Affair," in *Intolérance et indignation: L'Affaire Dreyfus*, ed. Jean-Max Guieu (Paris: Fischbacher, 2000), 200.

3. Georges Clemenceau, "Pour la force contre la pensée," in *Vers la réparation* (Paris: Stock, 1899), 506–10. This article originally appeared on 2 December 1898.

4. Charles-Brun, "L'Erreur du dilettantisme," *Le Sillon*, 10 January 1899, 38.

5. Clemenceau quoted in Linda L. Clark, *Social Darwinism in France* (University: University of Alabama Press, 1984), 60.

6. Reinach, *Histoire de l'affaire Dreyfus*, vol. 4: *La Révision*, 154, 155.

7. A. Cartault, *L'Intellectuel: Étude psychologique et morale* (Paris: Alcan, 1914), 45; P. Pichon, *Comment avoir une force d'Hercule* (Paris: Nilsson, 1914).

8. Eugen Weber, "Pierre de Coubertin and the Introduction of Organised Sport in France," *Journal of Contemporary History* 5, no. 2 (1970): 9, 10, 13, 18.

9. Louis Lumet, "Jean Richepin," *La Culture physique* 5, no. 80 (1 May 1908): 1042–43.

10. Mark Motley, *Becoming a French Aristocrat: The Education of the Court Nobility, 1580–1715* (Princeton, N.J.: Princeton University Press, 1990), 140–52.

11. "We can hypothesize as a general law that a sport is more likely to be adopted by a social class if it does not contradict that class's relation to the body at its deepest and most unconscious level, i.e., the body schema, which is the depository of a whole world view and a whole philosophy of the person and the body," Pierre Bourdieu writes in *Distinction: A Social Critique of the Judgement of Taste*, trans. Richard Nice (Cambridge, Mass.: Harvard University Press, 1984), 217–18.

12. Gilbert Andrieu, *L'Homme et la force: Des marchands de la force au culte de la forme (XIXe et XXe siècles)* (Joinville-le-Pont: Actio, 1988), 30–31, 121.

13. Jean-Pierre Yahi, "Duel, savate et boxe française: une nouvelle destinée des coups," in *Aimez-vous les stades? Les Origines historiques des politiques sportives en France (1870–1930)*, ed. Alain Ehrenberg (Paris: Recherches, 1980), 125; Jean-François Loudcher, "The Origins of French Boxing: Bare-Knuckle Duelling, Savate and Chausson, 1820–45," *International Journal of the History of Sport* 18 (June 2001): 168–78.

14. Charle has surveyed the social identities and pastimes professed by men featured in *Qui êtes-vous*, an annual Who's Who of the French elite. Charle found that wealthy businessmen tended to participate in traditional aristocratic pastimes like hunting and riding or new ones like automobile driving, while more cultured elites either opted for cycling and mountain climbing or sought to imitate the leisure activities of their more well-to-do contemporaries. Christophe Charle, *Les Élites de la République, 1880–1900* (Paris: Fayard, 1987), 403–5.

15. Paul Gerbod, "L'État et les activités physiques et sportives des années 1780 aux années 1930," *La Revue historique* 301 (January–June 1999): 322.

16. Désiré Séhé and G. Strehly, *Manuel des exercices physiques à l'usage des écoles primaires*, 2d ed. (Paris: Ch. Delagrave, 1891), 5; Dr Galtier-Boissière, "L'Exercice chez les bébés," *Bébé: Revue d'hygiène et d'éducation de la première enfance* 1, no. 10 (April 1904): 55–57.

17. Marcel Spivak, "Le Développement de l'éducation physique et du sport français de 1852 à 1914," *La Revue d'histoire moderne et contemporaine* 24 (January–March 1977): 37–38.

18. Marcel Boulenger, "L'Émotion sportive," *La Revue de Paris* 11, no. 5 (15 September 1904): 415.

19. Father Henri Didon, *L'Esprit militaire dans un nation* (Paris: J. Mersch, 1898), 5–6.

20. Ibid., 8, 10.

21. Ibid., 26.

22. Edmond Demolins, *A quoi tient la supériorité des Anglo-Saxons*, 2d ed. (Paris: Firmin-Didot, 1897), 81.

23. Ibid., 9.

24. Maurice Crubellier, *L'Enfance et la jeunesse dans la société française, 1800–1950* (Paris: Armand Colin, 1979), 199.

25. William M. Reddy, *The Invisible Code: Honor and Sentiment in Postrevolutionary France, 1814–1848* (Berkeley: University of California Press, 1997), 114–16; Paul Lapie, "La Hiérarchie des professions," *La Revue de Paris* 12, no. 5 (15 September 1905): 390–416.

26. Henry Jarzuel, *Petit catéchisme nationaliste* (Paris: Librairie antisémite, 1901), 11–12.

27. Unsigned, "Courrier de Paris," *L'Illustration*, no. 113 (18 March 1899): 166.

28. G. B. Sansom, "Sports and Physical Culture in French Schools," *Sandow's Magazine of Physical Culture and British Sport* 6 (April 1901): 266, 269.

29. R. W. Wood, "France and Its Physical Life," *Sandow's Magazine of Physical Culture and British Sport* 8 (January 1902): 445–46.

30. Gail Bederman, *Manliness and Civilization: A Cultural History of Gender and Race in the United States, 1880–1917* (Chicago: University of Chicago Press, 1995), 170–215.

31. Jean Izoulet, "Préface: Deux paroles sur la France," in Theodore Roosevelt, *La Vie Intense*, trans. Mme la princesse Ferdinand de Faucingy-Lucinge and Jean Izoulet (Paris: Flammarion, 1903), xvii, xviii.

32. Theodore Roosevelt, "Citizenship in a Republic," in *African and European Addresses* (New York: G. P. Putnam's Sons, 1910), 40–41.

33. Louis Dumont-Wilden, "La France nouvelle devant l'étranger," in Agathon [Henri Massis and Alfred de Tarde], *Les Jeunes Gens d'aujourd'hui*, 12th ed. (Paris: Plon, 1919), 125.

34. Captain Royet, *Les Éclaireurs de France* (Paris: Larousse, 1914), 31, 83.

35. Jean Rodes, "Pour faire des soldats," *L'Illustration*, no. 141 (8 March 1913): 195–96.

36. Weber, "Pierre de Coubertin," 21; Georges Jourmas, "L'Affaire Dreyfus: Une étape du Tour de France," *Histoire* 244 (June 2000): 24–25.

37. Charles de Saint-Cyr, *Manuel civique de la jeunesse: le sport, éducateur social* (Paris: Édition de "L'Auto," 1908), 16.

38. Richard Holt, *Sport and Society in Modern France* (London: Macmillan, 1981), 97; Paul M. Cohen, *Piety and Politics: Catholic Revival and the Generation of 1905–1914 in France* (New York: Garland, 1987).

39. Such, at least, was the conclusion that Ernest Psichari had reached. Cf. Robert Wohl, *The Generation of 1914* (London: Weidenfeld & Nicolson, 1980), 13.

40. Abbot H. Mocquillon, *L'Art de faire un homme: Conseils pratiques d'éducation moderne* (Paris: Librairie Molière, 1906); F.-A. Vuillermet, *Soyez des hommes: À la conquête de la virilité* (Paris: P. Lethielleux, 1909).

41. Bernard Deletang, "Le Mouvement sportif ouvrier: La République à l'épreuve du socialisme," in *Les Athlètes de la république: Gymnastique, sport et idéologie républicaine, 1870–1914,* ed. Pierre Arnaud (Toulouse: Privat, 1987), 345.

42. Jacques Léonard, *Archives du corps: La Santé au XIXe siècle* (Rennes: Ouest-France, 1986), 40.

43. Historians often associate the vitalist and antirationalist thought of the philosopher Henri Bergson with thinkers of the prefascist thought; yet a wide range of socialists adopted what Christophe Prochasson loosely terms a "vitalist" approach to politics. Exemplified in the writings of Jean-Richard Bloch and inspired by the works of Georges Sorel, Walt Whitman, and Romain Rolland, this socialist vitalism called for an *élan vital* that might regenerate a now decadent society. Prochasson, *Les Intellectuels, le socialisme et la guerre, 1900–1938* (Paris: Seuil, 1993), 72.

44. Pierre Jourda, *L'Exotisme dans la littérature française depuis Chateaubriand,* vol. 2: *Du romanticisme à 1939* (1938–56; reprint, Geneva: Slatkine, 1970), 217–42.

45. Cartault, *Intellectuel,* 276.

46. Mathieu Wolff, "Soyez forts!" *Univers israélite,* 15 December 1899, 398–400.

47. Unsigned, "Un Juif chef hottentot," *Archives israélites* 62, no. 34 (23 August 1906): 269.

48. Max Nordau, "Discours d'introduction (texte de) 'Sur le relèvement moral, matériel, physique et économique des Juifs,' donné au 5ème Congrès Sioniste, le 26 décembre 1901 à Bâle en Suisse (Premier jour)," *Echo sioniste,* 15 January 1902, 28.

49. A. Rokéach, "Le Rôle du sionisme," *Echo sioniste,* 20 November 1900, 2.

50. Michael Burns, *Dreyfus: A Family Affair* (New York: HarperCollins, 1991), 345–47.

51. Pierre Birnbaum, "La Citoyenneté en péril: Les Juifs entre intégration et résistance," in *La France de l'affaire Dreyfus,* ed. Pierre Birnbaum (Paris: Gallimard, 1994), 505–6.

52. Crubellier, *Enfance et la jeunesse dans la société française,* 314.

53. Maxime Rodinson, *Israel: A Colonial Settler State?* trans. David Thorstad (New York: Monad Press, 1973); Daniel Boyarin, *Unheroic Conduct: The Rise of Heterosexuality and the Invention of the Jewish Man* (Berkeley: University of California Press, 1997).

54. Hippolyte Prague, "L'Activité juive," *Archives israélites* 71, no. 33 (18 August 1910): 257.

55. Hippolyte Prague, "La Renaissance de la Palestine," *Archives israélites* 70, no. 9 (4 March 1909): 66. On the easing of tensions between assimilationists and Zionists, see Pierre Birnbaum, *Anti-Semitism in France: A Political History from Léon Blum to the Present,* trans. Miriam Kochan (Oxford: Blackwell, 1992), 53.

56. Georges Sorel, *Reflections on Violence,* trans. T. E. Hulme (London: Allen & Unwin, 1925), 272.

57. Ibid., 86.

58. Strictly speaking, Sorel expressly distinguished force from violence. The former, he claimed, was that whose object is "to impose a particular social system of minority rule, while *violence* aims at the destruction of that order." Sorel's celebration of rebellious proletarian violence nevertheless smacks of the combative understanding of force prescribed by Father Didon, particularly as it seemed to tap into the heroic and warrior ethos long abandoned by the bourgeoisie. His conception of violence was not an endorsement of lawlessness, but of a manly willingness to channel violence for productive ends. Quoting a study of Norwegian peasant behavior, Sorel agreed that "a soft and effeminate character is more to be feared than [a] feeling of independence, however exaggerated and brutal."

Ibid., 171–72, 206. One may draw parallels between Sorel's work and the therapeutic violence recommended in Georges Valois's *L'Homme qui vient*, where the men who are forced to labor through threat of the whip respond with gratitude to their brutal master: "Blessed be thy name, O victorious one, for the whip in your hand is like the desire we have to rise above ourselves. Strike us then, master, if you love us, and do not abandon us, so that we do not become like feral dogs again and do not return to the laziness of animals. Strike us so we that remain men." Georges Valois, *L'Homme qui vient: Philosophie de l'autorité* (1906; reprint, Paris: Nouvelle librairie nationale, 1923), 47–50. See also David Forgacs, "Fascism, Violence, and Modernity," in *The Violent Muse: Violence and the Artistic Imagination in Europe, 1910–1939,* ed. Jana Howlett and Rod Mengham (Manchester: Manchester University Press, 1994), 5.

59. Édouard Berth, *Les Méfaits des intellectuels* (Paris: Rivière, 1913), 49. Pascal Balmand's appraisal of the status of intellectuals in Berth's work is worth citing: "Somewhat like the Jews in the thought of Édouard Drumont, the intellectual was here perceived as the focal point of all the ills that afflicted society, as the location around which crystallised a whole series of anti-values and maladies. Where Berth himself made appeal to vitalism, the intellectual personified immobility; where action was required he embodied sterile abstraction; where, finally, there was need for virility and strength he symbolised femininity and impotence." Balmand, "Anti-Intellectualism in French Political Culture," in *Intellectuals in Twentieth-Century France: Mandarins and Samurais,* ed. Jeremy Jennings (New York: St. Martin's Press, 1993), 160.

60. Berth, *Méfaits des intellectuels,* 58–59. Berth looked for virility even in those who inspired him politically. Unlike Marx, who was "only an intelligence . . . and we confess that that is not much," or Nietzsche, a dilettante and a decadent, Proudhon embodied all that the young writer yearned for in a teacher. "For me he is much more than a mind and an intelligence; he is a conscience, a man, *vir* in the full sense of the word. . . . Proudhon is all force, all health, he is a true male!" Letter from Édouard Berth to Édouard Droz, 25 June 1908, in "À propos de Proudhon: Correspondance de Georges Sorel et Édouard Berth avec Édouard Droz," *Mil neuf cent* 10 (1992): 148.

61. Daniel Halévy, *Histoire de quatre ans: 1997–2001* (Paris: Cahiers de la Quinzaine, 1903). John Cerullo, "A Literary Sorel: Dirempting a Fin-de-Siècle Moralist," *History of Political Thought* 24 (Spring 2003).

62. Bram Dijkstra, *Idols of Perversity: Fantasies of Feminine Evil in Fin-de-Siècle Culture* (Oxford: Oxford University Press, 1986).

63. Albert Cim, quoted in Annelise Maugue, *L'Identité masculine en crise au tournant du siècle, 1871–1914* (Paris: Rivages, 1987), 145.

64. Ibid., 154.

65. Dr Georges Rouhet, "Aperçu d'esthétique," *La Culture physique* 5, no. 74 (1 February 1908): 862.

66. Andrieu, *Homme et la force,* 222–23.

67. Georges Demenÿ, *Les Bases scientifiques de l'éducation physique* (Paris: Alcan, 1902), 35.

68. Andrieu, *Homme et la force,* 222–23.

69. Alfred Binet, *Les Idées modernes sur les enfants* (Paris: Flammarion, 1909), 43.

70. Demenÿ, *Bases scientifiques,* 14.

71. Ibid., 24, 25. His colleague Georges Hébert was equally concerned about such trends, believing that physical force was best channeled into activities that were person-

ally and socially useful. For him the musclebound behemoths who captivated public attention were not worthy of emulation. "Il est d'autant plus nécessaire de combattre cette tendance que les jeunes gens, attirés par la masse de ces individus ou hypnotisés par la grosseur de leurs muscles, se laissent bien vite convaincre et perdent ainsi de vue le vrai but de l'éducation." Hébert, *L'Éducation physique raisonnée* (Paris: Librairie Vuibert, 190[?]), 167.

72. Dr Gilbert Lasserre, "Rapport du Dr Gilbert Lasserre, secrétaire général de la Ligue girondine," *La Revue des jeux scolaires* 13 (February 1903): 22.

73. Pierre de Coubertin, "La Psychologie du sport," *La Revue des deux mondes* 160 (1 July 1900): 178.

74. Binet, *Idées modernes*, 50–51.

75. F.-A. Vuillermet, *Soyez des hommes: À la conquête de la virilité* (Paris: P. Lethielleux, 1909), 250, 252.

76. Andrieu, *L'Homme et la force*, 199. See also Edmond Desbonnet, "Comment d'un accord parfait résulte une division" and "Notre programme," *La Santé par les sports* 1, no. 1 (15 July 1911): 3–4.

77. Edmond Desbonnet, *La Force physique: Culture rationnelle* (Paris: Berger-Levrault, 1901), 10–12.

78. Dr J.-E. Ruffier, "L'Exercice physique et le travail cérébral," *La Culture physique* 2, no. 18 (August 1905): 191.

79. Dr G. Rouhet, "De la nécessité de la culture physique," *La Culture physique* 1 (March 1904): 28–29.

80. Pierre Normat, "Questions d'éducation intellectuelle et morale," *La Culture physique* 5, no. 7 (1 January 1908): 796.

81. Albert Surier, "Aux éducateurs," *La Culture physique* 2, no. 20 (October 1905): 174.

82. Richard Andrieu, "Étude sur l'initiation à l'athléticisme par la culture physique," *La Culture physique* 3, no. 39 (15 August 1906): 637.

83. Advertisement, *La Culture physique* 5, no. 94 (1 December 1908), inside front cover. It would be wrong to see in this critique of the intellectual lifestyle a simple denigration of intelligence. Physical culturists lauded the virtues of intelligence as practiced by the bona fide athlete: a man who was complete, both intellectually and bodily. According to Albert Surier, the physician Georges Rouhet was "an intellectual of athleticism" who, by demonstrating that one could possess at once mental superiority and "formidable muscular power," proved that "physical force is not the exclusive endowment of brutes." Albert Surier, "Les Intellectuels de l'athléticisme: Le Docteur Georges Rouhet," *La Culture physique* 1 (August 1904): 116–18.

84. Louis Bally, preface to Desbonnet, *Force physique*, ix–x.

85. Ibid., x.

86. Albert Surier, *Comment on devient beau et fort* (Paris, 1905), 8–10.

87. Keith Walden, "The Road to Fat City: An Interpretation of the Development of Weight Consciousness in Western Society," *Historical Reflections/Réflexions historiques* 12 (Fall 1985): 356–57; Tamar Garb, *Bodies of Modernity: Figure and Flesh in Fin-de-Siècle France* (London: Thames & Hudson, 1998), 36.

88. Théophile Gautier, *De la mode* (Paris, 1858), 5–6, quoted in Philippe Perrot, *Fashioning the Bourgeoisie: A History of Clothing in the Nineteenth Century*, trans. Richard Bienvenu (Princeton, N.J.: Princeton University Press, 1994), 32.

89. Bess M. Mensendieck, *"It's Up to You"* (New York: Mensendieck System, 1931), 19.

90. Andrieu, "Étude sur l'initiation à l'athléticisme," 637. Andrieu was also the inventor of "la bobine Andrieu," which was regularly marketed in *La Culture physique* as a means of increasing the strength of the forearm.

91. *"Sa voix peut, tour à tour, nous tenir sous la charme / Et nous faire pâlir sous ses mâles accents. / Il sait nous entraîner dans tous les jeux puissants, / Façonner notre chair et redresser nos torses, / Elargir nos poumons et décupler nos forces. / Penseur illuminé d'un rêve audacieux, / Il veut régénérer, par son art précieux, / Les faibles, les chétifs, les vilains que nous sommes, / Nous rendre beaux et forts, faire de nous des hommes."* Unsigned, "Au Dr Rouhet," *La Culture physique* 3, no. 42 (1 October 1906): 717.

92. Unsigned, "La Culture physique chez soi: Entraînement par correspondance," *La Santé par les sports*, 15 August 1911.

93. Desbonnet, *Force physique*, 59.

94. William A. Ewing, *The Body: Photoworks of the Human Form* (London: Thames & Hudson, 1994), 168.

95. Advertisement, *La Culture physique* 3, no. 47 (15 December 1906).

96. Promotional poster, *La Culture physique* 3, no. 42 (1 October 1906), advertisement section.

97. F. Peyrou, "Pour guérir les dos ronds et redresser la colonne vertébrale il faut une simple opération instantanée et sans douleur," *La Santé par les sports* 1, no. 1 (15 July 1911): 17–18.

98. Dr J.-B. Wauquier, "L'Obésité: Gros ventre est synonyme de déchéance physique," *La Santé par les sports*, 8 March 1914, 5.

99. Payot, *Éducation de la volonté*, 172.

100. Desbonnet, *Force physique*, 31, 104.

101. Albert Surier, "La Guerre et le sport," *La Culture physique*, October 1904, 161–63.

102. Surier, *Comment on devient beau et fort*, 93. *La Culture physique* was peppered with such scorn for such weaklings, and in 1906 it informed its readers of a new society called "L'Élite" founded by the engineer Alfred Pichou, whose carefully screened members submitted to rigorous medical exams and agreed to procreate only amongst themselves. See Lehmann, "L'Élite," *La Culture physique* 3, no. 31 (1 April 1906), 438–39; Clark, *Social Darwinism in France*, 122–23.

103. Philippe Tissié, *La Fatigue et l'entraînement physical* (Paris: Alcan, 1897), 84–85. These observations are also traceable to the eighteenth century. For example, after bemoaning the fact that a nation's best men either died valiantly in battle or through the scourges of syphilis, the physician Antoine Le Camus recommended that weak, ugly, and otherwise "malformed men" be sent off to war in special regiments while superior men stayed home to reproduce healthy stock. Similar quasi-eugenic thought circulated widely during this time. See Anne C. Vila, *Enlightenment and Pathology: Sensibility in the Literature and Medicine of Eighteenth-Century France* (Baltimore: Johns Hopkins University Press, 1998), 87.

104. Robert A. Nye, *Crime, Madness, and Politics in Modern France* (Princeton, N.J.: Princeton University Press, 1984), 196–202.

105. See Pierre Normat, "Questions d'éducation intellectuelle et morale: La Peur des coups," *La Culture physique* 5, no. 75 (15 February 1908): 895.

106. L. Sauveroche, "Le Jiu-jitsu," *L'Illustration*, no. 126 (4 November 1905): 301.

107. The same police force would be criticized a few years later for its "weakness," due mainly to its officers' lack of exercise and tendency toward obesity. See Albert Surier,

"La Faiblesse de la force publique," *La Culture physique* 5, no. 92 (1 November 1908): 1434–37.

108. J. Lefèvre, "Une École de Jiu-Jitsu à Paris," *La Culture physique* 2, no. 15 (May 1905): 72.

109. J. Lefèvre, "Le Jiu-Jitsu," *La Culture physique* 2, no. 20 (October 1905): 184–85. For other techniques recommended for street fighting, see Edmond Vary, *Comment on se défend dans la rue et chez soi: manières multiples de se mettre partout en garde contre les agressions* (Paris: Nouvelle populaire, 1909). It would be an exaggeration to identify an interest in martial arts exclusively with manhood, for a number of self-defense manuals targeted women. Cf. A. Cherpillod, *Je me défends toute seule! Quelques coups de Jiu-Jitsu japonais à l'usage des dames* (Paris: Cart, 1907).

110. Lefèvre, "Jiu-Jitsu," 184.

111. Normat, "Questions d'éducation," *La Culture physique* 5, no. 75 (15 February 1908): 895–96.

112. Desbonnet, *Force physique*, 106.

113. Paul Leroy-Beaulieu, *La Question de la population* (Paris: Alcan, 1911), 350–51, quoted in Nye, *Crime, Madness and Politics*, 142.

114. Cartault, *Intellectuel*, 276. The same view was registered by Paul Vuibert in a book written in 1914 but published after the war: *Pour refaire la race: la méthode naturelle du lieutenant de vaisseau Hébert* (Paris: Librairie Vuibert, 1921), 35.

115. Nye, *Crime, Madness, and Politics*, 328–29.

116. Dr Paul Audollent, "Sans éducation physique, pas d'éducation intellectuelle ni morale," *La Santé par les sports*, 1 August 1911, 61.

117. Vuillermet, *Soyez des hommes*, 13–16.

118. René Delaporte, *Comment on fait des hommes: essai de viriculture* (Paris: Caron, 1911), 4. Pierre Bourdieu describes this debate as a reflection of tensions within the bourgeoisie itself: "To value *education* over *instruction*, *character* or *willpower* over *intelligence*, *sport* over *culture*, is to affirm, within the educational universe itself, the existence of a hierarchy irreducible to a strictly scholastic hierarchy which favours the second term in those oppositions. It means, as it were, disqualifying or discrediting the values recognized by other fractions of the dominant class or by other classes (especially the intellectual fractions of the petite-bourgeoisie and the 'sons of schoolteachers,' who are serious challengers to the sons of the bourgeoisie on the terrain of purely scholastic competence); it means putting forward other criteria of 'achievement' and other principles for legitimizing achievement as alternatives to 'academic achievement.'" Pierre Bourdieu, *Sociology in Question*, trans. Richard Nice (London: Sage, 1993), 121–22.

119. Binet, *Idées modernes*, 50–51.

120. Jean Daçay, "Le Renaissance athlétique en France," *La Culture physique* 136 (15 September 1910): 526. For a practical manual on how to do this, see Louis Kuypers, *Manuel pratique pour l'éducation physique des enfants (filles et garçons de 5 à 15 ans)* (Paris: Henry Paulin, ca. 1911), 5.

121. Émile Henriot, *A quoi rêvent les jeunes gens* (Paris: Champion, 1913), 12.

122. Étienne Rey, *La Renaissance de l'orgueil français* (Paris: Grasset, 1912), 31–32.

123. Agathon, *Jeunes gens d'aujourd'hui*, 6.

124. Georges Rozet, "La Jeunesse et le sport," in Agathon, *Jeunes gens d'aujourd'hui*, 134.

125. Fr.-Guillaume de Maigret, in Agathon, *Jeunes gens d'aujourd'hui*, 180, 183.

126. Henry du Roure, in Agathon, *Jeunes gens d'aujourd'hui*, 240.

127. Ernest Psichari, in Agathon, *Jeunes gens d'aujourd'hui*, 192.

128. Georges Rozet, "La Culture physique et l'université," *La Culture physique* 5, no. 93 (15 November 1908): 1475.

129. Georges Le Cardonnel, "Une Renaissance française: À propos d'enquêtes récentes," *Mercure de France*, 16 July 1913, 225–68.

130. Nye, *Crime, Madness and Politics*, 319.

131. Le Cardonnel, "Renaissance française," 238–40.

132. Hugues Le Roux, "La Culture de la force et la jeunesse d'aujourd'hui," *La Revue hebdomadaire* 26 (1912): 607–8.

Conclusion: An Affair to Remember

1. Robert Lambel, "La Caserne universitaire de la rue d'Ulm," *L'Illustration*, no. 3707 (14 March 1914): 196.

2. Martha Hanna, *The Mobilization of Intellect: French Scholars and Writers During the Great War* (Cambridge, Mass.: Harvard University Press, 1996), 60–65.

3. "Il faut de plus mâles sauveurs / Dans l'affreux orage où nous sommes: / Nous avons eu trop de rêveurs, / Soyez des hommes!" Victor de Laprade, "Soyez des hommes," quoted in Frédéric Godefroy, *Histoire de la littérature française: Depuis le XVIe siècle jusqu'à nos jours* (1878; reprint, Nendeln, Liechtenstein: Kraus, 1967), 2: 256.

4. Étienne Rey, *La Renaissance de l'orgueil français* (Paris: Grasset, 1912), 50.

5. Georges Hébert, *La Culture virile et les devoirs physiques de l'officier combattant* (Paris: G. Oudin, 1913), 149.

6. Martin Crotty, *Making the Australian Male: Middle-Class Masculinity, 1870–1920* (Melbourne: University of Melbourne Press, 2001); Michael S. Kimmel, *Manhood in America: A Cultural History* (New York: Free Press, 1996).

7. Hannah Arendt, *The Origins of Totalitarianism* (San Diego: Harcourt Brace, 1976), 45.

8. Jean-Marie Mayeur and Madeleine Reberioux, *The Third Republic from its Origins to the Great War, 1871–1914*, trans. J. R. Foster (Cambridge: Cambridge University Press, 1984), 206.

9. Bernard-Henri Lévy, *Adventures on the Freedom Road: The French Intellectuals in the 20th Century*, trans. Richard Veasey (London: Harville, 1995), 9.

10. Barbara Spackman, *Fascist Virilities: Rhetoric, Ideology, and Social Fantasy in Italy* (Minneapolis: University of Minnesota Press, 1996), 2.

11. Klaus Theweleit, *Male Fantasies*, vol. 1: *Women, Floods, Bodies, History* (Minneapolis: University of Minnesota Press, 1987); George Mosse, *The Image of Man: The Creation of Modern Masculinity* (New York: Oxford University Press, 1996); Joan Tumblety, "Revenge of the Fascist Knights: Masculine Identities in *Je suis partout*, 1940–1944," *Modern and Contemporary France* 7, no. 1 (February 1999): 11–20.

12. Luc Capdevila, "The Quest for Masculinity in a Defeated France, 1940–1945," *Contemporary European History* 10, no. 3 (November 2001): 423–45.

13. Roland Barthes, quoted in John M. Hoberman, *Sport and Political Ideology* (London: Heinemann, 1984), 115.

14. Gilles Perrault, quoted in Hoberman, *Sport and Political Ideology*, 105–6.

15. Andrew Hewitt, *Political Inversions: Homosexuality, Fascism, and the Modernist Imaginary* (Stanford, Calif.: Stanford University Press, 1996).

16. David Carroll, *French Literary Fascism: Nationalism, Anti-Semitism, and the Ideology of Culture* (Princeton, N.J.: Princeton University Press, 1995), 148.

17. Barbara Spackman, *Fascist Virilities: Rhetoric, Ideology, and Social Fantasy in Italy* (Minneapolis: University of Minnesota Press, 1996), 34.

18. Zygmunt Bauman, *Modernity and the Holocaust* (Ithaca, N.Y.: Cornell University Press, 1989).

Select Bibliography

PRIMARY SOURCES

Newspapers and Periodicals

L'Action française
Annales des sciences psychiques
Annales politiques et littéraires
Archives israélites
Aurore
Bébé: Revue d'hygiène et d'éducation de la première enfance
La Critique
La Croix
La Culture physique
L'Echo de Paris
L'Echo sioniste
L'Eclair
L'Essor
Le Figaro
La Fronde
Le Gaulois
La Gazette de France
Gil Blas
L'Illustration
L'Intransigeant
La Lanterne
La Libre parole
Le Matin
Mercure de France
Paris-Journal
Paris-santé illustré
Le Petit Bleu
Le Petit Journal
Le Petit Parisien
Psst . . . !
La Revue blanche
La Revue bleue
La Revue des deux mondes
*La Revue des jeux scolaire*s
La Revue hebdomadaire
Sandow's Magazine of Physical Culture and British Sport
La Santé par les sports
Le Siècle
Le Sifflet
Le Temps
L'Univers israélite

Books

Adam, Paul. *La Morale des sports.* Paris: Libraire mondiale, 1907.
Agathon [Henri Massis and Alfred de Tarde]. *Les Jeunes Gens d'aujourd'hui.* 12th ed. Paris: Plon, 1919.
Ajalbert, Jean. *Sous le sabre.* Paris: Éditions de La Revue blanche, 1898.
Aubry, Paul. *La Contagion du meurtre: Étude d'anthropologie criminelle.* Paris: Alcan, 1894.
Aumont, F. *L'Estomac des gens du monde: Neurasthénie digestive.* Paris: n.p., 1908.
Barbary, Fernand. *Les Misères du corps.* Paris: Société d'éditions scientifiques, 1901.
Barrès, Maurice. *Ce que j'ai vu à Rennes.* Paris: Sansot, 1904.

———. *Scènes et doctrines du nationalisme*. 1902. Reprint. Paris: Émile-Paul, 1926.

Benda, Julien. *La Jeunesse d'un clerc*. 1937. Reprint. Paris: Gallimard, 1964.

Bérenger, Henry. *Les Proletaires intellectuels en France*. Paris: Éditions de La Revue, 1896.

Berth, Édouard. *Les Méfaits des intellectuels*. Paris: Rivière, 1913. 2d ed. 1926.

Binet-Sanglé, *La Folie de Jésus: Ses connaissances, ses idées, son délire, ses hallucinations*. Vols. 1–4. Paris: A. Maloine, 1910.

Boisandré, André de. *Napoléon antisémite*. Paris: Librairie antisémite, 1900.

Bonnamour, George[s]. *Le Procès Zola: Impressions d'audience*. Paris: A. Pierret, 1898.

Bouchard, Charles. *Leçons sur les maladies par ralentissement de la nutrition*. Paris: Librairie F. Savy, 1890.

Brulat, Paul. *L'Affaire Dreyfus: Violence et raison*. Paris: Stock, 1898.

Carlier, F. *Les Deux Prostitutions*. Paris: E. Dentu, 1887.

Cartault, Augustin. *L'Intellectuel: Étude psychologique et morale*. Paris: Alcan, 1914.

Charpentier, Armand. *Les Côtés mystérieux de l'affaire Dreyfus*. Paris: Rieder, 1937.

Chevalier, J. *Une Maladie de la personnalité: L'Inversion sexuelle*. Paris: G. Masson, 1893.

Clemenceau, Georges. *La Honte*. Paris: Stock, 1903.

———. *L'Iniquité*. Paris: Stock, 1899.

———. *Vers la réparation*. Paris: Stock, 1899.

Cordier, Julien. *Une Bataille pour une idée*. Paris: Stock, 1901.

Cornély, Joseph. *Notes sur l'affaire Dreyfus*. Paris: Société française d'éditions d'art, 1899.

Corre, A. *Aperçu général de la criminalité militaire en France*. Lyon: A. Storck, 1891.

Coubé, Stéphen. *L'Âme du soldat*. Paris: Victor Retaux, 1899.

Delaporte, René. *Comment on fait des hommes: Essai de viriculture*. Paris: Caron, 1911.

Delcourt, Pierre. *Le Vice à Paris*. Paris: Alphonse Piaget, 1887.

Demenÿ, Georges. *Les Bases scientifiques de l'éducation physique*. Paris: Alcan, 1902.

Demolins, Edmond. *A quoi tient la supériorité des Anglo-Saxons*. 2d ed. Paris: Firmin-Didot, 1897.

Desbonnet, Edmond. *La Force physique: culture rationnelle*. Paris: Berger-Levrault, 1901.

Detois, E. *La Santé virile par l'hygiène*. Aurillac: Roux, 1901.

Dheur, Dr. *Comment on se défend contre l'obésité*. Paris: Société d'éditions scientifiques, n.d.

Didon, Henri. *L'Esprit militaire dans un nation*. Paris: J. Mersch, 1898.

———. *Influence morale des sports athlétiques*. Paris: J. Mersch, 1897.

Dreyfus, Mathieu. *L'Affaire Dreyfus telle que je l'ai vécue*. Paris: Grasset, 1978.

Droz, Gustave. *Monsieur, madame et bébé*, 116th ed. Paris: Havard, 1882.

Drumont, Édouard. *La France juive*. 2 vols. 1886. Reprint. Paris: Flammarion, 1912.

Duclaux, Émile. *Propos d'un solitaire*. Paris, 1898.

Escoffier, Léon. *Ohé les jeunes!* Paris: Ligue de l'encyclopédie, 1898.

Esterhazy, Ferdinand Walsin-. *Les Dessous de l'affaire Dreyfus*. Paris: Fayard, 1898.

Féré, Charles. *La Pathologie des émotions*. Paris: Alcan, 1892.

Gache, Ferdinand. *Mères et fils*. Paris: Henri Didier, 1909.

Gerschel, A. *Les Défenseurs de la justice*. Paris: Stock, 1898.

Ginevra, *Catholique-dreyfusard*. Paris: Société libre d'édition des gens de lettres, 1899.

Gohier, Urbain. *L'Armée contre la nation*. Paris: Éditions de La Revue blanche, 1898.

———. *Les Prétoriens et la congrégation*. Paris: Éditions de La Revue blanche, 1900.

Goncourt, Edmond de, and Jules de Goncourt. *Journal: Mémoires de la vie littéraire*. Edited by Robert Ricatte. 4 vols. Paris: Fasquelle 1959.

Grand-Carteret, John. *L'Affaire Dreyfus et l'image*. Paris: Flammarion, 1898.

———. *L'Affaire et l'image: 266 caricatures françaises et étrangères.* Paris: Flammarion, 1898.

———. *Derrière "lui" (homosexualité en Allemagne).* Paris: E. Bernard, 1907. Reprint. Lille: Cahiers Gai-Kitsch, 1992.

———. *Zola en images: 280 illustrations, portraits, caricatures, documents divers.* Paris: Librairie Félix Juven, 1908.

Grégoire, Abbé Henri. *Essai sur la régénération physique, morale et politique des juifs: Ouvrage couronné par la Société royale des sciences et des arts de Metz, le 23 août 1788.* Metz: Devilly, 1789. Reprint. Paris, Stock, 1988.

Guennebaud, Le lieutenant. *La Vie à la caserne au point de vue social.* Saint-Brieuc: Imprimerie René Prud'homme, 1906.

Halévy, Daniel. *Histoire de quatre ans: 1997–2001.* Paris: Cahiers de la Quinzaine, 1903.

———. *Regards sur l'affaire Dreyfus.* Edited by Jean-Pierre Halévy. Paris: Éditions de Fallois, 1994.

Hébert, Georges. *La Culture virile et les devoirs physiques de l'officier combattant.* Paris: G. Oudin, 1913.

———. *L'Éducation physique raisonnée.* Paris: Librairie Vuibert, 190–?

Herzl, Théodore, and Max Nordau. *Discours prononcés au IIe congrès sioniste de Bâle.* Translated by Jacques Bahar. Paris: Aux bureaux du Flambeau, 1899.

Laissus fils, Dr. *Considérations sur la cure de l'obésité.* Paris: A. Maloine, 1909.

Lemazurier, Jean. *Catéchisme dreyfusard.* Paris: Au Bureau du Siècle, 1898.

Lerne, J. de. *Comment devenir fort.* Paris: Baillière, 1902.

Leroy-Beaulieu, Anatole. *Israel Among the Nations: A Study of the Jews and Anti-Semitism.* Translated by Frances Hellman. New York: G. P. Putnam's Sons, 1904.

Livre d'hommage des lettres françaises à Émile Zola. Paris: Société libre d'Édition des Gens de Lettres, 1898.

Marmont, Le Maréchal. *De l'esprit des institutions militaires.* Paris: Librairie militaire, 1845.

Michelet, Jules. *Du prêtre, de la femme, de la famille.* 2d edition. Paris: Comptoir des imprimeurs-unis, 1845.

Mirbeau, Octave. *L'Affaire Dreyfus,* edited by Pierre Michel and Jean-François Nivet. Paris: Librairie Séguier, 1991.

Mocquillon, Abbot H. *L'Art de faire un homme: Conseils pratiques d'éducation moderne.* Paris: Librairie Molière, 1906.

Paléologue, Maurice. *My Secret Diary of the Dreyfus Case.* Translated by Eric Mosbacher. London: Secker & Warburg, 1957.

Payot, Jules. *L'Éducation de la volonté.* 1893. Reprint. Paris: Alcan, 1912.

[Capitaine Piétri] Capitaine de l'Armée active. *L'Officier et la crise française.* Paris, 1900.

Pouillet, Dr. *De l'onanisme chez l'homme.* 3d ed. Paris: Vigot Frères, 1897.

Pressensé, Francis de. *Un Héros: Le Colonel Picquart.* Paris: Stock, 1898.

———. *L'Idée de patrie.* Paris: P. Ollendorff, 1899.

Proust, Adrien, and Gilbert Ballet, *L'Hygiène du neurasthénique.* Paris: Masson, 1897.

———. and A. Mathieu, *L'Hygiène de l'obèse.* Paris: Masson, 1897.

Quillard, Pierre, ed. *Le Monument Henry.* Paris: Stock, 1899.

Reinach, Joseph. *L'Affaire Dreyfus: La voix de l'île.* Paris: Stock, 1898.

———. *Une Conscience: Le Lieutenant-colonel Picquart.* Paris: Stock, 1898.

———. *Histoire de l'affaire Dreyfus.* Vol. 1: *Le Procès de 1894.* Vol. 2: *Esterhazy.* Vol. 3: *La*

Crise. Procès Esterhazy. Procès Zola. Vol. 4: *Cavaignac et Félix Faure.* Vol. 5: *Rennes.* Vol. 6: *La Révision.* Vol. 7: *Index général.* Paris: Éditions de la Revue blanche, 1901–11.

Reinach, Théodore. "Juif." In *La Grande Encyclopédie,* 21: 256–80. Paris: H. Lamirault, 1894.

———. [Un intellectuel, pseud.]. *Gonse-Pilate et autres histoires.* Paris: Stock, 1899.

Réveillé-Parise, J. H. *Physiologie et hygiène des hommes livrés aux travaux de l'esprit.* Paris: Baillière, 1881.

Réville, Albert. *Les Étapes d'un intellectuel: À propos de l'affaire Dreyfus.* Paris: Stock, 1898.

Riant, Dr Aimé. *Hygiène du cabinet de travail.* Paris: Baillière, 1882.

Ribot, Théodule. *Diseases of the Will.* Translated from the 8th French ed. (1888) by Merwin-Marie Snell. Chicago: Open Court, 1894.

Roch, Mlle E. *Ce que vaut une femme: Traité d'éducation morale et pratique des jeunes filles.* Reims: Dubois-Poplimont, 1888.

Roosevelt, Theodore. *African and European Addresses.* New York: G. P. Putnam's Sons, 1910.

———. *La Vie intense.* Translated by Mme la princesse Ferdinand de Faucingy-Lucinge and Jean Izoulet. Paris: Flammarion, 1903.

Royet, Capitaine Maximin Léonce. *Les Éclaireurs de France.* Paris: Larousse, 1914.

Ruffier, Dr. *Le Traîtement de l'obésité par la culture physique.* Paris: Librairie de "Portez-vous bien!" 1912.

Séverine [Caroline Rémy]. *Vers la lumière: Impressions vécues.* Paris: Stock, 1900.

Sincère, Pierre. *Le Procès Dreyfus devant l'opinion.* Paris: Imprimerie E. Roux, 1898.

Sorel, Georges. *La Révolution dreyfusienne.* Paris: Librairie des sciences politiques et sociales, 1909.

Stock, P.-V. *Mémorandum d'un éditeur.* Paris: Stock, Delamain et Boutelleau, 1938.

Surier, Albert. *Comment on devient beau et fort.* Paris, 1905.

Szejko, Jadwiga. *Influence de l'éducation sur le développement de la neurasthénie.* Lyon: A Rey, 1902.

Thoinot, L. *Attentats aux moeurs et perversions du sens génital.* Paris: Octave Doin, 1898.

Tissié, Philippe. *La Fatigue et l'entraînement physique.* Paris: Alcan, 1897.

———. *L'Homme de demain: L'Éducation physique en France.* Brussels: Hayez, 1905.

Tissot, Samuel. *De la santé des gens de lettres.* 1768. Reprint. Geneva: Slatkine, 1981.

———. *Essai sur les maladies des gens du monde.* Paris: P.-F. Didot le jeune, 1771.

Toulouse, Édouard. *Enquête médico-psychologique sur les rapports de la supériorité intellectuelle avec névropathie: Introduction générale: Émile Zola.* Paris: Société d'éditions scientifiques, 1896.

Valois, Georges. *L'Homme qui vient: Philosophie de l'autorité.* 1906. Reprint. Paris: La Nouvelle Librairie nationale, 1923.

Vauthier, Maurice. *La France et l'affaire Dreyfus.* Paris: Stock, 1899.

Vérax, L. [Dr Oyon]. *Essai sur la mentalité militaire a propos de l'affaire Dreyfus.* Paris, 1898.

Villemar, H. [Hélène Naville]. *Dreyfus intime.* Paris: Stock, 1898.

———. *Essai sur le colonel G. Picquart.* Paris: Stock, 1899.

Vuillermet, F. A. *Soyez des hommes: À la conquête de la virilité.* Paris: P. Lethielleux, 1909.

Zola, Émile. *The Dreyfus Affair: "J'accuse" and Other Writings.* Translated by Eleanor Levieux. Edited by Alain Pagès. New Haven, Conn.: Yale University Press, 1996.

SECONDARY SOURCES

Accampo, Elinor A., Rachel G. Fuchs, and Mary Lynn Stewart, eds. *Gender and the Politics of Social Reform in France, 1870–1914*. Baltimore: Johns Hopkins University Press, 1995.

Adler, Laure. *Secrets d'alcôve: Histoire du couple de 1830 à 1930*. Paris: Hachette, 1983.

Agulhon, Maurice. *Marianne au pouvoir: L'Imagerie et la symbolique républicaine de 1880 à 1914*. Paris: Flammarion, 1989.

Andrieu, Gilbert. *L'Homme et la force: Des marchands de la force au culte de la forme (XIXe et XXe siècles)*. Joinville-le-Pont: Actio, 1988.

Arnaud, Pierre, ed. *Les Athlètes de la république: Gymnastique, sport et idéologie républicaine, 1870–1914*. Toulouse: Privat, 1987.

Aron, Jean-Paul. *Le Mangeur du XIXe siècle*. Paris: Robert Laffont, 1973.

Aron, Jean-Paul, and Roger Kempf. *La Bourgeoisie, le sexe et l'honneur*. Paris: Éditions complexe, 1984.

Arendt, Hannah. *The Origins of Totalitarianism*. New York: Harcourt Brace, 1951.

Badinter, Elisabeth. *The Myth of Motherhood: An Historical View of the Maternal Instinct*. Translated by Roger DeGaris. London: Souvenir Press, 1981.

Bakhtin, Mikhail. *Rabelais and His World*. Translated by Hélène Iswolsky. Bloomington: Indiana University Press, 1984.

Barnes, David S. *The Making of a Social Disease: Tuberculosis in Nineteenth-Century France*. Berkeley: University of California Press, 1995.

Barrows, Susanna. *Distorting Mirrors: Visions of the Crowd in Late Nineteenth-Century France*. New Haven, Conn.: Yale University Press, 1981.

Bauman, Zygmunt. "Allosemitism: Premodern, Modern, Postmodern." In Bryan Cheyette and Laura Marcus, eds., *Modernity, Culture and "the Jew."* Cambridge, UK: Polity Press; Stanford, Calif.: Stanford University Press, 1998: 143–56.

———. "Exit Visas and Entry Tickets: Paradoxes of Jewish Assimilation." *Telos* 77 (Fall 1988): 45–77.

———. *Modernity and the Holocaust*. Ithaca, N.Y.: Cornell University Press, 1989.

Bederman, Gail. *Manliness and Civilization: A Cultural History of Gender and Race in the United States, 1880–1917*. Chicago: University of Chicago Press, 1995.

Beizer, Janet. *Ventriloquized Bodies: Narratives of Hysteria in Nineteenth-Century France*. Ithaca, N.Y.: Cornell University Press, 1994.

Benjamin, Marina, ed. *Science and Sensibility: Gender and Scientific Enquiry, 1780–1945*. Oxford: Blackwell, 1991.

Benjamin, Walter. *Charles Baudelaire: A Lyric Poet in the Era of High Capitalism*. Translated by Harry Zohn. London: NLB, 1973.

———. *Illuminations*. Translated by Harry Zohn. New York: Schocken Books, 1969.

———. *Paris, capital du XIXe siècle*. Translated by Jean Lacoste. Paris: Éditions du CERF, 1989.

Berenson, Edward. *The Trial of Madame Caillaux*. Berkeley: University of California Press, 1992.

Birnbaum, Pierre. *Anti-Semitism in France: A Political History from Léon Blum to the Present*. Translated by Miriam Kochan. Oxford: Blackwell, 1992.

———, ed. *La France de l'affaire Dreyfus*. Paris: Gallimard, 1994.

Bleys, Rudi C. *The Geography of Perversity: Male-to-Male Sexual Behavior Outside the West and the Ethnographic Imagination, 1759–1918.* New York: New York University Press, 1995.

Bourdieu, Pierre. *Les Règles de l'art: Génêse et structure du champ littéraire.* Paris: Seuil, 1992.

Bowlby, Rachel. *Just Looking: Consumer Culture in Dreiser, Gissing, and Zola.* London: Methuen, 1985.

Boyarin, Daniel. *Unheroic Conduct: The Rise of Heterosexuality and the Invention of the Jewish Man.* Berkeley: University of California Press, 1997.

Boyarin, Jonathan, and Daniel Boyarin, eds. *Jews and Other Differences: The New Jewish Cultural Studies.* Minneapolis: University of Minnesota Press, 1997.

Braziel, Jana Evans, and Kathleen LeBesco, eds. *Bodies out of Bounds: Fatness and Transgression.* Berkeley: University of California Press, 2001.

Bredin, Jean-Denis. *The Affair: The Case of Alfred Dreyfus.* Translated by Jeffrey Mehlman. New York: George Braziller, 1986.

Brown, Frederick. *Zola: A Life.* London: Papermac, 1997.

Budd, Michael Anton. *The Sculpture Machine: Physical Culture and Body Politics in the Age of Empire.* New York: New York University Press, 1997.

Burns, Michael. *Dreyfus: A Family Affair.* New York: HarperCollins, 1991.

———. *France and the Dreyfus Affair: A Documentary History.* Boston: Bedford/St. Martin's, 1999.

Cahm, Eric. *The Dreyfus Affair in French Society and Politics.* London: Longman, 1996.

———. "Pour et contre Émile Zola: Les Étudiants de Paris en Janvier 1898." *Bulletin de la Société d'études jaurésiennes* 1978: 12–15.

Capatti, Alberto. *Le Goût du nouveau: Origines de la modernité alimentaire.* Paris: Albin Michel, 1989.

Carroll, David. *French Literary Fascism: Nationalism, Anti-Semitism, and the Ideology of Culture.* Princeton, N.J.: Princeton University Press, 1995.

Cerullo, John. "The Intellectuals and the Imagination of Heroism During the Dreyfus Affair." *Proceedings of the Western Society for French History* 25 (Fall 1997): 185–95.

———. "Religion and the Psychology of Dreyfusard Intellectualism." *Historical Reflections/Réflexions Historiques* 24 (Spring 1998): 93–114.

Charle, Christophe. *Les Élites de la République, 1880–1900.* Paris: Fayard, 1987.

———. *Naissance des "intellectuels," 1880–1900.* Paris: Minuit, 1990.

Corbin, Alain. *The Foul and the Fragrant: Odor and the French Social Imagination.* Cambridge: Harvard University Press, 1986.

———. *Women for Hire: Prostitution and Sexuality in France After 1850.* Translated by Alan Sheridan. Cambridge, Mass.: Harvard University Press, 1990.

Crubellier, Maurice. *L'Enfance et la jeunesse dans la société française, 1800–1950.* Paris: Armand Colin, 1979.

Datta, Venita. *Birth of a National Icon: The Literary Avant-Garde and the Emergence of the Modern Intellectual.* Albany: State University of New York Press, 1999.

Davidson, Neil R. "'The Jew' as Homme/Femme-Fatale: Jewish (Art)ifice, *Trilby,* and Dreyfus." *Jewish Social Studies* 8 (2002): 73–111.

Davy, Joseph. "La Vie privée d'Alfred Dreyfus." In *L'Affaire Dreyfus,* edited by Michel Winock, 93–97. Paris: Seuil, 1998.

Dean, Carolyn J. *The Frail Social Body: Pornography, Homosexuality, and Other Fantasies in Interwar France.* Berkeley: University of California Press, 2000.

Dijkstra, Bram. *Idols of Perversity: Fantasies of Feminine Evil in Fin-de-Siècle Culture.* Oxford: Oxford University Press, 1986.

Dobelbower, Nicholas. "Petits bleus et Billets doux: Dangerous Correspondence(s) of the Dreyfus Affair." In *Intolérance et indignation: L'Affaire Dreyfus,* edited by Jean-Max Guieu, 130–40. Paris: Fischbacher, 2000.

Doise, Jean. *Un Secret bien gardé: Histoire militaire de l'affaire Dreyfus.* Paris: Seuil, 1994.

Donzelot, Jacques. *The Policing of Families.* Translated by Robert Hurley. New York: Pantheon Books, 1979.

Driskel, Michael Paul. *Representing Belief: Religion, Art, and Society in Nineteenth-Century France.* University Park: Pennsylvania State University Press, 1992.

Drouin, Michel, ed. *L'Affaire Dreyfus de A à Z.* Paris: Flammarion, 1994.

Efron, John M. "Images of the Jewish Body: Three Medical Views from the Jewish Enlightenment." *Bulletin for the History of Medicine* 69 (1995): 349–66.

Ehrenberg, Alain. ed., *Aimez-vous les stades? Les Origines historiques des politiques sportives en France (1870–1930).* Paris: Recherches, 1980.

Finn, Michael R. *Proust, the Body, and Literary Form.* Cambridge: Cambridge University Press, 1999.

Fitch, Nancy. "Mass Culture, Mass Parliamentary Politics, and Modern Anti-Semitism: The Dreyfus Affair in Rural France." *American Historical Review* 97 (1992): 55–95.

Flambart, Alain. "L'Hystérie masculine en France à travers la littérature médicale." Doctoral diss., Faculté de Médecine, Université de Caen, 1981.

Forth, Christopher E. "Bodies of Christ: Gender, Jewishness, and Religious Imagery in the Dreyfus Affair." *History Workshop Journal* 48 (Autumn 1999): 18–38.

———. "Moral Contagion and the Will: The Crisis of Masculinity in Fin-de-Siècle France." In *Contagion: Historical and Cultural Studies,* edited by Alison Bashford and Claire Hooker, pp. 61–75. London: Routledge, 2001.

———. "Neurasthenia and Manhood in Fin-de-Siècle France." In *Cultures of Neurasthenia from Beard to the First World War,* edited by Roy Porter and Marijke Gijswijt-Hofstra, 325–57. Amsterdam: Rodopi, 2001.

Garb, Tamar. *Bodies of Modernity: Figure and Flesh in Fin-de-Siècle France.* London: Thames & Hudson, 1998.

Geller, Jay. "The Conventional Lies and Paradoxes of Jewish Assimilation: Max Nordau's Pre-Zionist Answer to the Jewish Question." *Jewish Social Studies* 1 (Spring 1995): 129–60.

Gerbod, Paul. "L'État et les activités physiques et sportives des années 1780 aux années 1930." *Revue historique* 301 (January–June 1999): 307–31.

———. "L'Éthique héroïque en France (1870–1914)." *Revue historique* 268 (July–December 1982): 409–29.

Gilman, Sander. *Franz Kafka, The Jewish Patient.* New York: Routledge, 1995.

———. *The Jew's Body.* New York: Routledge, 1993.

Goldstein, Jan. "The Hysteria Diagnosis and the Politics of Anticlericalism in Late Nineteenth-Century France." *Journal of Modern History* 54 (June 1982): 209–39.

———. "'Moral Contagion': A Professional Ideology of Medicine and Psychiatry in Eighteenth- and Nineteenth-Century France." In *Professions and the French State, 1700–1900,* edited by Gerald L. Geison, 207–8. Philadelphia: University of Pennsylvania Press, 1984.

Gordon, Rae Beth. *Why the French Love Jerry Lewis: From Cabaret to Early Cinema.* Stanford, Calif.: Stanford University Press, 2001.

Griffiths, Richard. *The Use of Abuse: The Polemics of the Dreyfus Affair and Its Aftermath.* New York: Berg, 1991.

Guieu, Jean-Max, ed. *Intolérance et indignation: L'Affaire Dreyfus.* Paris: Fischbacher, 2000.

Hall, Donald E., ed. *Muscular Christianity: Embodying the Victorian Age.* Cambridge: Cambridge University Press, 1994.

Hanna, Martha. *The Mobilization of Intellect: French Scholars and Writers during the Great War.* Cambridge, Mass.: Harvard University Press, 1996.

Harris, Ruth. *Murders and Madness: Medicine, Law, and Society in the Fin de Siècle.* Oxford: Clarendon Press, 1989.

Hause, Steven C., with Anne R. Kenney. *Women's Suffrage and Social Politics in the French Third Republic.* Princeton, N.J.: Princeton University Press, 1984.

Hayes, Peter. *The People and the Mob: The Ideology of Civil Conflict in Modern Europe.* Westport, Conn.: Praeger, 1992.

Hoberman, John M. "Otto Weininger and the Critique of Jewish Masculinity," In *Jews and Gender: Responses to Otto Weininger,* edited by Nancy A. Harrowitz and Barbara Hyams, 141–53. Philadelphia: Temple University Press, 1995.

———. *Sport and Political Ideology.* London: Heinemann, 1984.

Hoffman, Robert L. *More Than a Trial: The Struggle over Captain Dreyfus.* New York: Free Press, 1980.

Holt, Richard. *Sport and Society in Modern France.* London: Macmillan, 1981.

Howlett, Jana, and Rod Mengham, eds., *The Violent Muse: Violence and the Artistic Imagination in Europe, 1910–1939.* Manchester: Manchester University Press, 1994.

Hyman, Paula E. *The Jews of Modern France.* Berkeley: University of California Press, 1998.

Idt, Geneviève. "L''Intellectuel' avant l'affaire Dreyfus." *Cahiers de lexicologie* 15 (April 1968): 35–46.

Israël, Armand. *Les Vérités cachées de l'affaire Dreyfus.* Paris: Albin Michel, 2000.

Jennings, Jeremy, ed. *Intellectuals in Twentieth-Century France: Mandarins and Samurais.* New York: St. Martin's Press, 1993.

Johnson, Martin. *The Dreyfus Affair: Honour and Politics in the Belle Époque.* New York: St. Martin's Press, 1999.

Kassouf, Susan. "The Shared Pain of the Golden Vein: The Discursive Proximity of Jewish and Scholarly Diseases in the Late Eighteenth Century." *Eighteenth-Century Studies* 32, 1 (1998): 101–10.

Kimmel, Michael S. "Consuming Manhood: The Feminization of American Culture and the Recreation of the Male Body, 1832–1920." *Michigan Quarterly Review* 33 (Winter 1994): 7–36.

———. *Manhood in America: A Cultural History.* New York: Free Press, 1996.

Kleeblatt, Norman L., ed. *The Dreyfus Affair: Art, Truth, and Justice.* Berkeley: University of California Press, 1987.

———. "MERDE! The Caricatural Attack Against Émile Zola," *Art Journal* 52 (Fall 1993): 54–58.

Landau, Philippe E. *L'Opinion juive et l'affaire Dreyfus.* Paris: Albin Michel, 1995.

Lawrence, Christopher and Steven Shapin, eds. *Science Incarnate: Historical Embodiments of Natural Knowledge.* Chicago: University of Chicago Press, 1998.

Lears, T. J. Jackson. *Fables of Abundance: A Cultural History of Advertising in America.* New York: Basic Books, 1994.

———. "From Salvation to Self-Realization: Advertising and the Therapeutic Roots of the Consumer Culture, 1880–1930." In *The Culture of Consumption: Critical Essays in American History, 1880–1980,* ed. Richard Wighton and T. J. Jackson Lears, 1–38. New York: Pantheon Books, 1983.

Lehning, James R. *To Be a Citizen: The Political Culture of the Early French Third Republic.* Ithaca, N.Y.: Cornell University Press, 2001.

Léonard, Jacques. *Archives du corps: La Santé au XIXe siècle* (Rennes: Ouest-France, 1986).

Lévy, Bernard-Henri. *Adventures on the Freedom Road: The French Intellectuals in the Twentieth Century.* Translated by Richard Veasey. London: Harville, 1995.

Leymarie, Michel, ed. *La Postérité de l'affaire Dreyfus.* Villeneuve d'Ascq: Presses universitaires du Septentrion, 1998.

Lloyd, Rosemary. *The Land of Lost Content: Children and Childhood in Nineteenth-Century French Literature.* New York: Oxford University Press, 1992.

Loudcher, Jean-François. "The Origins of French Boxing: Bare-Knuckle Duelling, Savate and Chausson, 1820–45." *International Journal of the History of Sport* 18 (June 2001): 168–78.

Mackaman, Douglas Peter. *Leisure Settings: Bourgeois Culture, Medicine, and the Spa in Modern France.* Chicago: University of Chicago Press, 1998.

Maingueneau, Dominique. *Les Livres d'école de la republique, 1870–1914.* Paris: Le Sycomore, 1979.

Matlock, Jann. *Scenes of Seduction: Prostitution, Hysteria, and Reading Difference in Nineteenth-Century France.* New York: Columbia University Press, 1994.

Maugue, Annelise. *L'Identité masculine en crise au tournant du siècle, 1871–1914.* Paris: Rivages, 1987.

Marrus, Michael R. "'En Famille': The Dreyfus Affair and Its Myths," *French Politics and Society* 12 (Fall 1994), 77–90.

———. *The Politics of Assimilation: A Study of the French Jewish Community at the Time of the Dreyfus Affair.* Oxford: Clarendon Press, 1971.

Matsuda, Matt K. *The Memory of the Modern.* New York: Oxford University Press, 1996.

McAleer, Kevin. *Dueling: The Cult of Honor in Fin-de-Siècle Germany.* Princeton, N.J.: Princeton University Press, 1994.

McLaren, Angus. *Trials of Masculinity: Policing Sexual Boundaries, 1870–1930.* Chicago: University of Chicago Press, 1997.

Merrick Jeffrey, and Bryan T. Ragan, Jr., eds., *Homosexuality in Modern France.* New York: Oxford University Press, 1996.

Miller, Paul. *From Revolutionaries to Citizens: Antimilitarism in France, 1870–1914.* Durham, N.C.: Duke University Press, 2002.

Mosse, George. *The Image of Man: The Creation of Modern Masculinity.* New York: Oxford University Press, 1996.

Nerlich, Michael. *Ideology of Adventure: Studies in Modern Consciousness, 1100–1750.* Translated by Wlad Godzich. 2 vols. Minneapolis: University of Minnesota Press, 1987.

Nochlin, Linda. "Degas and the Dreyfus Affair: A Portrait of the Artist as an Anti-Semite." In *The Dreyfus Affair: Art, Truth, and Justice,* edited by Norman Kleeblatt, 96–116. Berkeley: University of California Press, 1987.

Nye, Robert A. *Crime, Madness, and Politics in Modern France: The Medical Concept of National Decline.* Princeton, N.J.: Princeton University Press, 1984.

——. "Degeneration, Neurasthenia and the Culture of Sport in Belle Époque France." *Journal of Contemporary History* 17 (January 1982): 51–68.

——. *Masculinity and Male Codes of Honor in Modern France.* New York: Oxford University Press, 1993.

——. *The Origins of Crowd Psychology: Gustave Le Bon and the Crisis of Mass Democracy in the Third Republic.* London: Sage, 1975.

Offen, Karen. "Depopulation, Nationalism, and Feminism in Fin-de-Siècle France." *American Historical Review* 89 (June 1984): 648–76.

——. "Feminism, Antifeminism, and National Family Politics in Early Third Republic France." In *Connecting Spheres: Women in the Western World, 1500 to the Present*, edited by Marilyn Boxer and Jean Quataert, 204–13. New York: Oxford University Press, 1987.

Oppenheim, Janet. *"Shattered Nerves": Doctors, Patients, and Depression in Victorian England.* New York: Oxford University Press, 1991.

Ory, Pascal, and Jean-François Sirinelli. *Les Intellectuels en France, de l'Affaire Dreyfus à nos jours.* Paris: Armand Colin, 1986.

Outram, Dorinda. *The Body and the French Revolution: Sex, Class and Political Culture.* New Haven, Conn.: Yale University Press, 1989.

Pick, Daniel. *Faces of Degeneration: A European Disorder, c. 1848–c. 1918.* New York: Cambridge University Press, 1989.

Prochasson, Christophe. *Les Intellectuels, le socialisme et la guerre, 1900–1938.* Paris: Seuil, 1993.

Rabinbach, Anson. *The Human Motor: Energy, Fatigue, and the Origins of Modernity.* Berkeley: University of California Press, 1990.

Rearick, Charles. *Pleasures of the Belle Epoque.* New Haven, Conn.: Yale University Press, 1985.

Reddy, William M. *The Invisible Code: Honor and Sentiment in Postrevolutionary France, 1814–1848.* Berkeley: University of California Press, 1997.

Revah, Louis-Albert. "Les Intellectuels juifs face à l'affaire Dreyfus." *Revue des études juives* 155 (January–June 1996): 201–11.

Roberts, Mary Louise. "Acting Up: The Feminist Theatrics of Marguerite Durand." *French Historical Studies* 19 (Fall 1996): 1103–38.

——. *Civilization without Sexes*: Reconstructing Gender in Postwar France, 1917–1927. Chicago: University of Chicago Press, 1994.

Robinson, Sally. *Marked Men: White Masculinity in Crisis.* New York: Columbia University Press, 2000).

Rosario, Vernon A. *The Erotic Imagination: French Histories of Perversity.* New York: Oxford University Press, 1997.

Schor, Naomi. "Zola et la carte postale." *Cahiers naturalistes* 38, no. 66 (1992): 303–13.

Schwartz, Hillel. *Never Satisfied: A Cultural History of Diets, Fantasies, and Fat.* New York: Anchor Books, 1986.

Schwartz, Vanessa R. *Spectacular Realities: Early Mass Culture in Fin-de-Siècle France.* Berkeley: University of California Press, 1998.

Shapiro, Ann-Louise. *Breaking the Codes: Female Criminality in Fin-de-Siècle Paris.* Stanford, Calif.: Stanford University Press, 1996.

Schehr, Lawrence R., and Allen S. Weiss, eds. *French Food: On the Table, on the Page, and in French Culture.* London: Routledge, 2001.

Silverman, Deborah L. *Art Nouveau in Fin-de-Siècle France: Politics, Psychology, and Style*. Berkeley: University of California Press, 1989.

Silverman, Willa Z. "Fin-de-Siècle Amazons: Antidreyfusard Women and the Affair." In *Intolérance et indignation: L'Affaire Dreyfus*, edited by Jean-Max Guieu, 199–200. Paris: Fischbacher, 2000.

———. *The Notorious Life of Gyp: Right-Wing Anarchist in Fin-de-Siècle France*. New York: Oxford University Press, 1995.

Spackman, Barbara. *Fascist Virilities: Rhetoric, Ideology, and Social Fantasy in Italy*. Minneapolis: University of Minnesota Press, 1996.

Stearns, Peter N. *American Cool: Constructing a Twentieth-Century Emotional Style*. New York: New York University Press, 1994.

———. *Be a Man! Males in Modern Society*. 2d ed. New York: Holmes & Meier, 1990.

———. *Fat History: Bodies and Beauty in the Modern West*. New York: New York University Press, 1997.

Taithe, Bertrand. *Defeated Flesh: Welfare, Warfare, and the Making of Modern France*. Manchester: Manchester University Press, 1999.

Taylor, Katherine Fischer. *In the Theater of Criminal Justice: The Palais de Justice in Second Empire Paris*. Princeton, N.J.: Princeton University Press, 1993.

Theweleit, Klaus. *Male Fantasies*. Vol. 1: *Women, Floods, Bodies, History*. Minneapolis: University of Minnesota Press, 1987.

Tosh, John. *A Man's Place: Masculinity and the Middle-Class Home in Victorian England*. New Haven, Conn.: Yale University Press, 1999.

Vigarello, Georges. *Concepts of Cleanliness: Changing Attitudes in France Since the Middle Ages*. Translated by Jean Birrell. Cambridge: Cambridge University Press, 1988.

———. *Le Corps redressé: Histoire d'un pouvoir pédagogique*. 1978. Reprint. Paris: Armand Colin, 2001.

Vila, Anne C. *Enlightenment and Pathology: Sensibility in the Literature and Medicine of Eighteenth-Century France*. Baltimore: Johns Hopkins University Press, 1998.

Vincent-Buffault, Anne. *A History of Tears: Sensibility and Sentimentality in France*. London: Macmillan, 1991.

Walden, Keith. "The Road to Fat City: An Interpretation of the Development of Weight Consciousness in Western Society." *Historical Reflections/Réflexions historiques* 12 (Fall 1985): 331–73.

Warner, Marina. *Monuments and Maidens: The Allegory of the Female Form*. New York: Atheneum, 1985.

Weber, Eugen. *France, Fin de Siècle*. Cambridge, Mass.: Belknap Press, 1986.

———. *Peasants into Frenchmen: The Modernization of Rural France, 1870–1914*. Stanford, Calif.: Stanford University Press, 1976.

———. "Pierre de Coubertin and the Introduction of Organised Sport in France." *Journal of Contemporary History* 5, 2 (1970): 3–26.

Whorton, James C. *Crusaders for Fitness: A History of American Health Reformers*. Princeton, N.J.: Princeton University Press, 1982.

———. *Inner Hygiene: Constipation and the Pursuit of Health in Modern Society*. Oxford: Oxford University Press, 2000.

Wilson, Stephen. *Ideology and Experience: Antisemitism in France at the Time of the Dreyfus Affair*. Rutherford, N.J.: Fairleigh Dickinson University Press, 1982.

Winock, Michel, ed. *L'Affaire Dreyfus*. Paris: Seuil, 1998.

Wistrich, Robert S. "Max Nordau and the Dreyfus Affair." *Journal of Israeli History* 16 (1995): 1–17.

———. "Three Dreyfusard Heroes: Lazare, Zola, Clémenceau." In *Les Intellectuels face à l'affaire Dreyfus alors et aujourd'hui: Perception et impact de l'affaire en France et à l'étranger: Actes du colloque de l'Université Bar-Ilan, Israël, 13–15 décembre 1994*, edited by Roselyne Koren and Dan Michman, 13–41. Paris: L'Harmattan, 1998. bv

Zeldin, Theodore. *A History of French Passions, 1848–1945*. Vol. 2: *Intellect, Taste and Anxiety*. 1977. Reprint. Oxford: Clarendon Press, 1993.

Index

Printed in the United Kingdom
by Lightning Source UK Ltd.
110148UKS00002B/52